Samuel Rawson Gardiner

History of England from the accession of James I.

to the outbreak of the civil war 1603-1642

Samuel Rawson Gardiner

History of England from the accession of James I.
to the outbreak of the civil war 1603-1642

ISBN/EAN: 9783742858306

Manufactured in Europe, USA, Canada, Australia, Japa

Cover: Foto ©ninafisch / pixelio.de

Manufactured and distributed by brebook publishing software (www.brebook.com)

Samuel Rawson Gardiner

History of England from the accession of James I.

HISTORY OF ENGLAND

FROM THE

ACCESSION OF JAMES I.

TO

THE OUTBREAK OF THE CIVIL WAR

1603–1642

BY

SAMUEL R. GARDINER, D.C.L., LL.D.

FELLOW OF MERTON COLLEGE, OXFORD, ETC.

IN TEN VOLUMES

VOL. VI.

1625–1629

NEW EDITION

LONGMANS, GREEN, AND CO.
LONDON, NEW YORK, AND BOMBAY
1896

All rights reserved

CONTENTS

OF

THE SIXTH VOLUME.

CHAPTER LV.

THE EXPEDITION TO CADIZ.

	PAGE
1625 Buckingham's intentions .	1
Breach of the engagements between Louis XIII. and the Huguenots . .	2
Determinatio of Charles to send out the fleet .	3
The Queen at Titchfield .	4
Rusdorf's diplomacy . .	5
The Treaty of Southampton	6
Buckingham to go to the Hague	7
The Essex trained bands at Harwich . . .	8
De th of Sir A. Morton—Sir J. Coke Secretary .	9
Sir E. Cecil appointed to command the expedition against Spain . .	10
He reports on the deficiencies of the troops .	11
The King and Buckingham at Plymouth . .	12
The fleet driven back by a storm . . .	13
It puts to sea . . .	14
Arrives at Cadiz . .	15
Attack on Fort Puntal .	16
Surrender of the fort . .	17
Cecil's march to the bridge	18
Failure of the expedition .	19
The look-out for the Mexico fleet . . .	20
Return of the fleet to England	21
No serious investigation into the causes of failure	23

CHAPTER LVI.

GROWING ESTRANGEMENTS BETWEEN THE COURTS OF ENGLAND AND FRANCE.

	PAGE
1625 Buckingham's intention to visit France . .	24
Objections of Louis . .	25
Buckingham's instructions	26
Blainville's interview with Charles . . .	27
His visit to Buckingham .	28
The Peers of the Opposition	29
Dismissal of Williams .	31
Coventry Lord Keeper .	32
The Opposition leaders of	

	PAGE		PAGE
the Commons made sheriffs	33	1626 Irritation of Louis	44
The Dunkirk privateers	34	Charles determines to relieve Rochelle	44
Buckingham visits the Hague and proposes to attack Dunkirk	35	The prize goods sold	45
The Congress of the Hague	35	The 'St. Peter' re-arrested	46
Treaty of the Hague	36	Interference of Charles in French politics	7
Prospect of war with France	37	The Queen refuses to be crowned	48
Difficulties about the Queen's household	38	Charles's coronation	49
Embassy of Holland and Carleton	39	Negotiation between Louis and the Huguenots	50
Difficulties about the law of prize	40	An agreement come to	51
Sequestration of the money on board the French prizes	41	The Huguenots look to Charles for support	52
		Richelieu proposes to join England against Spain	52
Orders given for the sale of prize goods	41	Charles rejects his overtures	53
Blainville protests	42	Fresh dispute between Charles and the Queen	56
Reprisals in France followed by an order for the restitution of the 'St. Peter'	43	Blainville ordered to absent himself from Court	57

CHAPTER LVII.

THE LEADERSHIP OF SIR JOHN ELIOT IN THE SECOND PARLIAMENT OF CHARLES I.

1626 Opening of Parliament	59	ings of the council of war	73
Eliot's position in the House	60	The councillors refuse to reply	74
He demands inquiry into past mismanagement	62	Charles supports them in their refusal	75
Laud's sermon	63	Dr. Turner's queries	76
The conference on Montague's books	64	Charles defends his minister	77
Case of the 'St. Peter' of Havre de Grace	65	Question of ministerial responsibility	78
Release of the ship and reprisals in France	66	Eliot counsels the Commons to persist	79
Inquiry in the House of Commons	66	Eliot's speech against Buckingham	80
State of feeling in the House of Lords	68	Charles refuses to accept the doctrine of ministerial responsibility	81
Fresh overtures from Richelieu	59	Coventry's declaration of the King's pleasure	82
The riot at Durham House	70	Buckingham's vindication of his proceedings	84
The marriage of Lord Maltravers	71	Remonstrance of the Commons	84
Arundel sent to the Tower	72		
The Commons wish to inquire into the proceed-		The Commons are allowed to proceed with their in-	

THE SIXTH VOLUME. vii

	PAGE		PAGE
quiry into Buckingham's conduct	85	Charles throws obstacles in the way of an agreement	88
They vote that common fame is a good ground for their action	86	Blainville leaves England	89
The French Government favours the English alliance	87	Treaty between France and Spain—End of the French alliance	90

CHAPTER LVIII.

THE IMPEACHMENT OF THE DUKE OF BUCKINGHAM.

1626 The House of Lords demands Arundel's liberation	91	Imprisonment of Eliot and Digges	109
Bristol's confinement at Sherborne	92	Carleton threatens the House with the danger of Parliaments falling into disuse	110
He is forbidden to come to Parliament	93	Digges cleared by the House of Lords	111
Petitions the Lords for his writ, comes to London and accuses Buckingham	94	Digges released, but Eliot kept in prison	112
Is accused by the King	95	The Commons suspend their sittings	113
Interference of the King in Buckingham's favour	97	Eliot released	113
Buckingham impeached by the Commons	98	Bristol's case before the Lords	114
Prologue by Digges	99	Liberation of Arundel	115
Charges brought against Buckingham	100	Buckingham elected Chancellor of Cambridge University	116
Eliot's summing up	103	The King demands supply	117
Buckingham compared to Sejanus	105	The Commons decide that remonstrance must precede supply	118
Charles's indignation	107	They demand Buckingham's dismissal	119
He replies to the Lords' demand for Arundel's liberation	108	Parliament dissolved	121

CHAPTER LIX.

THE RUPTURE WITH FRANCE.

1626 Proclamation for the peace of the Church	122	Demand of a free gift from the counties	125
Buckingham's case to be tried in the Star Chamber	123	Dismissal of justices of the peace	125
The Parliamentary managers refuse to countenance the trial	123	Wentworth's character and political position	126
		Nature of his opposition	127
The City refuses to lend money	124	His overtures to Buckingham	128
		His dismissal from office	129

	PAGE		PAGE
The free gift refused in the counties	131	Resistance spreading in the country	150
Ships demanded from the maritime counties	132	Pennington ordered to attack French ships at Havre	151
Willoughby's fleet at Portsmouth	133	1627 But finds no ships there	152
Disagreement between Charles and the Queen	134	Mutiny in Pennington's fleet	153
The Queen at Tyburn	135	Partial success of the loan	154
Dismissal of the Queen's French attendants	136	Growing resistance to it	155
Proposal to debase the coin	138	The chief opponents summoned before the Council	156
Defeat of Mansfeld and Christian IV.	139	Resistance of Hampden, Eliot, and Wentworth	157
Bassompierre's mission	141	Charles looks forward to a war with France	159
Capture of French prizes	142
The forced loan	143	Pennington's attack upon the French shipping	160
Sequestration of Eliot's Vice-Admiralty	144	Negotiations opened with Spain	160
Buckingham proposes to go to France	146	Interviews between Rubens and Gerbier	161
Seizure of the wine fleet at Bordeaux	147	Alarm of the Dutch ambassador	162
Buckingham prepares to go as ambassador to France	147	Agreement between France and Spain	163
Prospects of the loan	148	Progress of the war in Germany	164
Resistance of the judges—Dismissal of Chief Justice Crew	149	Morgan takes four regiments to the Elbe	165

CHAPTER LX.

THE EXPEDITION TO RHÉ.

1627 Walter Montague's mission	167	Becher carries a few recruits to Rhé	180
Preparations for the relief of Rochelle	168	Death of Sir John Borough	181
Buckingham's instructions	170	Supplies introduced into St. Martin's	182
Sailing of the fleet	171
Buckingham's landing in the Isle of Rhé	172	Buckingham resolves to carry on the siege	183
Marches to St. Martin's	173	Holland expected with reinforcements	184
Lukewarmness of the Rochellese	174	Rohan's insurrection meets with no general support	184
Commencement of the siege of St. Martin's	175	Failure of the negotiation with Spain	185
The siege converted into a blockade	175	Christian IV. overpowered	186
Need of reinforcements	176	Misery in Morgan's regiments	186
Eagerness of the King to support Buckingham	177	Seizure of a French ship in the Texel	187
Difficulties of the Exchequer	178	English feeling against Buckingham	188

	PAGE		PAGE
Delays in Holland's sailing	191	Landing of the French on the island	195
The King's anxiety	192	Buckingham attempts to storm the fort	196
Holland is unable to leave	192	The retreat from St. Martin's	197
Disorganisation of the Government	193	Slaughter of the English	198
The King constant to Buckingham	194	Re-embarkation of the troops	198
Gloomy prospects of the force at Rhé	195	Buckingham's part in the disaster	199

CHAPTER LXI.

PREROGATIVE GOVERNMENT IN CHURCH AND STATE.

1627	Buckingham's reception in England	201	The prisoners remanded	216
	Increased resistance to the loan	202	The sailors ready to mutiny	218
	Ecclesiastical parties	203	Bad conduct of the billeted soldiers	219
	Laud's royalism	204	Schemes for raising money	219
	Sibthorpe's sermon on Apostolic Obedience	206	Charles and Buckingham resolve to carry on the war	220
	Abbot sent into confinement for refusing to license it	207	Excise proposed in the Council	222
	Manwaring's sermons on Religion and Allegiance	208	A standing force proposed	223
	Manwaring's theory of government	209	1628 German horse sent for	224
	Eliot's petition from the Gatehouse	212	Abandonment of the proposed excise	225
	Five knights demand a *habeas corpus*	213	The prisoners released and Parliament summoned	225
	Arguments in the King's Bench on behalf of the five knights	214	Ship-money demanded and then abandoned	226
	Heath's argument for the Crown	215	Commission to inquire how excise can be levied	227
			Bad state of Denbigh's fleet	228
			The elections	229

CHAPTER LXII.

THE PARLIAMENTARY LEADERSHIP OF SIR THOMAS WENTWORTH.

1628	Laud's sermon	230	Secretary Coke acknowledges that the law has been broken	237
	Opening of the session	231	The Jesuits at Clerkenwell	238
	Coke's Imprisonment Bill	232	Secretary Coke tries to frighten the Commons	239
	Seymour and Eliot on grievances	233	Debate on the liberty of the subject	240
	Wentworth's demand	235		
	Comparison between Wentworth and Eliot	236		

	PAGE		PAGE
Sir E. Coke's statement of the law	240	A Good Friday's debate on martial law	254
The Commons' resolution against unparliamentary taxation	241	The Lords incline towards the King	256
Nethersole's argument from political expediency	241	The Commons refuse to proceed further with supply	257
The legal argument	242	Debate in the Upper House on the resolutions	258
Controversy between Coke and Shilton	243	The Lords' propositions	259
Anderson's judgment produced	244	Criticism of the Commons	261
The Commons' resolutions on imprisonment	245	Noy and Wentworth for a *Habeas Corpus* Act	262
Debate on supply	246	Coventry declares that the King's word must be taken	263
Debate on billeting	247	The Commons order the preparation of a Bill on the liberty of the subject	264
Question of pressing men for the army	249	The Bill brought in by Coke	264
Five subsidies voted in committee, but not reported	250	Wentworth proposes a Bill of his own	266
Wentworth proposes a Bill on the liberties of the subject	251	The King rejects Wentworth's terms	267
The King pleased at the vote of supply	252	Wentworth's appeal to the King	268
Arguments before the Lords on the resolutions	253	Coke's proposal	269
Further discussion on billeting	253	End of Wentworth's leadership	270

CHAPTER LXIII.

THE PETITION OF RIGHT.

1628			
Dissatisfaction of the House	272	The Commons persist in rejecting it	282
Coke proposes a Petition of Right	274	Wentworth proposes a further accommodation	283
The Petition of Right brought in	275	Eliot's rejoinder	284
The Petition before the Lords	276	Wentworth's reply	285
The King's defence of his claim to imprison without showing cause	276	The Commons decide against Wentworth	286
The Lords attempt to mediate	277	Fresh proposal by the Lords	287
Clause proposed by Williams	278	Buckingham opposes it	288
Clause prepared by Arundel and Weston adopted	279	The Lords give way	289
The clause rejected by the Commons	280	The petition passes both Houses	289
The Lords try to explain away the clause	281	The surrender of Stade	290
		Denbigh's failure to relieve Rochelle	291
		Resolution of Charles to make another effort	292
		Charles hesitates about the petition	293

Questions the judges	294
Consults the Council	296
Answer agreed on	297
Worthlessness of the answer	297
Eliot's resolution	298
His speech on the state of the nation	299
A Remonstrance proposed	301
The King tries to stop it	301
Distress of the House	302
Phelips proposes to ask leave to go home	303
Eliot stopped by the Speaker	304
Coke attacks Buckingham by name	305
Selden moves that the impeachment be renewed	306
Intervention of the Lords	306
Charles draws back	307
The Lords ask for a clear answer to the petition	308
Charles gives the Royal assent to the Petition of Right	309

CHAPTER LXIV

REMONSTRANCE AND PROROGATION

1628 The petition compared with Magna Carta	311
Impeachment of Manwaring	312
Pym's declaration of principle	313
Subsidies voted and the Remonstrance proceeded with	315
The Remonstrance voted	316
Charles will not give up Buckingham	318
Murder of Dr. Lambe	319
The King's answer to the Remonstrance	320
Buckingham seeks to meet the charges against him	321
Debate on tonnage and poundage	322
Remonstrance on tonnage and poundage	323
The King's speech	324
Parliament prorogued	325
Was tonnage and poundage included in the Petition of Right?	326
Ecclesiastical promotions	329
Buckingham's foreign policy	331
Carlisle's mission	332
Prospects of peace with France and Spain	333
Changes in the Government	334
Wentworth's peerage	335
Expectations held out to him of the Presidentship of the North	337
Wentworth's political position	337

CHAPTER LXV.

THE ASSASSINATION OF THE DUKE OF BUCKINGHAM.

1628 Lady Buckingham's overtures to Williams	339
Reconciliation between Buckingham and Williams	340
Influence of Carleton over Buckingham	341
Buckingham surrenders the Cinque Ports	342
Resistance of Rochelle	343
Buckingham prepares to relieve it	344
He welcomes Contarini's offer of Venetian mediation	345
The King hesitates	347
Forebodings of evil	347
Mutiny at Portsmouth	348

	PAGE		PAGE
Murder of the Duke by Felton	349	Mission of Rosencrantz	366
Seizure of the assassin	350	Influence of the Queen	367
Story of Felton	352	Charles rejects the terms offered	367
His popularity	353	Orders Lindsey to persevere	368
Towniey's verses	354	Surrender of Rochelle	369
Alexander Gill at Oxford	355	Charles's failure	370
Buckingham's funeral	356	A Spanish alliance suggested by Carlisle	371
His career	358	Arundel and Cottington in the Council	371
Felton threatened with the rack	359	Dorchester becomes Secretary	372
His execution	359	1629 The Council agrees to negotiate with France	373
Charles personally undertakes the government	360	Feeling of the nation about the war	373
Character and position of Weston	361	Dutch successes	374
Lindsey takes the fleet to the relief of Rochelle	363	End of the war period	375
Failure of the attempt	364		
Montague's negotiation	365		

MAPS.

MAP OF CADIZ HARBOUR . . . . *To face title-page*

„ „ THE ISLE OF RHÉ . . . . „ . *p.* 367

HISTORY OF ENGLAND.

CHAPTER LV.

THE EXPEDITION TO CADIZ.

THE gloomy anticipations of some of the members of the dissolved House of Commons with respect to their personal safety were not realised. Phelips and Seymour, Coke and Glanville returned in peace to their homes. Mansell, indeed, was summoned before the Council; but he answered boldly that he could not be touched without a violation of the liberties of Parliament, and was dismissed with nothing worse than a reprimand.[1]

<small>Aug. 12. The leaders of the Commons untouched.</small>

In fact it was no part of Buckingham's policy to drive the nation to extremity. Full of confidence in himself, he fancied that he had but to use the few months' breathing space allowed him to convince the electors that their late representatives had been in the wrong. The time had come which he had apparently foreseen when he conversed with Eliot at Westminster. He had asked for necessary support, and had been denied. A few days would show the King of France at peace at home, turning his sword against Spain and the allies of Spain abroad. A few months would

<small>Buckingham's intentions.</small>

---

[1] Johnston, *Hist. Rerum Britannicarum*, 666. Tillières to Louis XIII., Aug. $\frac{21}{31}$, *King's MSS.* 137, p. 121.

show the great English fleet returning with the spoils of Spanish cities and the captured treasures of the New World. Then a fresh Parliament would assemble round the throne to acknowledge the fortitude of the King and the prescience of his minister.

A few days after the dissolution news came from France which dashed to the ground the hopes which had been formed of the cessation of the civil war. Many persons about the Court of Louis had no liking for Richelieu's policy of toleration. The Prince of Condé, if report spoke truly, sent a hint to Toiras, who commanded the French troops outside Rochelle, that peace must in one way or another be made impossible. To carry such counsels into execution presented no difficulties to Toiras. The Rochellese, pleased with the news that peace had been made at Fontainebleau, pressed out without suspicion into the fields to gather in their harvest. Toiras directed his cannon upon the innocent reapers. Many of them were slain, and Toiras then proceeded to set fire to the standing corn. Loud was the outcry of the indignant citizens within the walls. It was impossible, they said, to trust the King's word. The ratification of the treaty was refused, and the war seemed likely to blaze up once more with all its horrors.[1] The English ships were now in the hands of the French admiral, and in a naval engagement which took place off Rochelle, on September 5, Soubise was entirely defeated, and driven to take an ignominious refuge in an English port.

The peace with the Huguenots comes to nothing.

Aug. 10.

Sept. 5. Defeat of Soubise.

Although such a calamity could hardly have been foretold by anyone, it was none the less disastrous to Buckingham's design of conciliating the English nation. All the long intrigue carried on with the assistance of Nicholas was rendered useless. The English ships were in French hands, and they would doubtless be used against Rochelle. It was easy to foresee what a handle would thus be given to Buckingham's accusers.

How it affected Buckingham.

[1] Resolution of the Town of Rochelle, Aug. $\frac{10}{20}$; Lorkin to Conway, Aug. $\frac{11}{21}$, *S. P. France.*

It is probable that the renewal of hostilities was already known to Charles when the Privy Council met at Woodstock on August 14, the Sunday after the dissolution. It was evidently the King's intention to show that he would take no serious step without the advice of the Privy Council. Its members unanimously approved of a proclamation for the banishment of the Roman Catholic priests, of the continuance of the preparations for sending out the fleet, and of the issue of Privy seals, to raise what was practically a forced loan, in order to meet its expenses.[1]

Aug. 14.

Banishment of the priests resolved on.

The fleet to go, and Privy seals to be issued.

If money had been needed for the fleet alone, there would have been no such pressing need. In addition to the 10,000*l.* borrowed in August, no less than 98,000*l.* were brought into the Exchequer in the months of August and September on account of the Queen's portion,[2] and Charles, before August was over, was quietly talking to the French ambassador of diverting part of the new loan to some other purpose.[3] In point of fact the order for preparing the Privy seals was not issued till September 17,[4] and the fleet was at sea before a single penny of the loan came into the King's hands. Charles, however, had many needs, and he may perhaps have thought that there would be less opposition to the loan if he demanded it for the purpose of fitting out the fleet.

Sept. 17. The Privy seals at last issued.

Charles had thus, after dismissing his Parliament, been able to convince or cajole his Privy Council. But he could neither convince nor cajole his wife. The promises lightly made when hope was young he had repudiated and flung aside. He was unable to understand why the Queen, who had, upon the faith of those promises, consented to leave her mother's care for a home in a strange land,

August. Charles's domestic troubles.

---

[1] Meautys's Note, Aug. 14, *S. P. Dom.* v. 41 ; Tillières to Louis XIII., Aug. $\frac{21}{31}$, *King's MSS.* 137, p. 121.

[2] *Receipt Books of the Exchequer.*

[3] Tillières to Louis XIII., Aug. $\frac{21}{31}$, *King's MSS.* 137, p. 131.

[4] The King to the Council, Sept. 17, *S. P. Dom.* vi. 70.

B 2

should feel aggrieved when the Catholics, whom she had come to protect, were again placed under the pressure of the penal laws. A few days after the dissolution he was at Beaulieu, hunting in the New Forest, whilst Henrietta Maria was estab-

The Queen at Titchfield. lished at Titchfield, on the other side of Southampton Water. There he visited her from time to time; but, in the temper in which they both were, there was little chance of a reconciliation. Charles never thought of taking the slightest blame to himself for the estrangement which had arisen between them. It was his wife's business, he held, to love and obey him, just as it was the business of the House of Commons to vote him money. Sometimes he sent Buckingham to threaten or to flatter the Queen by turns. Sometimes he came in person to teach her what her duties were. If he was blind to his own errors he was sharpsighted enough to perceive that his wife's French attendants were doing their best to keep her displeasure alive, and were teaching her to regard herself as a martyr, and to give as much time as possible to spiritual exercises and to the reading of books of devotion.[1]

Dispute about the Ladies of the Bedchamber. To counteract these tendencies in the Queen, Charles wished to place about her the Duchess of Buckingham, the Countess of Denbigh, and the Marchioness of Hamilton, the wife, the sister, and the niece of his own favourite minister, and he desired her at once to admit them as Ladies of the Bedchamber.

Although this demand was not in contradiction with the letter of the marriage treaty,[2] it was in complete opposition to its spirit, and the young Queen fired up in anger at the proposal. She told Charles that what he asked was contrary to the contract of marriage. Nothing, she told her own followers, would induce her to admit spies into her privacy.

[1] See a curious letter, said to be from a gentleman in the Queen's household (Oct. 15, *S. P. Dom.* vii. 85), which looks genuine. But even if it is not, the statements in it are in general accordance with what is known from other sources.

[2] By Article 11 all the attendants taken from France were to be Catholics and French, and all vacancies were to be filled up with Catholics. Louis had forgotten to provide for the case of Charles wishing to add Protestants when there were no vacancies.

The strife grew fierce. The guard-room at Titchfield was used on Sundays for the service of the English Church, according to the custom which prevailed in houses occupied by the King. Against this the Queen protested as an insult to herself, and argued that whilst Charles was at Beaulieu, she was herself the mistress of the house. Lady Denbigh, however, took part against her, and the service was not discontinued. At last the Queen lost all patience, made an incursion into the room at sermon time, and walked up and down laughing and chattering with her French ladies as loudly as possible. The preacher soon found himself a butt for the practical jokes of the Frenchmen of the household. One day, as he was sitting on a bench in the garden, a gun was fired off behind a hedge close by. The frightened man fancied an attempt had been made upon his life, and pointed to some marks upon the bench as having been made by the shot aimed at himself. Tillières, who had come back to England as chamberlain to the Queen, was called in to adjudicate, and, having sat down on several parts of the bench, gravely argued that as he could not sit anywhere without covering some of the marks, and as, moreover, the clergyman was very corpulent, whilst he was himself very thin, the shot which had made the marks must certainly have passed through the person of the complainant, if his story had been true.[1]

The English sermon at Titchfield.

Practical jokes upon the preacher.

If Charles was hardly a match for his wife, he had no doubt at all that he was a match for half the Continent. Those vast enterprises which he had been unable to bring himself to disavow in the face of the House of Commons had still a charm for his mind. In vain Rusdorf, speaking on behalf of his master, the exiled Frederick, urged upon him the necessity of concentrating his forces in one quarter, and argued that the ten thousand landsmen on board the fleet would be useless at Lisbon or Cadiz, but would be invaluable on the banks of the Elbe or the Weser, where

Rusdorf urges Charles to assist the King of Denmark.

---

[1] Tillières, *Mémoires*, 99–104; Rusdorf to Oxenstjerna, $\frac{\text{Sept. 30}}{\text{Oct. 10}}$, *Mémoires de Rusdorf*, ii. 73.

Christian of Denmark was with difficulty making head against Tilly.[1]

As the attack upon Spain was the first object with Charles, he listened more readily to the Dutch Commissioners, who had come to England in order to draw up a treaty of alliance. Naturally the Dutchmen cared more about the war with Spain than about the war in Germany, and when the treaty which they came to negotiate was completed it fixed accurately the part to be taken by the two countries in common maritime enterprise, whilst everything relating to hostilities on land was expressed in vague generalities The States-General had already agreed to lend Charles 2,000 English soldiers in exchange for the same number of recruits, and to send twenty vessels to join the fleet at Plymouth.[2] By the new treaty, which was signed at Southampton on September 8, an alliance offensive and defensive was established between England and the States-General. The Flemish harbours were to be kept constantly blockaded by a Dutch fleet, whilst the English were to perform the same task off the coast of Spain. Whenever a joint expedition was concerted between the two nations the States-General were to contribute one ship for every four sent out by England. The details of a somewhat similar arrangement for joint operations by land were left, perhaps intentionally, in some obscurity.[3]

The Dutch Commissioners in England.

Sept. 8. The Treaty of Southampton.

To Rusdorf the preference shown for maritime over military enterprise was the death-knell of his master's hope of recovering the Palatinate. Charles was far too sanguine to take so gloomy a view of the situation. He had now openly broken with Spain. He had recalled Trumbull, his agent at Brussels, and he had no longer any minister residing in the Spanish dominions. He had followed up this step by the issue of letters of marque to those who wished to prey on Spanish commerce. Yet he had no idea of limiting hostilities to a combat between England and Spain. "By the

Open breach with Spain.

---

[1] Rusdorf's advice, $\frac{\text{Aug. 31}}{\text{Sept. 10,}}$ *Mémoires de Rusdorf*, i. 611.

[2] Agreement, $\frac{\text{July 23}}{\text{Aug. 2,}}$ *Aitzema*, i. 468.

[3] Treaty of Southampton *ibid.* i. 469.

grace of God," he said to a Swedish ambassador who visited him at Titchfield, " I will carry on the war if I risk my crown. I will have reason of the Spaniards, and will set matters straight again. My brother-in-law shall be restored, and I only wish that all other potentates would do as I am doing." [1]

In fact, it was because Charles had not been content to pursue a mere war of vengeance against Spain, that he had entered upon those extended engagements which more than anything else had brought him into collision with the House of Commons. Those engagements he had no intention of abandoning, and he hoped that if some temporary way of fulfilling them could be found, the success of the fleet would give him a claim to the gratitude of his subjects, and would enable him to place himself at the head of an alliance more distinctly Protestant than when he had been hampered by the necessity of looking to France for co-operation. In the Treaty of Southampton the foundation for such an alliance had been laid, and it now only remained to extend it, with the needful modifications, to the King of Denmark and the North German Princes.

Buckingham to go to the Hague. It was therefore arranged that Buckingham should go in person to the Hague, where the long-deferred conference was expected at last to take place. It was useless for him to go with empty hands. If Charles could not procure the money which he had already bound himself to supply to the King of Denmark, it was hardly likely that Christian would care to enter into fresh negotiations with so bad a paymaster. Yet, how was the money to be found? One desperate resource there was, of which Charles had spoken already in a rhetorical flourish, and of which he was now resolved to make use in sober earnest. The plate and jewels of the Crown,

The Crown jewels to be pawned. the hereditary possession of a long line of kings, might well be pledged in so just and so holy a cause. In England, it was true, no one would touch property to which his right might possibly be challenged, on the ground that the inalienable possessions of the Crown could not pass, even for a time, into the hands of a subject; but on the Continent there

[1] Rusdorf to Frederick, Sept. $\frac{10}{20}$, *Mémoires de Rusdorf*, i. 623.

would be no fear of the peculiar doctrines of English law. The danger was that, if once the precious gems were sent to the Continent, there might be some difficulty in recovering them. At last it was decided that the plate and jewels should be carried by Buckingham to Holland. It was probably argued that in that rich and friendly country men might be found who would both accept the security and be faithful to their trust.[1]

Want of money is a sad trial to any Government, and in one part of England it had already brought Charles into difficulties with his subjects. Towards the end of August serious apprehensions were entertained for the safety of Harwich. It was known that Dunkirk was alive with preparations for war, and no part of England was so liable to attack as the flat and indented coast of Essex. Orders were therefore issued by the Privy Council to put Landguard Fort in repair, and to occupy Harwich with a garrison of 3,000 men, chosen from the Essex trained bands. So far everything had been done according to rule. Each county was bound to provide men for its own defence. But the Crown was also bound to repay the expenses which it might incur, and this time there was an ominous silence about repayment. Under these circumstances the Earl of Warwick, Holland's elder brother—who was now in high favour with Buckingham—made a proposition which looks like the germ of the extension of shipmoney to the inland counties. The adjacent shires, he said, were interested in the safety of Harwich. Let them, therefore, be called on to contribute to its defence in men and money. The adjacent shires, however, refused to do anything of the kind; and the vague promises of payment at some future time, which was all that the Government had in its power to offer, were met by the firm resolution of the Essex men that they, at any rate, would not serve at their own charges. Making a

<small>August.
The Essex trained bands at Harwich</small>

---

[1] The earliest mention of Buckingham's intended journey is, I believe, in Rusdorf's letter to Oxenstjerna. Sept. $\frac{9}{19}$ (*Mém.* ii. 63). The first hint about the jewels is in an order from Conway to Mildmay, the Master of the Jewel House, to give an account of the plate in his hands. Conway to Mildmay, Sept. 4, *Conway's Letter Book*, 227, *S. P. Dom.*

virtue of necessity, the Council ordered the men to be sent back to their homes, and directed Pennington, who, since his return from Dieppe, had been watching, with a small squadron, the movements of the Dunkirk privateers, to betake himself to the protection of Harwich. Thus ended Charles's first attempt so to construe the obligations of the local authorities as to compel them to take upon themselves the duties of the central Government.[1]

With all Charles's efforts to conciliate public opinion by a bold and, as he hoped, a successful foreign policy, there was no thought of throwing open the offices of State to those who were likely to be regarded with confidence by the nation. Yet it was not long before an opportunity occurred of which a wise ruler would have taken advantage. On September 6, Morton died of a fever which seized him a few days after his return from the Netherlands. The vacant secretaryship was at once conferred upon Sir John Coke, the only man amongst the Government officials who had incurred the positive dislike of the Opposition leaders of the Commons, in whose eyes the subserviency which he always showed to Buckingham more than counterbalanced the excellent habits of business which he undoubtedly possessed. The honesty of purpose upon which that subserviency was based was unlikely to make any impression on their minds.

Sept. 6. Death of Morton.

Sir John Coke, secretary.

Buckingham was not left without a warning of the danger he was incurring by his refusal to make any effort to conciliate public opinion. Lord Cromwell, who had left his service under Mansfeld for a more hopeful appointment in the new expedition, had brought back with him from the Netherlands his old habit of speaking plainly. "They say," he wrote to the Duke, "the best lords of the Council knew nothing of Count Mansfeld's journey or this fleet, which discontents even the best sort, if not all. They say it is a very

Sept. 8. Cromwell's letter.

---

[1] Coke to Buckingham, Aug. 25 ; Coke to Conway, Aug. 26 ; Order of Council, Aug. 30 ; Sussex to the Council, Sept. 9 ; Warwick to Conway, Sept. 10 ; Warwick to the Council, Sept. 18, 23 ; The Council to Warwick, Oct. 2, *S. P. Dom.* v. 85, 99 ; vi. 38, 44, 76, 98 ; vii. 4.

great burden your Grace takes upon you, since none knows anything but you. It is conceived that not letting others bear part of this burden now you bear, it may ruin you, which Heaven forbid."[1]

The expedition upon which so many hopes were embarked was by no means in a prosperous condition. For a long time the soldiers had been left unpaid. Before the end of August there was a new press of 2,000 men, to fill up the vacancies caused by sickness and desertion.[2] The farmers of South Devon, upon whom the soldiers were billeted, refused to supply food to their unwelcome guests as soon as they discovered that their pockets were empty. Like Mansfeld's men eight months before, the destitute recruits made up their minds that they would not die of starvation. Roaming about the country in bands, they killed sheep before the eyes of their owners, and told the farmers to their faces that rather than famish they would kill their oxen too.[3]

August. Bad condition of the troops at Plymouth.

At one time there had been a talk of Buckingham's taking the command in person, and a commission had been made out in his name; but he could not be at the Hague and on the coast of Spain at the same time, and he perhaps fancied that he could do better service as a diplomatist than as an admiral. At all events, whilst, much to the amusement of the sailors, he retained the pompous title of generalissimo of the fleet, he appointed Sir Edward Cecil, the grandson of Burghley and the nephew of Salisbury, to assume the active command, with the more modest appellation of general.[4] Cecil had served for many years in the Dutch army, with the reputation of being a good officer. He was now for the first time to be trusted with an independent command, and the selection was the more hazardous as he was entirely unacquainted with naval warfare. From the first he had attached himself closely to Buckingham, who had in vain supported his

Cecil to command the expedition.

---

[1] Cromwell to Buckingham, Sept. 8, *S. P. Dom.* vi. 30.
[2] The King to Nottingham and Holderness, Aug. 23, *ibid.* v. 62
[3] Commissioners at Plymouth to the Council, Aug. 12, Sept. 1, *S. P. Dom.* vi. 3.
[4] Eliot, *Negotium Posterorum.*

claims to the command in the Palatinate in 1620, but who had now sufficient influence to reverse the decision then come to in favour of Sir Horace Vere. The Earl of Essex, who was to go as Vice-Admiral, knew as little of the sea as Cecil himself; and the same might be said of the Rear-Admiral, the Earl of Denbigh, whose only known qualification for the post lay in the accident that he was married to Buckingham's sister.

<small>Essex and Denbigh.</small>

Whatever Cecil's powers as a general may have been, he had at least a soldier's eye to discern the deficiencies of the troops under his orders, and he professed himself as puzzled as the Commons had been to discover why, if no attempt had been made to convert the recruits into trained soldiers, they had been levied in May for service in September. Buckingham, too, he complained, had been recommending officers to him who were not soldiers at all, and whom 'he neither could nor durst return.' The arms which the men should have been taught to handle were still on board ship in the harbour. On September 8, only three out of the twenty Dutch ships promised had arrived at Plymouth.[1]

<small>Sept. 8. Cecil's report on the troops.</small>

There was, however, one direction in which Cecil's energy could hardly be thrown away. In answer to the complaints made in Parliament it had been announced that Sir Francis Steward would be sent out with a squadron to clear the English seas of the Sallee rovers. Steward's attempt had ended in total failure. According to the Mayor of Plymouth, his ships had been outsailed by the pirates. According to his own account the weather had been against him. Parliament, he said, instead of grumbling against the King's officers, ought to have passed an Act ensuring them a fair wind.[2]

<small>Measures taken against pirates.</small>

The outcry from the western ports waxed louder than ever. It was reported that danger had arisen from another quarter. No less than ten privateers had slipped through the Dutch block-

---

[1] Cecil to Conway, Sept. 8. *S. P. Dom.* vi. 36.

[2] The Mayor &c. to the Council, Aug. 12; Steward to Buckingham, Aug. 16, *S. P. Dom.* v. 36, 49.

ading squadron in front of Dunkirk,[1] and were roaming the seas to prey upon English commerce. Cecil, when he heard the news, sent out Sir Samuel Argall in search of the enemy. Argall, after a seven days' cruise, returned without having captured a single pirate or privateer; but he was followed by a long string of French and Dutch prizes, which he suspected of carrying on traffic with the Spanish Netherlands. Amongst these was one, the name of which was, a few months later, to flash into sudden notoriety—the 'St. Peter,' of Havre de Grace.[2]

Sept. 9. Argall's cruise.

On September 15[3] the King himself arrived at Plymouth to see the fleet and to encourage the crews by his presence. Charles went on board many of the ships, and reviewed the troops on Roborough Downs.[4] When he left, on the 24th, Buckingham, who had accompanied him, remained behind to settle questions of precedence amongst the officers, and to infuse, if it were possible, some of his own energetic spirit into the commanders. As usual, he anticipated certain success, and he was unwise enough to obtain from the King a public declaration of his intention to confer a peerage upon Cecil, on the ground that the additional rank would give him greater authority over his subordinates. It was given out that the title selected was that of Viscount Wimble-

The King and Buckingham at Plymouth.

---

[1] Hippisley to Buckingham, Sept. 9, *S. P. Dom.* vi. 67, 120.

[2] Narrative of the Expedition, Sept. 16; Examination of the masters of the prizes; *ibid.* vi. 67, 120.

[3] Cecil's Journal, printed in 1626, has been usually accepted as the authority for the voyage. But it should be compared with his own despatches, and with the letters of other officers, such as Sir W. St. Leger, Sir G. Blundell, and Sir T. Love, which will be found amongst the State Papers. We have also now Glanville's official narrative, edited by Dr. Grosart for the Camden Society. The Journal of the 'Swiftsure' (*S. P. Dom.* xi. 22) contains a full narrative of the proceedings of the squadron under Essex, whilst the proceedings of Denbigh and Argall are specially treated of in an anonymous journal (*S. P. Dom.* x. 67). Geronimo de la Concepcion's *Cadiz Ilustrada* gives the Spanish story. In the *Tanner MSS.* (lxxii. 16) there is a MS. copy of Wimbledon's Journal, annotated by some one hostile to the author, thus bearing witness to the correctness of his assertions where they are not questioned.

[4] *Glanville*, 3.

don, though there was not time formally to make out the patent before the sailing of the fleet. Buckingham seems to have forgotten that honours granted before success has crowned an undertaking are apt to become ridiculous in case of failure.

This was not the only foolish thing done by Buckingham at Plymouth. The sight of Glanville, the author of the last address of the Commons at Oxford, quietly fulfilling his duties as Recorder of the Devonshire port, inspired him with the idea of maliciously sending a Parliamentary lawyer to sea as secretary to the fleet. Glanville pleaded in vain that the interruption to his professional duties would cause him a heavy loss, and that, as no one but his clerk could, even under ordinary circumstances, decipher his handwriting, it was certain that when he came to set down the jargon of sailors, even that confidential servant would be unequal to the task.[1]

<small>Glanville sent on board the fleet.</small>

At last, on October 3, forty sail of the great fleet were sent on to Falmouth. The remainder lay in the Sound waiting for their Dutch comrades. They had not long to expect their coming; on the 4th the Dutch ships were descried, showing their topsails above the waves, as if, as men said, they had come to escort the English fleet upon its voyage. On the 5th the anchors were weighed, and the united fleet passed out of the harbour and rounded the point where the soft woods of Mount Edgcumbe slope down to the waters of the Sound. Its fair prospects were soon interrupted. The wind chopped round to the south-west, and began to blow hard. Essex, with the foremost vessels, took refuge in Falmouth, but the bulk of the fleet put back to its old anchorage. Plymouth harbour was no safe refuge in such a gale, in the days when as yet the long low line of the breakwater had not arisen to curb the force of the rolling waves. By the next morning all bonds of discipline had given way before the anxious desire for safety, and the waters of the Sound were covered with a jostling throng of vessels hurrying, regardless of the safety of each other, to the secure retreat of the

<small>Oct. 3. Sailing of part of the fleet.</small>

<small>The storm at Plymouth.</small>

---

[1] Glanville's reasons, Sept. (?) Woodford to Nethersole, Oct. 8, *S. P. Dom.* vi. 132; vii. 44. Was Glanville's objection the origin of the old joke, or did he use it for want of an argument?

Catwater. Orders, if given at all, met with but little attention, and Cecil himself was forced to get into a boat, and to pass from vessel to vessel, in order to exact the least semblance of obedience.

<small>Cecil's despondency.</small> Cecil had long ceased to look upon the expedition with his patron's confidence of success. Little good, he thought, would come of a voyage commenced so late in the season. The spectacle of disorder which he now witnessed left a deep impression on his mind. The discipline which comes from an energetic and well-arranged organisation was entirely wanting, and it was not replaced by the discipline which springs from old habits of comradeship, or from the devotion which makes each man ready to sacrifice himself to the common cause. Buckingham, who in 1624 had fancied that military power was to be measured by the number of enterprises simultaneously undertaken, fancied in 1625 that the warlike momentum of a fleet or army was to be measured by its numerical size. He had yet to learn—if indeed he ever learnt it—that thousands of raw recruits do not make an army, and that thousands of sailors, dragged unwillingly into a service which they dislike, do not make a navy. Cecil knew it, and the expedition carried with it the worst of omens in a hesitating and despondent commander.[1]

<small>Oct. 8. The fleet again puts to sea.</small> On the 8th the fleet, laden with the fortunes of Buckingham and Charles, put to sea once more. It sailed, as it had been gathered together, without any definite plan. There were general instructions that a blow should be struck somewhere on the Spanish coast before the treasure ships arrived, but no special enterprise had been finally selected. At a council held in the King's presence at Plymouth, Lisbon, Cadiz, and San Lucar had been mentioned as points of attack. The general opinion had been in favour of an attempt on San Lucar, which, if captured, might be used as a basis of operations against Cadiz and the expected treasure fleet. Objections had, however, been raised, and the whole question had been reserved for further discussion on the spot.

[1] *Glanville*, 7. Cecil to Coke, Oct. 8, undated in *Cab'a*, 370; Cecil to Buckingham, April 28, Sept. 26, 1626, *S. P. Dom. Addenda*.

As soon, therefore, as the fleet rounded Cape St. Vincent, Cecil called a council. The masters of the ships declared that it would be dangerous to enter the harbour of San Lucar so late in the year. Some who were present were strongly in favour of seizing Gibraltar as a place of great strength, and easy to be manned, victualled, and held if once taken. The majority concurred in rejecting the proposal, but hesitated between Cadiz and San Lucar. Upon this Argall observed that an easy landing could be effected at St. Mary Port in Cadiz Bay. From thence a march of twelve miles would bring the troops to San Lucar, a place which was certain to capitulate to so large a force without difficulty.

Oct. 20. The council of war at sea.

Argall's advice was adopted, and orders were given to anchor off St. Mary Port; but as the fleet swept up to the station a sight presented itself too tempting to be resisted. Far away on the opposite side of the bay lay twelve tall ships with fifteen galleys by their side,[1] covering a crowd of smaller vessels huddled under the walls of Cadiz. Essex, who led the way in Argall's ship, the 'Swiftsure,' disobeyed his orders, and dashed at once upon the prey.

Oct. 22. The fleet in Cadiz Bay.

No provision had been made for this conjuncture of affairs. To do him justice, Cecil did his best to repair his mistake. Sailing through Essex's division, he shouted orders to right and left to crowd all sail after the Vice-Admiral. But he shouted now as vainly in Cadiz Bay as he shouted a few weeks before in Plymouth harbour. The merchant captains and the merchant crews, pressed unwillingly into the service, had no stomach for the fight. Essex was left alone to his glory and his danger, and Cecil, who did not even know the names of the vessels under his command, was unable to call the laggards to account.

Of all this the Spanish commanders were necessarily ignorant. Instead of turning upon the unsupported 'Swiftsure,' they cut their cables and fled up the harbour. It was a

---

[1] There is a discrepancy about the numbers. I take them from Cecil's Journal. Glanville says there were fifteen or sixteen ships, and eight or nine galleys.

moment for prompt decision. Had a Drake or a Raleigh been in command, an attempt would doubtless have been made to follow up the blow. Cecil was no sailor, and he allowed his original orders for anchoring to be quietly carried out.

<small>Flight of the Spaniards.</small>

At nightfall a council of war was summoned on board the flagship. The project of marching upon San Lucar was abandoned, as it was discovered that the water at St. Mary Port was too shallow to allow the boats to land the men with ease. Though it was not known that a mere handful of three hundred men formed the whole garrison of Cadiz,[1] the flight of the Spanish ships had given rise to a suspicion that the town was but weakly defended. Some voices, therefore, were raised for an immediate attack upon the town. The majority, however, too prudent to sanction a course of such daring, preferred to think first of obtaining a safe harbour for the fleet. The council therefore came to a resolution to attack the fort of Puntal, which guarded the entrance, barely half a mile in width, leading to the inner harbour, where the vessels had taken refuge. The obstacle did not seem a serious one. "Now," said one of the old sailors, "you are sure of these ships. They are your own. They are in a net. If you can but clear the forts to secure the fleet to pass in safely, you may do what you will." Nothing could be easier, it was thought, than to take the fort. Sir William St. Leger alone protested against the delay. Part of the fleet, he argued, would be sufficient to batter the fort. The remainder might sail in at once against the ships whilst the enemy's attention was distracted. St. Leger, however, was not a sailor, and, good as his advice was, it was rejected by a council of war composed mainly of sailors.

<small>Puntal to be attacked.</small>

Five Dutch ships and twenty small Newcastle colliers were accordingly ordered to attack the fort at once. As Cecil watched the flashes of the guns lighting up the night, he flattered himself that his orders had been obeyed. But when morning dawned he learned

<small>Failure of the first attack.
Oct. 23.</small>

---

[1] *Geronimo de la Concpcion,* 458.

that the English colliers had taken advantage of the darkness to remain quietly at anchor, whilst the Dutchmen, overmatched in the unequal combat, had been compelled to draw off before midnight with the loss of two of their ships.

A rope at the yard-arm would doubtless have been Drake's recipe for the disease. Cecil was of a milder nature. Rowing from ship to ship, he adjured the cowards to advance for very shame. Finding that he might as well have spoken to the winds, he went on board the 'Swiftsure,' and directed Essex *Second attack.* to attack. The 'Swiftsure' was at once placed opposite the enemy's batteries, and was well seconded by her comrades of the Royal Navy. Nothing, however, would induce the merchant crews to venture into danger. Clustering timidly behind the King's ships, they contented themselves with firing shots over them at the fort. At last one of them clumsily sent a shot right through the stern of the 'Swiftsure,' and Essex, losing patience, angrily ordered them to cease firing.

Such an attack was not likely to compel the garrison to surrender, and it was only upon the landing of a portion of *Surrender of Puntal.* the troops that the fort at last capitulated. The Spanish commander, Don Francisco Bustamente, struck by the gallant bearing of the 'Swiftsure,' asked who was in command. "Do you know," was the reply, "who took Cadiz before?" "Yes," he said, "it was the Earl of Essex." "The son of that earl," he was told, "is in the ship." "Then," replied the Spaniard, "I think the devil is there as well." A request that he might be allowed to pay his respects to Essex was promptly accorded, and his reception was doubtless such as one brave man is in the habit of giving to another.

It was late in the evening before Puntal was in the hands of the English. By that time all hope of taking Cadiz by surprise *Reinforcements for Cadiz.* was at an end. Whilst Essex was battering Puntal Spanish troops were flocking into Cadiz, and that night the town was garrisoned by four thousand soldiers. It was true that the place was only provisioned for three days, but the Spanish galleys quickly learned that they could bring in succours in spite of the English, and Cadiz was soon provisioned as well as guarded.

On the morning of the 24th Cecil was busily employed in getting ashore the army of which, as a soldier, he wished to take the command in person. By his orders Denbigh called a council of war, which was to decide what was next to be done. The council recommended that provisions should be landed for the soldiers, that an attempt should be made to blockade Cadiz, and that the Spanish ships at the head of the harbour should at last be pursued.

<small>Oct. 24. The troops to be landed.</small>

Whilst the council was still sitting, a scout hurried in with intelligence that a large force of the enemy was approaching from the north, where the island, at the southern end of which Cadiz was situated, swelled out in breadth till it was cut off from the mainland by a narrow channel which was crossed by only one bridge. Fearing lest he should be taken between this force and the town, Cecil gave hasty orders to advance to meet the enemy. The Spaniards, however, were in no hurry to bring on an action against superior numbers, and prudently drew back before him.

<small>The march northwards.</small>

After a six miles' march the English discovered that no enemy was in sight. Cecil, however, did not appear to be in the least disconcerted. "It seemeth," he said to those who were near him, "that this alarm is false; but since we are thus forwards on our way, if you will, we will march on. It may be we may light on some enemy. If we do not, we may see what kind of bridge it is that hath been so much spoken of."[1]

Cecil, in fact, lighted on an enemy upon whose presence he had failed to calculate. In the hurry of the sudden march no one had thought of seeing that the men carried provisions with them. It is true that stores had been sent from the ships, in pursuance of the decision of the council of war. Yet even if these had been actually landed, they would hardly have reached the army, which was already engaged in its forward march, till too late to provide a meal for

<small>The soldiers among the wine-casks.</small>

---

[1] This would be almost incredible, if it did not stand on Cecil's own authority. The marginal note in the copy amongst the *Tanner MSS.* remarks: "The first time an army marched so far to answer a false alarm, and it were fit his Lordship would name those some of the council he spake to, that were not against his going to the bridge."

that day. As a matter of fact, they were never landed at all. The officer in command of Fort Puntal alleged that he had no orders to receive them, and sent them back to the ships. Cecil's force was thus in evil plight. Many of the soldiers had not tasted food since they had been landed to attack Puntal the day before. Ever since noon they had been marching with the hot Spanish sun beating fiercely on their heads. Cecil, in mercy, ordered a cask of wine to be brought out of a neighbouring house to solace the fasting men. Even a little drop would have been too much for their empty stomachs, but the houses around were stored with wine for the use of the West India fleets. In a few minutes casks were broached in every direction, and well-nigh the whole army was reduced to a state of raving drunkenness. Interference was useless, and the officers were well content that the enemy was ignorant of the chance offered him.

Disgraceful as the scene was, it had no appreciable effect upon the success or failure of the expedition. When morning dawned it was evident that the men could not be kept another day without food, even if there had been any object to be gained by their remaining where they were.[1] Leaving therefore a hundred poor wretches lying drunk in the ditches to be butchered by the Spaniards, Cecil returned to Puntal, to learn that the attack which he had ordered upon the Spanish ships had not

Oct. 25. Retreat to Puntal.

Failure of the attack upon the ships.

---

[1] Let Cecil be judged by his own Journal. "Now this disorder happening," he writes, "made us of the council of war to consider that since the going to the bridge was no great design, but to meet with the enemy and to spoil the country, neither could we victual any men that should be left there, and that the galleys might land as many men as they would there to cut them off: and that when my Lord of Essex took Cadiz, Conyers Clifford was taxed by Sir Francis Vere . . . with mistaking the directions that were given him to go no further from the town than the throat of the land, which is not above two miles, where he might be seconded and relieved, and be ready to relieve others; but he went to the bridge, which was twelve miles off; so in regard there was no necessity, this disorder happening and want of victuals, we resolved to turn back again, which we did." The marginal note to this is, "Why did his Lordship then go to the bridge without victuals and to lose time, having such a precedent against it?"

been carried out. Their commanders had made use of their time whilst the English were battering Puntal. Warping their largest vessels up a narrow creek at the head of the harbour, they had guarded them by sinking a merchantman at the entrance. Argall, to whom the attack had been entrusted by Denbigh, had only to report that the thing was impracticable. However great may be the risk in forming an opinion on imperfect data, it is difficult to resist the impression that a combined attack by sea and land would not have been made in vain, and that if Wimbledon, instead of wasting his time in pursuing a flying enemy, had contented himself with acting in conjunction with Argall, a very different result would have been obtained.

However this may have been, it was now too late to repair the fault committed. A reconnaissance of the fortifications of Cadiz convinced the English commanders that the town was as unassailable as the ships. The Mexico fleet, the main object of the voyage, was now daily expected, and there was no time to linger any longer. On the 27th the men were re-embarked. The next day Puntal was abandoned, and the great armament stood out to sea as majestic and as harmless as when it had arrived six days before.

Oct. 27. The men re-embarked.
Oct. 28.

On November 4 the English fleet arrived at its appointed station, stretching out far to seaward from the southern coast of Portugal. Though no man on board knew it, the quest was hopeless from the beginning. The Spanish treasure ships, alarmed by the rumours of war which had been wafted across the Atlantic, had this year taken a long sweep to the south. Creeping up the coast of Africa, they had sailed into Cadiz Bay two days after Cecil's departure.[1]

Nov. 4. The look-out for the Mexico fleet.

It may be that fortune was not wholly on the side of Spain. Judging by the exploits of the merchant captains before Puntal, it is at least possible that, if a collision had taken place, instead of the English fleet taking the galleons, the galleons might have taken the English fleet. At all events, if the Spaniards had trusted to flight rather than to valour, the English vessels would

[1] Atye to Acton, $\frac{\text{Dec. 28}}{\text{Jan. 7}}$, *S. P. Spain.* See, however, Mr. Dalton's *Life of Sir E. Cecil,* where is the best account of this voyage.

hardly have succeeded in overtaking them. With their bottoms foul with weeds, and leaking at every pore from long exposure to the weather, they found it hard to keep the sea at all. Cecil had at first resolved to keep watch till the 20th, but on the 16th he gave orders to make sail for home with all possible speed.

<small>Nov. 16. Return to England.</small>

There was indeed no time to lose. The officials who had been charged with supplying the fleet had been fraudulent or careless. Hulls and tackle were alike rotten. One ship had been sent out with a set of old sails which had done service in the fight with the Armada. The food was bad, smelling 'so as no dog in Paris Garden would eat it.'[1] The drink[2] was foul and unwholesome. Disease raged among the crews, and in some cases it was hard to bring together a sufficient number of men to work the ships. One by one, all through the winter months, the shattered remains of the once powerful fleet came staggering home, to seek refuge in whatever port the winds and waves would allow.

<small>Bad condition of the ships and men.</small>

It was certain that so portentous a failure would add heavily to the counts of the indictment which had long been gathering against Buckingham. Some indeed of the causes of failure were of long standing. In the King's ships both officers and men were scandalously underpaid, and many of them thought more of eking out their resources by peculation than of throwing themselves heart and soul into the service of their country. Nor was it fair to expect, after the long peace, that efficiency which is only attainable under the stress of actual warfare. Yet, if the actual conduct of the expedition were called in question, it would be in vain for Buckingham, after his defiant challenge to public opinion at Oxford, to argue before a new House of Commons that he was not answerable for Cecil's neglect of his opportunities at Cadiz, and still less for the accident by which the Mexico fleet had escaped.

<small>December. Buckingham's part in the matter.</small>

---

[1] Sir M. Geere to W. Geere, Dec. 11, *S. P. Dom.* xi. 49.

[2] Beverage, the term used in these letters, is the usual word in Devonshire now for common cyder, but it seems, from a passage in one of Cecil's letters (*Glanville*, xxxiv.), to have been made with sack. It was probably wine and water.

After all allowances have been made for exaggeration, is it easy to deny that the popular condemnation was in the main just? The commanders of the expedition, and the officials at home by whom the preparations were made, were Buckingham's nominees, and the system of personal favouritism, the worst canker of organisation, had never been more flourishing than under his auspices. Nor was it only indirectly that the misfortunes of the expedition were traceable to Buckingham. If, upon his arrival at Cadiz, Cecil had been too much distracted by the multiplicity of objects within his reach to strike a collected blow at any one of them, so had it been with the Lord High Admiral at home. Undecided for months whether the fleet was to be the mere auxiliary of an army which was to lay siege to Dunkirk, or whether the army was to be the mere auxiliary of a fleet of which the main object was the capture of the Plate fleet, he had no room in his mind for that careful preparation for a special object which is the main condition of success in war as in everything else.

If Cecil's errors as a commander were thus the reflection, if not the actual result, of Buckingham's own errors, the other great cause of failure, the misconduct of the merchant captains, brings clearly before us that incapacity for recognising the real conditions of action which was the fertile source of almost all the errors alike of Buckingham and of Charles. The great Cadiz expedition, of which Raleigh had been the guiding spirit, had been animated, like all other successful efforts, by the joint force of discipline and enthusiasm. A high-spirited people, stung to anger by a lifelong interference with its religion, its commerce, and its national independence, had sent forth its sons burning to requite their injuries upon the Spanish nation and the Spanish king, and ready to follow the tried and trusted leaders who had learned their work through a long and varied experience by sea and land. How different was everything now! It is hardly possible to doubt that the war of 1625 never was and never could have been as popular as the war of 1588 and 1597. Charles was not engaged in a national war, but in one which was political and religious, awakening strong popular sympathies, indeed, so long as the home danger of a

Spanish marriage lasted, but liable to be deserted by those sympathies when that danger was at an end. Nor, if enthusiasm were lacking, was its place likely to be supplied by discipline. The commanders were personally brave men, and most of them were skilled in some special branch of the art of war, but they had been utterly without opportunities for acquiring the skill which would have enabled them to direct the motions of that most delicate of all instruments of warfare, a joint military and naval expedition. It is possible that after eight or ten years of war so great an effort might have been successful. It would have been next to a miracle if it had been successful in 1625.

<small>No serious investigation.</small> The worst side of the matter was that Charles did not see in the misfortunes which had befallen him any reason for attempting to probe the causes of his failure to the bottom. Some slight investigation there was into the mistakes which had been committed in Spain; but nothing was done to trace out the root of the mischief at home. Sir James Bagg and Sir Allen Apsley, who had victualled the fleet before it sailed, were not asked to account for the state in which the provisions had been found, and they continued to enjoy Buckingham's favour as before. No officer of the dockyard was put upon his defence on account of the condition of the spars and sails. There was nothing to make it likely that if another fleet were sent forth in the next spring it would not be equally unprovided and ill-equipped. In the meanwhile the King and his minister had fresh objects in view, and it was always easy for them to speak of past failures as the result of accident or misfortune.

CHAPTER LVI.

CHARLES'S RELATIONS WITH FRANCE.

EVEN if the Cadiz expedition had not ended in complete failure, the difficulties resulting from the French alliance would *September.* have been likely to cause Charles serious embarrass-
The French ment. Every step which he had taken since the
alliance. meeting of his first Parliament had been in the direction of a closer understanding with the Protestant powers. He had begun again to execute the penal laws. He had signed a treaty with the Dutch, and he was about to send Buckingham to the Hague to sign another treaty with the King of Denmark and the princes of North Germany. When Parliament met again, he hoped to be able to stand forth in the character of a leader of the Protestantism of Europe.

Such schemes as these were fatal to the French alliance. Louis's idea of that alliance was evidently that of a man who
Bucking- wishes to play the first part. Buckingham wished to
ham's plans. play the first part too. He resolved to cross over at once to Holland, and then, when the foundations of a great
His proposed Protestant alliance had been surely laid, to pass on
visit to to Paris. Once more he would summon the King
France. of France to join England in open and avowed war against Spain and her allies, no longer, as he had done in May, as the representative of England alone, but as the leader of a mighty Protestant confederacy, offering to France the choice between the acceptance of English leadership or the isolation of neutrality.

Buckingham, indeed, had no difficulty in persuading himself that the offer which he was about to make was worthy of the acceptance of Louis. The Spanish treasure of which Cecil had gone in search was already his by anticipation. When the fleet returned there would be enough money to keep up the war in Germany for many a year, and the Flemish ports, so long the objects of his desire, would at last be snatched from Spinola's tenacious hold.[1]

There were reasons enough why the husband of Anne of Austria should be unwilling to receive a visit from the audacious upstart who had ventured to pay public court to the Queen of France; and Louis, as soon as he heard of the proposal, peremptorily instructed Blainville, the new ambassador whom he was despatching to England, to refuse permission to Buckingham to enter his kingdom.[2] Politics had

Objects of Louis.

---

[1] The views of the English Government may be gathered from a passage in the instructions drawn up as a guide to some one whom it was intended to send to Gustavus. "And because we are seated most properly and best furnished for maritime actions, we have undertaken that part, though it be of greatest cost, and which will, in a short time, by the grace of God, render all the land service easy and profitable to those that shall attempt it. And therefore we shall expect that both our dear uncle the King of Denmark and the King of Sweden will, upon your reasons heard, go on cheerfully for the stopping of the progress of the enemy's conquests by land, without calling to us for contribution in that, wherein principally must be regarded the present conservation of all the sea towns which might any way give Spain a port of receipt for their ships that may come from thence that may be bought or built in these parts, or may correspond with the ports of Flanders. And it will not be amiss when you shall fall into deliberation with that king, to consult and consider with him the great importance of taking away the harbours of Flanders from the King of Spain, and to prove how far he might be moved to join with us, our uncle of Denmark, and the States, to make one year's trial to thrust the King of Spain from the seacoasts of Flanders."—Instructions for Sweden, Oct. 17, *Rymer*, xviii. 212.

[2] "Je me passionne de sorte pour votre contentement que je ne crains point de vous mander si franchement mon avis, et vous êtes assez du monde pour pénétrer ce qui ne me seroit pas bienséant d'écrire," is Ville-aux-Clercs' explanation on giving the orders to Blainville, $\frac{\text{Sept. 24}}{\text{Oct. 4}}$, *King's MSS.* 137, p. 313.

undoubtedly as much part as passion in the matter. Not only was the question between Louis and Buckingham the question of the leadership of half Europe, but Louis had reason to suspect that he would have to guard against the interference of England nearer home. Buckingham, in fact, was instructed, as soon as he reached Paris, to require the immediate restoration of the English ships which had been used at Rochelle,[1] and to ask that an end should at once be put to the unnatural war between the King and the Huguenots.

<small>Demands to be made upon Louis.</small>

The demand, that Charles should be empowered to interfere between Louis and his subjects, was to be made in the most offensive way. Buckingham's instructions ran in the following terms:—"To the end they," that is to say, the French Protestants, "may not refuse the conditions offered them for the only doubt of not having them kept, you shall give them our Royal promise that we will interpose our mediation so far as that those conditions shall be kept with them; and if this will not satisfy them, you shall give them our kingly promise that if by mediation you cannot prevail for them, we will assist them and defend them." In other words, when Louis had once given his promise to the Huguenots, it was to be considered as given to the King of England, so that if any disputes again arose between him and his subjects, Charles might be justified in intervening in their favour if he thought fit so to do.

Buckingham, in fact, not content with taking the lead in Germany, was to dictate to Louis the relations which were to exist between himself and his subjects; and that too at a moment when the English Government was fiercely repudiating a solemn contract on the ground that it did not become a king of England to allow a foreign sovereign to intervene between

---

[1] Coke, who knew nothing of the circumstances which had induced Buckingham to surrender the ships, answers Lord Brooke's inquiries as follows: " For the French, I will excuse no error ; nor can give you any good account how the instruction for the ships not to be employed against them of the religion was changed. Only this I can assure your Honour, that I had neither hand nor foreknowledge of it. Now, our eyes are opened, and we shall endeavour by all means to recover the ships as soon as is possible."—*Coke to Brooke*, Nov. 5, *Melbourne MSS.*

himself and his people.[1] Before Buckingham left England, he had to learn that Louis had ideas of his own on the manner in which France was to co-operate with England. He was summoned back to Salisbury, where Charles halted on his return from reviewing the fleet at Plymouth, to hear what Blainville had to say.

On October 11 the new ambassador was admitted to an audience. He, indeed, had brought with him instructions to make proposals, if satisfaction could be given to Louis on other matters, which, as far as the war was concerned, ought not to have been unacceptable. Louis was ready to furnish 100,000*l.*, payable in two years, to the King of Denmark. He also promised to join Charles in giving support to Mansfeld's army, and consented to an arrangement, already in progress, for transferring that force to Germany, and placing Mansfeld under the command of the King of Denmark.[2] If Louis, however, was prepared to do as much as this, he was prepared to ask for something in return. He could hardly avoid asking for the fulfilment of Charles's promise to free the English Catholics from the penal laws; and now that Soubise had been defeated he would be likely to press for the entire submission of Rochelle, though he was ready to promise that the Huguenots should enjoy religious liberty, a privilege, as he afterwards wrote to Blainville, which was not allowed to the Catholics in England. In speaking to Charles, the Frenchman began in the tone of complaint. To his remonstrances about the English Catholics, Charles at first replied that he had only promised to protect the Catholics as long as they behaved with moderation. It was for himself to interpret this promise, and he took upon himself to say that they had not so behaved. He then added the now familiar argument that the secret article had never been taken seriously, even by the French Government.

Oct. 11. Blainville's audience. The French overtures.

[1] Conway to Carleton, Oct. 7, *S. P. Holland.* Instructions to Buckingham, *Rymer,* xviii.

[2] Louis XIII. to Blainville, Sept. $\frac{15}{25}$; Blainville to Louis XIII. Oct. $\frac{6, 11}{16, 21}$, *King's MSS.* 137, pp. 274, 350, 385; Villermont, *E. de Mansfeldt,* ii. 221.

The tone of the conversation grew warmer, and a fresh demand of the ambassador did not serve to moderate the excited feelings on either side. Soubise had brought with him to Falmouth the 'St. John,' a fine ship of the French navy, which he had seized at Blavet.[1] This ship Louis naturally claimed as his own property, which Charles was bound to restore. Charles, on the other hand, being afraid lest it should be used, as his own ships had been used, against Rochelle, hesitated and made excuses.

<small>The 'St. John' at Falmouth.</small>

The state of the Queen's household, too, ministered occasion of difference. Charles wished to add English officials to those who had been brought over from France, and he peremptorily refused to discuss the question with Blainville. He intended, he said, to be master in his own house. If he gave way, it would be from the love he bore to his wife, and for no other reason.

<small>The Queen's household.</small>

The next day the ambassador waited on Buckingham. The conversation was carried on in a more friendly tone than that of his conversation with Charles. In other respects it was not more satisfactory. Buckingham treated all the subjects in dispute very lightly. If anything had gone wrong the fault was in the necessities of the time. Instead of troubling himself with such trifles, the King of France ought to treat at once for an offensive league against Spain. As for himself, he was said to have ruined himself for the sake of France. He was now going to the Hague to save himself by great and glorious actions. If France pleased, she might take her place in the league which would be there concluded. If she refused, England would have all the glory.

<small>Oct. 12. Blainville visits Buckingham.</small>

Buckingham, as Blainville pointed out, had two irreconcilable objects in view. On the one hand he wished to ingratiate himself with English public opinion by placing himself at the head of a Protestant League; on the other hand he wished to show, by driving France to follow his lead on the Continent, that his original overtures to that power had not been thrown away.[2]

---

[1] See Vol. V. p. 304.

[2] Tillières, *Mémoires*, 105; Blainville to Louis XIII., Oct. $\frac{12, 16}{22, 26}$, *King's MSS.* 137, p. 409, 438.

Neither Louis nor Richelieu was likely to stoop as low as was expected of them. Blainville was instructed to announce that the 'Vanguard,' as being Charles's own property, should be given up, but that the merchant vessels, which had been expressly hired for eighteen months, would not be surrendered. He was to say that the Huguenots could not be allowed to carry on a rebellion against their lawful sovereign, and if Charles was so solicitous for religious liberty, he had better begin the experiment with his own Catholic subjects.[1] After this it was useless to lay before Charles the proposal for rendering assistance to Mansfeld which Blainville had been instructed to make under more favourable circumstances. Even the protest against Buckingham's visit to France was left unuttered for the present.

Bearing of the French Government.

Buckingham was too anxious to reach the Hague as soon as possible, to await the issue of these negotiations at Salisbury. But before he left the King, arrangements had been made for dealing in various ways with those Peers who had taken part in the opposition in the last Parliament. Of these Abbot might safely be disregarded. He had nothing popular about him except his firm attachment to the Calvinistic doctrine, and he had long been left in the shadow by James, who had displayed a strong preference for the cleverness and common sense of Williams, as Charles displayed a strong preference for the sharp decision of Laud.[2] It was a different matter to deal with Pembroke, the richest nobleman in England,[3] who commanded numerous

September. The opposition Peers.

Abbot and Pembroke.

---

[1] Memoir sent by De Vic, Oct. $\frac{16}{26}$; Louis XIII. to Blainville, $\frac{\text{Oct. 29}}{\text{Nov. 8}}$, *King's MSS.* 137, p. 470, 482.

[2] The idea, almost universal amongst historians, that Abbot was thrown into the shade by his accidental homicide in 1621, is not borne out by contemporary writers, and his want of influence may be easily accounted for from the causes mentioned above. Fuller is doubtless the original authority for the usual opinion, but Fuller's story has long ago been shown by Hacket to have been based upon a misapprehension of the facts.

[3] To the first subsidy of the reign Pembroke paid 700*l.*, standing alone; then came Northumberland. Rutland, and Devonshire, with 600*l.*; Buckingham, Derby, Cumberland, Hertford, Northampton, Petre, and

seats in the House of Commons,[1] and whose influence was not to be measured by the votes thus acquired. At first, indeed, Charles's temper had got the better of him, and on his journey to Plymouth he had treated Pembroke with marked disfavour. The Earl was not accustomed to be slighted, and replied with a counter-demonstration. As he passed through Sherborne he paid a formal visit to Bristol, who was still in disgrace. The significance of the step could not be misinterpreted, and Charles lost no time in renewing the old familiarity to which Pembroke was never insensible. Buckingham was with the King at Salisbury on his return journey, when he made an early call at Wilton; and, though Pembroke was still in bed and could not see him, it was afterwards understood that the temporary estrangement was at an end.[2]

Abbot and Pembroke belonged to that section of the Opposition which it was Buckingham's object to conciliate Arundel and Williams were in different case. As a great nobleman, not mixing much in the business of government, Arundel could hardly be touched; but Williams had incurred Buckingham's bitterest displeasure, and was easily assailable in his official position. His strong sense had led him to condemn alike the extravagances of the new reign and the shifts to which Charles had been driven in order to cover those extravagances from the popular view. He had shown a sad want of confidence in the success of those vast armaments in which Buckingham trusted, and he had been sufficiently uncourtierlike to dissuade the King from summoning the Commons to Oxford, and to suggest that if Charles had really given his word to the King of France that he would relax the penal laws, it was dangerous as well as impolitic to break it.

Arundel and Williams.

Robartes, with 400*l*. *Book of the Subsidy of the Nobility*, Oct. 2, *S. P. Dom.* vii. 6.

[1] Rudyerd to Nethersole, Feb. 3, 1626, *S. P. Dom.* xx. 23. 'All my Lord's letters were sent out,' means Pembroke's letters, not 'the Duke's,' as given in the *Calendar*. See also a letter from Sir James Bagg, in *S. P. Addenda*.

[2] North to Leicester, Sept. 28, Oct. 17; Pembroke to Leicester, Sept. 29, *Sydney Papers*, ii. 360, 363.

It was easier to resolve to get rid of the Lord Keeper than to find an excuse for dismissing him. At first he had been charged with entering upon conferences at Oxford with the leading members of the Opposition in the Commons. This charge, however, he was able to meet with a denial, though there is reason to believe that he was so convinced of Buckingham's folly in pitting himself against the House of Commons that he had boasted that if he were turned out of office, all England would take up his cause.[1] Charles was highly displeased with this language, but it was hardly possible to disgrace a Lord Keeper on the mere ground that he had vaunted his own popularity. At last some courtier reminded the King that his father had entrusted the Great Seal to Williams for three years on probation, and that the time fixed had now expired. Charles caught at the suggestion, and Williams, unable to defend himself against a form of attack in which no direct imputation on his conduct was necessarily implied, surrendered his office. Charles, glad to be rid of him, spoke to him fairly at the last, but the tone amongst Buckingham's followers was different. "May the like misfortune," wrote one of them to his patron, "befall such as shall tread in his hateful path, and presume to lift their head against their maker!"[2]

Oct. 25. Dismissal of Williams.

With Lord Keeper Williams worldly wisdom departed from the councils of Charles. If he could never have ripened into a great or a high-souled statesman, he had always at command a fund of strong common sense which saved him from the enormous blunders into which men more earnest and energetic than himself were ready to fall.

Greatness of the loss to Charles.

---

[1] "Your Lordship, I know, hath full information of all proceedings concerning the change of the Keeper, but happily hath not heard, and will hardly believe, that he was so confident in his party and the opinion of his worth, that he vaunted, if he were deposed, that he could have intercession made for him, not only by the strongest mediators now remaining, but by the generality of the land. Yet it pleased the good Bishop rather to submit himself to his Majesty's pleasure than to use his strength."—Coke to Brooke, Nov. 5, *Melbourne MSS*. This extract must be compared with Rushworth's story that Williams said that he meant to stand on his own legs.

[2] Not 'their heel,' as calendared. Suckling to Buckingham, Oct. 24; *S. P. Dom.* viii. 37.

Government was to him a balance to be kept between extreme parties. War was distasteful to him, and he cared little or nothing for Continental politics. Dogmatism of all kinds he regarded with the utmost suspicion. He had no sympathy with the persecution of Laud's friends by the House of Commons, and no sympathy with the coming persecution of the Puritans by Laud himself. Had Charles accepted him as an adviser, the reign would hardly have been eventful or heroic, but it would not have ended in disaster. England would have gained a great step on its way to liberty, by the permission which would, within certain broad limits, have been granted to the free development of thought and action. The last clerical Lord Keeper in English history was in reality less clerical than some of his successors.

The Great Seal was given to Coventry, whose legal knowledge and general ability were beyond dispute, and whose leanings were against all concessions to the Catholics. His accession to office therefore was one more announcement of the Protestant tendencies of Buckingham. "The Duke's power with the King," said a contemporary letter-writer, "for certain is exceeding great, and whom he will advance shall be advanced, and whom he doth but frown upon must be thrown down."[1] Heath succeeded Coventry as Attorney-General; and, with far less excuse, Shilton, whose only distinction was that he had been employed by Buckingham in his private affairs, followed as Solicitor-General.

Coventry Lord Keeper.

The meaning of the change was soon manifest, at least to the Catholics. The order for banishing the priests, given immediately after the dissolution, had not been followed at once by any attempt to interfere with the laity. On October 5, directions were given for a general disarmament of the recusants; but it was not till Coventry succeeded Williams that any further step was taken. On November 3 the blow fell. A commission was issued to provide for the execution of the penal laws, with instructions to pay over the fines levied to a special fund to be employed in the defence of the

Treatment of the Catholics.
Oct. 5. Disarmament of the recusants.
Nov. 3. The penal laws enforced.

[1] Ingram to Wentworth, Nov. 7, *Strafford Letters,* i. 28.

realm. On the 7th orders were given to prohibit all minors
from leaving England without licence from the King,
and to silence all schoolmasters whose teaching was open to
suspicion.[1]

<small>Nov. 7.</small>

Charles had probably an instinctive apprehension that the
persecution of the Catholics would not alone be sufficient to
secure for him the approbation of the next House of Commons;
but he was never keen-sighted in discerning the real causes of
popular dissatisfaction, and he ascribed the attack upon Buckingham
at Oxford to a mere ebullition of factious spite. The
inference was obvious. If by any means the assailants of his
minister could be excluded from seats in the coming Parliament,
the really loyal nature of Englishmen would find unimpeded
expression. It was like Charles, too, to fancy that if
only legal right were on his side no one could be justly dissatisfied.
With this idea in his head, nothing could seem simpler
than the course he adopted. A sheriff was bound to attend to
his duties in his own county, and if the Opposition leaders were
named sheriffs it was plain that they could not take their seats
at Westminster. Coke, Seymour, and Phelips were
of course marked out for the unwelcome honour.
With them were Alford, who had explained that the
subsidies voted in 1624 had not been voted for the recovery
of the Palatinate, and Sir Guy Palmes, who had referred
unpleasantly to the fate of Empson and Dudley. To these
five was added a sixth, Sir Thomas Wentworth.
It was not unknown to Charles that Wentworth had
little in common with Seymour and Phelips. He was
anxious, if possible, to obtain service under the Crown, and to
exercise his undoubted powers of government; but the war,
whether it was to be in Spain or Germany, was in his eyes sheer
madness, and it was plain that he would be as cool about the
King's Protestant crusade in 1626 as he had been cool about
his attack upon Spain in 1625. "Wentworth," said Charles, as
the names were read over to him, "is an honest gentleman."

<small>The Opposition leaders made sheriffs.</small>

<small>Wentworth's peculiar position.</small>

---

[1] Commission, Nov. 3, *S. P. Dom. Sign Manuals*, i. 87; the King to Buckingham, Nov. 7, *S. P. Dom.* Addenda.

The reasons for his exclusion were equally valid whether he were honest or not.¹

Such a manœuvre stands self-condemned by the very fact that it was a manœuvre. It had, however, at least one supporter amongst those who favoured the vigorous prosecution of the war. "The rank weeds of Parliament," wrote Rudyerd, "are rooted up, so that we may expect a plentiful harvest the next. I pray God so temper the humours of our next assembly that out of it may result that inestimable harmony of agreement between the King and his people."²

Rudyerd's opinion.

By this time Charles had hoped to receive news of great results from Buckingham's diplomacy in the Netherlands: but though the Lord Admiral, taking the courtly Holland with him, had left Charles at Salisbury in the second week of October, his voyage had been sadly delayed. On the 13th a terrific storm swept over the Channel and the North Sea. The Dutch fleet before Dunkirk was driven from its port, and great was the alarm in England when it was told that twenty-two vessels, it was said with 4,000 soldiers on board, had escaped to sea. The blow, however, fell upon the Dutch fishing vessels, and the English coast was spared.³

Oct. 13. The escape of the Dunkirk privateers.

With the Dunkirk privateers loose upon the world, the Lord Admiral could not cross without a convoy, and this was not easily to be found. The great fleet was still away at Cadiz, and three English ships had been cast away with all hands upon the cliffs between Calais and

Buckingham's voyage postponed.

---

¹ Ingram to Wentworth, Nov., *Strafford Letters*, i. 29. The name of Sir W. Fleetwood is here given as a seventh. He had not sat in the last Parliament, but in the Parliament of 1624. He was found ineligible for the shrievalty, and was neither a sheriff nor a member of the Commons in 1626. The first suggestion of making sheriffs in this way which I have met with, is in a letter from Sir G. Paul to Buckingham, Oct. 24; *S. P. Dom.* viii. 34.

² Rudyerd to Nethersole, Nov. 23, *S. P. Dom.* x. 16.

³ Downing to the Navy Commissioners, Oct. 19; Pennington to Buckingham, Oct. 23, *ibid.* viii. 5, 28.

Boulogne. What vessels were to be had must be hurried together for the defence of the country before the Duke's convoy could be thought of.

At last, however, ships were found for the purpose. On November 9 Buckingham was at the Hague, and was astonishing the sober citizens of the Dutch capital by the lavish splendour of his dress and the gorgeous display of pearls and diamonds with which it was adorned. He soon allowed it to be known that he had brought with him no friendly feeling towards France. "I acknowledge," he said, "the power of the King of France. But I doubt his good-will."[1]

<small>Nov. 9. Buckingham at the Hague.</small>

Buckingham had brought with him, too, his old plan for a joint attack with the Dutch upon Dunkirk. The effort, he told the Prince of Orange, should be made at once, as the Spaniards were in no condition to defend the place. The wary Prince knew too much about war to relish the idea of a siege to be begun in November, and refused to entertain the proposition till the spring. Then Buckingham asked that Sluys should be put in his master's hands, as a basis of operations for the English army which was to hem in the Flemish ports on the land side. The Prince met him with the same dilatory response. He was probably of opinion that the English army of which Buckingham spoke would never have any real existence;[2] and, even if it had been otherwise, he would certainly have been unwilling to confide to it the guardianship of so important a fortress.

<small>Nov. 11. He proposes to attack Dunkirk.</small>

The Congress of the Hague, when it met at last, was but a poor representation of that great anti-Spanish confederacy for which Gustavus had hoped when he first sketched out the plan. Though he was himself engaged in the Polish war, he had ordered his ambassador to take part in the assembly. Unhappily the ambassador fell ill, and died a few days before Buckingham's arrival. Sweden

<small>The Congress of the Hague.</small>

---

[1] Vreede, *Inleiding tot eene Geschiedenis der Nederlandsche Diplomatie,* ii. 2, 83.

[2] *Ibid.* ii. 2, 85, Note 2 ; Carleton to Conway, Nov. 14, *S. P. Holland.*

was therefore entirely unrepresented. The French minister stood aloof, and the North German princes took no share in the discussions. The representatives of the King of Denmark were there alone, to beg for money and men.

Christian IV. was indeed in sore need. Trusting to the promises made to him by Charles, he had gone to war. After the first month's contribution Charles had no money to send, and he was in no better plight in November than he had been in June. Buckingham's instructions, undoubtedly drawn up with his own concurrence, authorised him to acquaint the Danish ambassadors that the original offer of 30,000l. a month, or its equivalent in men, paid by the English exchequer, had only been made to give encouragement to the German princes. When those princes had once taken the field it was only to be expected that they would submit to provide a fair share of the expense. Buckingham was therefore to insist upon a large reduction of the monthly charge, though he was first to make sure that Christian was thoroughly embarked in the cause, lest by threatening to stop the supplies he might drive him to make his peace with the Emperor.[1]

It is probable that a little conversation with the Danish ambassadors convinced Buckingham that if the King of England thus withdrew from his engagements Christian would, without doubt, withdraw from the war. At all events nothing, so far as we know, was heard of the proposed reduction. On November 29 the Treaty of the Hague was signed between England, Denmark, and the States-General.

Nov. 29. Treaty of the Hague.

The Dutch agreed to supply the Danes with 5,000l. a month, whilst Buckingham engaged more solemnly than ever that the 30,000l. a month originally promised from England should be really sent.

Large as the sum was, there is reason to suppose that the promise was now made in good faith. Parliament would soon meet, and, as Buckingham hoped, all difficulties would then be smoothed away. For the immediate future he could

---

[1] Instructions to Buckingham and Holland, Oct. 17, *Rymer*, xviii. 211.

trust to the Crown jewels, which would soon be pawned to the merchants of Amsterdam. The disaster at Cadiz was as yet unknown, and every day might bring the happy news of victory. A new fleet was to be speedily prepared to relieve Cecil's force, and to take up the task of blockading the Spanish ports. The flood of mischief would thus be arrested at the fountain-head, as when gold no longer flowed from Spain, the armies by which Christain was assailed would break out into open mutiny.[1]

Dec. 5. Buckingham's expectations.

Proud of victories yet to be won, Buckingham had meditated a continuance of his journey to Paris, in order that he might add the name of the King of France to the signatures appended to the Treaty of the Hague. His hopes were cut short by the French ambassador, who plainly told him that, till better satisfaction had been given to his master's just demands in England, he would not be allowed to enter France.[2]

He is refused permission to enter France.

Buckingham therefore returned to England by the way that he had come. He was at once met by news of the failure at Cadiz and the return of the fleet. Alone, probably, of all Englishmen alive, Charles and Buckingham failed to realise the magnitude of the disaster, or the influence which it would exercise upon the deliberations of the coming session.[3] On December 16 the Lord Keeper was directed to issue writs for a new Parliament.[4]

News of the failure at Cadiz.

Dec. 16. Parliament summoned.

It was possible that Parliament might have work on hand even more serious than voting supplies for the King of Denmark. It was by no means unlikely that by the time the members were collected at Westminster, England would be at open war with France. Charles had been seriously vexed at the failure of his effort to frustrate the

Prospect of war with France.

---

[1] Buckingham to Christian IV, Dec. $\frac{5}{15}$, *S. P. Holland.*

[2] Louis XIII. to Blainville, Dec. $\frac{4}{14}$, *King's MSS* 137, p. 819.

[3] "Quod vero Regem et Buckinghamium attinet, illi non multum moventur aut indignantur." Rusdorf to Oxenstjerna. Dec. *Mémoires,* II. 138.

[4] *Rymer,* xviii 245.

employment of English vessels at Rochelle, and the first resolution taken in Council after Buckingham's return was that a new fleet should be sent out to succour Rochelle, and to bring home the ships by force.[1] Orders were accordingly issued that the soldiers who had come back from Cadiz should be kept under their colours for future service.[2]

<small>Dec. 16.</small>

Nor were the differences relating to the fulfilment of the marriage treaty in a fairer way to an accommodation. Louis, indeed, had sent messages to Buckingham after his return, that if the English Catholics were relieved from ill-treatment, and if his sister's household were permitted to remain as it had been arranged by the contract, he would make no further objection to receiving him in France.[3] On the first point Buckingham could not yield without alienating Parliament. On the second he could not yield without alienating the King.

<small>Difficulties about the marriage treaty.</small>

Whilst Buckingham was still at the Hague, Charles's exasperation at his wife's French attendants had risen to fever heat. To their interference, and not at all to his own failure to keep his promises, he attributed his domestic troubles, and he threatened to send them all back to France. More prudent counsels prevailed for a time, and he now contented himself with announcing to the Bishop of Mende, the Queen's almoner, his intention of introducing English ladies into her household. A man, he repeated once more, ought to be master in his own house. The utmost to which he would agree was to wait a few days till his resolve had been communicated to the Court of France.[4]

<small>The Queen's household.</small>

<small>Dec. 25.</small>

To Richelieu the threatened breach between France and England, bringing with it a death-struggle with the Huguenots

---

[1] Blainville to Louis XIII., Dec. $\frac{12}{22}$, *King's MSS.* 138, p. 948.

[2] Proclamations, Car. I., Dec. 16, No. 31, *S. P. Dom.*

[3] Louis XIII. to Blainville, Dec. $\frac{4}{14}$; The Bishop of Mende to Ville-aux-Clercs, received $\frac{\text{Dec. 27}}{\text{Jan. 6}}$, *King's MSS.* 138, p. 819, 1043.

[4] The King to Buckingham, Nov. 20, *Hardwicke S. P.* ii. 23. The Bishop of Mende to Louis XIII., $\frac{\text{Dec. 25}}{\text{Jan. 4}}$, *King's MSS.* 138, p. 1056.

of Rochelle, must have been infinitely displeasing. In spite of his master's strong feeling that he had been ill-treated, he contrived to obtain permission to address fresh overtures to Buckingham, assuring him of a good reception in France if certain conditions, of which we have no particular information, were fulfilled. If he could not come on these terms, let him at least send confidential ambassadors to smooth away the differences between the two Crowns.[1]

French offers to Buckingham.

The latter alternative was accepted. Holland was once more to go to Paris to make himself agreeable to the Queen Mother and the ladies of her court. The real business of the embassy was entrusted to Carleton, who had at last been recalled from the Hague, and was now Vice-Chamberlain and a Privy Councillor. A diligent, well-informed man, too dependent upon office to be likely to take a course of his own, and sympathising entirely with the movement against Spain without rising into any large view of contemporary politics, he was exactly suited for the service for which Buckingham required him, and was likely, as time went on, to establish himself firmly in his favour.

Embassy of Holland and Carleton.

Carleton's present work was to mediate a peace between the French Government and the Huguenots, and to persuade Louis to surrender the English ships and to join in the alliance of the Hague.[2]

Objects of the mission.

The differences between the two Courts were serious enough in themselves. Unhappily there was a political difference which was more serious still. In September, whilst the Cadiz

---

[1] "M. Bautru is on his way for England with letters from the Duke de Chevreuse and Marquis d'Effiat, but concerted with the Queen Mother and the Cardinal to invite my Lord Duke of Buckingham to come over, which many wish, but few hold it counselable."—De Vic to Conway, Dec. $\frac{16}{26}$. "We may not conceal what we understand, that what the Cardinal told us of Blainville's revocation was conditional, in case the Lord Duke of Buckingham came over upon such invitements as were sent him."—Holland and Carleton to Conway, Feb. 26, 1626, *S. P. France.* It can hardly be said, therefore, that Buckingham could not go to France without first declaring war.

[2] Instructions to Holland and Carleton, Dec. 30, *S. P. France.*

fleet was still at Plymouth, a string of French prizes had been brought in, charged with carrying goods for the use of the Spanish Netherlands. Under ordinary circumstances it is hard to persuade neutrals and belligerents to take the same view of the law of prize, and there was in this case a special difficulty arising from the fact that at Whitehall French neutrality was regarded as an underhand contrivance for reaping the benefits of war without sharing its burdens.

September. The neutrality of France.

There was clearly need of inquiry into the nature of the cargoes on board the vessels. Besides the French prizes, there were many of Dutch nationality, and a few from other parts of Europe. If they had on board goods which were the property of Spaniards, those goods, according to the ideas of the day, would be subject to immediate confiscation. Contraband of war again, being carried to Spain or the Spanish Netherlands, would be liable to seizure, whether it were Spanish property or not; but it was by no means a matter of universal agreement what contraband of war was. In the Treaty of Southampton indeed, England and the States-General had recently agreed upon a sweeping definition, including in that category provisions and the precious metals as well as munitions of war and materials used in shipbuilding,[1] and had declared not only such articles, but even the ships and men engaged in the traffic, to be lawful prize. Such an interpretation of the customary maritime law was not likely to commend itself to a neutral seafaring nation.

The French prizes.

Contraband of war.

Even if this knotty point had been settled, there was another behind it. What evidence was to be accepted that the contraband goods were or were not destined for Spanish use? Every one of the eleven French vessels seized had sailed from a Spanish port, and all of them, with one exception, were owned by Calais merchants.[2] It was, however, notorious that there were men at Calais whose business it was to pass goods as soon as landed over the frontier into Flanders,

Proof of destination.

---

[1] Art. 20 of the Treaty; *Dumont*, v. 2, 480.
[2] Examinations of the masters of the prize ships, Sept. 29, *S. P. Dom.* vi. 120.

in much the same way as goods were passed over into Russia from Memel in the time of the Crimean war.¹

It happened that Buckingham was at Plymouth when the prizes were brought in. Gold and silver being contraband of war, according to the view taken in England, he ordered 9,000*l*. or 10,000*l*. which were on board to be sequestered,² and the remainder of the goods to be placed in safe keeping. A few weeks later the cargoes were stowed again on board, and the prizes brought up to London, to pass through a legal investigation before the Court of Admiralty. By the beginning of November the number of captured French vessels had increased to twenty-two.³

<small>Sept. 27. The money on board sequestered.</small>

<small>October. The prizes sent to London.</small>

So far the French had no reasonable ground of complaint; but in the needy circumstances of the treasury the sequestered property was too tempting a bait to be long resisted. In October Buckingham had attempted to borrow 70,000*l*., in order that he might carry with him something to the Hague for the immediate supply of the armies of Christian IV. and Mansfeld. The security which Charles could offer fell short of the required sum by 20,000*l*., and Ley and Weston proposed to fill the gap by giving a lien upon the first sale of condemned prize goods. The suggestion in itself was innocent enough; but either it was not thought sufficient, or Charles fancied that he could do better. On October 27 the money already sequestered was taken to be spent on warlike preparations, and on November 5 orders were given to sell goods at once to the required value of 20,000*l*., without waiting for a sentence from the Court.⁴

<small>Oct. 27. Prize money taken and goods ordered to be sold.</small>

---

¹ Marten to Conway, Nov. 8 ; Joachimi to ⸺, *S. P. Holland*. ⸺ to Quester, *S. P. France*.

² Minutes by Nicholas Feb. (?) 1626, *S. P. Dom*. xxi. 99.

³ A minute of the replacing of the goods on board, is calendared in September, but should almost certainly be placed in October. Receipt by Marsh, Oct. 11, *ibid*. vi. 126 ; xxii. 12, 1. Blainville to Louis XIII., Nov. $\frac{6}{16}$, *King's MSS*. 138, p. 659.

⁴ Coke to Conway, Oct. 27, *S. P. Dom*. viii. 26. Warrant, Nov. 5, *Sign Manuals*, i. 90.

To Charles the difference may have seemed slight, as, if the decision of the Court were against him, he could refund the money. There was, however, another side of the question which he had forgotten to consider. Blainville reminded him that, as the cargoes had not been made up for the English market, they would not fetch anything like their full value on a compulsory sale in London.[1]

<small>Nov. 5.
Blainville protests.</small>

The impression produced by Charles's hasty act was likely to be worse than the act itself would justify. It gave to the Admiralty Court the appearance of being merely an official instrument for enforcing confiscation for the benefit of the Crown. Sir Henry Marten, the Judge of the Court, felt the indignity keenly. "For my part," he wrote, in answer to an appeal from Conway for arguments in support of the course which had been taken, "I can profess to know no other disposition yet intended, but that all the goods should be landed, inventoried, and appraised; and, on Saturday next, all who pretend to any of those ships or goods to appear and propound their claims."[2]

<small>Nov. 8.
Marten declines to support the seizure.</small>

Before this remonstrance Charles gave way for a time. Buckingham was absent at the Hague, and there was a period of indecision till the guiding spirit of the Government was once more in England. The Council took up the question, and on December 4 fresh orders were given to proceed with the sale, orders which were retracted shortly afterwards.[3] Sir John Coke, who was eager for money to enable him to meet the expenses of the fleet, and whose official mind could not catch sight of the larger aspects of the case, was anxious for instant and sweeping action. "If you shall limit the sales," he wrote to Conway, on hearing that some half-measure was in contemplation, "as I hear you intend, to goods which are out of question, I know not what goods can be sold; since there is neither ship nor particular goods therein to which no man doth pretend."[4]

<small>Charles's indecision.

Dec. 4.</small>

[1] Blainville to Louis XIII., Nov. $\frac{6}{16}$, *King's MSS.* 138, p. 659.
[2] Conway to Marten, Nov. 7, *Conway's Letter Book*; Marten to Conway, Nov. 8, *S. P. Dom.* ix. 32.
[3] Joachimi to ——, *S. P. Holland.*
[4] Coke to Conway, Dec. 17, *S. P. Dom.* xii. 1.

Before Charles had made up his mind, the mere announcement of his intention had called forth reprisals in France. Villars, the governor of Havre, was himself interested in the 'St. Peter' of that port, and on December 7 he arrested two English vessels lying at Rouen. A fortnight later it was known in London that the French authorities were contemplating a general embargo upon all English property in France, which was only delayed till there was some certain intelligence of the course finally adopted in England.

<small>Dec. 7. Reprisals in France.</small>

By this time Buckingham was again at Court, and the arrival of Richelieu's overtures had opened a prospect of averting the impending quarrel. "It is necessary for me," said Charles, "to preserve my friends and allies." Just as Holland and Carleton were starting, an Order in Council was drawn up to form a basis for the settlement of the dispute.[1]

According to this order the 'St. Peter' of Havre de Grace, against which the presumptions were less than against vessels belonging to the merchants of Calais, was to be delivered to its owners. Of the remaining ships and their cargoes, whatever was clearly French property should be given up at once. Against whatever was questionable proceedings should be taken, 'without any further restraint of sale or other proceeding warrantable by law or the course of the Admiralty.'[2]

<small>Dec. 28. Order in Council for the re-delivery of the 'St. Peter.'</small>

On January 11 the ambassadors had their first interview with Richelieu. He received them in the most friendly way: but he gave it to be understood that till the Huguenot rebellion was at an end there could be no open war with Spain, and that his master could not tolerate the interference of a foreign king between himself and his subjects. They might, however, rest assured that there was no intention of persecuting the Protestant religion in France. The 'Vanguard' would be restored as soon as the

<small>Jan. 11. Conference between Richelieu and the ambassadors.</small>

---

[1] *Commons' Journals*, i. 823; Palloyseau to Hippisley, $\frac{\text{Dec. 23,}}{\text{Jan. 2,}}$ *Harl. MSS.* 1583, fol. 171; Joachimi to the States-General, $\frac{\text{Dec. 27,}}{\text{Jan. 6,}}$ Jan. $\frac{7}{17}$, *Add. MSS.* 17,677 L. fol. 130, 119.

[2] Order in Council, Dec. 8, *S. P. Dom.* xii. 72.

prize taken by Soubise was given up. The other vessels had been hired from the merchants, and as long as Rochelle was in arms it was impossible to dispense with their services.

The irritation aroused at the French Court by the tone which Charles assumed was such as no minister, however anxious to avert war, could afford to disregard, and least of all was Richelieu likely to think lightly of the honour of his sovereign. Louis himself was particularly displeased at the proposal to include him in the treaty signed at the Hague without his concurrence. "The league," he wrote to his ambassador in the Netherlands, "is not aimed at the liberty of the Empire or the abasement of Spain, but at the abasement of the Catholic religion and of all the princes who profess it, and particularly of myself." One of his ministers expressed himself in much the same tone. "There is a great difference," he wrote, "between proposing to the King things done or things to be done. To communicate a design and to wish to do nothing without his advice would oblige his Majesty, but to propose to him to take part in a matter already arranged would have the contrary effect."[1]

<small>Feeling of Louis XIII.</small>

In Louis's place Charles would have felt precisely in the same manner; but he had not the tact to perceive that concession must be made to the feelings of others; and with the consciousness that he had himself contributed, or appeared to have contributed, to the misfortunes of Rochelle, he determined to support the town against its sovereign, at whatever cost to the interests of the rest of Europe. Pennington had for some time been getting ready a fleet at Plymouth, which was destined in case of necessity to escort Soubise with provisions for the blockaded Huguenots, and at a council held on January 20 it was resolved that the fleet should be at once despatched. In order to impart greater energy to the crews it was arranged that Buckingham should command in person. The deputies from the insurgent city, who were in England seeking for aid, were informed that the fleet would proceed to drive the

<small>Jan. 20. Charles determines to relieve Rochelle.</small>

[1] Extracts given by Vreede, *Inleiding tot eene Geschiedenis der Nederlandsche Diplomatie*, ii. 2, 85, 87.

troops of the King of France out of Rhé and Oléron, if the Rochellese would consent to leave the islands at Charles's disposal till the expenses of the undertaking had been repaid to him.

No secret was made of the resolution taken. Buckingham informed Blainville that his master could no longer remain neutral. He had contributed to the ruin of the Protestants by the loan of his ships, and now, with one voice, his Council and his people called upon him to undertake the defence of those whom he had so deeply injured. If war were once declared he would show the world that he was not so destitute of men and money as was commonly supposed.[1]

Blainville informed.

The resolution thus taken at Court could not fail to have its effects on the prospects of the owners of the French prizes. As far as the 'St. Peter' was concerned, everything had proceeded regularly. Suspicion only attached to some hides and a few other articles on board. Bonds were accepted in the Admiralty Court for the payment of their value, in case of their proving to be Spanish property, and on January 26 Marten gave orders for the delivery of ship and cargo to the owners.[2]

Jan. 26. Order for the restoration of the 'St. Peter.'

The proprietors of the other vessels had before this fancied that their difficulties were at an end. Soon after the Order in Council of December 28, goods to the value of 30,000*l.* were given up to them, as being beyond question legitimately French property. But when the news of the difficulties made in France about the surrender of the English vessels reached England, the Government took another tone. On January 24 the goods were again seized for the King, and out of that part of the cargo which was considered contraband by the Crown lawyers, though it had not yet been condemned by any court of law, property to the value of 7,000*l.* was sold by

Jan. 24. Sale of prize goods.

---

[1] Blainville to Louis XIII., Jan. 21, *King's MSS.* 138, p. 1206. Conway to Holland and Carleton, Jan. 21, *S. P. France.* Buckingham to Pennington, Jan. 7; Pennington to Buckingham, Jan. 17, *S. P. Dom.* xviii. 18, 75.

[2] Order for taking bonds, Jan. 21, *Book of Acts, Admiralty Court,* 159 fol. 30 b. Order for release, Jan. 26, *S. P. Dom.* xix. 52.

auction. Having made up his mind to war, it would seem that Charles no longer thought it necessary to keep terms with the subjects of the King of France.[1]

With the King and Buckingham in this temper, it was not likely that even the 'St. Peter' would be allowed to escape. As soon as the order had been issued for its release, Apsley, the Lieutenant of the Tower, remonstrated with the Lord Admiral, assuring him that he could bring as good evidence against that vessel as against the others. To Apsley's statements Buckingham gave too easy credence, and on February 4, having pre-

<small>Feb. 4.
The 'St. Peter' re-arrested.</small>

viously obtained the King's consent, he ordered the detention of the ship. It is perhaps not an unreasonable conjecture that the real motive in these proceedings was the desire to detain as many pledges as possible for the English ships at Rochelle, the recovery of which had been the subject of repeated messages to the ambassadors at Paris. Buckingham might well doubt his chances of obtaining from the approaching Parliament a favourable consideration of his policy, if Louis were still engaged in an attack upon the Huguenots with the help of English vessels.

All this time the despatches sent to Paris had been growing more peremptory. On January 23 the ambassadors were

<small>Jan. 23.
Negotiations in France.</small>

ordered to hasten home if the ships were not surrendered. On the 26th Charles was still unyielding. He had just received a letter from Holland and Carleton, telling him that Richelieu, in his master's name, insisted on the maintenance of the King's garrisons in Fort Louis and the islands of Rhé and Oléron, as well as on the right to send a Royal Intendant of Justice into Rochelle. The Huguenot deputies objected to all three points, and asked for the full execution of the treaty of Montpellier. After a time, however, they expressed their readiness to withdraw their demands. They would reluctantly agree to admit the Intendant, and to allow the garrisons to remain in the islands. Even

---

[1] Joachimi to ——, *S. P. Holland.* Joachimi to the States-General, Feb. $\frac{8}{18}$, *Add. MSS.* 17,677 L., fol. 143. Blainville to Louis XIII., $\frac{\text{Jan. 25}}{\text{Feb. 4}}$, *King's MSS* 138, p. 1270, 1273.

at Fort Louis they would not insist upon an immediate disarmament, if they could hope for its demolition in course of time.

The ambassadors were satisfied that peace was virtually made. Charles, however, was not satisfied. He thought that the conditions were insufficient for the safety of Rochelle. Nothing less than the terms of the Treaty of Montpellier should receive his assent. The ambassadors were also to ask for the immediate release of the ships, and if that were refused, they were to return at once to England.[1]

The English ships to be positively demanded.

The error of Louis was coming home to him. If he had been faulty in appending to his sister's marriage contract a condition which involved an interference with the administration of English law, Charles was now interfering far more incisively in French domestic politics. When once it was understood that the Huguenots were to owe their recovered independence to English help, a situation would be created which would be intolerable even to a king of France far less sensitive than Louis on all matters connected with his personal authority. In the preceding August Richelieu might wisely have argued that it would be better for the King to grant all the demands of his Protestant subjects, in order that he might turn his attention to external war. But it was one thing to grant such demands upon conviction; it was another thing to grant them to the menaces of the King of England. Rochelle, freed from the control of its own sovereign by Charles's interposition, would practically be an independent republic, resting for security upon the support of England. The work of uniting France, handed down as the task of centuries from one generation of monarchs to another, would receive a blow from which it would be hard to recover. An English Rochelle would be a far more potent instrument of mischief than even an English Calais had ever been.

Interference of Charles in French politics.

Such a view of the case was not likely to present itself to

[1] Buckingham to Holland and Carleton, Jan. 23; Holland and Carleton to Conway, Jan. 23; Conway to Holland and Carleton, Jan. 19, *S. P. France.*

Charles. All he saw was that, as his ships had been used for the defeat of Soubise, it was his business to take care that the Huguenots suffered no loss. By this time, moreover, he had a fresh grievance in his own domestic circle, which kept his mind in a state of irritation. He had arranged that his own coronation should take place before the opening of Parliament, and he fondly hoped that the Queen would be at his side on that solemn occasion. To his surprise he found that his young wife had religious scruples about taking part in a Protestant ceremony, and he at once appealed to her brother to convince her that she was in the wrong. The coronation, Conway wrote to the ambassadors, was but a form. "Yet," he added, "it is a wonder, it is a disorder, it is a misfortune, so apparent a declaration of a difference in judgment, obedience, and conformity." Charles got no help from Louis here. The view taken at the French Court was, that there would be no harm done if the Queen submitted to coronation, provided that none of the Protestant clergy took any part in the ceremony.[1]

The Queen refuses to be crowned.

Jan. 21.

As this was clearly inadmissible, Charles had to resign himself to be crowned alone. Such a consequence he ought to have foreseen when he decided upon marrying a Roman Catholic princess; but he was bitterly disappointed, and he threw the whole blame upon the French ambassador. Blainville, according to him, had made it his business, since his coming into England, to stir up ill-will between himself and the Queen. Blainville was certainly not conciliatory in his dealings with a Government against which he had many and bitter grievances, and he had listened more sympathisingly to the Queen's complaints than became an ambassador; but it is undeniable that Henrietta Maria's troubles had their root in causes which existed before he set foot in England.

Charles angry with Blainville.

The day fixed for the coronation was the 2nd of February. The curtained seat which had been prepared for Henrietta

[1] Louis XIII. to Blainville, Jan. $\frac{15}{23}$, *King's MSS.* 138. p. 1121. Conway to Holland and Carleton, Jan. 21, *S. P. France.*

Maria at a time when it was still hoped that she might be present as a spectator, if she would not take her part in the ceremony, was empty. Its emptiness must have reminded Charles bitterly of the misery of his home life and of the most conspicuous failure of his political life. Yet there was no want of loyalty in the hearty shout— the echo of that old cry which had once given to English kings their right to sit upon the throne—which greeted him as he stood in the pride of youthful dignity in the face of the assembled multitude. As yet, though the first enthusiasm which greeted his accession had passed away, no personal unpopularity had gathered round him. Whatever was ill-done was attributed to the influence of Buckingham.[1]

[1] Meade to Stuteville, Feb. 3; D'Ewes to Stuteville, Feb. 3, *Ellis*, ser. 1, iii. 220, 213. Mr. Forster is mistaken in supposing that the incident of Charles's stumbling, and of his answering, 'when Buckingham offered to assist him, "I have as much need to help you as you to assist me,"' took place 'when all was over, and the King and the Duke came wearily away.' It really happened before the coronation, and D'Ewes adds that the words were spoken 'with a smiling countenance.' Charles doubtless merely meant that he was able to recover his footing without help. It would not have been worth while mentioning this, but for the doubt which I entertain whether Mr. Forster was right in attributing any sort of foreboding of coming evil to Charles. There is no evidence either way; but my impression, from what I know of Charles's character and actions, is that he never foreboded evil, and that he was so convinced that he was always in the right, that the idea of Parliamentary opposition would not occur to him till he was called to face it.

As for the people not shouting at the coronation when Arundel first asked them to do so, I am content with D'Ewes's explanation : "Whether some expected he should have spoken more, or others hearing not so well what he said, hindered those by questioning which might have heard, or that the newness and greatness of the action busied men's thoughts, or the presence of so dear a thing drew admiring silence, or that those which were nearest doubted what to do, but not one word followed till my Lord of Arundel told them they should cry out, 'God save King Charles!' upon which, as ashamed of their first oversight, a little shouting followed. At the other sides where he presented himself there was not the like failing." Joachimi, as Ranke has observed, has no hesitation to tell of. He says the answer was given 'with great cry and shouting.'—Joachimi to the States-General, Feb. $\frac{3}{13}$, *Add. MSS.* 17,677 L, fol. 148.

The new king was thus, to use words spoken by his direction a few days later, married to his people. He chose on that day to be clothed in white,[1] as the sign of the virgin purity with which he came to play a bridegroom's part, instead of in the purple robe of sovereignty. *Amor civium, Regis præsidium* was the motto which in trustful confidence he placed upon the coins which bore the Royal arms impressed upon the sails of a ship careering through the waves, the emblem doubtless of that great naval victory with which he hoped to illustrate the annals of his reign. If Cecil had failed at Cadiz, Buckingham, he might think, would hardly fail at Rochelle. Charles, indeed, so far as it is possible to judge by the indications which have reached us, was preparing to meet the new Parliament with all the buoyancy of hopefulness. Neither Coke, nor Phelips, nor Seymour would be there to distract the hearts of his faithful Commons with factious opposition. So little did the King suspect that he would meet with any difficulty in the Upper House that he neglected the opportunity which the coronation afforded of raising to the peerage persons in whom he could confide. No additional votes were gained by the earldoms which he distributed amongst members of the existing peerage, and it was only a matter of personal importance to themselves that Lord Ley, for instance, would for the future be known as Earl of Marlborough, Viscount Mandeville as Earl of Manchester, and Lord Carew as Earl of Totness.

New earldoms.

There were yet a few days before the meeting of Parliament, and if Charles had been capable of rising into a statesmanlike view of his relations with France, he would have seized the opportunity of reconsidering his position which was then offered him. Holland and Carleton had left no stone unturned to bring about a pacification. The stumbling-block was Fort Louis. The French minister frankly averred that, unless the King kept up a garrison in it, he could have no security that when he was engaged in war abroad the Rochellese would not rise in insur-

Jan. 25. Negotiations between Louis XIII. and the Huguenots.

---

[1] Heylin, *Life of Laud*, 144. After Charles's death, this was pointed to as a presage of the innocence of martyrdom, as was also the text taken by the preacher, "I will give thee a crown of life."

rection, as they had done the year before. With equal energy the Huguenot deputies argued that unless the fort were demolished, they could have no security for the freedom of their commerce. On the evening of January 25 it was believed on both sides that the negotiation was at an end.

The next morning a chosen number of the French clergy were to have an audience, to declare to the King their readiness to open their purses in support of the holy war which they had done their best to render imminent. They had, however, reckoned without the Cardinal. Seizing a pretext for deferring the audience for a time, he had proposed a compromise through the English ambassadors. When at last the deputation swept into the Royal presence they found that they were too late. The Huguenot deputies were already on their knees before the King, and the baffled priests came only to witness the reconciliation of their Sovereign with his Protestant subjects.

<small>Jan. 26. An agreement come to.</small>

Unhappily the terms of reconciliation announced on the following day by the Chancellor, were such as by no means to preclude the probability of a renewal of the strife at no distant future. Under pressure from Holland and Carleton, the deputies agreed to give up all the points at issue, including the demolition of Fort Louis. In return they were to have from the King an assurance that 'by long services and continued obedience they might expect that which they most desired,' and that 'in fitting time he would listen to their supplications made with due respect and humility.'[1] Before the words were spoken a private exposition of their meaning was given by the French ministers, to the effect that they pointed to the eventual demolition of Fort Louis.[2]

<small>Terms of the agreement,</small>

Holland and Carleton had certainly taxed their authority

---

[1] Answer of the Chancellor in the name of the King of France, $\frac{\text{Jan. 27,}}{\text{Feb. 6,}}$ *S. P. France.* This date, however, must be merely that on which a written copy of the speech was delivered. It was spoken on $\frac{\text{Jan. 26}}{\text{Feb. 5}}$.

[2] Declaration by Holland and Carleton, $\frac{\text{Jan. 31}}{\text{Feb. 10}}$, *S. P. France.*

as mediators to the utmost. The deputies plainly told them that they had agreed to the treaty 'because they might now lawfully accept assistance from his Majesty.' When the ambassadors attended the Protestant church at Charenton on the following Sunday, they found themselves the objects of universal enthusiasm. The preacher took for his text, "How beautiful are the feet of them that preach the gospel of peace."

<small>Jan. 29. accepted by the Huguenots through expectations of English support.</small>

It was all very natural, but it was very dangerous. To thrust foreign mediation in the face of Louis was the very way to disgust him with the arrangement which had been made, and if Charles had been wise he would have kept his part in the treaty in the background. If the French Government were once engaged in earnest in the conflict with Spain, any renewal of persecution would be virtually impossible.

In such a course Charles would have had every assistance from Richelieu. The treaty was signed on the 28th, and the Cardinal at once assured the ambassadors that the English ships would be speedily restored, and that his master would practically, if not in name, join England in the war in Germany. On the 29th Holland and Carleton reported that the French ministers dealt with them more freely than they expected, 'for they have not denied those of the Religion any of their demands, so as all parties are satisfied.'[1]

<small>Richelieu ready to take up the conflict against Spain.</small>

On February 5 the ambassadors were able to write of offers still more definite. Richelieu had assured them that his master, besides carrying on the war in Italy, was ready to create a diversion in favour of the King of Denmark by sending into Germany an army nominally commanded by some German prince, but in reality supported jointly by France and England. In addition he would give the aid already promised to the King of Denmark. An army maintained in this manner would not cost Charles a third of

<small>Definite offers made by him.</small>

---

[1] Holland and Carleton to Conway, Jan. 27, 29; Declaration by Holland and Carleton, $\frac{\text{Jan. 31}}{\text{Feb. 10}}$; The state of Holland and Carleton's negotiations Aug. (?), *S. P. France.*

the expense of the force which he had proposed to send against Dunkirk, whilst it would be of far greater advantage to the common cause.¹

Whether Charles, after his numerous failures, would have been able to persuade the House of Commons to grant the supply necessary for this or for any other enterprise, may well be doubted: but it was at least in his power to meet Parliament with the proposal of a definite joint action with France, which was the very object at which he had been so long driving. In a few days the English ships would have returned and the establishment of peace in France would have justified the policy upon which their loan had originally depended, whilst it might be taken for granted that when once England and France were actively co-operating in Germany, there would be no disposition on the part of the French Government to return to that system of annoyance of which the Huguenots had previously complained, nor even to scrutinise very closely Charles's failure to observe the provisions of his marriage contract.

<small>Feb. 10. Satisfactory prospect.</small>

Such, however, was not the view which Charles took of the situation. On February 6, when the first news of the agreement had reached England, Conway was directed to write ironically to the ambassadors that his Majesty was confident that there must be in the treaty 'some excellent good warrants and reservations provided that are not expressed.'² The next day Charles had an opportunity of reading the treaty itself. "It seems," wrote Conway again, "something strange that your Lordships had concluded the peace with so little surety for those of the Religion, for aught appeared here; but his Majesty is persuaded—if your Lordships have, as it seems, placed the confidence of all those of the Religion and those of Rochelle upon him for the maintaining of their surety,—that you have some very good grounds that such underhand promises as may have been made, which appear not, shall be kept; or that, now that the King is satisfied in point of honour, of his goodness he will

<small>Feb. 6. Dissatisfaction of Charles.</small>

<small>Feb. 7. He complains of the agreement.</small>

---

¹ Holland and Carleton to Conway, Feb. 5, *S. P. France.*
² Conway to Holland and Carleton, Feb. 6, *ibid.*

presently withdraw all his forces from Rochelle, and will appoint a certain time when he will demolish the fort.

"His Majesty's pleasure is that you protest to that King and his ministers that, under the hope and confidence of the real and present performance of those things, you had employed your mediation, and had engaged the authority of his Majesty to move and almost constrain the deputies to accept the peace upon these conditions.

The ambassadors to demand a recognition of Charles's mediation.

"And further, you are, by the advice of the deputies, to move for such conditions as may be for their surety, and so to carry that business betwixt that king and those of the Religion that, if his Majesty's honour must be pledged for the due observation of the treaty, his Majesty may be called and admitted to that office by that king and those of the Religion; and that there may be some ground and possibility for such a surety to be in the power and possession of those of the Religion and those of Rochelle, in the strength of which they may subsist until such time as they may make their grievances known to his Majesty, and for him to apply his mediation and set his endeavours on work. But in these things his Majesty can give you no exact limits, but must leave you to that restraint or latitude your Lordships' own wisdom will take in your own negotiation. But it is his Majesty's precise commandment that you demand the present restitution of his Majesty's ship, and of the merchants' ships; and that in that point you admit no delay, but take a delay as a denial."

Charles, in short, blind to the fact that the force of circumstances under Richelieu's guidance was working for him, would be content with nothing less than an open acknowledgment of his position as mediator between Louis and his subjects. A few more despatches such as that which had just been sent, would make even Richelieu powerless to preserve peace between France and England.

Charles's mistake.

On the 11th the news of the French offer of co-operation in Germany had reached England. Sir John Coke was directed to answer as follows:—

"Concerning the raising of a new English-French army,—

which strange overture you have kept afoot by undertaking to procure an answer from hence,—that this may not serve them for any pretence to colour their withdrawing of contribution from the King of Denmark and Mansfeld, you are to lay before them his Majesty's great charges both by sea and land, and the impossibility of levying more armies of that kind ; and further directly to profess that if that king perform not what he hath promised for the support of those forces, his Majesty in like manner will presently hold his hand and employ all his means for the strengthening of his fleet, which he well knoweth to be the best support of his own honour and state, all the rest having a principal relation to his allies. And, since the diversion in Germany concerneth chiefly the security of France, against which the Imperial forces were evidently designed, if the King of Denmark had sat still ; you are to make them sensible of this interest and of his Majesty's resolution to bear that burthen no longer, if that king shall cast it off, or not contribute at least in an equal proportion."[1]

<small>Feb. 11. Charles persists in treating the offer of French co-operation with coolness.</small>

On such terms a working alliance was impossible. A foreign Government was to find now, as domestic parties were to find afterwards, that it was not enough to give way to Charles in some things, unless it was prepared to give way to him in all. What he asked was that a high-spirited and sensitive nation should first submit its domestic affairs to his arbitration, and should then enter upon a war precisely in such a manner and on such conditions as it pleased him to prescribe.

<small>An alliance impossible on these conditions.</small>

If knowledge of character be worth anything, it is to Charles rather than to Buckingham that these unsatisfactory despatches are to be ascribed. Charles, too, had annoyances at home which may well have served to put him in a bad temper during the days in which they were dictated. His dissatisfaction with his wife had reached a crisis. Parliament was opened on February 6, and arrangements had been made for the Queen to witness the procession from one of the windows of the banqueting hall at Whitehall. Charles, however, always anxious to

[1] Coke to Holland and Carleton, Feb. 11, *S. P France.*

separate her from her French attendants, and to bring her as much as possible in communication with the ladies of the Villiers family, expressed a wish that she should take a seat in a balcony occupied by the old Countess of Buckingham. The Queen assented, but when the time came she either saw or fancied she saw that it was raining, and asked to be excused from going out into the street in the wet. Charles, on the other hand, insisted that it did not rain, but finding that his words produced no impression, withdrew from the altercation. Dissatisfied at his rebuff,—so at least the French accounts of the affair assert,—he betook himself to Buckingham. "How can you expect," said the favourite, "to be obeyed by your Parliament if you cannot secure the obedience of your wife?" Charles, conscious perhaps of his own inability to impress the Queen with sufficient awe of his commands, sent Buckingham to try his powers upon her. Buckingham rated her soundly for her disobedience, and as Blainville, who had perhaps objected originally to her showing herself in Lady Buckingham's company, now advised submission, she took Buckingham's hand, and was led across the street to the house from which his mother was to view the procession.

Feb. 6. The Queen at the procession of the opening of Parliament.

Altercation with her husband.

Even this act of submission caused fresh umbrage to Charles. The Queen, it would seem, would not obey him, but would obey the French ambassador. With some reminiscence, perhaps, of the 'Taming of the Shrew,' he sent orders to her to come down from the window at which she was now seated, and with these orders Henrietta Maria meekly complied.

For three days Charles kept entirely aloof from his wife, waiting sulkily till she should come to beg his pardon. At last, weary of his silence, she sought him out and asked in what she had offended him. He expected her, he answered, to acknowledge her error. She was unable, she said, to accuse herself of anything wrong. Would he not tell her what her fault had been? The question seemed to take him by surprise. After some hesitation he answered: "You told me that it rained when I said that it did not rain." "I should never have

Ill-feeling between them.

Feb. 10. A reconciliation.

thought that to be an offence," she replied ; " but if you think so, I will think so too." Pleased with such evidence of humility, Charles took his wife in his arms, and kissed her.[1]

The quarrel was over for the time. The Queen had perhaps begun to open her eyes to the truth that with such a character as Charles's the outward appearance of complete and unreasoning obedience is the surest way to mastery in the end.

Unhappily this misunderstanding between man and wife became another element in the misunderstanding between two kingdoms. On the day after the offence was given, the courier who carried the despatch expressive of Charles's dissatisfaction with the Huguenot treaty. took with him a letter from Charles to Louis himself, asking for Blainville's recall, on the ground that he had done everything in his power to bring about a misunderstanding between himself and the Queen. At the same time he directed Conway to inform the ambassador that he would no longer be permitted to appear at Court.[2]

Feb. 7. Charles refuses to allow Blainville to appear at Court

Such were the conditions under which Charles met his second Parliament. A great French minister, amidst unexampled difficulties, had steered the vessel of state on to the track along which it was hereafter to be borne to victory on behalf of a noble cause. In spite of the hesitations of Louis and of the opposition of the clergy and of a large portion of the aristocracy, Richelieu had firmly planted the banner of monarchical France on the basis

Circumstances under which Charles meets Parliament.

---

[1] *Mémoires de Tillières*. It seems so unlikely that Charles should have quarrelled with Blainville on this point, that it is as well to give the words of the English narrative : " In the meantime a difference that fell out about the place for the Queen to see the King ride to Parliament (she affecting to stand in the Banqueting House, or in the Privy Gallery, when the King had given reasons for her better sight in the house of the Countess, mother to the Duke of Buckingham, next the gate in King Street), was a subject for some discontent, and so far as the Ambassador Blainville, seeming to his Majesty to have been the causer of it, had the next day a message brought him by the Lord Conway." Affair of Blainville, undated, *S. P. France*.

[2] Message sent to Blainville, Feb. 7. The King to Louis XIII., Feb. 7, *S. P. France*.

of toleration. He had gained his point by unwearied patience, by yielding in details whilst never losing sight of his main object, by the appearance of being but the servant of his king, whilst in reality he was bending the king and France itself to his own ends. One thing he yet wanted, that the ruler whom fortune had placed upon the English throne should be capable of understanding his meaning. As long as Charles was King of England no such good fortune was likely to be his.

CHAPTER LVII.

THE LEADERSHIP OF SIR JOHN ELIOT IN THE SECOND PARLIAMENT OF CHARLES I.

FEW and unimportant were the words which Charles addressed to the Houses at the opening of the session. "I mean to show," he said, in excuse for this brevity, "what I should speak in actions." Nor did the new Lord Keeper, who followed, add much to the knowledge of his hearers. He had nothing to say about the pressing wants of the Exchequer, nothing about the position which the King had taken up on the Continent; and, but for a passing allusion, no one would have gathered from Coventry's language that England was at war with Spain, still less that she had entered upon a serious diplomatic contest with France.

<small>Feb. 6.
Opening of the session.</small>

And yet money was sorely needed. The Privy seals were coming in slowly, and eight weeks later they had produced less than 28,000*l*.[1] The hopes which had been placed upon Buckingham's attempt to raise money in the Netherlands had proved still more fallacious. The Amsterdam merchants had refused to take the Crown jewels in pledge, unless they could also have security for their redemption within a limited period.[2]

<small>Want of money.</small>

When, on February 10, Rudyerd, the usual mouthpiece of the Government, rose to speak, he had still nothing to say about supply. He commended the King's zeal for religion as evinced by his late proceedings against the Catholics, and moved for a committee to consider how to increase the livings of the poorer clergy, and how to

<small>Feb. 10.
Rudyerd's motion.</small>

---

[1] Breviates of the receipts of the Exchequer.
[2] D. Carleton to Conway, Jan. 22, *S. P. Holland.*

deal with ministers who were leading immoral lives. The motion was adopted with an amendment by Pym that the committee should be empowered to consider all matters relating to religion. Charles evidently intended to stand upon his Protestantism. If he no longer protected the Roman Catholics, if he was ready to carry out practical reforms in the English Church, and if he was in close alliance with the States, why should not the Commons vote him large supplies to carry out so popular a policy.

Why should they not? Phelips was not there, to say him nay; nor Coke, nor Seymour, nor even Wentworth; and Sir John Coke could therefore rise hopefully to hint something about a grant of supply.[1] There was, however, one there who had been overlooked when the sheriffs had been pricked, and from whom no opposition was expected, but who had something to say before a motion for supply was carried. Eliot's last publicly spoken words at Oxford had been in defence of Buckingham's personal integrity.[2] The refusal of the favourite to submit his actions to the judgment of independent councillors, and the contempt shown for the House of Commons by the hasty dissolution, had since thrown him entirely on the side of the Opposition.

Supply suggested.

Eliot's position in the last Parliament.

Still Eliot was in no hurry to act. With a man of his warm and affectionate disposition the old personal ties which had bound him to Buckingham must still have counted for much. In the interval between the two Parliaments he had been anxiously watching the course of events. As Vice-Admiral of Devon he had special opportunities for noting the miserable results of a policy which his head and his heart alike condemned. He had been present at the sailing

1625. He watches events.

---

[1] Mr. Forster (*Sir J. Eliot*, i. 284) says—"The new secretary thereupon reminding the House of his Majesty's hint as to time, and that unreasonable slowness might produce as ill effect as denial, Eliot promptly rose." This is, I suppose, from the *Port Eliot Notes*, and must have referred to supply.

[2] The surprise at Eliot's turning against Buckingham in this Parliament, noticed by the Venetian Ambassador, as quoted by Ranke, *Engl. Gesch.* ii. 103, is one more piece of evidence that he never uttered the speech attributed to him in the *Negotium Posterorum*.

of the fleet, and when it sought refuge in Plymouth Sound from
its unlucky voyage, he had been witness of the miseries to which
those on board were doomed by a Government which had
launched them into the midst of the hazards of war without
sufficient means to provide for their daily wants. He knew
well how the poor wretches, torn from their homes a few short
months before, were wandering about the streets of Plymouth
without food or money ; how they were denied shelter by the
inhabitants ; and how, with nothing but their shirts on their
backs to ward off the wintry cold, they were dropping down
dead in the long December nights.[1]

Yet, whatever Eliot's thoughts may have been, there was no
open breach between him and the men in authority at Court.
At the end of December he appealed to Conway for
the reduction of an exorbitant demand made upon
his father-in-law by a Privy seal, and the wrong was
immediately redressed by a special resolution of the Council.[2]
A little later he wrote to request Pembroke, the Lord Lieutenant of Cornwall, for a deputy-lieutenancy which was reported
to be vacant, and his request would have been immediately
granted but for the discovery that there had been no foundation
for the report.[3]

Does not break with the Government.

Plainly, therefore, there was no expectation of any opposition
from Eliot ; and it is possible that if Charles had met Parliament in a different spirit—if he had made the
slightest acknowledgment of error, and had courted
inquiry instead of merely asking for money—Eliot's
first words in the new House might have been other
than they were. As it was, his whole soul was moved by that
which was passing before his eyes. To the high-hearted,
patriotic man it was bad enough that the failures of the past
should bring no warnings for the future ; but it was still worse that

1626. Feb. 10. Eliot in the new Parliament.

---

[1] The Commissioners of Plymouth to the Council, Jan. 4, *S. P. Dom.* xviii. 7.

[2] *Council Register*, Jan. 5. Eliot's letter to Conway, Dec. 31, *S. P. Dom.* xii. 95, is printed by Mr. Forster, *Sir J. Eliot*, i. 272.

[3] Eliot to his agent in London, Jan. 16, *S. P. Dom.* xviii. 68. Begg to ——, March (?), *Notes and Queries*, 4th ser., x. 325.

religion should be made the stalking-horse for political objects, and that Parliament should be asked to legislate for the Church as an inducement towards a grant of money.

When Eliot stood up, therefore, it was to ask that inquiry into past disasters should precede present supply. The accounts of the expenditure of the subsidies voted in 1624 must be laid fully before the House. Then, rising with the occasion, and feeling that this would not be enough, "Sir," he cried, "I beseech you cast your eyes about! View the state we are in! Consider the loss we have received! Weigh the wrecked and ruined honour of our nation! O the incomparable hopes of our most excellent sovereign checked in their first design! Search the preparation. Examine the going forth. Let your wisdoms travel through the whole action, to discern the fault, to know the faulty. For I presume to say, though no man undertook it, you would find the ancient genius of this kingdom rise up to be the accuser. Is the reputation and glory of our nation of a small value? Are the walls and bulwarks of our kingdom of no esteem? Are the numberless lives of our lost men not to be regarded? I know it cannot so harbour in an English thought. Our honour is ruined, our ships are sunk, our men perished: not by the sword, not by the enemy, not by chance, but, as the strongest predictions had discerned and made it apparent beforehand, by those we trust. Sir, I could lose myself in this complaint, the miseries, the calamities which our Western parts have both seen, and still feel, strike so strong an apprehension on me."

Eliot demands inquiry into the Cadiz voyage,

At this point, remembering doubtless that the special circumstances which gave a right of inquiring into the expenditure of the subsidies of 1624 did not convey a right of inquiry into the expenditure of any other money, Eliot paused for a moment, making, with the skill of a consummate orator, the half-retractation which he was about to utter an excuse for striking a yet harder blow. "Perchance, sir," he proceeded, "it will be said that this concerns us not —that our money was long since spent in other actions. To prevent such objection I will make this answer, that I know

and into earlier disasters.

nothing so preposterous[1] or good in those former actions that may extenuate, much less excuse, the faults of this. Upon both particulars, therefore, I will contract my motion; this of the war account, and that of the King's estate."

These questions—in short, inquiry into the past and provision for the future—should be discussed in special committees. Till this had been done, nothing should be said about the King's supply. The common cause must have the precedence.[2]

In spite, therefore, of the relegation of the leaders of the Opposition to their respective shires, a voice had been raised to resume the work which they had left unfinished. Instinctively Eliot had taken up ground which was unassailable. There was no personal attack upon Buckingham. The Lord Admiral's name had not even been mentioned. But there had been a plain assertion of the right of the Commons to ascertain by every means in their power whether the money for which they were asked would be used for the benefit of the country. No doubt such an inquiry contained within itself the germs of a mighty revolution. The Commons had certainly not been accustomed thus to pry into the secret actions of Henry VIII. or Elizabeth; but, even if they were as yet hardly fitted to occupy the place of sovereignty, it was not their fault that circumstances had changed, or that there was good reason for withdrawing from Charles I. the confidence which their fathers had reposed in his predecessors.

Weight of the speech.

It is possible that Eliot may have been irritated to some extent by the sermon preached by Laud at the opening of the session. "Jerusalem," the Bishop of St. Davids had told his hearers, "is builded as a city that is compact together." By unity alone could Church or State resist its foes. For the State the centre of unity was in the King. It was his to do judgment and justice, to appoint magistrates and to protect the oppressed. It was the part of the nation to surround him with loving reverence. "And never fear him," he said of Charles, "for God is with him. He will not depart from God's service; nor from the honourable care

Feb. 6. Laud's sermon.

---

[1] *i.e.* 'so preferable or excellent.'   [2] Forster, *Sir J. Eliot,* i. 285.

of his people ; nor from¹ wise managing of his treasure ; he will never undermine his own house, nor give his people just cause to be jealous of a shaking foundation." ²

Those who have been engaged in tracing out Charles's errors and failures will find it hard to understand how such words could be applied to him by any sane man. The difficulty, however, is not a great one. Laud was an ecclesiastic, not a statesman. He saw Charles's conscious wish to do right, and he took it for granted that his conduct was as prudent as his intentions were upright. Having every reason to doubt the fairness of the House of Commons towards the clergy of his own opinions, he thought that they were equally unfair in their opposition concerning political matters.

Laud's devotion to Charles.

Laud had been grieved at the resolution which the King had taken to withdraw his objection to the examination of Montague's opinions by the Commons, on the ground that he was one of the Royal chaplains. On January 16 four bishops, amongst whom were Andrewes and Laud, who had been asked to investigate the question, had reported that Montague's book was agreeable to the doctrine of the Church of England, and had recommended Charles to prohibit all further controversy on the disputed points.³ On the 11th and 17th of the following month a conference was held at Buckingham's house, in which Dr. Preston and Bishop Morton did their best to impugn the doctrines propounded in the incriminated books. Preston was a noted Puritan divine who had secured Buckingham's good-will, and had, in 1622, become Master of Emmanuel College in the University of Cambridge through his patron's influence. Buckingham had, however, for some time been pursuing courses which could not be agreeable to Preston, who had spoken with dislike of his advocacy of the French marriage, and of the concessions made in consequence to the Catholics. Preston now discovered that Buckingham repented of having offered his house for the purpose of the conference, and drew the inference that he had

Feb. 11. The conference about Montague's book.

---

[1] "for," as printed, but surely it should be "from."

[2] Sermon III., *Laud's Works*, i. 63.

[3] Neile, Andrewes, &c. to Buckingham, Jan. 16, *Harl. MSS.* 7000, fol. 193.

placed himself in the hands of the Bishops, and was indifferent or hostile to the triumph of Gospel truth.[1]

As far as it is possible to judge from the accounts which have reached us, the assailants failed to make their points good, as in insisting on a complete accordance with the formulas of the Church, they, in many cases, substituted their own interpretation for the obvious meaning of the formulas themselves. Yet, in spite of his controversial success, Montague was left to the judgment of Parliament. As might have been expected, the House of Commons pronounced strongly against him; but the session was brought to an untimely end before the opinion of the Lords could be taken, and he therefore escaped punishment for a time.

These Church questions would before long attract universal attention. At present the management of the war and the relations between England and the Continental powers were of more immediate interest. The four sub-committees of the Committee for Grievances were hard at work, and the one over which Eliot presided was busily occupied in investigating the case of the 'St. Peter' of Havre de Grace, and in inquiring incidentally why England was on the verge of a war with France without any apparent reason.

The 'St. Peter' of Havre de Grace.

The real history of the estrangement between the two Courts was known to but very few. Probably no one except Buckingham and one or two of his confidants had ever heard of the despatches by which Charles had met with icy coldness the overtures of Richelieu, or were acquainted with the course of the dispute about the French prizes; but the re-seizure of the 'St. Peter' was a fact patent to all. The merchants trading with France were in terror lest reprisals should be made on the other side of the Channel, and the Lord Admiral and the Privy Council were besieged with petitions for the release of the ship.[2]

Feb. 8. Consternation of the English merchants at its re-seizure.

---

[1] Ball's *Life of Preston* in *Clarke's General Martyrology.* 'The sum and substance of the Conference.' *Cosin's Works,* ii. 17. Buckingham presided, and certainly showed great shrewdness and ability.

[2] Petition of the merchants, Feb. 8, *S. P. Dom.* xx. 51. Act of Council, Feb. 12, *Council Register.*

When the ship had been seized, war with France had been imminent. As it was now known in England that the French civil war was at an end, and that the English vessels might soon be on their way home, Buckingham had no longer any interest in detaining the prize. He sent for Marten, and asked what he ought to do. Marten answered cautiously that the ship might be detained if there was fresh evidence against her, but that until he had seen the information on which Buckingham relied, he could not say whether it was sufficient or not. On the 15th the merchants' petitions were considered in the Council, and an order was given that, if the owners would enter into bonds to abide by the decision of the Court of Admiralty, the ship should be at once released.[1]

Feb. 9. Marten consulted.

Soon after this it was discovered that the evidence alleged by Apsley was absolutely worthless, and all further proceedings were tacitly withdrawn. This step, however, was taken too late. Even before the news of the re-seizure of the 'St. Peter' had reached France, the owners of the prize goods which had been sold, being convinced that they had nothing to hope from English justice, had petitioned to their own courts for redress. On the 7th the Judge of the Admiralty at Paris gave permission to all who had been wronged to seek redress by the seizure of English property in France, and on the 10th a similar order was issued by the Parliament of Rouen.[2]

Release of the 'St. Peter.'

Feb. 7. Reprisals in France.

Feb. 10.

Through this thicket of confusion, Eliot and his committee did their best to cut their way. Was it strange if they did not succeed in discovering the truth? It was clear that there was something behind of which they knew nothing. The second detention of the 'St. Peter' required an explanation which had not been vouchsafed to them. How Eliot would have branded with scorn the blunder of selling the prize goods if only he had become aware of the importance which it had in the eyes

Eliot's committee considers the seizure to have been made for Buckingham's private ends.

---

[1] Act of Council, Feb. 15, *Council Register*.

[2] List of proceedings about the ships, undated; Sentence of the Parliament of Rouen, Feb. $\frac{10}{20}$, *S. P. France*. In the subsequent correspondence the seizure of the 'St. Peter' is scarcely mentioned as complained of by the French. The sale of the prize goods is the sore point.

of the French, we can readily imagine ; but the seizure of the 'St. Peter' was all that met his eye, and being in ignorance of the fact that England had been at the time on the brink of a war with France, he had to account for the mystery as best he might. What wonder if he fancied that the Duke had done it all for his own advantage? He knew that some of Buckingham's officers had had charge of valuable articles which had been on board the 'St. Peter,' and that those articles had not been restored. The inference seemed obvious that they had gone to swell the Duke's private fortune, and that, for the sake of his own personal enrichment, he was embroiling the kingdom in an uncalled-for war.

Yet this was far from the truth. It was indeed an unequal contest upon which Eliot had entered. So unwise was the alienation of that State which was ready to become the ally of England, that so true a patriot could not but seek to probe the mystery to the bottom. The mystery could not be so probed. Charles and Buckingham had veiled their actions in secrecy as with a cloud. What Eliot learned had to be dragged from unwilling witnesses, themselves knowing but little, and anxious to tell as small a portion of that little as they could. When, therefore, Attorney-General Heath appeared before the House to defend his patron, he had an easy task before him. He was able to assert that the ship had been seized by the King's directions, and from public motives. It is 'not now,' he said, 'a particular or personal cause, but a national controversy.' It is true that he was not instructed to state what the grounds of that national controversy were ; but he was able to add, with perfect truth, that the seizure of the 'St. Peter' had nothing whatever to do with the embargo at Rouen. Heath's argument was successful with the Commons. By a small majority in a not very full House, they voted that the stay of the 'St. Peter' was not a grievance.[1]

March 6. Heath's defence.

Charles determined to strike while the iron was hot. On the very day on which Heath was pleading before the Commons,

[1] *Commons' Journals,* i. 831.

the Lords were asked to take into consideration the state of the realm. Already in a quiet way the Peers had given signs that they had no intention of being Buckingham's humble servants. Finding that the Duke held no less than thirteen proxies, the independent Lords, after a debate in which almost every official member spoke on the other side,[1] carried an order that for the future no peer should hold more than two proxies. Restlessness under Buckingham's supremacy did not, however, as yet imply readiness to reject a proposal brought to them with the authority of the Crown, and the House at once appointed a committee to take into consideration the question propounded on the King's behalf. The next morning the committee reported that it was advisable to set forth one fleet against Spain, and another for the defence of the English coast, and to maintain the armies of Mansfeld and the King of Denmark.[2]

Feb. 25. Order about proxies in the House of Lords.

March 7. The Peers consider the state of the realm.

With this suggestion the Commons were at once asked to comply. At the conference Buckingham prudently kept himself in the background, and Pembroke and Abbot were put forward to induce the Lower House to assent to the demands of the Government. After detailing the necessities of the fleet and of the Danish army, Pembroke held out hopes that a virtual alliance would be brought about with France.[3]

In the evening an attempt was made to carry the opinion of the Commons by storm. A hopeful despatch had been received from the ambassadors at Paris. Edward Clarke, the confidential servant of the Duke, who, when Charles left Madrid, had been entrusted with the secret orders to Bristol for the postponement of the marriage ceremony, and who, in 1625, had been imprisoned by the Commons for the strong language which he had used in defence of his patron,[4] went about the streets spreading the news that all difficulties had been

News from France.

---

[1] *Elsing's Notes,* 1624–1626, 113.
[2] *Lords' Journals,* iii. 517, 519.
[3] Speeches of Abbot and Pembroke, *Harl. MSS.* 4888, fol. 262.
[4] See Vol. V., pp. 118, 415.

removed, and that there was no longer any danger of a dispute with the King of France.¹

It was not Richelieu's fault that a good understanding had not long ago been effected. Though the news of Blainville's exclusion from Court had been very unwelcome to Louis, no hard language had been used, and Charles's objections to the French scheme of a joint army having been taken into consideration, a fresh offer was made that the King of France should confine himself to operations in Italy, whilst aiding Charles with money to carry on the war in Germany. On the commercial difficulty the French Government was equally conciliatory. Let the vessels seized on both sides, they said, be mutually restored, and then let there be some friendly arrangement to prevent disputes for the future.²

Feb. 21.
Negotiations
at Paris.

Feb. 26.

Charles's wisest course would undoubtedly have been to accept the offer. Unfortunately he was punctilious and keen to mark offences in others. The sense of injury caused in France by the sale of the prize goods he did not understand; and much less did it enter into his head that the strictness of the English law of prize might not commend itself to a neutral Government; but he discovered that, in the commercial treaty agreed on by Louis and his father, it was stated that embargoes were not to be laid on either side without previous notice, and he therefore demanded that France, by taking the first step in the restoration of vessels seized, should acknowledge herself to have been in the wrong. Even this was conceded to him, as Louis himself assured the ambassadors. "I will rely," he said, "upon your promise, and in confidence thereof will ordain a present release; but if in England what you undertake be not faithfully executed, and that such as . . . may be present at the definitive sentence advertise me that my subjects' goods are detained from them, the King my brother must not

March 3.
Charles
punctilious
about the
French
reprisals.

Conciliatory
overtures in
France.

---

¹ Blainville to Louis XIII., March $\frac{7}{17}$, *King's MSS.* 138, p. 1316.

² Holland and Carleton to Coke, Feb. 21; Holland and Carleton to Coke, Feb. 26, *S. P. France.*

take it ill if I do the like." This offer Louis followed up by sending immediate directions to the Admiral at Rochelle, directing him to send home to England the English ships under his charge, and by promising that the order for removing the embargo should be issued the next morning.[1]

March 4.

Such was the news which Clarke was spreading about the streets of London on the evening of March 7. Charles, however, was in a temper which tried the friendliness of the French Government to the utmost. In his anxiety to prove his Protestantism, he had inflicted a fresh blow upon Blainville which was not likely to make his relations easier with the ambassador's master. Blainville's lodgings were in Durham House, one of the mansions which in those days stood between the Strand and the river. It was the house where Raleigh had lived in the days of his splendour, and which was so extensive that the Bishop of Durham contented himself with occupying a small portion. A large part was given over to the French embassy. Blainville had his private chapel, and the mass, when celebrated there, was attended by throngs of the Catholics of London. To this abuse, as he considered it to be, Charles was determined to put an end. He gave orders to the Council to see that it was no longer tolerated, and on the morning of Sunday, February 26, a strong body of constables was posted at the gates, after mass had begun, with directions to seize all English subjects as they came out.

The mass at Durham House.

Interference with the attendance of English Catholics.

When the capture began it was impossible for the French gentlemen of the ambassador's suite to restrain their impatience. Charging upon the constables sword in hand, they rushed to the succour of their English friends. In the scuffle which ensued two men were injured, and one was dragged into the courtyard and borne in triumph before the window at which the ambassador was standing. By this time the noise of the tumult had attracted attention outside, and the population of the neighbourhood hurried up to take part in the fray. Fortunately the Bishop of Durham

Tumult which ensues.

---

[1] Holland and Carleton to Conway, March 3, 5, *S. P. France.*

arrived in time to part the combatants before further mischief was done.

<small>Blainville's anger.</small> Blainville of course was furious. "I wish," he said to the Bishop, as soon as he caught sight of him, "that my followers had killed the officers. The King my master will require reason for that which has been done against the law of nations."[1]

As a matter of law, Charles was plainly within his rights. His prudence in raising so irritating a question was not so certain. In the beginning of March, the very days in which matters were taking a favourable turn at Paris, he contrived, probably unconsciously, again to give offence to the French Court. He had long regarded Arundel with suspicion. In the last Parliament the Earl had been suspected of taking part in the opposition against Buckingham, and, like Williams and Wentworth, he had no sympathy with the warlike ardour of the King and his chief adviser. At the opening of the new Parliament, alone amongst the Privy Councillors he had sided with the independent Peers in the affair of the proxies, and it was not long before Charles found him interfering with his wishes on a more personal question.

<small>March. Arundel's opposition.</small>

Arundel's eldest son, Lord Maltravers, had fallen in love with Elizabeth Stuart, sister of the young Duke of Lennox, and niece of the Lord Steward of James I. His affection was warmly reciprocated. Charles had other views, and claimed, as head of the lady's house, to dispose of her hand as he pleased. The Earl of Argyle, a professed Roman Catholic, had long been an exile from his native country, and had spent many years of his life in the military service of the King of Spain. His son and heir, Lord Lorne, who was one day to be Charles's bitterest enemy as the Covenanting Marquis of Argyle, was not inclined to follow in his father's steps; and Charles hoped that by marrying him into a family so closely connected with the Court as that of Lennox, he might acquire an influence over his future life. Whilst Charles was scheming, the lovers

---

[1] A true relation, &c., *S. P. Dom.* xxi. 6

were acting. Lady Arundel favoured her son's pretensions, and she was not a woman accustomed to be thwarted. A clandestine marriage was hurried on, and, when it was too late to interfere, Arundel was told by his wife that he had better be himself the person to carry the news to the King, as he might safely assert that he had known nothing of the plot before it was carried into execution.[1]

His son's marriage.

Charles was at first not inclined to be very hard upon the Earl; but Arundel, or someone amongst his friends, thought it worth while to enlist the Queen's sympathy on his behalf. Either Charles was jealous of his wife's interference, or he saw in it some fresh plot of the detested Blainville. He at once ordered that Arundel should no longer be admitted to the meetings of the Council; and a fresh application from the Queen was followed by an order for his imprisonment in the Tower, whilst the ladies who had favoured the marriage were detained in various places of confinement.[2]

March 4. Arundel sequestered from the Council.

March 5. Sent to the Tower.

Charles's continued jealousy of the Queen did not augur well for the chances of a better understanding with her brother. Into the recesses of his councils indeed we have no means of penetrating; but the difficulties thrown in the way of the French alliance, the personal quarrel with Blainville, the punctilious hesitation about the release of the prizes, the demand to be recognised as a mediator between Louis and his subjects, all bear unmistakably the impress of Charles's quickness to take offence and reluctance to forget a real or fancied injury. Buckingham was more likely to snatch at the chance of bringing a French army into the field; and the one glimpse which we have of him during these days shows him anxiously desiring permission to go as ambassador to France, no doubt to cement that

Charles, not Buckingham, the cause of the difficulties with France.

---

[1] Meddus to Meade, March 10, *Court and Times*, i. 86. D'Ewes to Stuteville, March, *Harl. MSS.* 383, fol. 26.

[2] *Council Register*, March 4, Arundel to Lady Maltravers, March 5, *Harl. MSS.* 1581, fol. 390. Blainville to Louis XIII., March $\frac{7}{17}$; Blainville to the Bishop of Mende, March $\frac{7}{17}$, *King's MSS.* 138, pp. 1316, 1333.

friendly understanding which his master was doing everything to thwart.¹

<small>March 3. Inquiry directed by the Commons to the council of war.</small>
Whatever the truth may have been, it would have been hard to persuade the Commons that Buckingham was not wholly at fault. Partly from motives of policy, still more perhaps from traditional loyalty of disposition, the maxim that the King could do no wrong was deeply imprinted on their hearts. If they had failed to extract the whole truth about the French prizes, they hoped to be more successful in extracting from the council of war the advice which its members had given about the disposal of the subsidies voted in 1624, wishing probably to know whether Mansfeld's disastrous expedition had received the approbation of competent military authorities.²

<small>Heath's opinion.</small>
The House was, however, destined to disappointment. Heath, having been consulted by the King, gave it as his opinion that though, under the unusual provisions of the Act in question, the Commons would be justified in asking whether the council of war had issued warrants for any expenditure not provided for in the Act, they would not be justified in asking what advice any individual councillor had given, or to require him in any way to inculpate a third party by asking whether the advice given had or had not been followed.

¹ Holland to Buckingham, March $\frac{7}{17}$, *S. P. France*.

² In the *Eliot Notes* the proceedings in committee are given usually without the speaker's name; but the question of misemployment of the subsidies of 1624 is continually recurring in a way which fully bears out my view that the complaint was that they had been employed in too extensive warfare. Thus, on Feb. 27, "That the council of war may first satisfy the House what course hath been taken about the four ends, and what money hath been expended about fortifying our coasts." On Feb. 28, a cause of the war is said to be 'failing in the observation of the ratio [?] for the four ends in the statute 21° Ja.' On the 6th of March some one said 'that we gave our money for defence of our coasts.' The questions on which the councillors of war were to be examined are, 'Whether they met according to the Act, and how often, and when? What they advised and directed, and whether that advice were followed, or how hindered?' Upon the 17th of March it was voted that 'the misemploying of the money given 21 Ja., and the not employing it to the four ends, &c.' a cause.

The acts of the councillors, in short, were a fair subject for investigation, not their opinions.

The doctrine thus laid down is in our own day accepted by all parties in the State. It never occurs to the most inquisitive member of Parliament to ask what advice has been given in the privacy of the Cabinet. But if it has become possible to cover advice with a wise secrecy, it is because all those who act have submitted to a complete responsibility to Parliament for their actions. It was not without reason that when the councillors answered in accordance with Heath's opinion, the Commons felt that the partial satisfaction offered to them was illusory. In fact, the special stipulations of the Act of 1624 had been the beginning of a great change. It had recognised that certain special officials were to be responsible to Parliament as well as to the Crown. It had, however, effected either too much or too little, and the Commons were naturally of opinion that it had effected too little. If they came to the conclusion that the money had been spent on improper objects, how could they call to account the councillors, who might have acted under pressure or misrepresentation, whilst Buckingham was placed beyond inquiry?

March 7. The councillors refuse to reply.

The first thought of the Commons was to persist in their original demand. They informed each councillor that two days would be granted him for consideration, and that he would then be called upon individually to reply to the questions put to him.[1]

The Commons persist.

So strong was the current of feeling, that the old Earl of Totness—who, as Sir George Carew, had been Lord President of Munster in Elizabeth's days, and who was now one of the members of the council of war—thought that it was better that he and his fellows should bear the displeasure of the Commons than that the King's subsidies should be refused. "I beseech your Majesty," he said, "to regard your own ends. For it is better that we should suffer imprisonment than be the occasion of missing necessary subsidies, or breed any difference between you and the House

March 9. Interview between the King and Totness.

---

[1] Question and Answer, March 3 and 7; Heath's opinion, March, *S. P. Dom.* xxii. 16, 17, 18, 19.

of Commons: for we cannot do you better service." It was well and bravely spoken; but Charles saw plainly that his own authority was at stake. "Let them do what they list," he answered proudly. "You shall not go to the Tower. It is not you that they aim at, but it is me upon whom they make inquisition. And for subsidies, that will not hinder it. Gold may be bought too dear, and I thank you for your offer."[1]

The council, therefore, returned much the same answer as before, and the Commons, finding that no further information was to be had, desisted from their inquiry.[2]

<small>March 11.</small>

<small>Final answer of the council of war.</small>
As was usually the case, Charles was right on the narrow technical view of the transaction. He was also right in perceiving that, if there was to be a general inquiry into the past, his own authority would suffer grievously. A complete revolution was implied in the demand made upon him. Yet, after all that had happened, after the disaster which had attended Mansfeld's army, and the failure which had attended the expedition to Cadiz, after the French alliance, of which he had boasted so loudly, was changing, for some mysterious reason, into hardly-concealed hostility, was it reasonable to ask the Commons to entrust large sums to his wisdom and discretion, without that full and searching inquiry into the past, by which alone confidence once shaken could be restored?

This, however, was what Charles seriously proposed to do.

---

[1] Account by Totness, March 9, *S. P. Dom.* xxii. 51.

[2] It has hitherto been supposed that the King rested his objection simply on the impropriety of allowing the House to call his officers to account. Charles, however, acknowledged the right of the Commons to enquire into the employment of the money. "His Majesty," so stands the form of answer finally agreed on, "hath given us leave to give an account of our warrants to the Treasurers for the disbursements of the subsidies given last in the time of his Royal Father, which is clearly warranted by the Act of Parliament. But concerning our counsels, and the following thereof, his Majesty hath directly forbidden us to give any account, as being against his service to divulge those secrets, and expressly against our oath as councillors of war." Form of answer settled, with alterations, in Coke's letter of March 10, *S. P. Dom.* xxii. 57, 60.

The announcement made by Pembroke on the 7th, and the rumours spread abroad by Clarke in the same evening had produced no effect. On the 10th Weston delivered a message asking for an immediate supply for the necessities of State. The Commons were to vote the money, and to ask no questions.[1]

March 10. Supply demanded.

It was absolutely impossible that the Commons should accept the ignominious position thus assigned to them. Yet it was hard to say what course they were to follow. Since the old turbulent days when an adverse vote in Parliament had been enforced by actual or possible insurrection, ministerial responsibility had been a thing unheard of. The officers of the Crown under the Tudors were simply the agents of the sovereign, responsible for their conduct to him alone.

Difficult position of the Commons.

It may be that the straightforward way would have been the best in the end, and that a simple address assuring the King that no money could be voted till he could inspire the House with confidence that it would be wisely expended, would have placed the Commons in a position less logically assailable than any other. It was, however, certain that such a course would have given deep offence to Charles, and, on the other hand, a path was open which, strewed as it was with hidden dangers, appeared to offer a far more inviting prospect.

Two courses before them.

When men's minds are in a state of tension, it often happens that the thought with which all are occupied rises to the lips of some insignificant person, less able than others to weigh the full import of his words. It was thus that when the supply proposed by Pembroke and Abbot[2] was being discussed, Coke's son Clement, hitherto chiefly known for his quarrelsome disposition, flung out the taunt, "It is better to die by an enemy than to suffer at home."

Clement Coke's words.

Now that the King was pressing his demand by Weston, Dr. Turner, a man otherwise of no note, told the House that the cause of all their grievances was 'that great man, the Duke of Buckingham.' Common

March 11. Dr. Turner's queries.

[1] Message, March 10, *Harl. MSS.* 161, fol. 49.   [2] See p. 68.

fame had supplied him with certain queries which called for
an answer. Had the Duke guarded the seas against pirates?
Had he not, by the appointment of unworthy officers, caused
the failure of the expedition to Cadiz? Had he not engrossed
a large part of the Crown lands to himself, his friends, and his
relations? Had he not sold places of judicature and titles of
honour? Was he not dangerous to the State, his mother and
his father-in-law being recusants? Was it fit that he should,
in his own person, enjoy so many great offices?[1]

It has generally been supposed that the questions thus
put had been placed in Turner's mouth by others. However
this may have been, it marks a change of front on the part of
the Opposition. If there were no recent precedents for inquiring into the administrative acts of high officials, there were
the precedents of Bacon and Middlesex for inquiring into their
personal delinquencies. For some days a multitude
of facts damaging to Buckingham had been discovered by the various committees, and it may have
seemed a more hopeful task to induce Charles to abandon a
criminal of whose real character he had been ignorant, than to
surrender a minister to whose policy he had given his constant
approval.

Personal attack upon Buckingham.

If any such calculation as this passed over the minds of the
leading members, if, in short, the step which they were prepared
to take was the fruit of anything more than an honest
indignation against the man whom they had come
to regard as a criminal indeed, they had not taken
into account the extent to which Charles had given, not merely
his name, but his cordial support, to Buckingham's proceedings.
The attack upon his friend roused him to indignation, and he
sent to demand justice upon Coke and Turner. At the same
time the Commons took their stand against the King on
another most important principle. They directed
the King's Counsel in the House to bring in a Tonnage and Poundage Bill within a week, unless they wished to

March 14. Charles asks for justice.

Tonnage and poundage.

---

[1] I have abbreviated the Report in *Add. MSS.* 22, 474, fol. 11, which looks more like words actually spoken than that given in Rushworth.

see the farmers of the Customs called upon to explain by what authority those duties had been levied.[1]

It would evidently not be easy to establish ministerial responsibility. With a sovereign who does not pretend to govern or with a sovereign who is ready to make a scapegoat of an unpopular servant, it presents no difficulty. Charles at the same time claimed to rule the State and was too conscientious to throw over a minister whom he believed to have been unjustly accused. It needed two revolutions to make the doctrine current in England. Before the Commons could succeed in making ministers responsible, they had to re-establish in fact, if not in theory, the responsibility of the Crown.

Question of ministerial responsibility.

Under Eliot's guidance the House did its best to assure the King of its loyalty to himself. Coke and Turner were ordered to explain their words, and the King was assured that there was no wish to deprive him of the means necessary for carrying on a war. The wish of the Commons was to make him 'safe at home and feared abroad,' but they claimed a right to search out the causes of his wants, and to propose such remedies as they might think fitting.[2]

Loyal declarations of the Commons.

The Commons had not long to wait for an answer. Summoning them to Whitehall, Charles spoke his mind plainly. "Mr. Speaker," he said, "here is much time spent in inquiring after grievances. I would have that last, and more time bestowed in preventing and redressing them. I thank you all for your kind offer of supply in general, but I desire you to descend to particulars, and consider of your time and measure. For it concerneth yourselves, who are like first to feel it, if it be too short.

March 15. The King's answer.

"But some there are—I will not say all—that do make inquiry into the proceedings, not of any ordinary servant, but of one that is most near unto me. It hath been said, 'What shall be done to the man whom the King delighteth to honour?'

---

[1] *Rushworth*, i. 218; *Add. MSS.* 22, 474, fol. 12. *Commons' Journals*, i. 836.   [2] *Rushworth*, i. 216

But now it is the labour of some to seek what may be done against the man whom the King thinks fit to be honoured.

"In a former time, when he was an instrument to break the treaties, you held him worthy of all that was conferred upon him by my father. Since that time he hath done nothing but in prosecution of what was then resolved on, and hath engaged himself, his friends, and his estate for my service, and hath done his uttermost to set it forwards; and yet you question him. And for some particulars wherewith he hath been pressed, however he hath made his answer, certain it is that I did command him to do what he hath done therein. I would not have the House to question my servants, much less one that is so near me. And therefore I hope I shall find justice at your hands to punish such as shall offend in that kind."

He hoped, Charles concluded by saying, they would do him right with respect to Coke as well as to Turner. To their just grievances he would always be ready to listen.[1]

That the whole administration was one great grievance Charles could not be brought to understand. Yet this was precisely the belief to which the House was rapidly coming; and now Eliot took the lead in counselling that there should be no drawing back. "We have had a representation of great fear," he cried, "but I hope it shall not darken our understandings."[2] Coke might explain away his words: Turner, stricken with illness, perhaps the result of anxiety, might shrink back into the obscurity from which he had emerged for a moment;[3] but the thought which they had expressed had become the common property of the House.

March 17. Eliot's counsel.

During the following days the committees were busily at

---

[1] I quote the speech from a copy in *Add. MSS.* 22,474, fol. 19, which again looks more like the words actually spoken than the form given by Rushworth.

[2] Mr. Forster (*Sir J. Eliot*, i. 500) has happily restored this exclamation to its proper place.

[3] I cannot share the opinion of those who speak disparagingly of Dr. Turner's letter. It seems to me a manly and outspoken production. He was afterwards one of the Straffordians, so that he can hardly have been a timid man.

work accumulating fresh evidence against Buckingham. Charles impatiently urged the immediate consideration of supply, and after the House had once more listened to an explanation of the necessities of the Exchequer from Sir John Coke,[1] the 27th was fixed as the day for taking the subject into consideration. On the 29th, Buckingham, if he wished, might make answer to the charges collecting against him.

Supply again demanded.

On the 27th, after a persuasive speech from Rudyerd, Eliot rose. Commencing with a graceful allusion to the day, as the first anniversary of the King's accession, he threw aside the argument which had been so often the refuge of timid reasoners in the last Parliament, that the subject was unable to give. The only question, he justly argued, was whether the subject was willing to give. Yet how could men be willing when one miscarriage had followed another, and when these disastrous enterprises 'were undertaken, if not planned and made, by that great lord the Duke of Buckingham.'

March 27. Eliot's speech.

Foreign miscarriages.

Nor were affairs at home much better. "What oppressions have been practised," the orator continued, "are too visible; not only oppressions of the subject, but oppressions on the King. His treasures are exhausted, his revenues are consumed, as well as the treasures and abilities of the subject; and though many hands are exercised, and divers have their gleanings, the harvest and great gathering comes to one. For he it is that must protect the rest. His countenance draws all others to him as his tributaries; and by that they are enforced not only to pillage for themselves but for him, and to the full proportion of his avarice and ambition. This makes the abuse and injury the greater. This cannot but dishearten, this cannot but discourage, all men well affected, all men well disposed to the advancement and happiness of the King. Nor, without some reformation in these things, do I know what wills or what abilities men can have to give a new supply."

Domestic oppressions.

Yet it was not Eliot's intention to dissuade the House from

[1] *Add. MSS.* 22,474, fol. 13.

granting supply. He had two precedents to quote. In the reign of Henry III., Hubert de Burgh, 'a favourite never to be paralleled but now having been the only minion both to the King then living and to his father which was dead,' had been removed from office, and supply, refused before, was at once granted. "The second precedent," he then said, "was in 10th of Richard II.; and herein I shall desire you to observe the extraordinary likeness of some particulars. First, for the placing and displacing of great officers. Then, within the space of two years, the treasurer was changed twice, the chancellor thrice, and so of others; so that great officers could hardly sit to be warmed in their places. Now you can ask yourselves how it is at present, and how many shifts, changes, and re-changes this kingdom can instance in like time to parallel with that. Secondly, as to moneys. I find that then there had been moneys previously granted and not accounted for; and you know that so it is yet with us. Thirdly, there were new aids required and urged by means of a declaration of the King's occasions and estate; and this likewise, as we know, agrees with our condition. Yet then, because of these and other exceptions made against De la Pole, the Earl of Suffolk, the minion of that time, of whom it was said that he misadvised the King, misemployed his treasures, and introverted his revenues, the supply demanded was refused, until, upon the petition of the Commons, he was removed both from his offices and the Court."

<small>Precedents quoted.</small>

Then, after a bitter reference to the Crown 'jewels, the pride and glory of this kingdom,' now offered in vain to the merchants of Amsterdam, Eliot concluded by proposing that the resolution for the three subsidies and three fifteenths asked for by Rudyerd should be passed, but that it should not be converted into a Bill till grievances had been redressed. The position thus pointed out was at once taken up by the House.[1]

It was the misfortune of the situation that unless Charles had been other than he was, he could not accept the hand thus

---

[1] Forster, *Sir J. Eliot*, i. 515.

offered to him. Believing, and it may safely be added being justified in believing, that Buckingham's character was not that compound of avarice and self-seeking which had been described by Eliot, his apprehension was too dull to realise the full meaning of the late disasters, or to understand the state of mind into which they would throw a patriotic Englishman anxious to fathom the causes of his country's misfortunes. Evils, if they existed at all, if they were not the result of mere ill-luck or of the parsimony of former Parliaments, were to be brought before his notice in a respectful and decorous fashion. It never occurred to him that, if Buckingham was well-intentioned, he might be vain, rash, and incapable, still less, that his own ability for government was no greater than that of his minister.

Charles not to be won.

To such a man it would seem a plain duty to hold his own. He knew enough of history to be aware that the fall of Hubert de Burgh had been followed by the insurrection of Simon de Montfort, and the fall of Michael de la Pole by the revolution which placed Henry IV. on the throne. He would take care to guard in another fashion the crown which he had received from his father. That the crown itself was attacked he had no doubt whatever. The leaders of the Commons, he fancied, were taking advantage of the necessities of the position into which their advice had brought him, to raise themselves above the throne.

With such thoughts in his mind, Charles summoned the Commons into his presence on the 29th, the day on which Buckingham had been invited to give an account of his proceedings to the House. As soon as they appeared they were addressed by Coventry. The King, said the Lord Keeper, would have them to understand the difference between liberty of counsel and liberty of control. Not only had they refrained from censuring Coke and Turner, but they had followed in the steps of the latter by founding their charges upon common fame. In their attack upon Buckingham they had assailed the honour of the King and of his father, and they had refused to trust him with the reformation of abuses. It was therefore his Majesty's express command that they should

March 29. Coventry's declaration.

desist from this unparliamentary inquisition, and commit their real grievances to his wisdom and justice. Further, he was to say that the supply proposed was insufficient, and that the mode in which it had been offered was dishonouring to his Majesty. If they could not give a better answer in three days, he could not promise that the session would continue longer.

Charles had a few words of his own to add. "Now, that you have all things according to your wishes," he said, after reminding his hearers that he had entered upon the war in compliance with their advice, "and that I am so far engaged that you think there is no retreat, now you begin to set the dice, and make your own game; but I pray you to be not deceived: it is not a Parliamentary way, nor it is not a way to deal with a king. Mr. Coke told you it was better to be eaten up by a foreign enemy than to be destroyed at home. Indeed, I think it more honour for a king to be invaded and almost destroyed by a foreign enemy, than to be despised by his own subjects. Remember, that Parliaments are altogether in my power for their calling, sitting, and dissolution; therefore, as I find the fruits of them good or evil, they are to continue, or not to be."[1]

Additions by the King.

Not so! Precedent might be met by precedent, and the history of the Constitution might be ransacked for evidence that England had, at one time or another, been either almost a republic or almost an absolute monarchy; but the right of control, as opposed to the mere right of giving counsel, was not to be won or defended by such arguments as these. In the long run it would lie with those by whom it was best deserved.

Weakness of his position.

The Commons, moved as they were by grave necessity, stood firm. At Eliot's advice they resolved to draw up a remonstrance to explain their position to the King.[2] Before the resolution could take effect they were summoned to a conference to hear Buckingham explain away Charles's threat of immediate dissolution, and

March 30. Eliot proposes a remonstrance.

[1] *Parl. Hist.* ii. 56.   [2] Forster, *Sir J. Eliot,* i. 529.

announce that a committee was to be selected by the King from both Houses to consider the state of the finances.

Buckingham did not stop here. With magnificent assurance he proceeded to draw a picture of his own actions in startling contrast with that which had been presented by Eliot three days before. He told the House of the eagerness with which, after his return from Spain, he had thrown himself into the business of the State, and of his unceasing efforts to carry out the warlike policy of Parliament, frustrated, alas! by accident, or by the faults of others. Then, after an assurance from Conway that nothing of all this had been done without counsel, he again rose to tell the true story of the ships which had been used against Rochelle, revealing the secret that all the solemn orders and injunctions into which the Commons had been so laboriously inquiring were a mere farce. He had, he said, 'proceeded with art,' and had done his best to avert the surrender of the ships. If he had not succeeded in this, everything had turned out for the best for the Huguenots, 'for the King of France, thereby breaking his word, gave just occasion for my master to intercede a peace for them, which is obtained, and our ships are coming home.'

Buckingham vindicates himself.

Tells the truth about the ships.

After a few words from Pembroke, who added that at the time when the ships were surrendered it was believed that they would be used against Genoa, the meeting came to an end.[1] Of the effect which this astounding revelation produced at the time we have no information; but as the Commons never took the slightest notice of what they had heard, it may be concluded that they disbelieved the entire story. How indeed could they be assured that the man who openly boasted that he had cheated the King of France, would not, on some future occasion, take credit for having cheated them. At all events they returned to their own House, resolved to vindicate, in the remonstrance which they were preparing, their claim to call in question the highest subjects who were found grievous to

Effect of this revelation.

April 4. Remonstrance of the Commons.

[1] Our knowledge of this conference has hitherto ended with Conway's speech. But the whole can now be read in *Add. MSS.* 22,474, fol. 22 b–31 b.

the commonwealth. On April 4 the Remonstrance was presented to Charles, and at his request the Houses adjourned at once for the Easter recess, to give him time to re-consider his position.

<small>April 13.
They are
allowed to
go on.</small>
When the Commons re-assembled on the 13th they found that no further obstacle was to be opposed to their proceedings. The King advised them to lay aside lesser things for greater ;[1] but further than that he did not go.

<small>Probable
motives of
Charles.</small>
Charles's motives for this change of language are mere matter of conjecture ; but, on the whole, it is most probable that Buckingham's speech in his own defence appeared to him to be so entirely conclusive that he fancied that, unless he provoked the Commons by opposition, it could not fail in having its fitting effect.[2]

<small>April 17.
Proceedings
in the House.</small>
In these expectations, if he ever entertained them, Charles was speedily to be undeceived. On the 17th a sub-committee met to discover the cause of causes, or, in other words, to fix the grievances upon Buckingham, and on the 18th a Committee of the whole House was ordered to consider the evils, causes, and remedies.

<small>April 18.
Carleton's
narrative.</small>
In order that this Committee might be freed from the fear of an impending war with France, Carleton, who had just returned from his embassy, was directed to give an account of the position of affairs. Besides telling how the 'Vanguard' and its comrades would soon be back, and how the order for the release of the English ships and goods had been granted, he had to tell of the hope of co-operation with France upon the Continent. All now, he said, rested on his Majesty's answer to the French King's proposals, 'and the King resteth upon the Parliament.'

Either, however, the Commons disbelieved Carleton's story,

---

[1] Weston's message, *Sloane MSS.* 1710, fol. 289.

[2] " And for his own particular, the Duke gave so pertinent answers to those things which were cast upon him for faults, as I conceive the greatest part and most indifferent men went away well satisfied."—Conway to Wake, April 14, *S. P. Venice.*

or they considered it irrelevant to the point at issue. They went steadily on with the charges against the Duke, and they replied to a fresh message demanding an increase of the subsidies voted, unless they wished his Majesty to 'be driven to change his counsels,' by a resolution that they would go on with the matter in hand forenoon and afternoon, so as to be able to take the King's wish into consideration on the 25th.

Persistence of the Commons.

April 20.

By this time the charges against Buckingham were in so forward a state that it was necessary to clear the way for them by considering the objections which had been raised to the ground upon which they were based. For many weeks the whole band of courtiers had been sneering at those who were attacking a minister upon mere common fame, as if the House had based its action upon rumour alone. One morning's debate sufficed to blow the fiction to the winds. Eliot and Pym were not the men to ask the House of Lords to accept the gossip of Paul's Walk as evidence against the meanest Englishman alive. The difficulty, such as it was, was of a purely technical character. In the cases of Bacon and Middlesex inquiry had been preceded by the presentation of a petition from some person who felt himself aggrieved. The question was whether the House could institute an inquiry when no private person had complained. In either case the real justification of the action taken would be the inquiry conducted by the House, and, in deciding that a petition was unnecessary, the Commons undoubtedly decided in accordance with the dictates of common sense. "Else," as Selden argued, "no great man shall, for fear of danger, be accused by any particular man." If Buckingham could not be called in question till some one out of the House was hardy enough to appear against him, his opponents within the House might have waited long enough.[1]

Proceeding on common fame.

When this point had once been settled, the charges were speedily voted, the one relating to the 'St. Peter' of Havre de Grace being replaced amongst them. In order to point out distinctly that no attack was intended

May 1.
The charges voted

[1] *Commons' Journals,* i. 844–848.

upon the King, the Commons passed a resolution for a fourth subsidy, to be included in the Bill which was to be brought in as soon as grievances had been redressed.

Another subsidy voted.

Whatever Buckingham's faults may have been, history cannot, like the House of Commons, turn away its eyes from the faults of Charles. During these weeks in which he had been struggling to defend his favourite, the French alliance, which he had risked so much to bring to pass, had been melting away before his eyes.

Charles and the French alliance.

There can be very little doubt that in the beginning of March, Louis as well as Richelieu, meant honestly to co-operate with England on the Continent. The terms of the peace were accepted at Rochelle, and orders were sent to the King's commanders to withdraw their troops from before the walls;[1] but there was a large party at the French Court which viewed with grave displeasure a peace with the Huguenots and a war with Spain, and this party had a useful instrument in Du Fargis, the French ambassador at Madrid.

March 4. The French Government favourable to the English alliance.

Without instructions from his own Government, Du Fargis drew up, in concert with Olivares, the draft of a treaty putting an end to the disputes existing between the two monarchies. When it reached Paris the question whether this treaty should be adopted or not formed the battle-field between Richelieu on the one side and the friends of the clergy on the other.

Treaty with Spain prepared by Du Fargis.

French historians have much to tell us of the strength of this clerical party, and of the hold which it gained upon the mind of the King. All this, however, was as true in January as it was in March. If this party did not prevent Louis from signing the treaty with the Huguenots, why did it prevail upon him to sign the treaty with Spain? The answer is not very difficult to give. If Charles and England had been ready to support the French movement towards hostility with Spain, Du Fargis's treaty would surely have been

Question of its acceptance.

[1] Louis XIII. to Blainville, March $\frac{4}{14}$, *King's MSS.* 138, p. 1283.

rejected; but if Charles were lukewarm, or threatening to interfere on behalf of the King's Protestant subjects, then its acceptance would become an act of imperative necessity, not only for Louis, but even for Richelieu himself. No French Government could prudently engage in war in Italy or Germany, leaving the great seaport on the Atlantic coast to the chances of a hostile occupation by the King of England.

All through March and April Charles was doing his best to throw Louis into the arms of Spain. On March 7 Holland and Carleton announced that, in addition to the orders despatched to restore the English ships and to withdraw the troops from Rochelle, a day was fixed for the consideration of the best way of assisting Mansfeld and the King of Denmark, and that, in spite of the clamour of the French merchants, directions had been given for removing the embargo on English property. The English ambassadors, on their part, had made some excuse for the seizure of the 'St. Peter.' "But," they wrote, "for former proceedings in ill-treatment of the Frenchmen which were taken in those prizes, in embezzling and selling their goods, in suffering them to live in want and misery whilst their cause was in trial, in delay of justice after his Majesty had resolved of restitution of their goods at Hampton Court, we wish we had been better furnished with matter than we were to answer their complaints, which were made the cause of these reprisals, though not justifiable by the treaties." Yet, in spite of his just ground of complaint, Louis, though asking that Blainville should be admitted to a formal audience, offered to recall him, and to appoint another ambassador of a more conciliatory disposition.[1]

<small>March 7. Charles's treatment of the French Government.</small>

The next day the ambassadors wrote again. They had been unable to accept the removal of the embargo, because it was granted on condition that they would engage that the French prizes in England should be liberated within three weeks. Charles refused utterly to believe in the sincerity of the French Government. Instead of giving his ambassadors orders to show signs of friendliness, he

<small>March 8. Question of reciprocity in releasing goods seized.</small>

---

[1] Holland and Carleton to Coke, March 7, *S. P. France.*

left them without instructions about the embargo or the assistance offered to Denmark, expressed his suspicion that the French meant to attack Rochelle, and finally recalled them. On March 28 Holland and Carleton left Paris.[1] So plain was the folly of such conduct that even the obsequious Conway, for once in his life, raised an objection to the proceedings of his master. He perceived, he informed Buckingham, 'that, by the whole scope of the present estate of things, the French King hath no desire to fall in disorder with his Majesty, and that what had passed in Paris declared an intention rather to oppose the public enemy than to maintain the broils at home.'[2]

<small>March 1 Charles's suspicions.</small>

For a time it seemed that Conway's advice would be taken. In the beginning of April, five ships were released in England. Blainville was received with all ceremony at an audience at which he was to take leave. The deputies of Rochelle, whose presence in England gave umbrage to Louis, were about to return home.[3] These bright hopes, however, were but of short continuance. There were fresh seizures of French vessels at sea, and the English goods were still detained in France till better news came from beyond the Channel.[4]

<small>April 19. Blainville received at an audience.</small>

A few seizures more or less might easily have been got over, if there had been any desire to remove the cause of the evil; but Charles maintained steadily that his view of the law of prize was right, and that the French view was wrong. There was no effort made to come to an understanding on this point, any more than any effort was made to come to an understanding about the German war. As the prospect of a close alliance with England faded away, the French Government became the more reluctant to fulfil the hopes which it had held out to the Huguenots when that alliance appeared to be attainable. One day the deputies from Rochelle

<small>April 27. Doubts entertained in France of the English alliance.</small>

---

[1] Holland and Carleton to Conway, March 11; Coke to Holland and Carleton, March 16, 17, *ibid.*

[2] Conway to Buckingham, March, *S. P. France.*

[3] Blainville to Louis XIII., March $\frac{19}{29}$, *King's MSS.* 138, p. 1429.

[4] Louis to Conway, April 22, 27 : *S. P. France.*

were told that Fort Louis could not be demolished, at all events not till new fortifications were erected on the Isle of Rhé. They appealed to Charles for aid, and Charles at once replied that he was ready to support them in their lawful demands.[1]

<small>April 30.
The Peace of Barcelona.</small>
Even if there was to be no actual war with England, if there was to be nothing worse than coolness between the two Courts, it was a pressing necessity for Louis to make up his quarrel with Spain. On April 30, Du Fargis's draft was converted into the Treaty of Barcelona. Richelieu gave a consent, doubtless unwillingly enough, but it was a consent which was under the circumstances inevitable. To succeed in the policy which he had adopted, it was necessary that Charles should give to it his active support. As soon as it was beyond doubt that this support was not to be given, Richelieu, as prompt to seize the conditions of action as Charles was dull, faced round for a time, till he could pursue his own object again without the necessity of asking for the good word of so <small>End of the French alliance.</small> unintelligent an ally. The alliance between England and France was at an end. It was but too probable that a war between England and France would not be long in following.

[1] Deputies of Rochelle in France to the Deputies in England, $\frac{\text{March 29,}}{\text{April 3,}}$ April $\frac{5}{15}$; Instructions to Barrett, April 30, *S. P. France.*

CHAPTER LVIII.

THE IMPEACHMENT OF THE DUKE OF BUCKINGHAM.

ALTHOUGH it was impossible that Parliament should have any real knowledge of the course of the negotiations with France,

April. Details of the negotiations with France not generally known.

it can have been no secret that the relations between the two crowns were anything but satisfactory. It was a matter of common conversation that Blainville had for some weeks been refused admission to Court, that English ships and goods had been sequestered in France, and that French ships and goods were still being brought as prizes into English ports. There was enough in this to throw serious doubt on Carleton's assertion that the King was only waiting for Parliamentary supplies in order to join France in open war. If this had been the whole truth, why did not Charles give further information of the objects at which he was aiming, and of the means by which he expected to attain them?

Such general distrust of a Government is certain to vent itself in personal attacks upon those of whom it is composed. In the course of the past weeks the committees of the Commons had been busily bringing together all kinds of charges against Buckingham, thinking that here was to be found the explanation of that which was otherwise so inexplicable. The House of Lords too, unluckily for Buckingham, had a grievance

Case of the Earl of Arundel.

of its own. Charles had probably forgotten that by sending Arundel to the Tower whilst Parliament was sitting, he might be accused of violating the privileges of the House of Lords; but the Peers were not disposed to be equally forgetful, and, after no long delay, they demanded an account of the absence of a member of their House from his place in Parliament. During the Easter recess Arundel was allowed to exchange his cell in the Tower for confinement in one of his own houses. Agreeable as the change may have been to himself, it did not affect the grievance of the Peers, and on April 19 they drew up a remonstrance vindicating their right to demand the presence of any member of their House who was not accused of treason, felony, or refusal to give security against breach of the peace.[1]

Interference of the House of Lords.

April 19. Their remonstrance.

At this juncture a fresh champion raised his voice on behalf of the privileges of Parliament, a champion whose co-operation was all the more valuable to the leaders of the Lower House, because he could speak with official knowledge of the actions which he denounced, and was not, as they had been, compelled to extract the truth from the mouths of unwilling witnesses.

Bristol appears on the scene.

When Charles first ascended the throne he had missed the opportunity of putting an end gracefully to his long altercation with Bristol. He assured his father's late ambassador that, though he was quite aware that he had not offended in any matter of honesty, he could not acquit him of trusting too implicitly to the Spanish ministers. Bristol must therefore acknowledge his error if he wished to be received into favour, though the slightest acknowledgment would be sufficient.

1625. May. Charles's message to Bristol.

Slight as the acknowledgment required was, it was more than Bristol could give, unless he were first convinced that he had committed an error at all. When once Charles's overtures had been rejected, and Bristol's confinement at Sherborne was maintained, a grievance had been established of which that cool and practised disputant was certain sooner or later to avail himself. For, loose as the

Bristol's confinement continued.

---

[1] Joachimi to the States-General, April $\frac{15}{25}$, *Add. MSS.* 17,677, L, fol. 184 b, *Lords' Journals*, iii. 558, 564, 566.

notions on the right of imprisonment by prerogative had been, it was difficult to argue that the King was justified in depriving a subject of his liberty on the simple ground that the subject thought that he had been right when the King thought he had been wrong.

Even Charles seems to have had the glimmering of a suspicion that everything was not as it should be. He sent directions to Bristol to abstain from presenting himself at his first Parliament, but he excused himself on the ground that he had as yet had no time to examine the causes of his restraint.

<small>June 10. Bristol forbidden to come to Parliament.</small>

Months passed away, and there were no signs that the requisite leisure would ever be found. Bristol quietly remained at Sherborne till the approaching coronation gave him an excuse for asking for liberty. He also reminded the King that the instructions which he had received commanded him to remain in the confinement in which he had been at James's death. As, however, his late master had ordered his liberation, it was hard to know what was precisely intended.

<small>1626. January. He asks to be present at the Coronation.</small>

Charles perhaps thought that Bristol was laughing at him, and flashed into anger. Forgetting that he had already pronounced the Earl to be guiltless of any real offence, he now accused him of having attempted to pervert him from his religion when he was in Spain, and of having given his approval to the proposal that the Electoral Prince should be educated at Vienna.

Violent as the King's letter was, it contained no intimation of any intention to bring Bristol to trial. The incriminated man saw his advantage. In his reply he plainly showed it to be his opinion that, though he could not, as a subject, demand from his sovereign a trial as a right, the charges which had been brought against him were such as could only be fairly met in open court.[1]

<small>Bristol answers that he is ready for a trial.</small>

At any other time Bristol would probably have been com-

<small>The whole correspondence is printed in the sixth volume of the *Camden Miscellany*.</small>

pelled to remain quietly at Sherborne without hope of liberty. Parliament, however, being again in session, the Earl, who, for a second time had received no writ of summons, forced Charles's hand by petitioning the Lords to mediate with the King that he might either be brought to trial or allowed his rights as a subject and a Peer.[1]

<small>March 22. He petitions the Lords for his writ.</small>

Here at least Bristol was sure of a favourable hearing. The Peers had already expressed a strong opinion in Arundel's case that the King had no right to deprive their House of the services of any one of its members without bringing him to trial, and a committee to which Bristol's petition was referred reported that there was no instance on record in which a Peer capable of sitting in Parliament had been refused his writ. The King, answered Buckingham, would grant the writ, but he had intimated to Bristol that he did not wish him to make use of it. So transparent a subterfuge was not likely to be acceptable to the Lords. Lord Saye and Sele, always ready to protest against arbitrary proceedings, moved that it should be entered in the Journal Book that, at the Earl's petition, his Majesty sent him the writ ;—and no more. Saye's proposal was at once adopted, and no trace of Charles's unlucky contrivance is to be found in the records of the House.[2]

<small>March 30. The Lords support Bristol.</small>

Bristol had another surprise in store for Charles. As soon as he received the writ from Coventry, with the accompanying letter informing him that he was not to use it, he replied with inimitable irony that as the writ, being under the King's great seal, took precedence of a mere letter from the Lord Keeper, it was his duty to obey the Royal missive by coming to London.[3]

<small>April. Bristol comes to London.</small>

When Bristol reached London he proceeded to lay his correspondence with Coventry before the Peers. For two years, he added, he had been a prisoner simply because Buckingham was afraid of him. He therefore desired to be heard 'both in the point of his wrongs, and of the accusation of the said Duke.'

<small>April 17. Attacks Buckingham.</small>

---

[1] *Lords' Journals*, iii. 537.   [2] *Elsing's Notes*, 1624–1626, p. 135.
[3] Earl of Bristol's Defence, *Camden Miscellany*, vi. Pref. xxxv.

Charles and Buckingham seemed to be powerless in the hands of the terrible Earl. They had but one move left in a game in which their adversary had occupied all the positions of strength in advance. Though Charles had emphatically declared that Bristol had committed no actual offence, and had been guilty of nothing worse than an error of judgment, he was now compelled to accuse him of high treason, if he was not to allow him to take his seat triumphantly and to attack Buckingham from the very midst of the House of Lords.

April 17. Is accused by the King of high treason.

That House had suddenly risen to a position unexampled for many a long year. Its decision was awaited anxiously on the gravest questions. It was called upon to do justice on Bristol, on Buckingham, and, by implication, on the King himself. By this time too it was becoming evident that the sympathy of the House was not with Buckingham. There was a sharp debate on the question whether Bristol should be allowed to take his seat till his accusation had been read. The supporters of the Government were compelled to avoid an adverse decision by an adjournment, and prevent further discussion by hurrying on the accusation.

April 29. Was Bristol to take his seat?

On May 1, therefore, Bristol was brought to the bar, to listen to the allegations of the Attorney-General. Before Heath could open his mouth the prisoner appealed to the House, urging that the object of the charge was merely to put him in the position of a person accused of treason, so as to invalidate his testimony against Buckingham. He called Pembroke to witness how, when he first returned from Spain, Buckingham had proposed to silence him by sending him to the Tower. Buckingham, he said, was now aiming at the same object in another way.

May 1.

If there had ever been any intention of getting rid of Bristol's charges upon technical grounds it could hardly be pressed after this. It was finally decided that, though the Attorney-General was to have the precedence, the two cases were to be considered as proceeding

The charges to proceed simultaneously.

simultaneously, so as to allow Bristol to say what he liked without hindrance.[1]

Hitherto the contest had been very one-sided. In Bristol's hands Charles and Buckingham had been as novices contending with a practised gladiator. In truth they had but little to say. Many of Heath's charges related to mere advice given as a councillor, and those which went further would hardly bear the superstructure which was placed upon them. The attempt to change the Prince's religion of course figured in the list, as did also an elaborate argument that if Bristol had not advised the continuance of the marriage negotiations in spite of his knowledge that the Spaniards were not in earnest, Charles would not have been obliged to go to Madrid to test the value of the ambassador's asseverations. Still more strange was the accusation that Bristol, in expressing a doubt of the accuracy of Buckingham's narrative in the Parliament of 1624, had thrown suspicion upon a statement which the present King had affirmed to be true, and had thereby given 'his Majesty the lie.'

_{The charges against Bristol.}

Bristol's charges against Buckingham were then read. His main point was that Buckingham had plotted with Gondomar to carry the Prince into Spain in order to effect a change in his religion, and that Porter, when he went to Madrid in the end of 1622, was cognisant of this plot. When Buckingham was in Spain, he had absented himself from the English service in the ambassador's house, and had gone so far as to kneel in adoration of the Sacrament, in order 'to give the Spaniards a hope of the Prince's conversion.' Far worse conditions had been imposed by Spain after the Prince's visit than had been thought of before, and if England was now free from them it was because Buckingham's behaviour was so intolerable that the Spanish ministers refused to have anything further to do with him. Other charges of less importance followed, and then Bristol proceeded to accuse Conway of acting as a mere tool of the man whom he was accustomed to style his most gracious patron.

_{Bristol's charges against Buckingham.}

[1] *Elsing's Notes*, 1624-1626, p. 154.

Even if Buckingham, as was probably the case, had been the dupe rather than the confederate of Gondomar, and if he had merely played with the Spaniards in their hopeless design of converting the Prince, in order that he might gain his own ends the better, the weight of Bristol's charges against him tells far more heavily than those which he was able to bring against Bristol. Not one of the latter can compare in gravity with that one of his own actions which is known beyond doubt to have actually taken place, namely, that he formed a plan with a foreign ambassador for carrying the Prince to Spain, and that he concealed the design for nearly a whole year from the reigning sovereign.

<small>Case between Bristol and Buckingham.</small>

No wonder that Buckingham and Buckingham's master had been anxious to avoid the terrible exposure. They were probably aware that Bristol had in his possession the letters which had been carried by Porter to Spain; and, though we have no means of knowing what those letters contained, there can be little doubt that there was much in them which neither Charles nor Buckingham would wish to make public.[1] As soon as it was known that the Lords meant to go into the evidence on both sides, Charles sent them a message that Bristol's charges were merely recriminatory, and that he was himself able to bear witness to their untruth. Though Carlisle did his best to irritate the Peers against Bristol by calling the attention of the House to the Earl's disrespect to their lordships in sending a copy of his charges to the Commons, they refused to notice an act in committing which the prisoner had evidently intended to secure for himself the publicity of which he feared to be deprived.[2]

<small>May 2. Interference by the King.</small>

The investigation therefore was left to take its course. On the 6th, in the midst of a defence conducted with consummate ability, and in which Bristol pointed out that whatever he might have said in Spain about the Prince's conversion was caused by Charles's deliberate ab-

<small>May 6. Bristol's defence.</small>

---

[1] In the *Sherborne MSS.* are the interrogatories which Bristol, in his subsequent trial in the Star Chamber, put to Porter, asking him whether each of these letters, of which the first words were quoted, was genuine or not.   [2] *Elsing's Notes,* 1624-1626, p. 163.

stention from contradicting the rumours which were abroad of his intended change of religion, the accused Earl extracted from Pembroke an admission that he knew of Buckingham's proposal to send him to the Tower on his return from Spain. Such an admission, by showing how indifferent Buckingham had been to the wishes of James, went far to strengthen the suspicions which were generally entertained, that he was now no less indifferent to the wishes of Charles.

Every step of this great process was marked by some fresh interference of the King. He now sent to contest the right of the Lords to allow Bristol the use of counsel, as being contrary to the fundamental laws of the realm. This and the preceding message, in which Charles had tendered his personal evidence, were very coolly received by the Peers. The question of the propriety of admitting the King's evidence was referred to the Judges. The question of counsel was debated in the House. In the course of the discussion one of the Peers mentioned that in 1624, when Charles himself was a member of the House, counsel had been allowed to persons accused before the Lords.[1]

May 8. Question of allowing counsel.

The discussion was at its height when fresh actors appeared upon the scene. A deputation from the Commons, with Carleton, a most unwilling spokesman, at its head, had come to demand a conference that afternoon, with the intention of proceeding with the long-prepared impeachment of the Duke.

Buckingham impeached by the Commons.

In the afternoon, therefore, eight managers on behalf of the Commons, together with sixteen assistants, appeared to read and to explain the charges. To the surprise of many, though it was not strictly in contravention of precedent,[2] Buckingham himself was present, taking up a position directly opposite to the managers, and even, it is said, expressing his contempt for them by laughing in their faces.[3]

---

[1] *Elsing's Notes*, 1624-1626, p. 128. Charles afterwards argued that Middlesex, in whose case the order was made, was not accused of high treason, whereas Bristol was.

[2] The theory which seemed likely to prevail in Bristol's case, was that the accused person might keep his seat till his accusation had been read.

[3] Meade to Stuteville, May 13, *Ellis*, ser. 1, iii. 266.

The prologue was entrusted to Digges. "The laws of England," he said, after a preamble in which he attributed to the Duke all the calamities which had befallen the nation, "have taught us that kings cannot command ill or unlawful things. And whatsoever ill events succeed, the executioners of such designs must answer for them."

Prologue by Digges.

It has been said that no one rises so high as he who knows not whither he is going. Little did the Commons think of all that was implied in these words. By the mouth of Digges they had grasped at the sovereignty of England.

Importance of his declaration.

By his constant personal interference Charles had shown that he knew better than the House of Commons how much his own authority was at stake. They fancied that Buckingham had been the author of everything that had been done; had taken advantage of the King's youth and docility; had deceived him, misadvised him, even plundered him, without his knowing anything about the matter. Charles knew that it was not so; that he had himself been a party to all that had been done, either by agreeing to it beforehand or by approving of it afterwards. As this was so, he would never abandon Buckingham to his adversaries. Everything, he assured the Houses again and again, had been done by him or with his consent. It was not his fault if the Commons would not face the larger question of royal responsibility before entering upon the smaller question of ministerial responsibility. He at least was perfectly clear about royal responsibility. The king, he held, as Laud had taught him, was responsible to God alone. When the king had said that a thing had been well done, there was an end of the matter. The weakness of the position of the Commons was that they would not look this assertion in the face. They maintained that by impeaching Buckingham they were strengthening the King's hands, whereas they were in reality weakening them, and were making the King indirectly responsible, whilst they would be the first to deny that he was responsible at all.

Meaning of the personal interference of Charles.

The Commons had need to take good care to say no more than they could prove. Yet how was this possible? The records of State affairs were not accessible to them. No Blue Books were issued in those days to enlighten them on the words spoken and the policy supported by a minister.

Difficulty of reaching the truth.

Since Charles's accession the acts of Government had been veiled in deeper secrecy than ever before. If James had sometimes changed his mind, he had never failed to speak out the thought which ruled him for the time being. Charles said as little as possible, and no one was commissioned to say much on his behalf.

Besides the difficulty of knowing what had really been done, the Commons had made another difficulty for themselves by their resolution to spare the King. Again and again, in the course of their investigations, they reached the point in which Buckingham's acts ran into the acts of the King. In such a case silence was their only resource. They could not tell all they knew.

The first charge was entrusted to Edward Herbert, one day to be the Attorney-General who took part in the impeachment of the five members. He spoke of the danger to the State from the many offices held in one hand : of the purchase of the Admiralty from Nottingham, and of the purchase of the Cinque Ports from Zouch. Selden had then to speak of the failure to guard the Narrow Seas, and of the detention of the ' St. Peter' of Havre de Grace. To Glanville was entrusted the tale of the money exacted from the East India Company, and of the ships lent to serve against the Protestants of Rochelle.

The first day of the impeachment.

Can it be wondered that Buckingham, conscious of his superior knowledge, should smile as he heard each story, told only as these men were able to tell it? Did he not know that in paying money to Nottingham and Zouch he had only conformed to the general custom? Could the failure to guard the seas be judged irrespectively of the wisdom of the other employment to which the ships had been destined in preference, or the exaction of money from the East India Company irrespective of the share which James had had in the transaction? To come to a true conclusion about the seizure of the ' St. Peter,' or the loan of the ships for Rochelle, it was

Criticism on these charges.

necessary to know the whole truth about the relations between England and France; and though the whole truth would have told even more against the Court than the charges brought by the Commons, Buckingham may perhaps be excused for thinking more of the weakness of his opponents' case than of the weakness of his own. Still more had they missed the mark in charging him with the assumption of many offices in his own person. The Mastership of the Horse was a mere domestic office in the King's household. There was a direct advantage to the State in the accumulation of the Admiralty and the Wardenship of the Cinque Ports in the hands of one person. The real grievance was not that Buckingham nominally held three offices, but that, although he was incompetent for the task, he virtually controlled the action of the occupants of all other offices.

On May 10 the remainder of the charges were heard. This time the Duke absented himself from the House. Sherland declared that Buckingham had compelled Lord Robartes to buy a peerage against his will. He had also sold the Treasurership to Manchester, and the Mastership of the Wards to Middlesex. Pym spoke effectively of the honours dealt out to Buckingham's poor kindred, entailing upon the Crown the necessity of supporting them. Buckingham had himself received from the Crown lands producing a rental of more than 3,000*l.*, and ready money to the amount of upwards of 160,000*l.*, to say nothing of valuable grants of other kinds. What these grants were worth no man could discover; for the accounts of the revenue were in such confusion that it was impossible to say how much had come into the Duke's hands by fictitious entries. One last charge remained, that of administering medicine to the late King on his death-bed. Wentworth's friend, Wandesford, did not venture to allude to the rumours of poison, which were at that time generally credited; but he justly characterised the act as one of 'transcendent presumption.'

May 10. Second day of the impeachment.

That the facts thus disclosed deserved the most stringent investigation it is impossible to deny. On the other hand it must be remembered that the lavish grants of James to Buckingham and his kindred were a reproach rather to the giver than to the receiver, and, further, that the looseness of the manner in which the accounts were kept, which has been such as to baffle every serious investigator into the financial history of the time, is susceptible of another explanation than that which was given by Pym. Nothing can be asserted positively, but there is every reason to believe that the real accounts, if they were ever to be recovered, would tell more in Buckingham's favour than against him. Sums were paid into his hands, there can be little doubt, which were used by him not for his personal objects, but for the service of the State, or for purposes to which the King wished them to be applied.[1]

Need of reform. Reform, in short, was absolutely needed, a reform to which the expulsion of Buckingham from power would be the first step. Yet, with all his faults, the Buckingham of history is very different from the Buckingham of the

[1] This seems to have been the case with the money received from Manchester and Cranfield (Middlesex). Robartes's money was paid to Buckingham, but it does not follow that it was not used for the fleet or some other public object. *See* Robartes's petition, March (?) 1626, and the depositions of Robartes and Strode, *S. P. Dom.* xxiii. 118, lxvii. 40, i. Thus, too, in Pym's charge we have a statement that amongst moneys employed for his own use, the Duke had the 60,000*l.*, which were paid to Burlamachi on Oct. 7, 1625 (*Lords' Journals*, iii. 614). The Declared Accounts, *Audit Office* (Agents for Special Services, roll 3, bundle 5), show us that 60,000*l.* was ordered to be paid to Burlamachi out of the Queen's portion money by a Privy Seal of August 5, and that of this, 52,313*l.* 15*s.* were paid before Michaelmas, 1625, and 6,300*l.* between Michaelmas and Easter, 1626. It also appears that Burlamachi was 'allowed for monies paid to the Duke of Buckingham, and such as he appointed to receive the same for secret services, and by him issued, most part upon his warrants and the rest upon his verbal significations, as by several acquittances of those who received the same may appear, the sum of 58,689*l.* 13*s.*' Nothing can be looser than this, but does it follow that the money was not employed by Buckingham upon the public service? Probably this is the same money as that mentioned in Buckingham's defence (*Lords' Journals*, iii. 666), as 58,880*l.* Of the sum there named, 26,000*l.* is said to have been spent on the Navy, and the rest by his Majesty's directions. Again, Buckingham stated that on the 15th and 28th of January, he received of free gift 50,000*l.*; but it was for the fleet, and that the 'Duke's name was only used for that his Majesty was not willing to have that intention publicly discovered at that time.' This seems a very probable explanation.

impeachment. Though it would go hard with him if he had to prove that he had any one qualification fitting him for the government of a great nation, he would have no difficulty in showing that much which had been said by the Commons was exaggerated or untrue.

It remained to sum up the different charges, and to embody the general feeling of the House in a few well-chosen words. To none could the task better be entrusted than to Eliot, who above all others had urged on the preparation of the charges with unremitting zeal, and who believed, with all the energy of burning conviction, in the unutterable baseness of the man against whom he was leading the attack. The oratorical and imaginative temperament pervaded the conclusions of Eliot's judgment. The half-measures and compromises of the world had no place in his mind. What was right in his eyes was entirely right ; what was wrong was utterly and irretrievably wrong. So too in his personal attachments and hatreds. Those whom he believed to be serving their country truly he loved with an attachment proof against every trial. Those whom he believed to be doing disservice to their country he hated with an exceeding bitter hatred. Such a nature as Buckingham's, with its mixture of meanness and nobility, of consideration for self and forgetfulness of self, of empty vanity and real devotion, was a riddle beyond his power to read. In his lofty ideal, in his high disdain for that which he regarded as worthless, in his utter fearlessness and disregard of all selfish considerations, Eliot was the Milton, as Bacon had been almost the Shakspere, of politics.

Eliot sums up.

The doctrine that the King's command relieved the subject from responsibility found no favour in Eliot's eyes. "My Lords," he said, in speaking of the loan of the ships to serve against Rochelle, "I will say that if his Majesty himself were pleased to have consented, or to have commanded, which I cannot believe, yet this could no way satisfy for the Duke, or make any extenuation of the charge ; for it was the duty of his place to have opposed it by his prayers, and to have interceded with his Majesty to make known the dangers, the ill consequences, that might follow.

Eliot on responsibility.

And if this prevailed not, should he have ended here? No; he should then have addressed himself to your lordships, your lordships sitting in council, and there have made it known, there have desired your aids. Nor, if in this he sped not, should he have rested without entering before you a protestation for himself, and that he was not consenting. This was the duty of his place ; this has been the practice of his elders ; and this, being here neglected, leaves him without excuse."

It was characteristic of Eliot to approach the subject from the moral rather than the political side. It was nothing to him that he was lightly dashing into ruin the whole scaffolding upon which the Tudor monarchy had rested—the responsibility of ministers to the sovereign alone. He called upon every man to profess openly, in the eye of day, his personal conviction of right as the basis of action. With such a faith, whatever mistakes Eliot might commit in the immediate present, he had raised a standard for the future which could never be permanently dragged in the dust. Not in fidelity to constitutional arrangements, not in obedience to the orders of a king or in obedience to the votes of a Parliament, lay the secret of political capacity. The ideal statesman was to be the man who had the open eye to discern his country's wants, the tongue to speak freely the counsel which his mind had conceived, and the heart and the resolution to suffer, if not to die, in the defence of his belief.

To such a man as Eliot the faults of Buckingham—his heedlessness, his wanton profusion—must have seemed infinitely mean, altogether meaner than they really were. Buckingham's power, he said, was in itself a wonder; it needed a party to support it. To that end 'he raised and preferred to honours and commands those of his own alliance, the creatures of his kindred and affection, how mean soever.' Having thus got all power into his hands, he 'set upon the revenues of the Crown, interrupting, exhausting, and consuming that fountain of supply.' "What vast treasures," cried Eliot, "he has gotten ; what infinite sums of money, and what a mass of lands ! If your lordships please to calculate, you will

Attack upon Buckingham's power and wealth.

find it all amounting to little less than the whole of the subsidies which the King hath had within that time. A lamentable example of the subjects' bounties so to be employed! But is this all? No; your lordships may not think it. These are but collections of a short view, used only as an epitome for the rest. There needs no search for it; it is too visible. His profuse expenses, his superfluous feasts, his magnificent buildings, his riots, his excesses,—what are they but the visible evidences of an express exhausting of the State, a chronicle of the immensity of his waste of the revenues of the Crown? No wonder, then, our King is now in want, this man abounding so. And as long as he abounds the King must still be wanting."

Worse was still to come. Eliot had to make reference to the administration of medicine to the late King, perhaps too in some covert way to the graver suspicions which attached to that act even in the eyes of men who, like Bristol, had little sympathy with mere popular rumour. "Not satisfied," Eliot continued, "with the wrongs of honour, with the prejudice of religion, with the abuse of State, with the misappropriation of revenues, his attempts go higher, even to the person of his sovereign. You have before you his making practice on that, in such a manner and with such effect as I fear to speak it, nay, I doubt and hesitate to think it. In which respect I shall leave it, as Cicero did the like, *ne gravioribus utar verbis quam natura fert, aut levioribus quam causa postulat*. The examination with your lordships will show you what it is. I need not name it.

"In all these now your lordships have the idea of the man; what in himself he is, and what in his affections. You have seen his power, and some, I fear, have felt it. What hopes or expectations then he gives I leave it to your lordships. I will now only see, by comparison with others, where I may find him paralleled or likened; and, so considering what may now become him, from thence render your lordships to a short conclusion.

"Of all the precedents I can find, none so near resembles him as doth Sejanus, and him Tacitus describes thus: that he was *audax; sui obtegens, in alios criminator; juxta adulatio et superbia.* If your lordships please to measure him by this, Parallel with Sejanus. pray see in what they vary. He is bold. We have had experience lately; and such a boldness I dare be bold to say as is seldom heard of. He is secret in his purposes, and more; that we have showed already. Is he a slanderer? Is he an accuser? I wish this Parliament had not felt it, nor that which was before. And for his pride and flattery, what man can judge the greater? Thus far, I think, the parallel holds. But now, I beseech your lordships, look a little further. Of Sejanus it is likewise noted amongst his policies, amongst his arts, that, to support himself, he did *clientes suos honoribus aut provinciis ornare.* He preferred his clients to second, to assist him. And does this man do the like? Is it not, and in the same terms, a special cause in our complaint now? Does not this kingdom, does not Scotland, does not Ireland speak it? I will observe one thing more, and end. It is a note upon the pride of Sejanus, upon his high ambition, which your lordships will find set down by Tacitus. His solecisms, his neglect of counsels, his veneries, his venefices; these I will not mention here:[1] only that particular of his pride, which thus I find. In his public passages May 10. and relations he would so mix his business with the prince's, seeming to confound their actions, that he was often styled *laborum imperatoris socius.* And does not this man do the like? Is it not in his whole practice? How often, how lately have we heard it? Did he not, in this same place, in this very Parliament, under colour of an explanation for the King, before the committees of both Houses, do the same? Have not your lordships heard him also ever mixing and confusing the King and the State, not leaving a distinction between them? It is too, too manifest.

"My Lords, I have done. You see the man. What have been his actions, whom he is like, you know. I leave him to your judgments."

[1] "Such expressions," Mr. Forster observes, "could not of course have been directly applied to Buckingham. They are insinuated only through Sejanus."

Eliot had one other parallel to draw. "And now, my Lords," he said, "I will conclude with a particular censure given on the Bishop of Ely in the time of Richard I. That prelate had the King's treasures at his command, and had luxuriously abused them. His obscure kindred were married to earls, barons, and others of great rank and place. No man's business could be done without his help. He would not suffer the King's council to advise in the highest affairs of State. He gave *ignotis personis et obscuris* the custody of castles and great trusts. He ascended to such a height of insolence and pride that he ceased to be fit for characters of mercy. And therefore, says the record of which I now hold the original, *per totam insulam publice proclametur, Pereat qui perdere cuncta festinat; opprimatur ne omnes opprimat.*" [1]

Comparison with the Bishop of Ely.

Such was the terrible invective, glowing with the fire of inmost conviction, and strong with the roused indignation of an angry people collected into one burning focus, which poured that day from the lips of the great orator. Much, if not all, that he said went true to the mark. The vanity and self-confidence of the man, the assumption of almost regal dignity, the immense wealth heaped up when the royal exchequer was drained of its last resources, were depicted with unerring accuracy. And yet the portrait, as a whole, was untrue to nature. It was false that Buckingham was a Sejanus. It was false that he had been guilty of sordid bribery. It was false that he had used the powers of government in his own hands simply for his own private ends, and not for that which for the time he believed to be the best interest of the State.

How far was this portrait true?

If this is now plain to anyone who will carefully and dispassionately study the records of Buckingham's misdeeds, what must have been the effect of the speech upon Charles, who believed as implicitly in the wisdom as in the innocence of his minister, and who felt that he was himself attacked through Buckingham. "If the Duke is Sejanus,"

Anger of Charles.

---

[1] Forster, *Sir J. Eliot*, i. 324-330.

he is reported to have said, "I must be Tiberius."[1] The next day, in a speech prepared for him by Laud, he tried to enlist the sympathies of the Peers in his favour. In the attack upon Buckingham, he told them, their honour had been wounded. He had himself taken order for the punishment of the offenders. If he had not done so before, it was because Buckingham had begged that the impeachment might proceed, in order that his innocency might be shown. Of his innocency there could be no doubt whatever, 'for, as touching the occasions against him,' he could himself 'be a witness to clear him of every one of them.'

May 11. The King's speech to the Lords.

It was only in words that Charles attempted to conciliate the Peers. Two days before they had petitioned for 'a gracious present answer' to their request for the liberation of Arundel. At these words he had taken fire. "I did little look," he replied, "for such a message from the House, and did never know such a message sent from the one House to the other. Therefore, when I receive a message fit to come from you to your sovereign, you shall receive an answer."

His answer about Arundel.

Before a reply could be given by the House, Sir Nathaniel Rich appeared, on behalf of the Commons, to ask that Buckingham might be put under restraint during the impeachment, a request with which the Lords refused for the present to comply, on the ground that the charges against him had not yet been formally reported. But this concession to the Court, if concession it was, was more than counterbalanced by the reply returned to the King's message. As soon as it was understood that Charles's special objection was to the demand of a 'present answer,' Saye and Sele proposed that it should be explained to him that the word 'present' only meant 'speedy.' Manchester, catching at the suggestion, moved that the petition might be amended so as to ask for 'a gracious speedy answer.' "Leave out the word 'speedy' also," cried

The Commons demand Buckingham's imprisonment.

The Lords' reply about Arundel.

---

[1] D'Ewes gives the words (*Harl. MSS.* 383, fol. 32) apparently as part of the King's speech which follows in the text. But, though this seems to be incorrect, Charles may very likely have used the words in private.

Buckingham. Yes, was the reply, but leave out the word
'gracious' too. The House accordingly voted that they would
merely ask for 'your Majesty's answer.'[1]

It was but a little thing in itself, but it indicated plainly the
temper into which the Lords had been brought.

The claim of the King to imprison members during the
session, maintained as yet in the face of the Lords, was to
receive a more daring application in the face of the
Commons. When Rich returned after delivering
his message, he found the Lower House in great
commotion. It was discovered that neither Eliot nor Digges
were in their places, and on inquiry it appeared that they had
been sent for to the door, and had been hurried off to the
Tower. Shouts of Rise! Rise! sounded on all sides. In vain
Pym, not yet aware of the true state of the case,[2] did his best
to quiet the tumult. The House broke up in discontent. In
the afternoon an informal assembly gathered in Westminster
Hall, and serious words were interchanged on this unexpected
attack upon the liberties of Parliament.

Imprisonment of Eliot and Digges.

The next morning, when the Speaker rose, as usual, at the
commencement of business, he was at once interrupted. "Sit
down!" was the general cry. "No business till we
are righted in our liberties." Carleton attempted to
defend his master's conduct. He had much to say
of the tartness of Eliot's language. But the main offence, both
of Digges and Eliot, was that they had pressed 'the death of
his late Majesty, whereas the House had only charged the
Duke with presumption.' Eliot had hinted that more had taken
place than he dared to speak of. Digges had even suggested
that the present King had had a hand in his father's murder.
In speaking of the plaister given to James, he had added, 'that
he would therein spare the honour of the King.' It was for
the House to consider whether they had authorised such a

May 12. Carleton defends the King.

---

[1] *Elsing's Notes.*

[2] Which shouts 'Mr. Pym, not well understanding, stood up,' &c.
Meade to Stuteville, May 13, *Harl. MSS.* 390, fol. 57. This seems
more likely than that Pym should have objected, if he had known what
happened.

charge as this. The two members, in short, were punished as having gone beyond the directions of the House.

Carleton had something yet more startling to add. "I beseech you, gentlemen, he said, "move not his Majesty with trenching upon his prerogatives, lest you bring him out of love with Parliaments. In his message he hath told you that if there were not correspondency between him and you, he should be enforced to use new counsels. Now I pray you to consider what these new counsels are, and may be. I fear to declare those that I conceive. In all Christian kingdoms you know that Parliaments were in use anciently, until the monarchs began to know their own strength ; and, seeing the turbulent spirit of their Parliaments, at length they, by little and little, began to stand upon their prerogatives, and at last overthrew the Parliaments throughout Christendom, except here only with us." Then he went on to speak of the scenes which he had lately witnessed in France, of the peasants looking like ghosts rather than men, of their scanty covering and wooden shoes, as well as of the heavy taxation imposed upon them. "This," he ended by saying, "is a misery beyond expression, and that which yet we are free from."[1]

With great difficulty the Commons were restrained from calling Carleton to the bar. The danger with which they had been threatened was, in their opinion, best met by a firm pursuance of the course which they had already chosen. On the one hand they ordered a protest to be signed by every member disclaiming all part in the imputation upon the King in relation to his father's death, which had been attributed to Digges. On the other hand they prepared a vindication of their own liberties to be laid before Charles.[2]

Answer of the Commons.

Carleton's speech had neither made nor deserved to make the slightest impression ; but it was not, as it is usually repre-

---

[1] Though no country is named, I have no doubt that his last visit to France was intended. Such scenes were not to be witnessed amongst Dutch or Venetian peasants. Besides, the subsequent words about men taxed to *the King*, show what Carleton was thinking of.

[2] *Rushworth*, i. 360.

sented, either ridiculous or illogical. If it had been possible
to grant his premisses, and to allow that the Commons were factiously taking advantage of the danger
of their country to advance their own position in the
State, Carleton's warnings might well have been listened to
with respect, in their substance, if not in their form. There is
no law of nature to save Parliaments any more than kings,
when they forget the interests of the nation which they are
appointed to protect. If Carleton and his master were in the
wrong, it was because whatever mistakes the Commons might
have committed, the interests of the nation were safer in their
hands than in those of the King.

Remarks on Carleton's speech.

If Charles erred in his general view of the case, it soon
appeared that he was no less wrong in his knowledge of the
particular circumstances. As soon as the report
of the proceedings at the Conference was read in the
Upper House it was seen that, if that report could be
trusted, Digges had said something different from
that which was alleged against him. Buckingham, however,
was not satisfied. With a warmth which may easily be excused
in a man against whom a charge of having poisoned his bene-
factor had been brought, he protested his own innocence, and
then expressed an opinion that the report was not altogether
correct. Manchester, by whom that portion of the report had
been drawn up, admitted that, as his notes had been rapidly
taken, he had afterwards consulted Digges on their accuracy,
and that Digges had 'mollified' the wording. According to
the notes, Digges had said that he wished 'not to reflect upon
the person either of the dead or of the present King.' That is
to say, cried Buckingham, 'on the dead King touching point of
government; upon this King touching the physic.' A protest
was at once raised by North and Devonshire. "This," added
Saye, "may trench on all our loyalties." Each Peer, it was
then suggested, should be called upon to declare whether he
had heard anything 'that might be interpreted treason.' In
spite of an interruption from Buckingham, that he wanted
Digges's words, not his meaning, Saye rose and protested that
Digges had not spoken the words alleged, nor did he con-

May 15. The Lords question Digges's words.

ceive that he had the intention ascribed to him. The great majority of the Peers followed Saye's example. A few only, on various grounds, refused to make the declaration. In the end, thirty-six Peers, Buckingham's brother-in-law Denbigh amongst them, signed a protest that Digges had said nothing contrary to the King's honour.

Before they parted, the Peers took another step in opposition. They replied to the King's message urging that to allow Bristol the use of counsel was contrary to the fundamental laws of the realm, by respectfully assuring him that he was altogether mistaken. On the other question of the King's right to tender evidence against a subject, which had been referred to the judges, Charles himself had already seen fit to waive his pretensions for the present. He had directed the judges to give no resolution on that point, 'not knowing how dangerous it may be for the future.'[1]

Question of counsel for Bristol.

May 13.

After what had passed in the Lords, it was impossible to keep Digges any longer in the Tower, and the next morning he reappeared in his usual place. Charles could not be so easily induced to relax his hold upon Eliot, the guiding spirit of the attack upon his government. If he should plead the precedents of Elizabeth's reign, he would none the less find in the Commons the same bitter opposition which his treatment of Arundel had raised in the Lords. It seemed to him better to evade the difficulty; and, dropping the original complaint, he ordered Weston to acquaint the Commons that Eliot was charged 'with things extrajudicial to the House.' Weston, who was directed by the Commons to inquire what was the meaning of the word 'extrajudicial,' informed them that Eliot's crimes had been committed out of the House.

May 16. Digges released.

New ground taken in Eliot's case.

May 17. Weston's explanations.

It was not likely that the Commons would be beguiled by so transparent a subterfuge. The feeling of the House was unmistakeable. In vain Carleton urged that they should clear Eliot of all that he had done as a member, and ask the King to

---

[1] *Elsing's Notes.* 1624–1626, p. 193; *Lords' Journals,* iii. 627.

release him out of favour to themselves. It was the very thing which they absolutely refused to do. They were well aware that a member might have done things which no Parliamentary privilege could cover. He might have committed high treason, or highway robbery; but they wished to have an opportunity of judging for themselves whether anything so unlikely had really happened. When, therefore, Carleton, pushed to the wall, entreated them to give his Majesty time to prove his accusation, they at once complied with his request and suspended their sittings till the 19th. It is hardly likely that anyone present took Charles's explanations seriously. "The King," wrote one of the members to a friend, in speaking of Eliot's imprisonment, "hath sent him to the Tower for some words spoken in Parliament, but we are all resolved to have him out again, or will proceed to no business."[1]

The Commons suspend their sittings.

Charles, in fact, had still to discover the charges upon which he had elected to take his stand. That Eliot had been instigated by Blainville to prefer the complaints relating to the 'St. Peter' was too probable a solution of all that had passed not to present itself to him : but it was a long step from mere suspicion to actual evidence. In vain Eliot's study was searched for proof. In vain Eliot was himself subjected to an examination. Not one scrap of evidence was producible to show that the slightest intercourse between him and the ambassador had ever taken place. Charles had forgotten that the very imperfect manner in which that part of the charge against Buckingham had been produced was in itself the strongest evidence that the French ambassador had not been consulted. With Blainville's assistance Eliot would have drawn up a far more telling case than he had succeeded in doing.

May 18. Fresh charges against Eliot.

There was therefore nothing for it but to set Eliot at liberty. When the Commons re-assembled they were informed by Carleton that his imprisonment was at an end. The House, however, was not to be so easily

May 19. Eliot released,

---

[1] Forster, *Sir J. Eliot*, i. 561.

VOL. VI.   I

contented. The next morning Carleton was compelled to go over one by one the objections which he had originally taken to the epilogue delivered before the Lords. With a mixture of sarcasm and pleasantry, Eliot answered them in detail. One reply was peculiarly felicitous. He had been accused of speaking slightingly of the Duke as 'the man.' The word, he answered, had been commonly applied to Alexander and Cæsar, 'which were not less than he.' It was therefore no dishonour to the Duke to be so called, 'whom yet he thinketh not to be a god.' In the end, both Eliot and Digges were unanimously cleared of the imputations brought against them.

<small>May 20. and cleared by the House.</small>

The attempt and its failure were alike characteristic of Charles. Prone to act upon impulse, he had been thrown off his balance by the suggestion, which the words reported to him seemed to convey, that he had himself been implicated in his father's murder. Taking it for granted that the facts were as he supposed them to be, taking it for granted too that he had the right, by the precedents of Elizabeth's reign, to punish the offenders, he had been startled when the House of Lords denied his facts, and the House of Commons denied his right. The whole opposition of the protesting Lords and the sternly resolute Commons which started up before him, was thoroughly unprovided for in his plan of action. Like an inexperienced general who has forgotten to allow for the independent action of the enemy, he had no resource but to take refuge in the first defence which offered itself as a means of prolonging the contest. The new device shivered in his hands, and he stood unarmed and discredited in the face of the nation.

<small>Charles's failure.</small>

In the House of Lords, too, the tide was running strongly against his hopes. Already he had been driven to withdraw his pretension to deprive Bristol of the help of counsel; and as soon as the accused Earl had had time to bring in his answer to the charges against him, the Lords warmly took up their claim to see Arundel restored to their House. Nor was it only the exclusion of their members that they dreaded. Grandison had just been

<small>May 17. Bristol's case in the Lords.</small>

created Baron Tregoze in the English Peerage, and Carleton had been snatched away from the assaults of the champion of the Commons to sit on the benches of the Upper House as Lord Carleton of Imberville. The independent Lords regarded these promotions as a preliminary to an attempt to pack the House by a creation on a far larger scale, and some were even heard to suggest the extreme measure of depriving the new Peers of their votes till the end of the session.[1]

<small>May 19.</small>

In vain, therefore, Charles alleged, as he had alleged against Eliot, that he had fresh charges to bring against Arundel. The Peers would listen to no excuses. On June 5 the Earl recovered his entire liberty,[2] and on the 8th he was in his place amongst the Peers.

<small>June 5. Liberation of Arundel.</small>

In the meanwhile the Commons had been busy reinforcing their attack upon Buckingham by a simultaneous declaration of the illegality of the collection of tonnage and poundage, unless voted by themselves, and of their own readiness to settle an ample revenue upon the King if he would conform to their wishes.

<small>May 24. Tonnage and poundage declared illegal unless granted by Parliament.</small>

Before long, however, an incident occurred which must have convinced the most reluctant that it was in vain to hope that either fear or persuasion would induce the King to abandon Buckingham. On May 28 Suffolk died, leaving the Chancellorship of the University of Cambridge vacant. "I would Buckingham were Chancellor," said Charles, when he heard the news. The idea took firm possession of his mind, and the next morning a chaplain of the Bishop of London[3] carried to Cambridge an intimation of the royal pleasure. The Bishop himself soon followed; and the whole party which had seen with displeasure the continued attacks of the Commons upon Montague and his book rallied round the Duke. The Masters of Trinity, of Peter-

<small>May 28. The Cambridge Chancellorship.</small>

---

[1] Joachimi to the States-General, $\frac{May\ 31}{June\ 10}$, *Add. MSS.* 17,677 L, fol. 225.

[2] Conway to Arundel, June 5, *S. P. Dom. Addenda*

[3] *i.e.* Bishop Montaigne; not Laud, as Mr. Forster stated by an oversight.

house, and of Clare Hall used all their influence in his favour; and the influence of the Head of a house, who thought more of the object to be gained than of his own character for impartiality, was no slight weight in the scale. Yet, discouraging as the prospects of the Calvinists were, they chose at the last moment a candidate in the person of the Earl of Berkshire, the second son of the late Chancellor; and so strong was their party numerically, that though there was no time to obtain assurance of their candidate's consent, they secured no less than 103 votes in his favour. Buckingham, it was true, obtained 108; but it was known that many had voted for him sorely against their wishes, and it was whispered amongst Berkshire's supporters that, even as it was, an impartial scrutiny would have converted their opponents' victory into a defeat.[1]

<small>June 1.
Election of Buckingham.</small>

Deep offence was taken by the Commons at this new honour conferred upon a man whom they had charged with holding too many offices already. Venturing upon unsafe ground, they resolved to send for a deputation from the University and to demand an account of the election, a resolution which was met by positive orders from the King to proceed no further in that direction, as the University was entitled to elect anyone it pleased.[2] The reply of the House was the conversion of the remonstrance upon freedom from arrest into a general statement of grievances.

<small>June 5.
Displeasure of the Commons.

June 6.

June 8.</small>

On the day when this new appeal to the King was to be drawn up, Buckingham laid his defence before the Lords. Prepared, it is said, by Nicholas Hyde, in all probability under Heath's supervision, and submitted to the friendly criticism of Laud,[3] the Duke's answer displayed no common ability. Rebutting—as with their

<small>Buckingham's defence.</small>

---

[1] Meade to Stuteville, June 3, *Ellis*, ser. 1, iii. 228. Certain Considerations, &c., *Harl. MSS.* 161, fol. 134.

[2] —— to Meade, June 9, *Harl. MSS.* 390, fol. 73.

[3] Of Laud's part there is no doubt. See *S. P. Dom.* xxvii. 25. Hyde's part we learn from *Whitelocke's Memorials*, 8. For Heath, see the King's warrant to assist Buckingham, *S. P. Dom. Addenda.*

superior knowledge its authors were well able to do—many of the accusations, in the form at least in which they had been brought, they were able to assert that in other respects the Duke had either acted by the King's orders, or that, if he had gone wrong, he had done so either from inadvertence or through compliance with customs already established when he came to Court. "Who accused me?" said Buckingham— "Common fame. Who gave me up to your Lordships?—The House of Commons. The one is too subtle a body, if a body; the other too great for me to contest with. Yet I am confident neither the one nor the other shall be found my enemy when my cause comes to be tried."

The confidence thus expressed was doubtless a genuine expression of feeling. Buckingham could not hope to have the issue tried on more favourable ground. He knew that he had witnesses to prove that on many important points the Commons had been in error;[1] and he had only to close his eyes to the political antagonism which he had aroused, to imagine that an acquittal would be the probable termination of the affair.

<small>Buckingham's confidence.</small>

The news, however, that the Commons had embarked upon a general remonstrance cannot have been without effect even upon Buckingham. To Charles it must have been absolutely decisive. Believing as he did that his minister was the victim of a factious combination, he had submitted to wait till the worthlessness of the evidence against him had been proved; but if the Commons were about to demand that, whether their charges were proved or not, he should dismiss his minister, he would only be strengthened in his opinion that the honour of his crown was at stake. He therefore peremptorily demanded that, happen what might, the Subsidy Bill should be passed before the end of the following week. If it were not, he should be forced 'to use other resolutions.'[2]

<small>June 9. The King demands supply.</small>

---

[1] Nicholas, for instance, seems, from the notes prepared by him (*S. P. Dom.* xxvii. 105–111), to have been ready to tell the truth, and to call upon Pennington to tell the truth, about the ships lent to the French.

[2] *Lords Journals*, iii. 670.

Before the Royal message was taken into consideration, the Commons took a further step, which indicated plainly enough the spirit by which they were animated. They ordered the committee to which the framing of the remonstrance had been entrusted to send for the Parliament roll containing the declaration made by Buckingham after his return from Spain, and to require the young Lord Digby, by whom his father's charges against the Duke had formerly been communicated to the House, to prove, if he was able, that Parliament had been abused on that occasion.[1] On the previous day the Lords had given a similar indication of their feeling by ordering the Attorney-General to take charge of Bristol's case, so as to give to it those official advantages which had been accorded to the King's accusations.

<small>June 10. Further steps of the Commons.

June 9. Bristol's case taken up by the Lords.</small>

The Commons probably intended to incorporate Bristol's charges in their remonstrance; but time pressed, and it was doubtful whether, if they embarked upon such a work, they would be allowed to finish it. The question which they met to discuss on the morning of the 12th was whether the remonstrance or the supply should be presented first. After a long and stormy debate, a large majority voted that the remonstrance should have the precedence.[2]

<small>June 12. The remonstrance to precede supply.</small>

From the ground thus taken up by the Commons it would in the long run be found impossible to drive them. After running over the charges which they had brought against the Duke, they expressed their reprobation of those new counsels which had been held before their eyes by Carleton, and denied that tonnage and poundage could be lawfully raised without their consent. Then, turning upon Buckingham, they declared that the articles which they had sent up to the Lords were not the measure of their objections to his 'excessive and abusive power.' These they had

<small>Substance of the remonstrance.</small>

---

[1] *Commons' Journals*, i. 870. Digby may be a slip for Bristol; but the young lord, having presented his father's complaint, had a *locus standi* before the House.

[2] Meddus to Meade, June 16, *Court and Times*, i. 110.

been 'enforced to insist upon, as matters' lying under their 'notice and proof;' but, beyond them, they believed him to be an enemy to both Church and State. It was therefore grievous to them to find that he had ' so great power and interest in ' the King's 'princely affections,' so as, under his Majesty, 'wholly in a manner to engross to himself the administration of' the realm, 'which by that means is drawn into a condition most miserable and hazardous.' They therefore begged that he would remove the Duke from his presence, and would not 'balance this one man with all these things and with the affairs of the Christian world, which all do suffer, so far as they have relation to this kingdom, chiefly by his means.'

"For we protest," they went on to say, "before your Majesty and the whole world, that until this great person be removed from intermeddling with the great affairs of State, we are out of hope of any good success; and do fear that any money we shall or can give will, through his misemployment, be turned rather to the hurt and prejudice of this your kingdom than otherwise, as by lamentable experience we have found in those large supplies formerly and lately given."

The Commons, in short, had again taken up the position which they had occupied at the close of the Oxford meeting. They would give no money where they could place no confidence. No impartial reader of the long story of the mishaps of the Government can deny that they were thoroughly in the right in refusing their confidence to the man who was mainly responsible for these misfortunes.

<small>What this implied.</small>

In one respect indeed the Commons were slow to perceive the whole consequence of their change of position. If they had been able to substantiate the criminal charges which they had brought against Buckingham, if they could have proved him to be false, corrupt, and venal, Charles could have parted with him without loss of honour. To ask the King to abandon his minister on the ground that the Commons could not trust him, though the acts at which they took umbrage had been done, always nominally and often really, by the authority of Charles, was to ask him to surrender himself as well as Buckingham. Neither Elizabeth nor even his father had allowed anyone to dictate the choice of counsellors. If the advisers of the Crown and the officers of State were to be accepted or dismissed at the will of the House of Commons, the supremacy of that House would soon be undisputed. Would such a change carry with it merely a constitutional re-arrangement? Could a popular body form a government? Would not anarchy and confusion ensue to the nation, personal danger to the King? To yield now might be to launch the barque of Royalty without chart or compass on that sea of violence and intrigue which was to be descried by the anxious king in those annals of the Middle Ages to which the Commons so cheerfully appealed. To him the precedents of Eliot spoke not of justice executed, but of riot and disorder. "Let us sit upon the ground," they seemed to say,

> "And tell sad stories of the death of kings:
> How some have been deposed, some slain in war,
> Some haunted by the ghosts they have deposed,
> Some poisoned by their wives, some sleeping killed,—
> All murdered."

To acknowledge Buckingham's responsibility was indirectly to acknowledge his own. Where was that to end? Perhaps it was too late for him now to learn a better way, and to discern that alike behind the despotism of the Tudors and the violence of the Middle Ages a deeper principle had been at work—a principle which called upon rulers to guide, and not to force, the national will. Precedents might be quoted for almost any iniquity on either side; but the great precedent of all, from which all worthy precedents received their value, the tradition of a healthy national life handed down by father to son from the remotest days, was guarded in the heart of the English nation by defences against which Charles would dash himself in vain.

The King's choice was soon made. As he had said earlier in the session, he would give liberty of counsel, not of control.

June 14. A dissolution resolved on. In vain Heath, with lawyer-like appreciation of the weakness of the articles of impeachment, pleaded hard for delay. In vain the Peers begged earnestly for a prolongation of the situation by which they were constituted supreme arbitrators between the nation and the Crown. To their urgent entreaty that Charles would grant them but two days more, he replied impatiently, "Not a minute." On June 15 the Parliament of 1626 ceased to exist.¹

June 15. The dissolution.

"Let compounds be dissolved."² The words with which Wotton had closed the epitaph of the great philosopher and statesman who had passed away from his earthly work almost unnoticed amidst the contentions of the session now brought to a close, might fitly be inscribed over the tomb of the constitutional theories which Bacon had striven hard to realise. The King and the House of Commons no longer formed constituent parts of one body. On either side new counsels would prevail. The King would demand to be sole judge of the fitness of his own actions, and to compel the nation to follow him whithersoever he chose to lead. Parliament would grasp at the right of control as well as the right of counsel, and would discover that the responsibility of ministers could only be secured by enforcing the responsibility of kings. At last, after a terrible struggle, teeming alike with heroic examples and deeds of violence, a new harmony would be evolved out of the ruins of the old.

Future of the constitution.

¹ Heath to Buckingham, June 14 (?), *S. P. Dom. Addenda. Lords' Journals*, iii. 682. —— to Meade, June 15, *Harl. MSS.* 390, fol. 776.
² "*Composita dissolvantur.*"

CHAPTER LIX.

THE RUPTURE WITH FRANCE.

IN trying the effect of those 'new counsels' with which the Commons had been so often threatened, Charles, it may be safely said, had no intention of deliberately treading under foot the laws of England. Holding, as he did, that a few factious men had preferred their own ambitious schemes to the welfare of the country, he believed himself to be justified in putting forth for a time the powers of that undefined prerogative which was given him for use in special emergencies when the safety of the nation was at stake.

<small>June 15. New counsels.</small>

Charles's first thought was to issue a proclamation for the establishing of the peace and quiet of the Church of England. On April 17 Pym had reported to the Lower House a long string of charges against Montague,[1] and, if time could have been found before the dissolution, his impeachment would doubtless have followed. In his proclamation Charles spoke of 'questions and opinions' lately broached in matters of doctrine, 'which at first only being meant against the Papists, but afterwards by the sharp and indiscreet handling and maintaining by some of either parts, have given much offence to the sober and well-grounded readers and hearers of these late written books on both sides, which may justly be feared will raise some hopes in the professed enemies of our religion, the Romish Catholics, that by degrees the professors of our religion may be drawn into schism, and after to plain Popery.'

<small>June 16. Proclamation for the peace of the Church.</small>

[1] *Faws'ey Debates*, App. 179.

Charles's remedy for the evil was to reduce both parties to silence. No new opinions were to be introduced by tongue or pen; no innovation to be allowed in Church or State. As both Pym and Montague claimed to set forth the original doctrine of the Church of England, it was not unlikely they would both interpret the proclamation in their own favour. It was, however, probable that those who carried it into execution would interpret it in favour of Montague rather than of Pym.[1]

The next day a fresh proclamation was issued ordering the destruction of all copies of the remonstrance of the Commons.[2]

June 17. Charles calls in the Remonstrance. Charles, however, took care not to inflict the slightest punishment upon the offending members of either House, with the exception of Bristol and Arundel; and he might fairly argue that if the two obnoxious Peers had committed faults at all, they were faults which had nothing to do with their position as members of the House of Lords.

Commitment of Bristol and Arundel. Arundel was therefore relegated to confinement in his own house,[3] and Bristol was sent to the Tower, to prepare for a Star Chamber prosecution. If wrong was done, the wrong did not this time take the shape of a breach of privilege.

It was Charles's intention that Buckingham was still to be allowed, in spite of the dissolution, to bring his defence to a triumphant issue. Heath was accordingly directed to request the managers of the impeachment to carry on their case before the Star Chamber.[4] The plan broke down in consequence of the steady refusal of the managers to have anything to do with the matter. "We," Eliot answered in their name, "entreat you to take knowledge that whatsoever was done by us in that business was done by the command of the House of Commons, and by their directions some proofs were delivered to the Lords with the charges, but what other proofs the House would have used, according to the liberty reserved to themselves,

Buckingham's case to be tried in the Star Chamber.

June 19. The Parliamentary managers refuse to take part in the trial.

---

[1] *Rymer*, xviii. 719.　　[2] *Ibid.* 721.
[3] Salvetti's *News-Letter*, June $\frac{16}{26}$.
[4] Heath to Eliot and others, June 17; Forster, *Sir J. Eliot*, i. 350.

either for the maintenance of their charge or upon their reply,
we neither know nor can undertake to inform you." The next day Eliot was pressed to give a better answer. "My first knowledge and intelligence," he replied, "happening in Parliament, after discharge of mine own particular duties to the House, I remitted to that again wholly the memory and consideration thereof." It was no private charge which he had brought. The accusation had sprung from the House of Commons, and if the King wished it to be carried further, he must provide for the resuscitation of Parliament. Charles, however, thought that he could carry on the accusation without having recourse to so formidable an instrument. The charges were formally repeated and formally answered, and the Star Chamber gave a sentence in favour of the Duke which inspired no confidence in anyone who was not already convinced of his innocence.[1]

June 20. Eliot's defence of their refusal.

Such sentences were easily obtainable. It was less easy to provide money for the war which Charles was resolved to carry on. A loan of 100,000*l.*, on the security of the Crown jewels, was demanded from the City; but the City firmly refused to lend, and it was only upon strong pressure from the King himself that the aldermen agreed personally to provide him with the fifth part of the sum named.[2]

The City refuses a loan.

More general measures were required if the Exchequer was to be filled. For some time rumours of a Spanish force gathering in the ports of Biscay had been rife in England, and Charles was well content to make more of these rumours than they were really worth. To meet the danger, a fleet of a hundred sail was to be brought together to guard the coast, and another fleet of forty sail, with the assistance of a Dutch contingent, was to seek out the enemy in his own harbours.[3] In order to find means to support so large an expenditure, Charles's first thought had been to

June 15. Plan for asking the freeholders to vote subsidies.

---

[1] Forster, *Sir J. Eliot*, i. 350.

[2] Rudyerd to Nethersole, July 9, *S. P. Dom.* xxxi. 39. Salvetti's *News-Letters*, $\frac{\text{June } 30}{\text{July } 10}$, July $\frac{7}{17}$. —— to Meade, June 30, *Court and Times*, i. 116.

[3] Rusdorf to Oxenstjerna, June 15, *Mem.* ii. 190.

order the sheriffs to assemble the freeholders in the several counties, and to take their votes for a direct grant of the subsidies to which a factious Parliament had refused to agree.[1] The project was, however, abandoned in this hazardous form, and on July 7 letters were despatched to all justices of the peace, bidding them to acquaint their counties with the requirements of the State, and to exhort them that, as the House of Commons had judged four subsidies to be needed for the defence of the country, they should, in a case of such necessity, be a law to themselves, and should lovingly, freely, and voluntarily supply that which might have been levied by law if the Act had passed.[2] In order to show that, in calling on his subjects for contributions, he did not intend to spare his own courtiers, Charles gave orders that, for two years to come, no suits involving any charge on the revenue should be brought before him.[3]

<small>July 7. A free gift proposed.</small>

If Charles was to extract money directly from his subjects' purses it was necessary for him to go through the form of asking their consent. Tonnage and poundage, according to the view taken by the Crown lawyers, could be levied without any such formality. Once more, as after the dissolution at Oxford, orders were given to continue the collection of the duties, the King declaring that he could not do without them, and that they must therefore be gathered in till Parliament had leisure to make the usual arrangements.[4]

<small>July 8. Tonnage and poundage to be levied.</small>

Almost at the moment when Charles was appealing to the people for a free gift, he purified the Commission of the Peace by the dismissal of those persons who were likely to oppose that measure. Eliot and Phelips,

<small>Dismissal of justices of the peace.</small>

---

[1] Intended Proclamation, June 15, *S. P. Dom.* xxx. 2.

[2] The King to the Justices, July 7, *ibid.* xxxi. 30, 31. The official view of these proceedings is expressed in a letter from Sir John Coke. "His Majesty," writes the Secretary, "had sought his assistance, resolving to take no violent or extraordinary way to levy monies, but in a common danger to rely upon a common care and affection, that all men must have that will not wilfully be guilty of abandoning their religion, Prince, and country, to the enemy's power."— Coke to Brooke, July 2, *Melbourne MSS.* [3] *Ibid.*

[4] Act of Council, July 8, *Council Register.* Commission, July 26, *Rymer,* xviii. 737.

Seymour and Alford, Mansell and Digges ceased to bear the honours of justice of the peace in their respective counties. On the list of those judged unworthy to serve the Crown stands the name of Sir Thomas Wentworth, once more associated with those of the leaders of the Opposition, as it had been upon the sheriffs' list the year before.[1]

<small>Wentworth amongst them.</small>

A Government which could alienate men so opposed to one another as Eliot and Wentworth must indeed have gone far astray. Eliot's course in the last Parliament was too decided to call for any additional explanation of the causes which made all further co-operation between him and Buckingham impossible. Wentworth stood on a very different footing with the Court. He was himself longing to enter the service of the Crown, and his frequent overtures to the governing powers have exposed him to the suspicion of those who misunderstand alike his character and his principles.

<small>Position of Wentworth.</small>

The reforming spirit was strong in Wentworth. To him England was a stage on which there was much to be done, many abuses to be overthrown, many interested and ignorant voices to be silenced. Since the days when Bacon had been a member of the House of Commons no man's voice had been raised so frequently in favour of new legislation. Legislation was the only mode in which, as a member of the House of Commons, he could proceed to action. There could be little doubt, however, that he would prefer a shorter course. Power in his own hands would be very welcome to him, from whatever quarter it came. At first he was content to ask for local authority in his native Yorkshire. He had long ago driven his rival Sir John Savile from the post of

<small>Wentworth a reformer.</small>

<small>His desire for power.</small>

---

[1] Wentworth's name is happily on the list in Coventry's letter to the Clerk of the Crown, July 8 (*Harl. MSS.* 286, fol. 297), from which I have at last, after giving up the search entirely, been able to recover the date of his dismissal, and to bring the fact into connection with the known events of history. The list contains fifteen names for ten counties. It is manifestly imperfect, as we learn that Phelips was also dismissed from the *Hist. MSS. Commission Reports*, iii. 182.

Custos Rotulorum of the West Riding. Having that dignity in his hands, he had, during the last years of James, been constantly seeking for higher employment.

A courtier in the ordinary sense of the word Wentworth never was,—never by any possibility could become. He could not learn like the Conways and the Cokes, to bear a patron's yoke. Whatever his heart conceived his mouth would speak. In any position occupied by him he was certain to magnify his office. If he had been in Becket's place he would have striven for the King as Chancellor, and for the Church as Archbishop. As a member of the Commons in 1621 he had rebelled against James's attempt to refuse to the assembly of which he formed a part the right of giving counsel to its sovereign. In 1624 the tide of affairs seemed to have stranded him for ever. To his mind the King and the nation appeared to have gone mad together. What side was he to choose when all England rushed with one consent into war with Spain? All war, unless it were a war of defence, was hateful to Wentworth. He would leave the Continent to itself, to fight its own battles. England, he thought, had enough to do within her own borders. Whilst Buckingham was planning fantastic schemes, and Coke and Phelips were cheering him on to shed the blood of Englishmen like water, Wentworth could but stand aside and wait till the excitement had run its course, and till there was again time to think of legislation and reform for England.

<small>Wentworth in earlier Parliaments.</small>

In 1625 the tide had begun to ebb. If Wentworth had little sympathy with the leaders of the Opposition, yet his place was naturally by their side. Yet, if he was ready to join them in refusing or paring down the supplies which Buckingham needed for the war, he joined them as one who would gladly be spared the task of resisting the wishes of his sovereign.

<small>1625. He opposes Buckingham,</small>

Wentworth, in short, was with the Opposition, but not of it. Charles acknowledged the difference between his resistance and that of Seymour and Phelips. Though he took care to include him in the penal list of sheriffs, he spoke of him with kindness, as one who might yet be won. Wentworth justified the preference.

His objection was not against Charles's system of government, but against the policy pursued by the King and his minister.

<small>but is not thorough in his opposition.</small> Consequently, he refused to take measures to evade the restriction placed upon him. "My rule," he said, "which I will never transgress, is never to contend with the prerogative out of Parliament, nor yet to contest with a king but when I am constrained thereunto or else make shipwreck of my peace of conscience, which I trust God will ever bless me with, and with courage too to preserve it." He would for the present 'fold himself up in a cold, silent forbearance, and wait expecting that happy night that the King shall cause his chronicles to be read, wherein he shall find the faithfulness of Mardocheus, the treason of his eunuchs, and then let Haman look to himself.'[1]

Even if Haman here meant Buckingham, the feeling thus expressed had nothing of the fierce earnestness which drove Eliot to track out the footsteps of misgovernment with the enduring steadfastness of a bloodhound. Nothing would induce Wentworth to make himself partaker in Haman's misdeeds; but he had no objection to pay a stately court to Haman, or to accept from him such favours as might be consistent with an honourable independence. In January 1626, before Parliament met, having heard a rumour that Lord Scrope was about to resign the Presidency of the Council of the North, he wrote to Conway to ask for the appointment.[2] In such a post there would be nothing to implicate him in the foreign policy which he disliked. The rumour proved false, and Wentworth gained nothing by his request. Later in the spring, however, he drew still more closely to the Court. Whilst the Commons were bringing their charges against Buckingham, he came up to London and was introduced by his friend Weston to the Duke. Buckingham assured him of his desire 'to contract a friendship with him.'[3]

<small>1626. Wentworth asks for the Presidency of the Council of the North.</small>

<small>His overtures to Buckingham.</small>

Whether Wentworth meant anything more by these over-

---

[1] Wentworth to Wandesford, Dec. 5, 1625, *Strafford Letters*, i. 32.
[2] Wentworth to Conway, Jan. 20, *S. P. Dom.* xviii. 110.
[3] Wentworth to Weston, undated, 1626, *Strafford Letters*, i. 34.

tures than that he was ready to conform to the custom of the time in paying his court to Buckingham, it is impossible to say; for, though his friend Wandesford took a leading part in the Duke's impeachment, it is by no means unlikely that he may have himself regarded the proceedings of the Commons with disfavour. That the Commons might give counsel to the King, and that, if that counsel were rejected, they might proceed to a refusal of subsidies, was a doctrine which Wentworth had advocated by word and action. But he had never shown any inclination to support the theory that the Commons had the right of meddling directly or indirectly with the King's ministers; and though he would doubtless have been well pleased if Charles had dismissed Buckingham of his own motion, he may very well have refused his sympathy with an attempt to force him to dismiss his minister whether he wished it or not. Wentworth was just the man to doubt whether the King's government could be carried on under such conditions.

Did he favour the impeachment?

The dissolution of Parliament in June had left Buckingham triumphant. It was speedily followed, on July 8, by a letter from the Lord Keeper dismissing Wentworth from the official position which he held in his own county. When it reached York, Wentworth was sitting as High Sheriff in his court. The letter was handed to him, and the proud, high-spirited man learnt that he was no longer to call himself a justice of the peace. The office of *Custos Rotulorum*, for which he had struggled so hard, was given to his detested rival, Sir John Savile.[1]

July. Dismissal of Wentworth.

That Wentworth felt the insult keenly it is unnecessary to say; but he was not the man to betray weakness. In a few measured words he protested his loyalty to the King. He called those around him to witness that he had always loved justice. "Therefore," he added, "shame be from henceforth to them that deserve it. For I am well assured now to enjoy within myself a lightsome quiet as

Wentworth's justification.

---

[1] This we learn from a note to the list in Coventry's letter; see p. 126. In the same way Sir D. Foulis succeeded Sir Thomas Hoby in the North Riding, and the Earl of Hertford Sir F. Seymour in Wiltshire.

formerly. The world may well think I knew a way which would have kept my place. I confess indeed it had been too dear a purchase, and so I leave it."[1]

Explanation of his dismissal.
The bystanders doubtless understood this language better than those who have, perhaps not unnaturally, seen in the attack made upon Wentworth the fountain of his opposition in the next Parliament. If words mean anything, Wentworth was deprived of office because he was already in opposition. It was not a thunderbolt out of a clear sky which struck him. He distinctly intimated that he might have kept the place if he had chosen. There was something which he might have done, which he had refused to do.

What that was is entirely matter for conjecture; but it is highly probable that Wentworth had been asked to countenance the collection of the free gift, and that he had refused to do so. It is at all events certain that he could not possibly have used his official influence in its support without sacrificing his self-respect. The old doctrine of the constitution was that money needed for war must be voted by Parliament. Wentworth would feel probably more than any other man in England the importance of maintaining this doctrine intact. To spend money upon the war with Spain was, in his eyes, as bad as throwing it into the sea. Was he to become the tool of such a policy as this? Was he to go round amongst the freeholders, begging them to support the Crown in so ruinous an infatuation? Well may he have refused to demean himself so low.

It was the necessary consequence of the unhappy course which Charles was pursuing that he could not fail to alienate all who had it in their power to serve him best; yet he still believed himself to be possessed of the confidence of the people. On July 8, the very day on which the dismissal of the justices was resolved on, orders were issued for carrying on the usual musters with more than ordinary diligence. It looks as if Charles wished to appeal from a faction to the body of the nation.[2]

July 8. Orders for the musters.

[1] Wentworth's speech, *Strafford Letters,* i. 36.
[2] Instructions for Musters, July 8, *S. P. Dom.* xxxi. 34.

In the hands of Charles such a policy was not likely to be successful, especially when it took the shape of a demand for money. The first attempt to collect the free gift was made in Westminster Hall. Cries of "A Parliament, a Parliament!" were raised on every side, and only thirty persons, all of them known to be in the King's service, agreed to pay. In the rest of Middlesex and in Kent similar failures were reported, and the Council was driven to gild the pill by a declaration explaining away the compulsory character of the demand. There was no intention, they said, of asking for four subsidies as if the Commons' resolution had been in any way binding upon the nation. All that was meant had been to show what was the opinion of Parliament on the amount required for the defence of the country.[1]

The free gift in Middlesex.

July 26.

In a few days answers to the demand made in this new fashion began to pour in. All through August and the first fortnight of September the tale of resistance went up with almost uniform monotony. Here and there a handful of loyalists offered a poor tribute of a few pounds. Here and there a county based its refusal on its poverty rather than on its disinclination to give; but the great majority of refusers spoke out clearly. They would give in Parliament. Out of Parliament they would not give at all. The figment of a nation passing by its representatives to fly to the support of its King was demonstrated to be without a shadow of foundation.[2]

August. Refusal of the counties.

After this, unless Charles was prepared either to make peace with Spain, or to summon another Parliament, one course only remained. The English constitution had grown up round the belief that the King was in very truth the centre of the national life. Precedents as ancient, and to the full as continuous, as the protests against tyranny and misgovernment which had been quoted in the House of

Charles resolves to follow precedents.

[1] Meade to Stuteville, July 24, *Court and Times*, i. 130. *Council Register*, July 26.

[2] The answers will be found amongst the Domestic State Papers in August and September. Berkshire was the first to refuse, on August 5.

Commons, told how the Kings of England had been accustomed to call, not in vain, upon their subjects, to put no strict construction upon their local or individual rights in times of national danger. In reality nothing could be more perilous than to gather up these precedents as a rule of government at a time when the spirit which had animated them was being violated at every turn. Yet this peril, apparently without the least suspicion that there was any peril at all, Charles was determined to confront.

One of these precedents had already been followed before the appeal for the free gift had been made. The fleet which had taken Cadiz in Elizabeth's reign had been partly supplied with ships by a levy on the maritime counties. The same course had been adopted now, and the shires along the coast had been ordered to join the port towns in setting out a fleet of fifty-six ships.[1] Few of the shires were hardy enough to dispute the precedent, and most of them contented themselves with an effort to shift as much as possible of the burden upon their neighbours. The Dorsetshire magistrates, who took higher ground, were sharply reprimanded by the Council. "State occasions," they were told, "and the defence of the kingdom in times of extraordinary danger, do not guide themselves by ordinary precedents." The City of London, having ventured to argue that the twenty ships at which it was assessed were more than had been required in former times, was still more soundly rated. "Whereas," answered the Council, "they mention precedents, they may know that the precedents of former times were obedience and not direction, and that there are also precedents of punishment of those who disobey his Majesty's commandments signified by the Board in the case of the preservation of the State, which they hope there shall be no occasion to let them more particularly understand."

Ships to be found by the maritime counties.

July 24. Resistance of the City of London.

Aug. 11.

On the 15th the City gave way.[2] It would, however, be some

---

[1] List of ports charged with furnishing ships, June, *S. P. Dom.* xxx. 81.

[2] Proceedings in Council, July 24, Aug. 11, 15, *Council Register.*

time before the ships thus obtained would be ready for sea. In the meanwhile a fleet of thirty-nine ships had been gathering at Portsmouth, under the command of Lord Willoughby. It had been given out that it would sail on August 12,[1] to fall upon the transports in the Biscay harbours, and if possible to intercept the Mexico fleet, and to succeed where Cecil had failed the year before. But August 12 came, and nothing was ready. Provisions for the voyage were not forthcoming, and the men, left without the necessaries of life, were deserting as fast as they could.[2] By Buckingham's own confession the King was incurring a debt of 4,000*l.* a month because he could not lay his hand upon 14,000*l.* to discharge some utterly useless mariners by paying off their arrears.[3]

<small>Aug. 15. The City gives way.</small>
<small>Aug. 12. Willoughby's fleet at Portsmouth.</small>

New efforts were therefore made to get money. On August 18 the Council directed the sale of 50,000 oz. of the King's plate. On the 26th 20,000 oz. more were disposed of in the same way.[4] Even Buckingham, sanguine as he was, felt in some measure the seriousness of his position. Having broken hopelessly with the leaders of the Commons, he would do his best to attach the nobility to his cause. A marriage was contrived between his little daughter and another child, the son of Pembroke's brother, Montgomery. Pembroke himself, incurring, if report spoke truly, no slight obloquy by his compliance with Buckingham's wishes,[5] was raised to the dignity of Lord Steward, whilst Montgomery succeeded him as Chamberlain. The Earls of Dorset, Salisbury, and Bridgewater, who had supported Buckingham in the last session, were admitted to the Privy Council. If Arundel was still under a cloud, no attempt was made to press hardly upon him, and the advancement of Wallingford, the brother-in-law of the new Earl of Suffolk, to the Earldom of Banbury, may probably be regarded as an overture to the Howards.

<small>Aug. 18 Sale of plate.</small>

---

[1] List of ships, *S. P. Dom.* xxxii. 74.
[2] Gyffard to Nicholas, Aug. 24, 27, *S. P. Dom.* xxxiv. 28, 39.
[3] *Council Register*, Aug. 23.
[4] *Ibid.* Aug. 18, 26.
[5] Advice from England, Sept. 12, *Brussels MSS.*

Buckingham and his master had need of more support than could be found in the House of Lords. Nothing had been done to improve the King's relations with France. A commission had, indeed, been issued, to inquire into the law of prize,[1] but as the French were not convinced that Charles had any intention of withdrawing his extreme pretensions, a fresh collision might arise at any moment. This was the time chosen by Charles to effect a domestic revolution, perhaps justifiable in itself, but certain to cause bitter mortification to his wife and to exasperate her brother more than ever.

For months Charles had felt that, as long as the Queen's French attendants were in England, he could hardly call his wife his own. Her ladies taught her to look upon English men and women with distrust. Her priests taught her to display ostentatiously more than the ordinary humiliations which found favour with her Church. Her complaints of her husband's broken promises met with a warm response in their sympathetic bosoms. When she was in private with her chosen companions she was merry enough, dancing and laughing as if no shadow of misfortune had ever crossed her path. She reserved her ill-humour for her husband, and in his presence bore herself as a martyr. The winter before he had thought of sending the whole company back to France; but the marriage contract was against him, and he desisted for a time. Then came fresh disputes and recriminations. The Queen wished to name some amongst her French attendants to take charge of her jointure. Charles refused his permission. One night, after the pair were in bed, there were high words between them. "Take your lands to yourself," said the offended wife. "If I have no power to put whom I will into those places, I will have neither lands nor houses of you. Give me what you think fit by way of pension." Charles fell back upon his dignity. "Remember," he said, "to whom you speak. You ought not to use me so." In reply, she broke out into mere fretfulness. She was miserable, she said. She had no power to place servants,

---

[1] Commission, July 11, *Rymer*, xviii. 730.

and businesses succeeded the worse for her recommendation. She was not of that base quality to be used so ill. She ran on for some time, refusing to listen to her husband's explanation. "Then," wrote Charles afterwards, in giving an account of the scene, "I made her both hear me, and end that discourse."[1]

Charles's displeasure is not likely to have been softened by any real insight into his wife's difficulties, or by sympathy with the poor child's natural clinging to those who alone shared her feelings and her prejudices in a strange land. It was not long before a fresh cause of offence arose. On June 26[2] the Queen obtained leave to spend some time in retirement, in order to give herself to a special season of devotion. After a long day passed in attendance upon the services of her Church at the chapel at St. James's, she strolled out with her attendants to breathe the fresh evening air in St. James's Park. By-and-by she found her way into Hyde Park, and by accident or design directed her steps towards Tyburn. In her position it was but natural that she should bethink herself of those who had suffered there as martyrs for that faith which she

The Queen at Tyburn.

---

[1] Instructions for Carleton, printed in Ludlow's *Memoirs*, (ed. 1751), 459. I rather suspect the date given as July 12, should be July 22, as the other instructions (*S. P. France*) are dated July 23.

[2] This date of the Jubilee is distinctly given in Salvetti's letter, June 30, July 10, and is nearly in agreement with Bassompierre's statement (*Ambassade*, 185) that more than six weeks passed between the visit to Tyburn and the notice taken of it on July 31. If the 26th of June was the day, there would be exactly five weeks, and Bassompierre may be allowed a little exaggeration. Miss Strickland's notion (*Queens of England*, 237) that the visit to Hyde Park took place in 1625, founded on a blunder in an English translation of Bassompierre's speech, receives no countenance from the original (*Ambassade*, 185). If Miss Strickland consulted Pory's letter in the *Court and Times*, in which the visit is said to have taken place on St. James's Day last, its date as there given, July 1, may have confirmed her in her idea that 'St. James's Day last' meant July 25, 1625. But the Queen was not in London at that date, and the date July 1 is a blunder of the editor. In the original it is July 5, as printed by Sir H. Ellis (ser. 1, iii. 244). Internal evidence, however, shows that it was really written on Aug. 5, and Pory must therefore have meant July 25, 1626, an impossible date. St. James's Day perhaps arose out of some confusion with St. James's Park.

had come to England to support. What wonder if her heart beat more quickly, and if some prayer for strength to bear her weary lot rose to her lips?

A week or two probably passed away before the tale reached Charles, exaggerated in its passage through the mouths of men. There was no compassion in him for the disappointment to which he had given rise in his young wife's heart, by the promises which had been made only to be broken—a disappointment which was none the less real because she could frolic amongst her companions with all the gaiety of her nation and her age. The Queen of England, he was told, had been conducted on a pilgrimage to offer prayer to dead traitors who had suffered the just reward of their crimes. The cup of his displeasure was now full. Whatever the contract might say, those who had brought her to this should no longer remain in England.

The story told to Charles.

Something, however, must be done to diminish the indignation with which the news would be received in France. An excuse was found for sending Carleton on a special embassy to Louis, in order that he might be at hand to explain everything away. As soon as it was known that Carleton was safely on the other side of the Channel, Charles proceeded to carry out his intentions.

On July 31 the King and Queen dined together at Whitehall. After dinner he conducted her into his private apartments, locked the door upon her attendants, and told her that her servants must go. In the meanwhile Conway was informing the members of her household that the King expected them to remove to Somerset House, where they would learn his pleasure. The Bishop of Mende raised some objections, and the women 'howled and lamented as if they had been going to execution.' The yeomen of the guard interfered, and cleared the apartments.

July 31. The dismissal of the French.

Charles had a less easy task. As soon as the young Queen perceived what was being done, she flew to the window and dashed to pieces the glass, that her voice might once more be heard by those who were bidding her adieu for the last time. Charles, it is said, dragged her back

The Queen's anger.

into the room with her hands bleeding from the energy with which she clung to the bars. The next day Conway visited Somerset House and told the angry crowd that they must leave the country, with two or three exceptions which had been made at the Queen's entreaty. Presents to the amount of 22,000*l.* were offered them, and they were told that if anything was owing to them it should be paid out of the remainder of the Queen's portion, which had been detained in France in consequence of the misunderstanding between the Courts.[1]

They refused to obey, and clung to England as their right. For some days they remained at Somerset House, in spite of all orders to the contrary. Charles lost his patience. "I command you," he wrote to Buckingham, "to send all the French away to-morrow out of town ; if you can, by fair means—but stick not long in disputing—otherwise force them away, driving them away like so many wild beasts until ye have shipped them, and so the Devil go with them."

Aug. 7. The French finally expelled.

The King's pleasure was executed. At first the French refused to move till they were ordered by their own King to do so. The next morning the yeomen of the guard were marched down to Somerset House, and there was no more resistance. With the exception of a few personal attendants specially named, all the foreigners were conducted to Dover, and were there embarked for France as soon as the wind served.[2]

Aug. 8.

What would Louis say to this high-handed transaction? Carleton told his story in France as well as he could. The King answered him sharply. His sister, he said, had been treated cruelly. Charles had plainly broken his promise. An ambassador of his own, Marshal Bassompierre, should be sent to investigate the affair. When

Aug. 11. Resentment of Louis.

---

[1] Pory to Meade, Aug. 5 (not July 5), *Ellis*, ser. 1, iii. 237. Private instructions to Carleton, July 23 ; Conway to Carleton, Aug. 9, *S. P. France.* Richelieu, *Mémoires*, iii. 176. Contarini to the Doge, Aug. $\frac{11}{21}$, *Ven. Transcripts, R.O.*

[2] The King to Buckingham, Aug. 7 ; Pory to Meade, Aug. 11, 17 ; *Ellis*, ser. 1, iii. 244, 245, 247.

he had received his report he would say what he would do
From this resolution Carleton was never able to move him, and
was finally recalled to England, having effected nothing.[1]

It was a badly chosen moment to offend the King of France
The want of money was more crying every day. On August 17
some two hundred soldiers and sailors, hopeless of
obtaining their pay at Portsmouth, flocked up to
London, stopped the Duke's coach, and presented their complaint. Buckingham promised to satisfy them later in the day,
slipped home by water, and placed himself beyond their reach.[2]

Distress for money.

All attempts, too, to fill the Exchequer were breaking down
The free gift had come to nothing. A resolution to issue
Privy seals in the old way was not persisted in.[3] For
a time much was hoped from the issue of debased
coin, and the Mint had been busy for some weeks in
preparing the light pieces. The City merchants, however, remonstrated strongly, and Sir Robert Cotton was heard on their
behalf before the Council. The King himself was present, and
in spite, it is said, of the opposition of Buckingham, refused to
agree to the iniquitous proposal. The new pieces were declared
by proclamation not to be current coin of the realm.[4]

Proposal to debase the coin.

In the face of all these increasing difficulties, there were
men at Court who held high language still. Dorset, who had
completely thrown in his lot with the high prerogative doctrines which now found favour with Charles,
talked of the impossibility of a rebellion in a country
where there were no fortresses, and asserted that, as it was the
duty of the people to maintain the war, the King would only
have to take irregularly what he had failed to obtain from
Parliament.[5]

High language at Court.

In the midst of these perplexities, bad news arrived from
Germany. To all outward appearance the position of the King

---

[1] Carleton to Conway, Aug. 13, *S. P. France.*
[2] Pory to Meade, Aug. 17, *Ellis,* ser. 1, iii. 247.
[3] The King to the Council, Aug. 14, *S. P. Dom.* xxxiii. 101.
[4] —— to Meade, Sept. 8, *Court and Times,* i. 145.
[5] Contarini to the Doge, $\frac{\text{Aug. 25}}{\text{Sept. 4}}$, *Ven. Transcripts, R. O.*

of Denmark at the opening of the campaign of 1626 was extremely strong. He had one army under his own command in Lower Saxony. Another army under Mansfeld was on the east bank of the Elbe. Other troops were pushing forward in Westphalia. The peasants had risen in Austria. Bethlen Gabor had engaged to fall upon the Emperor's hereditary dominions from the east. It was true that Christian had now to do with another enemy in addition to Tilly. Wallenstein had brought against him that strange army, self-supporting and self-governed, which, in the name of the Emperor, was so soon to become a power in the Empire almost independent of the Emperor himself. Yet it seemed not unlikely, judging from numbers alone, that Christian and his allies would be strong enough to make head against Tilly and Wallenstein combined. From the beginning, however, one circumstance was against him. His finances were inadequate to meet the strain. He had calculated that Charles would and could keep his word, and that 30,000*l.* a month would flow into his military chest from the English exchequer. Then had come the refusal of subsidies by Parliament. The payments, scarcely begun in May 1625, stopped altogether. Christian had levied soldiers on the faith of the English alliance, and his soldiers were clamouring for their pay.[1] To stand on the defensive, without money, was impossible, and there was no unity of command in the united armies. In May Mansfeld made a dash southwards, and was defeated by Wallenstein at the Bridge of Dessau. Before the summer ended he was hurrying through Silesia with Wallenstein hard upon his heels, hoping to combine with Bethlen Gabor for a joint attack upon Austria and Bohemia.

The campaign in Germany.

Mansfeld's defeat.

Then came the turn of Christian of Denmark. To him a defensive war was impossible without Charles's money. An attempt to slip past Tilly and to make his way towards Bethlen Gabor in Bohemia proved vain. Tilly, reinforced by some of Wallenstein's regiments, started in pursuit and overtook him at Lutter. After a sanguinary

Aug. 17. Christian's defeat at Lutter.

[1] Anstruther's despatches (*S. P. Denmark*) give a good insight into these financial difficulties.

battle the Danish King was completely defeated, and North Germany lay open to the Imperialists.

The news of the disaster, for which the English Government was so largely responsible, reached Charles on September 12.[1]

<small>Sept. 12. Charles receives the news.</small> Now that it was too late, he talked of raising 10,000 men for his uncle's service, and ordered the sale of a large quantity of plate. He came at once to London, and sat for four hours in the Council, a feat which he had seldom performed before. When the Council was over he sent for the Danish Ambassador, and assured him that he would stake his crown and his life in his master's defence. With the tears almost standing in his eyes, he reminded the Dane that he was in distress for his own personal needs.

The matter was discussed anxiously in the Council. The <small>The four regiments in the Netherlands to go to Denmark.</small> most feasible project seemed to be to send on the four volunteer regiments in the Netherlands, whose term of service would expire in November. There was, however, a difficulty in the way. The men, like most others in Charles's service, had not been paid for some months, and how was money to be found?[2]

The first instinct of the Government was to apply to the City for a loan; but the Lord Mayor and Aldermen had not forgotten the sharp message about the ships, and closed their purses tightly.

<small>[1] If, as seems almost certain, the following undated letter was written at this time, we get from it Buckingham's feeling about the matter :—'My dear Master,—This noble lord hath this day behaved himself like your faithful servant. He is able to relate to you what hath passed. I will only say this, that already your brother and sister are thrust out of their inheritance. If the news be true that runs current here, your uncle is in a very ill estate. There is much difference between the cases. The one, with the help of your people, brought you into this business, and yourself brought the other. The times require something to be done and that speedily, and the more it appears to be yours, certainly the better success will follow. Strike while the iron is hot, and let your uncle at the least see you were touched with the news. So, in haste, I kiss your Majesty's hands, as your humble slave, STEENIE.' Buckingham to the King, *Harl. MSS.* 6988, fol. 74.

[2] Contarini to the Doge, Sept. $\frac{15}{25}$, *Ven. Transcripts, R. O.* —— to Meade, Sept. 15, *Court and Times,* i. 148.</small>

Such was the position of affairs when, on September 27,
Bassompierre arrived in London. Everything had
been done by Charles, since the expulsion of the
French, to soothe the injured feelings of the Queen.
A new household of noble English ladies, amongst whom
Buckingham's wife and mother and sister were of course numbered, was formed to minister to her dignity. But
the deprivation which she suffered from the absence
of the old familiar faces, and the silence of the old familiar
accents of her mother-tongue, weighed heavily upon her spirits,
and, in spite of the sedulous attentions of her husband, a sullen
melancholy pervaded her features.[1]

Sept. 27 Bassompierre's arrival.

Treatment of the Queen.

The King's desire to please his wife did not extend to a
desire to please her countrymen. To the Venetian ambassador
he complained openly of the treachery and insincerity
of the French. Buckingham was still more bitter.
He gave orders that Bassompierre should be treated
on his arrival with studied rudeness. He summoned Soubise
to London, and talked with him for hours about the state of
France.[2]

The King's feeling about France.

If any man was capable of smoothing away the difficulties
in his course it was Bassompierre. He knew the world well,
and he had that power of seizing upon the strong point of his
opponent's case which goes far to the making of a successful
diplomatist. To the young Queen he gave the best possible
advice; told her to make the best of her situation, and warned
her against the folly of setting herself against the current ideas
of the country in which she lived and of the man to whom she
was married. In the question of the household he
was at the same time firm and conciliatory. He acknowledged that Charles had a genuine grievance,
that the Queen would never be a real wife to him as
long as she was taught by a circle of foreigners to regard herself as permanently a foreigner; whilst at the same time he
spoke boldly of the breach of the contract which had been

October. Bassompierre's negotiation on the household.

---

[1] Contarini to the Doge, $\frac{\text{Aug. 25}}{\text{Sept. 4}}$, *Ven. Transcripts R. O.*

[2] *Ibid.* $\frac{\text{Sept. 23}}{\text{Oct. 3}}$.

committed. In the end he gained the confidence both of the King and of Buckingham, and with the assent of the King of France a new arrangement was agreed to, by which a certain number of French persons would be admitted to attend upon the Queen, whilst a great part of the household was to be formed of natives of England.

The maritime questions at issue were discussed by Bassompierre in the same spirit. He was ready to admit the reasonableness of the English in objecting to a large trade being carried on between Spain and Flanders under the French flag; but he wished to see some arrangement come to by which the perpetual interference of the English cruisers could be obviated. But for events which occurred to exasperate both nations, a commercial treaty laying down the terms on which neutrals should be liable to arrest might perhaps have been the result of Bassompierre's mission.[1]

<small>On the commercial disputes.</small>

Unfortunately Charles was not disposed to withdraw any one of his pretensions whilst the negotiations were pending. In October Lord Willoughby's fleet contrived at last to put to sea; but, having met with a severe storm in the Bay of Biscay, against which the ill-found vessels were incompetent to struggle, was driven back to the English ports without accomplishing anything. Before it sailed, a squadron under Lord Denbigh had captured three Rouen vessels of immense value, on the suspicion that they were laden with Spanish property.[2] Public opinion in France was greatly excited, and a fresh decree was issued by the Parliament of Rouen for the sequestration of English goods.[3] Yet the English Court did not contemplate the probability of a breach. In the beginning of November it was announced that Sir George Goring would go to France to clear up all difficulties. Buckingham was by this time once more in that frame of mind in which all things seemed

<small>Willoughby's fleet.</small>

<small>Sept. 18. Three French ships taken by Denbigh.</small>

<small>Oct. 10.</small>

<small>November. Goring to go to France.</small>

---

[1] *Ambassade de Bassompierre.*

[2] Denbigh to Buckingham, Sept. 21, *S. P. Dom.* xxxvi. 31.

[3] An English merchant at Rouen to Ferrar, Oct. $\frac{11}{21}$, *S. P. France.*

easy, all the more because he had reason to believe that the financial difficulties which had plagued him so long were at last at an end.

The forced loan. In the course of September some clever man, not improbably Sir Allen Apsley,[1] suggested that though the King had found difficulties in raising a so-called free gift, there might be less difficulty in the way of raising a forced loan. The Statute of Benevolences, it may have been urged, stood clearly in the way of any attempt to make the gift compulsory; but forced loans under the name of Privy seals were perfectly familiar to all Englishmen, and it would only be necessary to extend the system a little further. It is only due to Charles that he should be heard in defence of the proposal.

Sept. 21. The King's circular. In a letter which Abbot was required to circulate in all the dioceses of England, Charles called upon the Church to aid the necessities of the State. After dwelling at length upon the evil consequences of the defeat of Lutter, the King went over the old story how he had been led into war by the counsel of Parliament. "This," he wrote, "upon their persuasions and promises of all assistance and supply we readily undertook and effected, and cannot now be left in that business but with the sin and shame of all men :— sin, because aid and supply for the defence of the kingdom and the like affairs of State, especially such as are advised by Parliamentary counsel, are due to the King from his people by all law both of God and men; and shame if they forsake the King while he pursues their own counsel just and honourable, and which could not, under God, but have been successful if he had been followed and supplied in time, as we desired and laboured for." The greatest evil of Church and State, Charles went on to say, was the breach of unity. The clergy were to preach unity and charity, and to exhort the people to prayers for themselves and for the King of Denmark.[2]

[1] At least he afterwards claimed to have been the cause of bringing 400,000*l.* to his Majesty. And though the loan produced less than 300,000*l.*, I am at a loss to think of any other scheme which produced nearly so much. Apsley to Nicholas, Feb. 2, 1628, *S. P. Dom.* xcii. 18.

[2] The King to Abbot, Sept. 21, *Wilkins*, iv. 471.

Two days after this letter was written, and before there was time to put it in circulation, a first attempt to collect the loan was made in the county of Middlesex. The sum to be paid was fixed at five subsidies, an amount far greater than had ever been raised upon Privy seals. The Commissioners appointed to collect the loan were directed, first to lend money themselves, and then to summon before them all men rated in the subsidy books. Anyone who refused to lend was to be required to swear whether he had been prompted in his refusal by another person, and if he would neither lend nor swear, then to be bound over to answer for his contempt before the Privy Council.[1]

<small>Sept. 23. The commission for Middlesex.</small>

Westminster was chosen as the scene of the first meeting of the Commissioners. In the parishes of St. Margaret's and St. Martin's, lying as they did under the very eye of the Court, little difficulty was made. In the parishes about the Strand there was more disturbance. When the inhabitants of the country parts of Middlesex were summoned, the majority of those who came agreed to pay, and the Government was thus encouraged to apply to the other counties in the neighbourhood of London.[2]

<small>October. Proceedings in Westminster.</small>

The moment when success seemed to be dawning upon Charles was chosen by him to deal a blow at the man who had done more than anyone else to frustrate his hopes. As soon as Eliot returned home, all the swarm of Buckingham's adherents fell upon him. Foremost of all was Sir James Bagg, the man who coveted Eliot's office, and who never signed a letter to the Duke without subscribing himself his 'humble slave.' Charges and complaints were easy to bring together when they were welcome to those who received them, and on October 25 they were brought into such shape as to induce the Privy Council to pronounce Eliot unworthy any longer to exercise the duties of his office. The Vice-Admiralty of Devon was made over to Sir James Bagg, and to a kindred spirit, Sir John Drake.

<small>Oct. 25. Sequestration of Eliot's Vice-Admiralty.</small>

Buckingham's heart was again full of triumph. In the

---

[1] Commission and Instructions, Sept. 23, *S. P. Dom.* xxxvi. 42, 43.
[2] —— to Meade, Oct. 6, 20, *Court and Times,* i. 154, 159.

beginning of November it had not only been finally decided to send the four regiments in Holland to the assistance of the King of Denmark, but arrangements had been made for paying them, at least for a time.¹ In his conversations with Bassompierre, Buckingham had much to say about the revival of the French alliance, and on November 5 he adroitly took the opportunity of a magnificent entertainment given by himself to the ambassador at York House to signify the hopes which he had founded on the renewal of amity with France. In the masque which the spectators were called upon to admire, Mary de Medicis was represented as enthroned in the midst of the celestial deities upon the sea which separated England and France, welcoming the Elector and Electress Palatine, as well as her three daughters, with their husbands the Kings of England and Spain and the Prince of Piedmont.² It was the old dream of 1623, with the substitution of Henrietta Maria for the Infanta. In his conversations with Bassompierre Buckingham talked freely of the difficulties caused by want of money, and something was said of an arrangement to be brought about in Germany by French influence.³

Nov. 5. The entertainment at York House.

So smooth had the waters been running at home since Bassompierre's arrival that everything seemed possible. The Queen—with occasional outbursts of petulance—was at last on good terms with her husband, and was even carrying on friendly intercourse with the English ladies of her Court, and through them with Buckingham himself. But it was not easy to make amends for the want of foresight which had postponed so long the settlement of the maritime quarrel between the two countries. An angry crowd interested in the French trade had lately gathered round Bassompierre's door, and had loaded the ambassador with insults. On November 9 a formal petition was presented to the Council by the merchants, asking for the further stay of the French prizes

The Queen and Buckingham.

Nov. 9. The merchants trading with France protest against the liberation of the prizes.

¹ The King to the States-General, Nov. 3, *Add. MSS.* 17,677, L, fol. 292.
² Salvetti's *News-Letter*, Nov. 10.
³ Contarini to the Doge, Nov. $\frac{17}{27}$, *Ven. Transcripts, R. O.*

till the goods sequestered at Rouen had been liberated.¹
Buckingham's spirits only rose with the occasion. The
knot was worthy of his own personal intervention. Bassompierre should go without the prizes. He should carry with
him a few priests set free from prison, but the further concessions promised to the Catholics should for the present be
<small>Buckingham proposes to go to France.</small> postponed. The extraordinary ambassador about to start for Paris should go to the heart of the difficulty, and propose a reasonable settlement of the law of
prize, to be followed by a renewed understanding on the
general affairs of Europe. Goring was no longer considered
fit for a negotiation of such extended dimensions. There was
but one man in England believed by Buckingham to be equal
to the task, and that man was himself.²

Events were hurrying on too rapidly for Buckingham's
control. The example of the Rouen Parliament proved in-
<small>Fresh seizures at Rochelle.</small> fectious. Four English vessels were stopped off Rochelle. Again the merchants flocked round the Council, begging for letters of marque against the
French, and the Council was beginning to share in their
excitement. Though, for the present, the King refused to issue
letter of marque, orders were drawn up for a further seizure
of French property in England. Fresh news might at any
time provoke an act which would involve the two countries
in war.³

Such news was already on its way.⁴ The Duke of Epernon,
Governor of Guienne, was one of the many amongst the French
aristocracy who were opposed to Richelieu and his policy. If
his motive was to frustrate that policy and to create a breach
between France and England he could hardly have acted more

---

¹ Petition, Nov. $\frac{9}{19}$. Bassompierre to Herbault, Nov. $\frac{12}{22}$, *Neg.* 257, 259.

² The Duke's intention is mentioned by Bassompierre in his letter of Dec. $\frac{2}{12}$, but Contarini knew of it on Nov. $\frac{17}{27}$.

³ Contarini to the Doge, $\frac{\text{Nov. 24}}{\text{Dec. 4}}$, *Ven. Transcripts, R. O.*

⁴ It reached Bassompierre at Dover on the 24th of November, but was not known in London till later.

cleverly than he did. As a fleet of two hundred English and
Scottish vessels, laden with the year's supply of wine,
was sailing from Bordeaux, he ordered the seizure
of the whole. When the news reached England, it
was regarded as a peculiar aggravation of the offence that he
had waited till a new duty of four crowns a tun had been paid,
and had thus secured both the money and the wine. This
time not the merchants only, but all who drank wine were up
in arms. It was known that the last year's supply would soon
be exhausted, and its price consequently went up rapidly.[1]

<small>The wine fleet seized at Bordeaux.</small>

Even before these last tidings from Bordeaux reached
Buckingham, he had discovered that others had not as much
confidence as himself in his diplomatic powers.
Bassompierre hinted to him pretty plainly that his
presence would not be acceptable in France—advice
which may to some extent have been founded on the recollection of Buckingham's insolent behaviour to the Queen, but
which was fully justified by dislike of the impetuous character
of the Duke. Nor was resistance wanting from Buckingham's
own family. His wife, his mother, and his sister threw themselves on their knees, imploring him to desist from so hazardous
an enterprise.[2] When the news arrived from Bordeaux the
enterprise became more hazardous still. The Council was in
favour of instant retaliation. Buckingham himself began to partake of the general exasperation; but he was all the more convinced that his own personal intervention would clear away the
difficulty. Summoning back Bassompierre, who had
already reached Dover on his return home, he went
down to Canterbury to meet him, and offered to
cross the Straits at once in his company, to set matters right.
Bassompierre had some difficulty in persuading him to wait
till an answer could be received from the French Court.[3]

<small>Buckingham's projected embassy.</small>

<small>Dec. 4. Buckingham offers to go at once.</small>

---

[1] Contarini to the Doge, Dec. $\frac{1}{11}$, *Ven. Transcripts, R. O.* —— to Meade, Dec. 9, *Court and Times,* i. 180.

[2] Bassompierre to Herbault, $\frac{\text{Nov. 30}}{\text{Dec. 10}}$, *Neg.* 297. Contarini to the Doge, Dec. $\frac{8}{18}$, *Ven. Transcripts, R. O.*

[3] Bassompierre to Louis XIII., Dec. $\frac{10}{20}$, *Neg.* 307.

It was hardly likely that this overture would be favourably received. On December 3, before Buckingham started for Canterbury, an Order in Council was issued for the seizure of all French ships and goods in English waters.[1]

<small>Dec. 3. French ships and goods to be seized.</small>

Yet even then Buckingham still talked of going to Paris, as if nothing had happened. He said that till he heard that the King of France had himself refused to see him, he would not believe that his overtures had been rejected. He may well have hesitated to acknowledge that war was inevitable. Every day he was receiving signs of the unpopularity of which he was the object. At Court it was believed that his only aim was to seek an opportunity of making love once more to the Queen of France; whilst reasonable men explained his desire to go to France by his eagerness to be out of England during the session of Parliament which was now naturally enough presumed to be inevitable. When he set out to meet Bassompierre at Canterbury, the mob followed him with curses, shouting after him, "Begone for ever!"[2]

Hard pressed as he was, Charles had not the slightest intention of meeting a Parliament. Yet the prospects of the loan were far less favourable in December than they had been at the beginning of November. At first, when the money had been demanded only from the five counties nearest London, it seemed as if a little firmness would bear down all opposition. In Essex, Sir Francis Barrington and Sir William Masham were committed to prison for a few days for refusing to sit upon the commission, and thirteen poorer men were sent down to Portsmouth to serve on board the fleet, as a punishment for their refusal to pay, though they were allowed to go home again after a short detention. After this, little further resistance was made, and the Government, congratulating itself that its difficulties were at an

<small>October. Prospects of the loan.</small>

<small>November.</small>

---

[1] Order in Council, Dec. 3, *S. P. Dom.* xli. 15.

[2] Contarini to the Doge, Dec. $\frac{8}{18}$, *Ven. Transcripts, R. O.* The idea about making love to the Queen is frequently mentioned by Contarini, but, I think, without much belief on his part.

end, prepared to despatch to more distant shires the Privy Councillors who were to take part in the commissions in order that they might overawe the counties by their presence.

Suddenly opposition arose from an unexpected quarter. The judges had hitherto borne their share of Benevolences and *Resistance of the judges.* Privy seals without murmuring; but though they still expressed their readiness to pay their quota towards the new loan, they now unanimously refused to acknowledge its legality by putting their hands to paper to express their consent to the demand. Charles, as soon as he heard the objection, hastily sent for the Chief Justice, Sir Randal Crew, and, finding that he would not give way, dismissed him on the spot from his office, as an example to the rest.[1]

Nov. 10. Dismissal of the Chief Justice.

If Charles expected to intimidate the other judges he was quickly undeceived. One and all they refused to give the required signatures unless they were allowed to add that they signed simply to please his Majesty, without any intention of giving their authority to the loan.[2]

A successor was easily found for Crew in Sir Nicholas Hyde, who had been the draftsman of Buckingham's defence. The Chief Justiceship of the Common Pleas, which was vacant by Hobart's death, was filled by Serjeant Richardson, who gave a pledge of his subserviency by marrying a kinswoman of the Duke before he was admitted to the Bench.[3] But the wound inflicted by Charles upon his own authority was not so easily healed. When at any future time he appealed to the

---

[1] Meddus to Meade, Oct. 27, Nov. 4, *Court and Times*, i. 160, 165.

[2] "Sur ce refus, le Roy a envoyé quérir au principal des juges, lequel ayant refusé de signer, le Roy l'a desmis au mesme instant de sa charge, et puis a envoyé presenter ledit livre aux autres juges, lesquels y ont mis cette clause, que non pour donner exemple au peuple, ny le convier à faire la mesme chose, mais qu'estant interpellés et pressés, pour eviter de fascher sa Majesté ils ont souscrit." Bassompierre, *Neg.* 263. Compare Contarini's Despatch, Nov. $\frac{17}{27}$; Meddus to Meade, Nov. 10, 17, *Court and Times*, i. 167, 170. Hyde's formal appointment was on Feb. 5, 1627; *Rymer*, xviii. 835.

[3] Meddus to Meade, Dec. 1, *Court and Times*, i. 175.

judges against what he regarded as the encroachments of the Commons, it would be remembered that they were no longer disinterested umpires, and that the highest of their number had been dismissed from office because he refused to say that to be legal which he believed to be illegal. The judges, in short, were to be appealed to as impartial arbiters when they were on the side of the Crown; but to be treated with scorn when they ventured to have opinions of their own.

The news that the judges had made objections spread like wildfire. Fifteen or sixteen of the Peers—amongst them Essex, Lincoln, Warwick, Clare, Bolingbroke, and Saye— refused to lend. In Hertfordshire a large number of persons who had already given their subscriptions, declared that the opinion given by the judges had set them free. In the Council the fiery Dorset urged the immediate imprisonment of the recalcitrant Lords. The majority, however, was against him, and it was resolved to await the effect of the visits of the Privy Councillors to the counties.[1]

<small>Further refusals.</small>

<small>Nov. 27. Debate in the Council.</small>

Not even the risk of a failure of the loan could induce Charles to change his policy towards France. On December 3, as has been seen, the order was issued for the seizure of French vessels On the 8th Bassompierre left Dover with a promise to send back the message which would virtually imply peace or war.[2] In the meanwhile everything that passed in France was regarded with jealous scrutiny. The evident determination of Richelieu to make France a maritime nation, that she might no longer go a begging to foreign powers for the means of repressing rebellion amongst her own people, was treated at Whitehall as an insult to the English supremacy at sea, an encroachment upon Charles's rights which Buckingham was bent on resisting by any means in his power.

<small>December. Fear of French maritime force.</small>

A plan was soon formed. As in 1625, Pennington was entrusted with the secret. Of the twenty ships wrung from the

---

[1] Meade to Stuteville, Nov. 25; Meddus to Meade, Dec. 1, *Court and Times*, i. 172, 175. Rudyerd to Nethersole, Dec. 1, *S. P. Dom.* xli. 3.

[2] Hippisley to Buckingham, Dec. 8, *S. P. Dom.* xli. 50.

City with so much difficulty, some were now ready and were lying under Pennington's command in the Downs. On the 22nd Charles wrote to Buckingham that six or eight ships purchased by the French King in the Low Countries were at Havre. As they were intended to be employed against England he was to see that they were sunk or taken.[1] Two days later Buckingham sent Pennington his instructions. "When you shall come where these ships ride," he wrote, "you are, according to your best discretion to give the captains or commanders of them some occasion to fall out with you and to shoot at you; and thereupon presently, with the best force you can make, you are to repulse the assault, and so to set upon them with your own and all the ships of your fleet as that, having once begun with them, you may be sure, God willing, not to fail to take them, or, if they will not yield, to sink or fire them. If, because they are but a few ships, and, as I am informed, not well manned, they shall not dare, upon any occasion, to meddle first with you, then you are to take occasion to pick some quarrel with them upon some suspicion of their intent to lie there to colour enemy's goods or countenance his ships, and so to assure or take them, or otherwise to sink them and fire them. In which you are, as you see occasion, to make as probable and just a ground of a quarrel as may be, and, if you can, to make it their quarrel, not yours. But howsoever, if you can meet with them you may not fail to take, sink, or fire them."[2]

With his usual readiness to obey orders as soon as he understood what they meant, Pennington prepared to obey. He had 'now fifteen ships altogether;' but he complained that the Londoners had taken no trouble to make the vessels extorted from them worthy of his Majesty's service. The ships themselves were 'very mean things.' They were undermanned, and those who had been sent on board were chiefly landsmen and boys. With two of the King's ships he would undertake to beat the whole fleet.[3]

[1] The King to Buckingham, Dec. 22, *S. P. Dom.* x'ii. 67.
[2] Secret instructions from Buckingham to Pennington, Dec. 24, *S. P. Dom.* xlii. 81.   [3] Pennington to Buckingham, Dec. 28, *ibid.* xlii. 100.

The value of Pennington's squadron was not to be tested this time. Buckingham had been completely misinformed. Havre roads were empty, and after a few days' cruise Pennington arrived at Falmouth, having done nothing at all, except that he had fired into ten Dutch men-of war, believing them to be Dunkirkers. He was himself not well pleased with the result. "Consider," he wrote to Buckingham, "what a desperate employment you put upon me, to be sent out at this time of year with three weeks' victual, having long dark nights, base ships, and ill-fitted with munition and worse manned, so that if we come to any service it is almost impossible we can come off with honour or safety."[1]

<small>1627. January. Pennington does nothing.</small>

Whilst Pennington was still at sea, Louis's final determination was placed in Charles's hands.[2] Bassompierre's plan for settling the Queen's household, which had been even more favourable to France than a scheme of which Louis had expressed his approval in October,[3] was now entirely disavowed. The King of France, Charles was to be informed, was unwilling to accept anything short of the complete execution of the marriage contract. Nevertheless, at his mother's intercession, he would consent to some changes, though they were to be far fewer than those to which his ambassador had agreed. As for the ships, if the King of England would fix a day for liberating the French prizes, he would do the same on his side.

<small>Final demands of France.</small>

The answer was regarded in England as a personal affront. Buckingham informed Richelieu that his master now considered himself free from all former obligations about the household, and that France, having begun the seizure of the English vessels unjustly, must be the first to make reparation.[4]

<small>Their rejection.</small>

Open war could hardly be averted much longer. The

---

[1] Pennington to Buckingham, Jan. 10, *S. P. Dom.* xlviii. 26.

[2] The letter in Bassompierre's *Negotiations* (312) is undated, but was written in the end of December.

[3] Louis XIII. to Bassompierre, Oct. $\frac{21}{31}$, *Neg.* 153.

[4] Buckingham to Richelieu, Jan. (?) 1627, Crowe's *History of France*, iii. 515.

marriage treaty of 1624, so fair in its promise, had borne its
bitter fruits. The attempt to bind too closely nations
differing in policy and religion had failed. The
English Government had made up its mind to involve Catholic France in a declared war in defence of Protestantism in Germany. The French Government had made up its mind to secure toleration for the English Catholics. When hopes that should never have been entertained failed to be realised, there was disappointment and irritation on both sides. Then came the interference of Charles on behalf of Rochelle, the quarrel about the prize goods, and the quarrel about the Queen's household, all of them perhaps matters capable of settlement between Governments anxious to find points of agreement, but almost impossible of settlement between Governments already prepared to take umbrage at one another's conduct.

Cause of the rupture with France.

How was a Government which had failed so signally in making war against Spain, to make war against France and Spain at the same time? Even at Charles's Court it was acknowledged that, in the long run, the contest which had been provoked would be beyond the strength of England. Yet there were those who thought—and Buckingham was doubtless one of the number—that the English superiority at sea was so manifest that it would be possible to re-establish the independence of Rochelle and to drive the French commerce from the seas, before either France or Spain would be strong enough to make resistance.[1]

How was England to fight France and Spain?

Was it certain, however, that even this temporary superiority at sea would be maintained? Again and again, during the autumn and winter, mobs of sailors had broken away from discipline, and had flocked up to London to demand their pay by battering at the doors of the Lord Admiral or the Treasurer of the Navy; and now Pennington's crews were breaking out into open mutiny at Stokes Bay. The three months for which the City fleet had been lent were nearly at an end, and when orders were given to weigh anchor and to make sail for the westward, the men responded with

Mutiny in Pennington's fleet.

---

[1] This is the substance of an undated paper amongst the *State Papers, France*, which seems to have come from some one of authority.

shouts of 'Home! home!' and refused to touch a rope unless they were assured that they would be allowed to return to the Downs.¹

Commission of inquiry into the state of the Navy. After the return of Willoughby's fleet, the state of the Navy had at last compelled Charles to order a special commission of inquiry, and the defects of the King's ships were being daily dragged to light. The workmen at Chatham, the Commissioners discovered, had not received their wages for a year. The sailors on board some of the ships were in the greatest distress. They had neither clothes on their backs nor shoes on their feet, and they had no credit on shore to supply these deficiencies.²

Yet, in spite of all these disclosures, orders were given to prepare a great fleet of eighty ships for the summer. French prizes were now beginning to come in, and would doubtless meet part of the expense. The revenue had been anticipated to the amount of 236,000*l.*³ The utmost economy was practised in the Royal household. If only the loan could be collected, all might yet be well for a season.

Progress of the loan. In January the Privy Councillors and other persons of note appointed to act as Commissioners for the loan started for the counties assigned to them. It was thought that men who had closed their purses tightly in the presence of the local Commissioners would be chary of offering a refusal to the Lords of the Council. In the majority of cases, the effect produced was doubtless great. Of the reports sent up in the first three months of the new year, the greater part of those preserved must have been tolerably satisfactory to the King. Berkshire made but little difficulty. The university and city of Oxford showed alacrity in the business. In Cheshire there was ready obedience.⁴ In Somerset, Hereford, Shropshire, Stafford, Durham, all but a small number were ready to pay.⁵ Nor does this afford matter for surprise. The immediate risk

---

¹ Philpot to Buckingham, Jan. 15, *S. P. Dom.* xlix. 37.
² Order of the Commissioners, Jan. 16, *ibid.* xlix. 68.
³ *Ibid.* xlvii. 55.
⁴ *S. P. Dom.* xlix. 12, 36; lvi. 72.
⁵ *Ibid.* liii. 88, liv. 28, lvi. 89, lix. 6.

was great. The refuser might be cast into prison, or sent to be knocked on the head in some chance skirmish in the German wars. Except for the most resolute and self-sacrificing, the temptation to escape the danger by the payment of a few shillings, or even a few pounds, was too strong to be resisted. Yet, small as the number of refusers was, the Government could not afford to pass lightly over their denial. It represented a vast amount of suppressed discontent, and the men from whom it proceeded were often in the enjoyment of high personal consideration in their respective neighbourhoods. In some counties their example spread widely amongst all classes. In Essex some of the local Commissioners themselves refused to pay.[1] In Northamptonshire twenty-two of the principal gentry, followed by more than half the county, offered so decided a resistance that the itinerant Privy Councillors at once bound over the gentlemen to appear before the Board at Whitehall, and sent up a number of refractory persons of lesser quality to be mustered for service under the King of Denmark. In Gloucestershire twelve out of twenty-five Commissioners refused to pay, and the example thus given was widely followed.[2] In Lincolnshire, at the end of January, only two or three persons had given their consent.[3] The Council was in no great hurry to proceed to strong measures. Most of the members were absent from London as Commissioners, and during the greater part of February some twenty gentlemen were allowed to remain in confinement without receiving any summons to appear before the Board. When no signs of submission appeared they were called up and commanded to obey the King. The threat produced no impression on them. The flower of the English gentry refused to admit the justice of the

Growing resistance.

---

[1] *S. P. Dom.* liv. 47.

[2] Manchester, Exeter, and Coke to Buckingham, Jan. 12 : Northampton and Bridgeman to the Council, Feb. 17, *ibid.* xlix. 8, liv. 28.

[3] Contarini to the Doge, Feb. $\frac{2}{12}$, *Ven. Transcripts, R. O.* —— to Meade, Feb. 2, *Court and Times,* i. 191. The story of the riot and attack on the house in which the Commissioners were sitting is contradicted by Meade on the evidence of a Lincolnshire gentleman. The rumours of the day contained in this correspondence must be received with great caution.

demand, and every one of the offenders was sent back to the restraint from which he had come.

The battle once engaged had to be fought out to the end. It would never do to accept payment from the weak and to allow the strong to go free. A fresh attempt to overcome the opposition in Lincolnshire ended somewhat better than the former one. Still there were sixty-eight recusants. Ten of them, who were Commissioners, were sent up to answer for their refusal before the Council. Others followed not long afterwards. The Earl of Lincoln was detected in agitating against the loan, and was sent to the Tower.[1]

<small>March. The Earl of Lincoln sent to the Tower.</small>

Reports of the confusion which prevailed poured in from every side. Soldiers were wandering about the country, to the dismay of quiet householders. "And besides," wrote Wimbledon to Secretary Coke, "there are many vagabonds that, in the name of soldiers, do outrages and thefts." The laws seemed to be powerless against them, and yet "there was never time more needful to have such laws put in execution, in regard of the great liberty that people take, more than they were wont." These obstructions to the well-being of the commonwealth must be cleared away 'rather at this time than at any other, for that the world is something captious at all things that are commanded without a parliament.' Wimbledon's remedy was the appointment of a provost-marshal in every shire. This advice was adopted, and the men were thus brought under martial law.[2]

The spirit of resistance was abroad. On February 28 orders were given by the Council to press fifty of the Essex refusers for the King of Denmark; but the poorer classes were learning, from the example of the gentry, to stand upon their rights. With one consent the men refused to take the press-money, the reception of which would consign them to bondage. On March 16 there was a long debate on their case in the Privy Council, and some of its members, with more zeal than knowledge, recommended

<small>February. Resistance of the poorer classes.</small>

<small>March.</small>

---

[1] *S. P. Dom.* lvi. 39. Meade to Stuteville, March 17, *Court and Times,* i. 207.

[2] Wimbledon to Coke, Feb. 23, *Melbourne MSS.*

that they should be hanged, under the authority of martial law. Coventry was too good a lawyer to admit this doctrine. Martial law, he explained, was applicable to soldiers only, and men who had not yet received press-money were not soldiers. The order given for sending these bold men of Essex to the slaughter was accordingly rescinded, and they were left to be dealt with —if they could be dealt with at all—in some other way.[1]

The names of these obscure men have been long ago forgotten ; but that persons of no great repute should have been found on the list of those who were willing to suffer persecution for their rights as Englishmen is a thing not to be forgotten. It was the surest warrant that the resistance, though led by an aristocracy, was no merely aristocratic uprising. The cause concerned rich and poor alike, and rich and poor stepped forward to suffer for it—each class in its own way. The day would come, if they were pressed hard, when rich and poor would step forward to fight for it.

Amongst the names better known to the England of that day are to be found three which will never be forgotten as long as the English tongue remains the language of civilised men. John Hampden, the young Buckinghamshire squire, known as yet merely as a diligent Member of Parliament, active in preparing the case against Buckingham in the last session,[2] but taking no part in the public debates, was amongst the foremost on the beadroll of honour to be called up to London, on January 29, to answer for his refusal to pay the loan. Eliot's summons in May and his subsequent imprisonment need no explanation. With Hampden and Eliot and many another whose names are only less honoured than theirs, was Sir Thomas Wentworth.

Hampden, Eliot, and Wentworth.

If Wentworth had good reasons for opposing the free gift, he had still better reasons for opposing the forced loan. Scarcely a shred was left of that freedom of choice which, at least in appearance, accompanied the

Wentworth's opposition.

---

[1] Meade to Stuteville, March 17, 24, *Court and Times*, i. 207, 208. This hearsay evidence is corroborated by the order in the *Council Register*, March 19, for rescinding the directions for the press.

[2] Forster, *Sir J. Eliot*, i. 290.

former demand. An attempt to draw money illegally from Wentworth's purse was an insult which he would have been inclined to resent even if Charles had intended to employ it for purposes of which he approved. He knew that the present loan was to be employed for purposes of which he entirely disapproved. To talk to him about the patriotism of lending money for a war with Spain, and, for all he knew, for a war with France too, was adding mockery to the insult. What he wanted was to see the Crown and Parliament turning their attention to domestic improvement. Instead of that, Charles and Buckingham were ruining the sources of their influence by forcing the nation to support unwillingly an extravagant and ill-conducted war.

That the forced loan was not a loan in any true sense it was impossible to deny. There was no reasonable prospect of its repayment, and money thus given was a subsidy in all but name. That Parliament alone could grant a subsidy was a doctrine which no Englishman would be likely directly to deny, and which few Englishmen not living under the immediate shadow of the Court would be likely even indirectly to deny.

Wentworth, however, as usual contented himself with passive opposition. His old rival, Sir John Savile, threw himself into the vacancy which Wentworth had made, and was able to report in April that the success of the loan in Yorkshire was entirely owing to his exertions.[1] For the present Wentworth was suffered to stand aloof, taking his ease at his ancestral manor of Wentworth Woodhouse. At last, as the summer wore on, he was summoned before the Council, answered courteously but firmly that he would not lend, and was placed under restraint. Before the end of June he was sent into confinement in Kent. The last resource of the King was to banish the leading opposers of the loan to counties as far away as possible from their own homes.[2]

The forced loan in Yorkshire.

At Court the views which prevailed on the subject of the

---

[1] Savile to Buckingham, April 4, 1627, *S. P. Dom.* lix. 35.

[2] *Council Register*, June 16, 20, 27, 29. Manchester to the King, July 5, *S. P. Dom.* lxx. 32.

war with France were diametrically opposed to those which commended themselves to Wentworth. Charles did not indeed either abandon his wish to recover the Palatinate or conceal from himself the hindrance which a French war would be to the accomplishment of that design; but he was deeply persuaded that, whatever the consequences might be, he could not act otherwise than he had done. His explanation of the whole matter was very simple. Richelieu had at first meant well. But he was a priest after all. He had been bribed by the Court of Rome with an offer of the high position of Papal Legate in France, to set his whole mind upon the extirpation of the Huguenots.

January. Charles's opinion of the war with France.

Believes Richelieu to be bought by the Pope,

If such an estimate of Richelieu's character strikes those who hear of it at the present day as too monstrous to have been seriously entertained, it must not be forgotten that good judges of character are rare, and that Charles had neither the materials before him which are in our days accessible in profusion, nor the dispassionate judgment which would have enabled him to extract the truth from what materials he had. On one point he was quite clear. He himself had been always in the right. The treaty between France and England had been directly violated by the seizures of English ships and goods in France. What had been done in England had been a necessity of State policy. The Queen's household had intrigued with the English Catholics and had sown distrust between himself and his wife. Bassompierre had set matters straight, but had been disavowed by Louis in a fit of ill-temper.[1]

and himself to have been always right.

If Charles and his ministers misunderstood the motives and underrated the difficulties of the great statesman with whom they had to do, they were equally blind to the secret of his power. They watched the struggles of the inhabitants of Rochelle, and fancied that strength was there. They watched the seething discontent of the French

Has no doubt of the weakness of France.

[1] This is the main result of the language used by Holland to Contarini in giving an account of the opinion prevailing at Court. Contarini to the Doge, $\frac{\text{Jan. 26}}{\text{Feb. 5}}$, *Ven. Transcripts, R. O*

aristocracy, and fancied that strength was there. They thought that they had but to strike hard enough, and the overthrow of the Cardinal would be the work of a few months. They did not see that they were aiming, not at the abasement of a minister but at the disintegration of a nation, and that the effective strength of the nation would fly in the face of the audacious foreigners who based their calculations on its divisions.

In one point Charles was not deceived. The French had nothing afloat which could look the English Navy in the face.

<small>March. Pennington attacks the French shipping.</small>
In March Pennington was let loose upon the French shipping,[1] and English cruisers swept the seas from Calais to Bordeaux. The goods on board the prizes were sold without delay. The effect was instantaneous. In the winter sailors and soldiers alike had been on the verge of mutiny. Rioters had thronged the streets of London, crying out upon the Duke for the pay of which they had been defrauded. Before the summer came the preparations for the great expedition were going gaily forward. There was money in hand to pay the men for a time, and to buy provisions. France, it seemed, would provide the means for her own ruin.

Buckingham was this time to go himself in command.

<small>February. Buckingham's overtures to Spain.</small>
With the prospect of increased responsibility, even he looked uneasily at the enormous forces of the two great monarchies which he and his master had provoked. He determined to make overtures to Spain.

The proposal was not to be made through any accredited agent of the Crown. In proportion as the policy of the English Government came to revolve round the favourite minister, there sprang up a new swarm of courtier-like diplomatists, whose chief qualification for employment was to be found in their dependence on the great Duke. Such a one was Edward Clarke, who had been employed on many a delicate mission by Buckingham, and who had been reprimanded by the Commons at Oxford on account of the indecent warmth with

[1] Instructions to Pennington, March 3, 11, 12, *S. P. Dom.* lvi. 18, 85, 90.

which he defended his patron. Such a one too was Balthazar Gerbier, architect and connoisseur, born in Zealand of French refugee parents,[1] and settled in England—a man at home in every nation and specially attached to none. In 1625 he had accompanied Buckingham to Paris, and had there met Rubens, who was engaged to paint Buckingham's portrait, and who coveted the distinction of a diplomatist as well as that of a painter. Rubens then talked fluently to the Duke of the advantages to England of peace with Spain; but as yet the tongue of the great artist had no charm for Buckingham. The Cadiz expedition, with all its expected triumphs, was still before him.

In January, 1627, Gerbier was again in Paris, where he seems again to have met Rubens, who held much the same language as he had done two years before.[2] Buckingham, when he heard what had been said, resolved to avail himself of the opportunity offered to him, but, to do him justice, when he now sent Gerbier to Brussels to take up the broken thread of these conversations, it was no cowardly desertion of his allies which he was planning. Just as when he made war with Spain he was sanguine enough to suppose that he could get everything he wanted by plunging into war, so now that he was ready to make peace, he was sanguine enough to expect to get everything he wanted for the mere asking. Gerbier was ostensibly to open negotiations for the purchase of a collection of pictures and antiques, but in reality to propose that a suspension of arms should be agreed upon with a view to peace. This suspension of arms was to include the Dutch Republic and the King of Denmark.

Such a proposal was doomed to rejection, unless Charles was ready to abandon the Dutch. With them Spain would make neither truce nor peace unless they would open the Scheldt, and tacitly abandon their claim to independence.[3]

---

[1] Sainsbury, *Papers relating to Rubens*, 316.

[2] That the overture came from Rubens was afterwards stated by Buckingham, and is implied in an undated letter from Gerbier to Rubens in the Archives at Brussels.

[3] The Infanta Isabella to Philip IV., Feb. $\frac{18}{28}$, *Brussels MSS.*

Rubens, of course, by the direction of the Infanta Isabella, replied courteously to Gerbier; but he assured him, with truth,[1] that the King of Spain had no longer any great influence in Germany, and could do nothing in a hurry about the King of Denmark. There would be a difficulty, too, about the Dutch, who insisted upon receiving the title of independent States. The best thing would be to treat for a separate peace between Spain and England. If Charles, in short, would throw over his allies he would then see what Spain would think fit to do for him.[2] The claims put forward by Spain, were, however, out of all proportion to her strength. The siege of Breda had completely exhausted the treasury. Never, wrote the Infanta, had she been in such straits for money. If the enemy took the field she saw no means to resist him.[3]

<small>Answer of Rubens.</small>

Before the end of February Gerbier was in London, telling his story to Buckingham. Baltimore, the Calvert of earlier days, was for the first time since his dismissal from office summoned to consultation with the favourite. Buckingham failed to see that, at a time when England had ceased to have any terrors for Spain, it was madness to expect to impose on her such a peace as he designed. He sent Carleton to acquaint the Dutch ambassador, Joachimi, with all that had passed. Joachimi was to be asked to consult the States-General, assuring them that nothing would be done without their consent.

<small>Gerbier returns to London.</small>

<small>Joachimi informed.</small>

Joachimi was frightened. He could not understand how Buckingham could seriously expect, under the circumstances, to bring about a general pacification in Germany and the Netherlands, and he not unnaturally fancied that the proposal made to him was only the prelude to a separate peace between England and Spain. He was the more uneasy as Charles was absent at Newmarket, and he supposed, whether correctly or

---

[1] The Infanta's correspondence in the previous year, 1626, is full of accounts of an abortive attempt at an alliance with the Emperor.

[2] *Sainsbury*, 68–76.

[3] The Infanta Isabella to Philip IV., March $\frac{10}{20}$, *Brussels MSS.*

not cannot now be known, that Charles was to be kept in
ignorance till it was too late for him to remonstrate. His
suspicions were increased when he learned that Conway knew
nothing about the matter, and that when that usually submis-
sive Secretary was informed of what was passing, he burst out
into angry talk, and actually called his 'most excellent patron'
a Judas.

What Buckingham might have been induced to do, it is
impossible to say. Most probably he had, as yet, no fixed
design. At all events, if he had meant to keep the
secret from Charles, he was now obliged to abandon
the idea. Taking Baltimore with him, he went to
Newmarket, and invited all the Privy Councillors on the spot
to discuss the matter in the King's presence. Their opinions
were not favourable to the chances of the negotiation. Charles
himself, though he would not refuse to listen to anything that
the Spaniards might have further to say, positively declined to
abandon either his brother-in-law or the States-General. It was
finally arranged that Carleton should go as ambassador to the Hague, upon a special mission for which
it was easy to find an excuse. In reality he was
to take the opportunity of persuading the Dutch to accept
any reasonable offers of peace which might reach him from
Brussels, and Gerbier was directed to inform Rubens that
England would not treat apart from the States-General. The
pacification of Germany might, however, be left to a separate
negotiation.[1]

Feb. 28. The King consulted.

Terms on which the negotiation is to proceed.

Whilst the Spanish Government was amusing England
with negotiations which it had no expectation of being able
to bring to a conclusion satisfactory to itself,[2]
Olivares was making use of Buckingham's overtures in another direction. He showed his letters
from Brussels to the French ambassador at Madrid, and, by

Agreement between France and Spain.

---

[1] Joachimi to the States-General, March $\frac{3, 9}{13, 19}$. *Add. MSS.* 17,677,
M, fol. 43, 48. Contarini to the Doge, $\frac{\text{Feb. 27}}{\text{March 9}}$, March $\frac{\ }{19}$. *Ven. Transcripts, R. O.* Sainsbury, 76-80.

[2] Philip IV. to the Infanta Isabella, $\frac{\text{May 22}}{\text{June 1}}$, *Brussels MSS.*

holding up before his eyes the unwelcome prospect of peace between Spain and England, frightened him into signing an engagement between France and Spain for common action against England. This engagement was at once ratified in Paris.¹ It was so clearly against the political interests of Spain to support the growing power of France, that it has generally been supposed that the Spanish Government had no intention of fulfilling its promises. It has, however, been forgotten that at Madrid religious took precedence of political considerations. The letters written by Philip IV. at the time leave no doubt that he contemplated with delight the renewal of an alliance with a Catholic country, and that if he afterwards failed to assist Louis in his hour of danger, it was his poverty rather than his will that was at fault.²

March 16.

April 10.

Between Charles and Buckingham there was much in common. Both were ever sanguine of success, and inclined to overlook the difficulties in their path. But whilst Buckingham was apt to fancy that he could create means to accomplish his ends, Charles was apt to fancy that he could accomplish his ends without creating means at all. In the midst of his preparations for war with France, he still thought it possible to intervene with effect in Germany. In the spring of 1627 there was indeed just a chance of retrieving Christian's defeat at Lutter if Charles could have given efficient support to his uncle. With the merely nominal support which he was now able to give, there was practically no chance at all.

The war in Germany.

The one bright spot in Christian's situation was that for a time he had to contend with Tilly alone. Wallenstein was away in Hungary, keeping Mansfeld and Bethlen Gabor at bay. Before long, however, he reduced Bethlen Gabor to sue for peace. Mansfeld, hopeless of success, directed his course towards Venice, and died on the way. Wallenstein, relieved from danger, was thus enabled to

Wallenstein in Hungary.

---

¹ Philip IV. to the Infanta Isabella, April $\frac{1,}{11,}$ May $\frac{22}{\text{June 1}}$. Philip IV. to Mirabel, $\frac{\text{May 22}}{\text{June 1}}$, *Brussels MSS.*

² Richelieu, *Mémoires*, iii. 282 ; Siri, *Mem. Rec.* vi. 257.

bring back his troops to North Germany before the summer was over. Yet, if Charles had been an ally worth having at all, he would by that time have enabled Christian to strike a blow which might have changed the whole complexion of affairs.

Charles had at his disposal only the four regiments which had been sent to defend the Netherlands in 1624. Their term of service was now expired. The offer to place them at the King of Denmark's service sounded like a mockery to Christian. He calculated that, by the treaty of the Hague, 600,000*l.* were now due to him from England, and Charles, who had no money to spare, offered to send him jewels instead. There was no demand for jewels in Denmark, and Christian complained bitterly. "Let God and the world," he said, "judge whether this be answerable or Christianlike dealing."[1] Even the four regiments were not what they ought to have been. They should have numbered 6,000 men, but their commander, Sir Charles Morgan, reported in April that when the men were mustered to go on board ship at Enkhuisen, only 2,472 answered to their names.[2] The others had fallen a prey to the general disorganisation of the English administration. The pay had come in slowly. Many of the officers knew nothing of military service, and were living in England whilst the soldiers were left to their own devices in the Netherlands.

Such as they were, the skeletons of the four regiments were shipped for the Elbe. From time to time recruits were sent from England to fill up their numbers. Men pressed against their will, and men sent abroad because they had refused to pay the loan, were expected to hold head against Tilly's triumphant veterans. With all the efforts of the English Government the numbers never reached their full complement. On June 1, Morgan had not quite 5,000 under his command. Disease and desertion soon thinned the ranks, and it was found impossible to keep up even that number. A

---

[1] Statement by the King of Denmark, Feb. 26, *S. P. Denmark.*
[2] Morgan to Carleton, March 27; Memorial, April 7, *S. P. Denmark.*

jewel which Charles sent proved entirely useless. It was valued at 100,000*l.*, but no one in Denmark would advance such a sum upon it.[1] One more failure was about to be added to the many which had baffled the sanguine hopes of Buckingham and his master.

[1] Anstruther to Conway, June 16, *S. P. Denmark.*

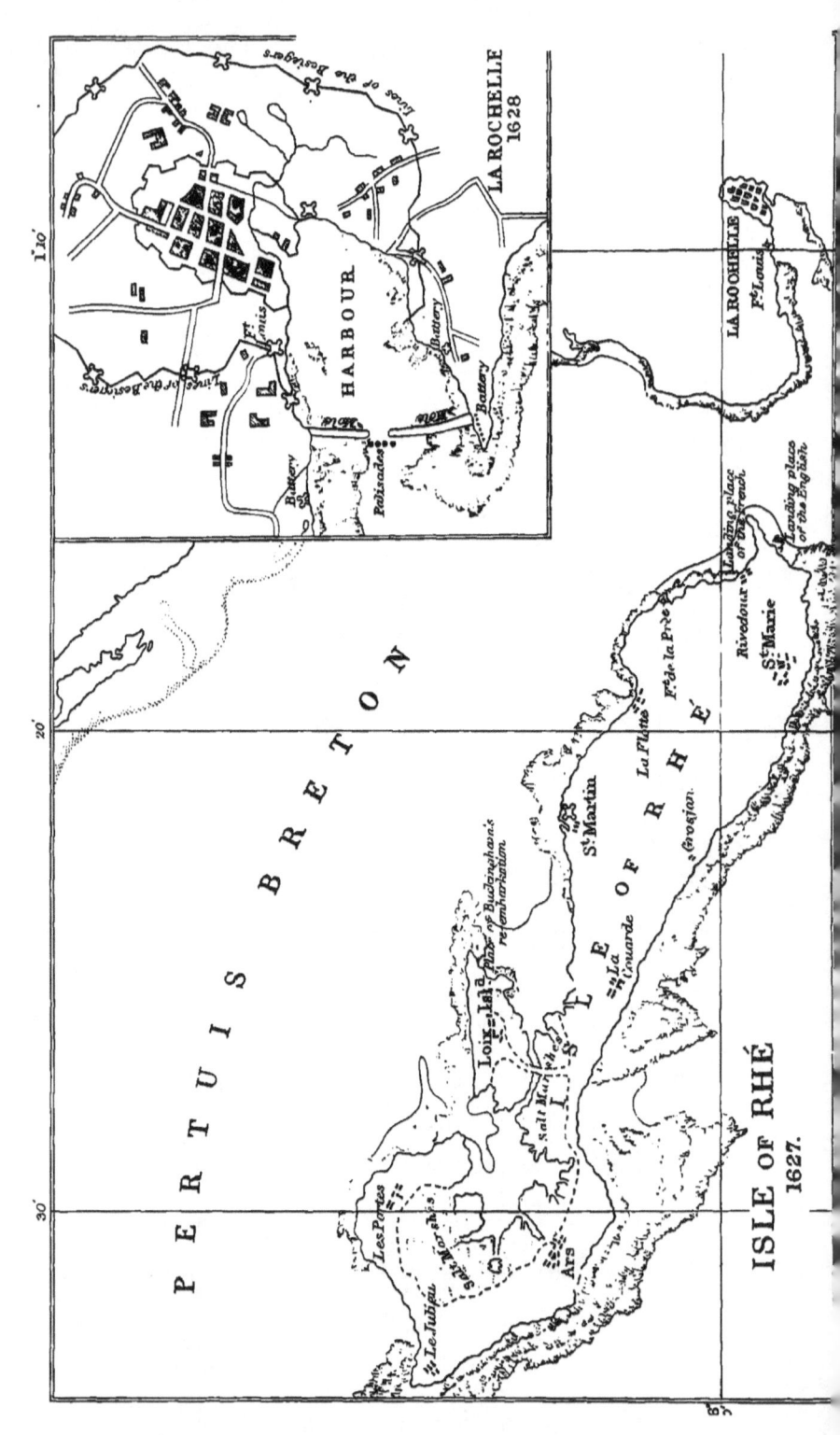

CHAPTER LX.

THE EXPEDITION TO RHÉ.

To fight in Germany still formed part of the plan of the English King, but his heart—and, what was of still greater importance, the heart of the favourite—was now elsewhere.

April. Charles hopes for success against France.

Charles was deeply wounded by the refusal of the King of France to agree to Bassompierre's plan for his household arrangements, and by Richelieu's evident intention to make France powerful by sea. He fell into the mistake into which others have fallen before and after him, of fancying that any weapon was good enough to be used against a hostile Government, and that if he could raise a sufficient number of adversaries against Richelieu it would be unnecessary for him to inquire what cause they represented or what moral weight they possessed.

That the French aristocracy were highly discontented with Richelieu was no secret to anyone, and Charles and Buckingham determined to send an agent to fan the flame of their discontent. Walter Montague, the youngest son of the Earl of Manchester, one of those sprightly young men who sunned themselves in the light of Buckingham's favour, was selected for the mission. In Lorraine it was expected that he would find the Duchess of Chevreuse, whose bright eyes and witty tongue were inspired by a genius for political intrigue, and who had been exiled from France in consequence of the part which she had taken against the Cardinal. She had been a partisan of the English alliance from the beginning, and it is believed that in 1624 she counted the English

Montague's mission.

ambassador Holland amongst her numerous lovers. Buckingham now hoped that she would allure the Duke of Lorraine to attack France from the east, whilst the communications which she still kept up with her friends at home would be of service in preparing trouble for the French Government nearer Paris. Still greater hopes were founded on the Court of Turin. The restless Charles Emmanuel, who had spent his youth in attacking France and his middle age in attacking Spain, was now believed to be willing to turn his arms once more against his first enemy. With him was the Count of Soissons, a French Prince of the Blood, who disliked the government of the Cardinal, and was pressing for a Savoyard force to enable him to invade his native country.

Such were the allies with whose help Buckingham hoped to effect a diversion for his great enterprise. The great enterprise itself had something in it of a loftier strain. Cool reason may suggest that the continued independence of the French Protestants was in the long run likely to bring ruin on themselves ; but the dangers attending upon complete submission to a Catholic Government were so patent that wiser men than Buckingham might easily have become enthusiastic in the defence of Rochelle. For such a defence the time appeared favourable. The Duke of Rohan, whose authority was great in the south of France, was to raise the Protestants of Languedoc, and to welcome Soissons on the one side, whilst he gave his support to the Rochellese on the other.[1]

All through the spring preparations were going on in England. In the beginning of May the new levies which were to make up the wrecks of the Cadiz regiments to 8,000 men were beginning to gather round Portsmouth, but the reports which were sent to the Government were not encouraging. Of 200 furnished by the county of Hants, 120 were 'such base rogues' that it was useless to keep them. No money had been sent down to meet the wants of the men.[2] The troops gathered at Southampton and

May. Preparations in England.

---

[1] Buckingham's plans from time to time may be gathered far best from Contarini's despatches.
[2] Blundell to Buckingham, May 1. *S. P. Dom.* lxxii. 6.

Winchester were ready to mutiny for want of pay.¹ The deputy lieutenants, whose duty it was to collect the men and send them forward, were hard put to it to satisfy the King and their neighbours too. In Dorsetshire the Isle of Purbeck refused to send men at all, and the officials who had advanced the money required for the clothing and support of the levies on the march to Portsmouth, complained that the county had refused a rate for the purpose, and that they had heard nothing of any order from the Lord Treasurer for their repayment.² A few days later came a fresh order for 150 more men. The men were found, and were sent away amidst the tears and cries of their wives and children. On June 3, Sir John Borough, the old soldier who was going as second in command of the expedition, wrote that the surgeons' chests were still unfurnished. A warrant had been given for the money, but it was not paid, nor likely to be. If men were to be expected to fight, care must be had to preserve them when they were hurt. Shirts, shoes, and stockings too were wanting, and the arms had not yet arrived. Yet he hoped that, when 'armed and clothed, the men would be fit to be employed.'³

In spite of every drawback, the armament, with the help of the French prize-money, was approaching completion. The King went down to Portsmouth to see the fleet, dined on board the Admiral's ship, and talked merrily about the prospects of the voyage.⁴ The Duke followed soon afterwards, boasting as he went of what he would do to re-establish the reputation of the English Navy, which had been tarnished by the failure at Cadiz and by Willoughby's disaster.⁵

June 11. The King at Portsmouth.

The instructions issued to Buckingham were dated on June 19.⁶ The view which Charles took of his relations to the

---

¹ Mason to Nicholas, May 7, *ibid.* lxii. 70.
² Deputy Lieutenants of Dorsetshire to the Council, May 30, June 8, *ibid.* lxv. 19, lxvi. 41.
³ Burgh to Buckingham, June 3, *ibid.* lxvi. 19.
⁴ Mason to Nicholas, June 11, *ibid.* lxvi. 67.
⁵ Contarini to the Doge, June $\frac{19}{29}$, *Ven. Transcripts, R. O.*
⁶ Instructions to Buckingham, June 19, *S. P. Dom.* lxvii. 57.

French Government was very much the same as that which he had taken of his relations to the House of Commons. Both had urged him to war with Spain. Both, for their own objects, had basely deserted him. As Seymour, Phelips, and Eliot wished to make themselves masters of England, Richelieu wished to make himself master of the sea. Charles was therefore only acting in self-defence. "Our nearest allies," he maintained, "even those who have counselled us to the same war, have taken advantage to encroach upon our rights, to ruin our friends, and to root out that religion whereof by just title we are the defender. Our resolution therefore is, under the shield of God's favour, to prosecute our just defence." Buckingham was therefore to consider as his first business how to suppress all attempts on the part of Spain or France to interfere with English commerce and to destroy or capture the ships of either nation. Secondly, he was to conduct to Rochelle certain regiments which were needed by the French Protestants in consequence of the refusal of Louis to carry out the stipulations of the treaty of the preceding year. He was to explain to the Rochellese that there was no intention of raising a rebellion in France on any pretence of English interests, but that he was come on hearing that they were shortly to be besieged in defiance of the treaty, for the maintenance of which the King of England's honour had been engaged. He was then to ask them if they still required assistance, and were willing to enter into mutual engagements with England. If the answer was 'negative or doubtful,' all the land soldiers not needed for other purposes were to be sent back to England. If the answer was in the affirmative, the troops were to be handed over to Soubise, who was to accompany the expedition. Buckingham was then to go on with the fleet to recover the English vessels detained at Bordeaux, and, having made good his claim to the mastery of the sea on the coast of France, was to pass on to break up the trade between Spain and the West Indies and between Spain and Flanders. After scouring the coasts of Spain and Portugal, he was, if he thought fit, to despatch divisions of his fleet to the Mediterranean, to the Azores, and even to Newfoundland, in search of French or Spanish prizes.

Such were the instructions, drawn up doubtless with Buckingham's full concurrence, under which the fleet was to sail. In them the aid to Rochelle is mentioned almost in an apologetic manner, as if it were only secondary to the greater object of maintaining the dominion of the seas. It may be that doubts were already entertained at the English Court of the extent to which any meddling with the French national feeling was likely to find favour in France. At all events it was already rumoured in London that not a few amongst the Huguenot population of the South were unwilling to join a foreign invader against their own sovereign, and that doubts had been expressed even in Rochelle itself of the feasibility of resisting the forces opposed to the city with the aid of such help as Buckingham, variable and inconstant as he was, was likely to bring to its succour.[1]

On June 27 the fleet, numbering some hundred sail, and carrying 6,000 foot and 100 horse,[2] left Stokes Bay with a favourable wind. Except a few Dunkirkers, who made all haste to escape, Buckingham saw nothing of any enemy. The first part of the Admiral's instructions, which enjoined upon him the duty of sweeping the Spaniards and French from the seas, could not be fulfilled because Spaniards and French alike kept carefully within their ports. A poetaster of the day seized the glorious opportunity of declaring that King Charles was superior to Edward III. or Elizabeth. Whilst they had only conquered their enemies, he found no enemy willing to meet him.[3]

Sailing of the fleet.

---

[1] Contarini to the Doge, May $\frac{10}{20}$, *Ven. Transripts, R. O.*

[2] *Herbert* (Philobiblon Society's edition), 46. The common soldiers embarked numbered 5,934. *S. P. Dom.* lxxxii. 431.

[3] May (*S. P. Dom.* lxviii. 74) made Neptune address the King thus :—

> "I saw third Edward stain my flood
>   By Sluys with slaughtered Frenchmen's blood :
>   And from Eliza's fleet
>   I saw the vanquished Spaniards fly.
>   But 'twas a greater mastery,
>   No foe at all to meet ;
>   When they, without their ruin or dispute,
>   Confess thy reign as sweet as absolute."

On the evening of July 10, Buckingham cast anchor off St. Martin's, the principal town of the Isle of Rhé, lying on the shore towards the mainland, and guarded by the new fort which had been recently erected, and which, with the smaller fort of La Prée on the island and with Fort Louis on the mainland, served to hold in check the commerce of Rochelle. The next day was spent in collecting the fleet as it came in, and in battering La Prée. On the morning of the 12th a council of war was held. Sir William Becher, accompanied by Soubise and an agent of Rohan, was to go to Rochelle to discover whether the citizens would accept the hand held out to them. The English troops were to be landed at once upon the island.

July 10.
Buckingham at Rhé.

July 11.

July 12.

There were reasons apart from the decision of the Rochellese which made Buckingham anxious to place himself in possession of Rhé. If only it could be brought into English hands it would be a thorn in the side of the rising French commerce. Its ports within the still waters of the strait which divided it from the mainland would be an admirable gathering-place for English privateers, whilst its situation in the close neighbourhood of the Protestant populations of Southern France would open the door to a skilful use of religious and political intrigue. Its salt marshes too, which were in high repute all over Europe, would offer a valuable source of revenue to the English exchequer.

In the afternoon the preparations for landing near the eastern point of the island were completed. Buckingham, on his first day of actual warfare, showed no lack of spirit or intelligence. He was to be found everywhere, listening to information and urging on the men. When the troops descended into the boats it was evident that opposition would be offered. Toiras, the Governor of St. Martin's, the commander who had insidiously broken peace with Rochelle two years before, had collected a force of some 1,200[1] foot and 200 horse to dispute the landing of the English. Covered by

The landing.

---

[1] The numbers vary in different accounts from one to more than two thousand.

the fire of the ships the boats put off. The great defect of the English army was at once made manifest. There was no cohesion amongst the men, no tradition of customary discipline. There were some who hastened to take up their place in rank as good soldiers should. There were others, and that too not merely raw recruits, who, weary with the long voyage, lingered on shipboard and turned a deaf ear to the orders of their commanders, or who, even when they reached the shore, hung about the water's edge dabbling their hands in the waves. Among this helpless mass Buckingham, cudgel in hand, went to and fro, 'beating some and threatening others.' When two regiments were on shore, he had to throw himself into a boat and go back to do the like on shipboard. Sir William Courtney's regiment had refused to leave their safe position in the vessels, and without the personal presence of the Duke nothing could be done.[1]

Toiras saw his opportunity. The French horse charged down upon the disordered clusters, and drove them headlong into the sea. Many a brave man, carried away by the rush, perished in the waters. The two colonels, Sir John Burgh and Sir Alexander Brett, did their duty well. Buckingham, perceiving what had happened, hurried back to the post of danger. At last a line was formed, and before the French infantry had time to come up, the horsemen, leaving on the ground nearly half their number, many of them bearing some of the noblest names in France, drew off from the unequal combat. It was thought in the English ranks that, if the enemy's foot had hastened up, the day must have gone otherwise than it did.

The march towards St. Martin's. Of personal bravery Buckingham had shown that he possessed his full share, and in his march towards St. Martin's he gave proof of that consideration for the needs and feelings of others which is no slight element of

---

[1] The account of the early history of the expedition is taken from Graham's journal (*S. P. Dom.* lxxi. 65) compared with another journal (*ibid.* lxxi. 60), and the printed books of Herbert (*The Expedition to the Isle of Rhé*), Philobiblon Society's edition; Isnard (*Arcis Sammartinianæ Obsidio*); *Le Mercure François,* tom. 13, &c.

success. He refused a large sum of money offered him for the ransom of the bodies of the slain Frenchmen, and allowed them to be taken freely away by their friends for burial. He tended his wounded enemies as if they had been his own personal friends. Not content with issuing the usual orders against pillage, he directed that none of his soldiers should even enter a village, and he himself set an example to men less delicately nurtured than himself, by sleeping under a cloak in the open fields. He neglected nothing which would conduce to the comfort of his men. With his own eyes he took care to see that the provisions were landed in due time, and on one occasion he risked his life to save a poor wretch who had been left on a sandbank surrounded by the rising tide.

If only military and political capacity had been granted to Buckingham, he might well have become the idol of his soldiers; but already the unstable foundations on which his enterprise was raised were beginning to make themselves manifest.

Answer from Rochelle. Before he reached St. Martin's he knew that the Rochellese, instead of springing into his arms at a word, were doubtful and hesitating. Soubise thought that they were like slaves too long held in captivity to venture to claim their freedom. Becher thought that the magistrates had been bribed by the King of France. But whatever the explanation might be, the fact was certain that they would not stir till they had consulted their brother Huguenots in the interior of the country. A miserable handful of eighteen volunteers, gradually swelling to 250 men, was all that Rochelle had to offer to her self-constituted deliverer.[1]

According to the letter of the Admiral's instructions, he should have turned elsewhere as soon as he found that no real support was to be expected from Rochelle; but it was one thing for Buckingham to contemplate in England the abandonment of the main object of the expedition, it was another thing for him to turn his back upon the enemy in the Isle of Rhé.

---

[1] Soubise to Buckingham, July $\frac{12}{22}$ (not $\frac{\text{July 22}}{\text{Aug. 1}}$, as calendared). *Becher's Journal.* Symonds to Nicholas, Aug. 15, *S. P. Dom.* lxii. 74, lxxii. 22; i. lxxiv. 9. *Mém. de Rohan,* 211.

He resolved, unsupported as he was, to remain on the island, and to push on the siege of the fort of St. Martin's.

At first all seemed to promise well. Guns were landed and placed in position and the English officers hoped to reduce the place in a short time. A fortnight later they were of another mind. The fort was well garrisoned and vigorously defended. The soil around was rocky and ill-suited for the operations of a siege. What was worse still, there was no longer any cordial co-operation between Buckingham and his chief officers. Men who had served in the hard school of actual warfare were restless under the command of a novice, and the Duke, with his resolute desire to look into everything with his own eyes, may easily have given offence without any intention of being overbearing to those beneath him. Whilst his own forces were diminishing, the French armies were gathering around. Ships were fitting out along the coast, and a land army, under the Duke of Angoulême, was firmly established in the neighbourhood of Rochelle.

<small>July 17. St. Martin's besieged.</small>

To do him justice, Buckingham saw clearly into the heart of the situation. He knew that his chance of obtaining auxiliaries in France depended entirely upon his success or failure at St. Martin's. If force failed, a blockade must be kept up till the fortress surrendered from sheer starvation, and if this was to be done in the face of the threatened succour from the mainland, reinforcements of every kind must be sent from England, and that soon.[1]

By the middle of August the works surrounding the fort had been completed. On the sea side the passage was guarded by the fleet, and a floating boom was thrown round the landing-place to make ingress impossible. In order that hunger might do its work the more speedily, the wives and female relations of the soldiers of the garrison were collected from the town on the 11th, and driven towards the fort. They were told that if they returned they would be

<small>August. The siege turned into a blockade.</small>

---

[1] De Vic to Conway, July 27; Buckingham to Conway, July 28, *Hardwicke S. P.* ii. 23, 27.

put to death without mercy. Toiras at first turned a deaf ear to the cries of these miserable creatures; but the English soldiers knew how to appeal to him in a way which he was unable to resist. Again and again they fired into the midst of the shrieking crowd. One at least, a mother with a child at her breast, was killed on the spot. The demands of the fathers, husbands, and brothers within could no longer be resisted, and the fort received the helpless fugitives, to burden yet more its failing resources.[1] After this barbarity, excused doubtless in the eyes of the English officers as a necessity of war, there is little satisfaction in reading how the commanders corresponded with one another in terms of high-flown courtesy, how Buckingham sent to Toiras a present of a dozen melons, and how Toiras returned the compliment by sending some bottles of citron-flower water to his assailant.

It was well known in the English camp that the resources of the besieged were limited; but the numbers of the besiegers, too, were wasting away, and it was uncertain whether they would be able to hold out long enough to enforce the hoped-for surrender. Reinforcements were therefore absolutely needed, all the more because there was little prospect of aid from the allies from whom so much had been expected.

<small>Reinforcements needed.</small>

The Duke of Lorraine had listened to Montague, but had done no more. The Duke of Savoy was thinking of designs upon Geneva and Genoa, and wanted the aid of an English army before he would stir. Soissons asked that some strong place—Sedan, Stenay, or Orange—might be given up to him before he moved, and that he might marry a daughter of the titular King of Bohemia, with a rich provision from her uncle the King of England. Rohan was agitating the South of France, and promised to take the field in September or

---

[1] *Isnard*, 101. *Herbert* (84) makes light of the whole matter, talks as though the Duke had performed an office of piety in sending the women to their husbands, and suggests that if any were shot it was by the French. But a letter from the camp says coolly: 'Afterwards they were often shot at by our men.' Symonds to Nicholas, Aug. 15, *S. P. Dom.* lxxiv. 9.

October.[1] Whilst the aid upon which Buckingham had counted was not forthcoming, Rochelle promised to be a burden rather than a support. The neutral position which the citizens had taken up was fast becoming untenable. No French commander could endure to leave them unassailed whilst an English army was on the Isle of Rhé. Angoulême accordingly let them know that they must make up their minds. They must be subjects of the King of France or subjects of the King of England. The Rochellese upon this began to draw closer to Buckingham; but they approached him to ask for succour, not to offer him assistance.[2]

Louder and louder grew Buckingham's entreaties for aid from home. Men and provisions were diminishing sadly, and the work was still undone. His own personal risks he could pass over lightly, and he scarcely mentioned the danger which he had run from a French deserter who had attempted to assassinate him; but the army under his command must not be neglected.[3]

A sanguine miscalculation of the state of feeling in France had left Buckingham isolated in the Isle of Rhé. Had he not equally miscalculated the state of feeling at home?

Of one thing at least he might be sure. The King would stand by him stoutly. The quarrel with France was as much Charles's as Buckingham's. No sooner therefore had the fleet left Portsmouth than Charles threw himself with unwonted vigour into the conduct of affairs. Up to this time he had been content to leave everything to Buckingham's energetic impulse. If he appeared on rare occasions at the Council table, it was but to give the sanction of his authority to schemes which Buckingham would

July. The King's eagerness to support the expedition.

---

[1] Montague's relation, July 5; Instructions to Montague, July 13, *S. P. Savoy*. Rohan to Soubise, $\frac{\text{July 29}}{\text{Aug. 8}}$, *S. P. France.*

[2] De Vic to Conway, Aug. 14, *Hardwicke S. P.* ii. 35.

[3] Buckingham to Nicholas, Aug. 14 [?], *Hardwicke S. P.* ii. 34. Buckingham to Becher, Aug. 14; Symonds to Nicholas, Aug. 15. An account of what happened at Rhé, Aug. 15, *S. P. Dom.* lxxiii. 91, lxxv. 53; i. lxxiv. 9, 10.

have to carry into effect. In Buckingham's absence the duty of rousing the sluggish from their apathy and directing the energies of the active devolved upon him alone.

As far as urgency went Charles left little to be desired by his favourite. Marlborough and Weston, whose business it was, as Treasurer and Chancellor of the Exchequer, to furnish supplies, were not long in feeling the application of the spur.

July 17. "I will not think," wrote Charles on July 17, "that now, in my absence, delaying answers will serve me." Ten days later, finding that nothing had been done, he sent Carlisle to see what they were about. "I confess," he complained, "these delays make me impatient even almost beyond patience, if I did not hope that the goodness of your answer should in some measure recompense the slowness of it. One item, and so an end. Let not my monies go wrong ways."[1]

Such exhortations were of little avail. Charles could call upon others to do the work, but he had no practical suggestion of his own to give. Yet the position of the Exchequer was one in which a single practical suggestion would be worth a whole torrent of exhortations. The great source which had made the fitting out of the expedition possible—the sale of French prize goods—had suddenly dried up. The supremacy of the English at sea was so complete that the enemy's vessels refused to venture from their harbours. The only resource left was the loan money. Since Buckingham's departure the loan money had been gathered in with a more unsparing hand. Many gentlemen in custody were sent into places of confinement in counties as far distant from their own homes as possible, so as to be a standing token of his Majesty's displeasure, and fresh batches of refusers were summoned before the Council.[2] For the present this rough discipline was successful. A large part of the loan was paid, grudgingly and angrily no doubt, but still it was paid. On July 17, 240,000*l.* had thus come into the Exchequer.[3]

Difficulties of the Exchequer.

[1] The King to Marlborough and Weston, July $\frac{17}{27}$; printed by Mr. Bruce in his *Calendar of State Papers*, Preface, viii.
[2] Holles to Wentworth, Aug. 9, *Strafford Letters*, i. 40.
[3] Manchester to Conway, July 17, *S. P. Dom.* lxxi 25.

It was like pouring water on the sand. The money was paid out as soon as it was paid in. 10,000*l.* a month by estimate, amounting to nearer 12,000*l.* in practice,¹ had to be paid for Sir Charles Morgan's troops in the Danish service, and claims of all kinds arising from the fitting out of the expedition had to be paid by the help of the loan.

Immediately upon the sailing of the fleet the Council had come to the conclusion that 2,000 recruits should be levied, and some days later it was agreed to be necessary to spend 12,615*l.* upon provisions for the seamen already at Rhé.² The money was not to be found. Marlborough was too old to lay the difficulty very deeply to heart, and took refuge in telling all applicants for payment that their case would be taken into consideration to-morrow.³ Weston growled over every penny he was called upon to spend, but was powerless to raise supplies from an alienated nation. Ordinary applicants for money due to them were driven to despair. One of them declared that when he waited on the Lord Treasurer he was treated 'like a cur sent by a dog,' and ordered out of the room ; when he applied to the Chancellor of the Exchequer he was set upon like a bear tied to the stake.⁴ The King could not be treated thus : but if he met with more civil treatment, he did not get more money than his subjects.

On August 1 Charles wrote again. Becher had come from Rhé to urge on the reinforcements. The Council had at last despatched orders for the levy of the 2,000 men, and there was a talk of finding half the sum needed for the provisions for the sailors.⁵ Charles took even this as a promise of better things, and charged his officers to go on in the course they were pursuing. "For if," he wrote, "Buckingham should not now be supplied, not in show but substantially, having so bravely, and, I thank God,

August. Fresh urgency of the King.

---

[1] Manchester to the King, July 20, *S. P. Dom.* lxxi. 44.
[2] Manchester to the King, June 29 ; Estimate for victuals, July 5, *ibid.* lxviii. 28, lxx. 37.
[3] Coke to Conway, June 20, *ibid.* lxvii. 76.
[4] Belou to Conway, July (?) July 30 (? , *ibid.* lxx. 1, lxxii. 41.
[5] Coke to Conway, July 31, *S. P. Dom.* lxxii. 48 ·

successfully begun his expedition, it were an irrecoverable shame to me and all this nation; and those that either hinders, or, according to their several places, furthers not this action as much as they may, deserves to make their end at Tyburn, or some such place ; but I hope better things of you."[1]

Something at last was to come of all these consultations. The King was able to announce to Buckingham on August 13,

Reinforcements promised. that in eight days Becher would sail with provisions and 400 recruits, as well as with 14,000*l.* of ready money. Two thousand men were to follow on September 10. Two thousand more were getting ready in Scotland.[2] Besides this, a fresh force of about the same number was in an advanced state of preparation.

The King's calculations had outstripped reality. More than three weeks passed before the money was actually provided,[3]

Progress of the siege. and contrary winds prevented Becher from sailing till September 16. He arrived at the Isle of Rhé on the 25th.[4] An Irish regiment had anticipated him, and had joined the army in the beginning of the month.[5]

When Becher landed, matters were looking more hopefully for the besiegers. The recruits had done something towards filling up the gaps in the English ranks. Food was known to be scarce within the citadel, and desertions were becoming numerous. Buckingham, at least, cannot be accused of misunderstanding the requirements of his position. Everything, he knew, depended upon keeping up the strength of the army and stopping the ingress of supplies by sea. He erected a floating battery to watch the sea face of the fort, and when this was broken down by the violence of the waves he barred the passage with a strong boom which, though it was in its turn

---

[1] The King to Marlborough and Weston ; *Calendar of Domestic State Papers*, Preface, ix.

[2] The King to Buckingham, Aug. 13, *Hardwicke S. P.* 17, 13.

[3] Long to Nicholas, Aug. 18, *S. P. Dom* lxxiv. 40, 74, 81. Conway to Coke, Aug. 22 ; the King to Marlborough and Weston, Aug. 23.

[4] Becher to Conway, Sept. 27, *ibid.* xxv. iii. 16. *Hardwicke S. P.* ii. 46.

[5] Sir E. Conway to Conway, Sept. 4, *Hardwicke S. P.* lxxvi. 26.

snapped by the beating waters, was subsequently replaced by a barrier of hawsers stretched from ship to ship.

These failures increased the gloom which was spreading in the army. Sir John Borough, Buckingham's second in command, had been killed by a shot. The hot words which had caused a rupture between him and the Duke had been long ago forgiven, and the two had worked together in the face of difficulty.

<small>September.
Difficulties
of the siege.</small>

Buckingham did not conceal from himself the extent of the danger. The French army was gathering on the opposite coast, and if it should effect a landing before the fort surrendered, he would hardly be able to meet it. One attempt at negotiation was tried by Buckingham. Sending his kinsman Ashburnham to Paris, on September 4, he made overtures for peace. The suggestion was taken by the French Government as a confession of weakness. Ashburnham was told that as long as an English soldier stood upon French soil, no peace was to be had.[1] Even before this answer reached Buckingham he was crying out for further reinforcements to be sent at all costs.[2] "The army," wrote Sir Edward Conway on September 20 to his father the Secretary, "grows every day weaker; our victuals waste, our purses are empty, ammunition consumes, winter grows, our enemies increase in number and power; we hear nothing from England."[3]

A week later confidence had returned. With the exception of a few boats which had slipped in from time to time, all attempts at victualling St. Martin's had hitherto being baffled. Deserters were thrust back into the fort, to increase the number of mouths. On the 25th a request that a gentleman might be sent out 'to treat of a matter of importance,' was refused unless he came to treat for a surrender. All men in the English camp were 'full of hope and confidence.' On the 27th the offer to surrender was actually made. The officers who brought it were to come back in the afternoon to specify the conditions. When the appointed hour arrived, a

<small>Sept. 27.
Proposed
surrender of
the fort.</small>

---

[1] *Isnard*, 135. *Herbert*, i. 19. Richelieu to Louis XIII., Sept. 20; Richelieu to Toiras, Sept. 22, *Lettres de Richelieu*, ii. 609, 620.

[2] Buckingham to the King, Sept. 19, *Hardwicke S. P.* ii. 45.

[3] Sir E. Conway to Conway, Sept. 20, *S. P. Dom.* lxxviii. 71.

message was brought asking for a further delay till the next morning.¹ In three days more the provisions of the defenders would be exhausted.²

Much, however, might be done before the next morning dawned. A flotilla of thirty-five boats had been hindered by contrary winds from attempting to bring relief to the garrison. On the 27th, while Toiras was negotiating, the wind changed and blew strongly from the north-west. The night was dark and gloomy, and the waves were running high. About three hours after midnight, the Frenchmen, guided by beacon fires within the fort, dashed into the heart of the English fleet. Buckingham, roused by the firing, hurried on board. The combat was carried on almost at hazard in the thick gloom. At one point the hawsers which defended the passage were severed, and twenty-nine boats laden with supplies succeeded in depositing their precious burden under the walls of the fortress. After morning dawned a fire-ship was sent in after them by the besiegers; but the wind had dropped and the garrison had no difficulty in thrusting off the dangerous assailant. In the afternoon a second fire-ship was let loose, with much the same result. Buckingham had all his work to recommence.³

<small>Sept. 28.
The fort supplied.</small>

On the 29th a council of war was summoned to consider what was now to be done. The citadel had been furnished with supplies which would last for more than a month. The delay could not be a long one. Yet the prospects of the besiegers were not promising. Sickness was making sad havoc in the ranks, and there were

<small>Sept. 29.
A council of war resolves to abandon the siege.</small>

---

¹ Becher to Conway, Oct. 3, *Hardwicke S. P.* ii. 48. Isnard (157) spreads the negotiation over the 27th and 28th.

² Letter from the French camp, Oct. $\frac{8}{18}$, *S. P. France*.

³ Becher to Conway, Oct. 3, *Hardwicke S. P.* ii. 48. Symonds to Ashburnham, Oct. 4, *S. P. Dom.* lxxx. 43. Letter from the French camp, Oct. $\frac{3}{18}$, *S. P. France*. Herbert, 145. *Isnard*, 157. I give the number of boats entering from the French letter, which is in accordance with Isnard. The writer had the information from Audoin, who led them in. The English fancied only 14 or 15 had got through. The dates I give from Symonds. Becher gives the 28th wrongly as the day of the offer of surrender.

only 5,000 men fit for duty. The winter was coming on, and it would be harder than ever to watch the access to the fort; provisions were growing scarce, and as only unground corn had been sent out,[1] whenever the wind lulled the windmills were rendered useless and the men were all but starved. The French forces on the mainland were gathering thickly, and an attempt to relieve the garrison might be expected at any moment.

On these grounds the council of war unanimously voted for giving up the attempt. Buckingham reluctantly gave his consent, and part of the siege material was carried on board ship. Before long new considerations were presented. Soubise and the Rochellese pleaded hard for delay. Their town was by this time girt about with the entrenchments of the Royal army, and they knew that they must make their choice between submission to their own King and a thorough alliance with England. They offered to find quarters in the city for a thousand sick men, to supply the troops with provisions, and to send boats to assist in guarding the approach to St. Martin's. Nor did the offer of the Rochellese stand alone. Dulbier, Mansfeld's old commissary-general, who was now Buckingham's chief military adviser, brought news from England that the long-wished-for reinforcements would soon be on the way. The Earl of Holland was coming with supplies in men and money which would make the army safe for the winter.[2]

Oct. 3. It retracts its opinion. The council of war was again summoned on October 3. With only one dissentient voice it retracted its former decision and voted for a continuance of the siege.[3]

The resolution thus taken has been severely criticised. It is possible that the officers may have yielded, against their better judgment, to Buckingham's urgency; but even if this were the

---

[1] Like the green coffee afterwards sent to the Crimea.

[2] Becher to Conway, Oct. 3; De Vic to Conway, Oct. 12, *Hardwicke S. P.* ii. 48, 51. *Herbert,* 154.

[3] This, which is distinctly stated in Becher's letter, puts an end to the theory, hitherto, I believe, generally accepted, that Buckingham remained on the island in opposition to the officers. Their vote may have been reluctantly given, but given it undoubtedly was.

case it would have been hard to affirm that the military situation was already desperate. October had been marked out for Rohan's rising, and if that rising were to take place, the French commanders, with a fortified city before them, would be in no position to send further aid to St. Martin's. Even if Rohan's rising came to nothing, Holland's reinforcement, if it really arrived, would place any landing of French troops out of the question. The 6,000 foot and 300 horse which the enemy was preparing to throw upon the Isle of Rhé, would indeed be a formidable diversion to Buckingham's 5,000 soldiers ; but they would be powerless in the face of the 13,000 which the army was expected to number upon Holland's arrival;[1] and, indeed, there is every reason to believe that if the reinforcements had been furnished promptly no attempt would have been made by the French to land troops on the island at all.[2] The only question would, then, be whether, with greater care and a larger number of ships, it would be possible to frustrate any fresh attempt to revictual the fort.

The difficulties before Buckingham, in short, were, in October as they had been in August, rather political than military. Rohan, indeed, kept his word, and before the end of October was at the head of 5,500 men.[3] In his own country, and in the midst of a Protestant population, he could not but meet with some support, but there was no general enthusiasm in his cause. Buckingham's theory that Richelieu was bent upon the suppression of Protestantism as a religion, in order to please the Pope, was entirely at variance with fact. The assurances of the French Government that only the political independence of the Protestant towns was at stake, found ready credence.

<small>Rohan's insurrection.</small>

[1] Statement &c., Oct. 19, *S. P. Dom.* lxxxii. 35.
[2] I say this on the authority of Richelieu himself. "Il faut faire cet effet devant que le secours d'Angleterre arrive, d'autant qu'estant renforcés de trois ou quatre mil hommes, il pourroit arriver que nous ne serions pas en estat de deffaire nos ennemis." Mémoire, Sept. $\frac{6}{16}$, *Lettres*, ii. 603. The whole memoir should be read by those who think that Buckingham's failure was a foregone conclusion.
[3] *Mém. de Rohan*, 235.

Disappointed of the support which he had looked for from the French Protestants, Buckingham was equally disappointed in his hopes of a French aristocratic rebellion. Montague had been sent back to Turin, and on October 13 he reported that the Duke of Chevreuse had made up his quarrel with Richelieu, that the Duke of Savoy and the Count of Soissons talked much of an attack upon France, but that they would do nothing till St. Martin's was taken. "Your Majesty's present undertakings," was Montague's conclusion, "grow upon their own roots, and can be nourished by nothing but their own natural heat and vigour."[1]

<small>Oct. 13. Montague again at Turin.</small>

His Majesty's undertakings had, indeed, need of all the heat and vigour obtainable. Before the middle of September it was known that the negotiation carried on by Gerbier and Rubens had broken down utterly.[2] It would be well if Olivares did not send an actual reinforcement to the French army before Rochelle. While all Charles's attention was thus directed to the Isle of Rhé, the fortunes of the King of Denmark were crumbling away in North Germany. England had helped him just enough to spur him on to the enterprise, not enough to save him from ruin. Even if Morgan's troops had been duly paid, they formed but a slight instalment of the aid which Charles had promised at the beginning of the war. In point of fact pay came to the poor men with the greatest irregularity. On July 23 Morgan reported, from his post near Bremen, that his men would probably refuse to fight if the enemy attacked them.[3] Just as Buckingham was sailing, his confidant, Edward Clarke, was sent to the King of Denmark to assure him that order was taken for the money, and to console him for the past by informing him that the expedition to Rhé had been sent out 'to weaken and divert our joint enemies, that our burden might be easier to our dear uncle.' The uncle must have been possessed of no incon-

<small>Failure of the negotiation with Spain.</small>

<small>Misfortunes of the King of Denmark.</small>

<small>July. Morgan's regiments.</small>

---

[1] Montague to the King, Oct. 13, *S. P. Savoy.*
[2] Sainsbury, *Rubens,* 85-105.
[3] Morgan to Conway, July 23, *S. P. Denmark.*

siderable control over his temper if he did not burst out into angry reproaches when he received the message.¹

Clarke reached the seat of war with a month's pay just in time to prevent Morgan's regiment from breaking up; but he might as well have left the 1,400 recruits he brought at home. No sooner had they set foot on shore than they deserted in troops of a hundred or two at a time, to hire themselves out to other masters who knew the value of a soldier. The one service which was plainly intolerable to an Englishman, was the service of the King of England. Some of them were recaptured and brought back to their colours, but it was easy to foretell that they would be at best of little use in the field.²

At last the crisis was come. A peace with Bethlen Gabor had released Wallenstein from Hungary. Crushing the Danish garrisons in Silesia as he passed, he met Tilly at Lauenburg towards the end of August. The plan of the joint campaign was soon arranged. Christian, with his finances in disorder and his forces diminished, dared not offer resistance. Only 8,000 men gathered round his standards. Throwing them into garrisons as best he might, he took ship at Glückstadt and fled hurriedly to his islands. On August 28 Wallenstein was marching past Hamburg at the head of 25,000 men. A few days later one of his lieutenants smote heavily upon the Margrave of Baden at Heiligenhafen. Excepting three or four fortified towns there was nothing to resist the Imperialists but the ocean.³

September.
The King of Denmark overpowered.

The remnants of Morgan's men were called across the Elbe. The money brought by Clarke had proved useless. There was some confusion in the accounts, and the merchant who was to pay the bills of exchange refused to do so. Morgan borrowed 3,000 dollars on his own credit; but this would not last long. "What service," he wrote in despair, "can the King expect or draw from these unwilling men? Thus I have been vexed all this summer, and could do nothing but what pleased them. Their officers had little com-

Misery of Morgan's men.

---

¹ Instructions to Clarke, July 27, *S. P. Denmark*.
² Clarke to Conway, Aug. 20, *ibid*.
³ Anstruther to Conway, Sept. 1; Clarke to Conway, Sept. 7, *ibid*.

mand over them, and by these reasons the King had no great services from us. . . . I could have wished our men had died at the point of the sword, rather than live to see those miseries we are in, and like to be still worse." [1]

It was not owing to Charles's wisdom that he had war with only half Europe on his hands. The art of giving up his rights from motives of policy was entirely unknown to him. All through the summer, when it was of the utmost importance to conciliate the Germans of the North, an English fleet, under Sir Sackville Trevor, had been lying off the Elbe and stopping the whole commerce of Hamburg by prohibiting trade with France or Spain. At last Trevor was recalled, to take measures against a State more powerful than Hamburg. When Carleton was sent to the Hague, he was ordered to watch the progress of some ships which were building in Holland for the French, and to remonstrate with the Dutch on the use which was being made of their harbours. Carleton's remonstrances proving fruitless, Trevor was ordered to sail into the Texel and bring out every French vessel that he could find. On the night of September 27, whilst the French boats were dashing in to relieve St. Martin's, Trevor sailed along the front of the Dutch vessels at anchor. Ranging up unexpectedly alongside of a French ship he poured a broadside into her. She was but half-manned, and her captain hastily struck his colours. The next morning, before the Dutch authorities had time to remonstrate, Trevor set sail with his prize to the English coast, leaving Captain Alleyne behind him, with orders to look out for other French ships which were known to be fitting out in Holland.[2]

Blockade of Hamburg.

A French ship seized in the Texel.

If the Dutch had been as easy to provoke as Charles or Louis, so flagrant a violation of a neutral harbour might easily have brought on an open rupture. The Dutch, however, wished merely to draw as much assistance as possible from each of the rival nations. To please the French they sent a

[1] Morgan to Carleton, Sept. 7, *S. P. Denmark*.
[2] Carleton to Coke, Sept. 29, *S. P. Holland*. *Alleyne's Journal*, Oct. 2 ; Duppa to Nicholas, Oct. 3, *S. P. Dom*. lxxx. 13, 26 *Mém. de Richelieu*, iii. 386.

commission to the Texel to seize upon Alleyne's ships; but at the same time the Prince of Orange sent a secret message to Carleton, urging him to direct Alleyne to be gone before the Commissioners arrived, and suggesting that, 'for fashion's sake,' Alleyne and the Dutch officials should fire in the air over one another's heads as he sailed out of the harbour.[1] The imperturbable refusal of the Dutch to take offence is the more noteworthy, as Charles, weary with their delay in giving him satisfaction for the Amboyna massacre, had just seized upon three Dutch East Indiamen, and had lodged them safely under the guns of Portsmouth.

All these tidings of failure before the enemy and provocation to allies came dropping in upon the ears of Englishmen during

<small>October.
State of feeling in England.</small>

the month of October, whilst the Government was straining every nerve to get ready the reinforcements for Buckingham. What wonder if the feeling against Buckingham grew more bitter every day? So strong was it that it left its impression even on the letters of those who were nearest and dearest to the absent man. His wife, whose clinging tenderness was not to be turned aside by his many infidelities, had been saddened by the absence of him who was to her the head and front of all mankind. He had promised to see her

<small>Letters of the Duchess of Buckingham.</small>

before he went, and he had broken his promise. "For my part," she wrote when she first knew that he had slipped away from her, "I have been a very miserable woman hitherto, that never could have you keep at home. But now I will ever look to be so, until some blessed occasion comes to draw you quite from the Court. For there is none more miserable than I am now; and till you leave this life of a courtier, which you have been ever since I knew you, I shall ever think myself unhappy."[2] After the bad news of the introduction of supplies, a sense of her husband's personal danger mingled with the thought of her own loneliness. Some hint he seems to have given of an intention of throwing himself into

---

[1] Carleton to Coke, Oct. 5, *S. P. Holland*.

[2] The Duchess of Buckingham to Buckingham, June 26 (?), *S. P. Dom.* lxviii. 3. This and the other letters have been quoted in part in the Preface to Mr. Bruce's *Calendar*, 1627-8.

Rochelle. Against this, in writing to Dr. Moore, a physician in the camp, she protests with her whole soul. "I should think myself," she says, "the most miserablest woman in the world if my lord should go into the main land; for though God has blessed him hitherto beyond all imagination in this action, yet I hope he will not still run on in that hope to venture himself beyond all discretion; and I hope this journey hath not made him a Puritan, to believe in predestination. I pray keep him from being too venturous, for it does not belong to a general to walk trenches; therefore have a care of him. I will assure you by this action he is not any whit the more popular man than when he went; therefore you may see whether these people be worthy for him to venture his life for."[1]

Buckingham's mother, as a good Catholic, wrote in another tone, scolding her son for his blindness and presumption.

Buckingham's correspondents.

"Dear mother," he had written from Rhé, "I am so full of business as hardly have I time to say my prayers, but hardly passes an hour that I perceive not His protecting hand over me, which makes me have recourse to your prayers to assist me in so great a duty. For my coming home, till I have means from England wherewithal to settle this army here, I cannot with any honour leave them. If it be possible for you to lend me some money, do it."[2] The Countess had plenty of good advice to give, but no money. "I am very sorry," she wrote, "you have entered into so great a business, and so little care to supply your wants, as you see by the haste that is made to you. I hope your eyes will be opened to see what a great gulf of businesses you have put yourself into, and so little regarded at home, where all is merry and well pleased, though the ships be not victualled as yet, nor mariners to go with them. As for moneys, the kingdom will not supply your expenses, and every man groans under the burden of the times. At your departure from me, you told me

---

[1] The Duchess of Buckingham to Moore, Oct. 20 (?), *S. P. Dom.* lxxxii. 42.

[2] Buckingham to the Countess of Buckingham. Printed from the Earl of Denbigh's collection in the *Fourth Report of the Hist MSS. Commission*, 256.

you went to make peace, but it was not from your heart. This is not the way; for you to embroil the whole Christian world in war, and then to declare it for religion, and make God a party to these woful affairs, so far from God as light from darkness, and the highway to make all Christian princes to bend their forces against us, that otherwise, in policy, would have taken our parts."[1]

Most of Buckingham's correspondents, however, wrote in a different strain. The Earl of Exeter told him that his success at Rhé was 'miraculous.' Dorset assured him that he had only to let him know his will, for if he failed to obey it he deserved to be 'whipped with double stripes.'[2] Yet even amongst those who were entirely dependent on his favour there were some whose anxieties would not allow them to conceal from him the misery at home. On September 21, amidst the difficulties of getting Holland's reinforcement ready, Sir Robert Pye, whose position as Auditor of the Exchequer gave him every opportunity of knowing the truth, uttered a note of warning. "Pardon me, I beseech you, if I humbly desire that you would advisedly consider of the end, and how far his Majesty's revenue of all kinds is now exhausted. We are upon the third year's anticipation beforehand; land, much sold of the principal; credit lost; and at the utmost shift with the commonwealth. I would I did not know so much as I do, for I do protest I would not for 500*l*. but I had been in the country. Deputy lieutenants are not active, and justices of the peace of better sort are willing to be put out of commission, every man doubting and providing for the worst, so that all our fears increase at home. I know I please not, but I cannot see one I am so much bound unto and not inform him my reason. I know no way to advise, but by some speedy accommodation of these loans, for nothing pleaseth so long as this is on foot, and of late no money, or little, hath been paid thereupon. For my own

September. Pye's warning.

---

[1] The Countess of Buckingham to Buckingham, Aug. 26 (?), *S. P. Dom.* lxxv. 22.

[2] Exeter to Buckingham, Nov. 3; Dorset to Buckingham, Aug. 21, *S. P. Dom.* lxxxiv. 16. Preface to Bruce's *Calendar*, p. i.

particular, I will lay myself to pawn for your Lordship, but so soon as the fort is taken I could wish your Lordship were here." [1]

<small>Delays in Holland's expedition.</small> "So soon as the fort is taken" was easily said; but the taking of the fort depended on Holland's speedy setting out, and the difficulties in the way of Holland's expedition were almost insuperable. Weston might be, as Sir Humphrey May asserted, 'not a spark, but a flame of fire, in anything that concerned' the Duke, but the words with which this assertion was prefaced were none the less true. "It is easy for us to set down on paper ships, and money, and arms, and victual, and men, but to congest these materials together, especially in such a penury of money, requires more time than the necessity of your affairs will permit." [2]

The whole frame of government was unhinged. Lord Wilmot, a veteran who had seen hard service in Ireland, was to command the reinforcements which were to be shipped on board Holland's fleet. On October 6 he was waiting at Plymouth for supplies from London.[3] The warrant for the money needed for feeding the troops was only issued three days <small>Oct. 9.</small> later.[4] On the same day Sir James Bagg, Buckingham's creature who had succeeded Eliot in the Vice-Admiralty of Devon, wrote that no money had been sent him to purchase provisions, or to hire ships for his patron's relief. <small>Oct. 10.</small> Of the new levies which were ordered to rendezvous at Plymouth, large numbers had, as was now usual, escaped the hateful service by desertion.[5] On the 11th, <small>Oct. 11.</small> Wilmot again wrote that the supplies from London had not arrived, that he had no arms with which to train the men, and that the population of the county was exasperated

---

[1] Pye to Buckingham, Sept. 21, *S. P. Dom.* lxxix. 2.
[2] May to Buckingham, Oct. 7, *ibid.* lxxx. 60.
[3] Wilmot to Conway, Oct. 6, *ibid.* lxxx. 55.
[4] Docquet, Oct. 9, *S. P. Docquet Book.*
[5] Commissioners at Plymouth to the Council, Oct. 10, *S. P. Dom.* lxxxi. 4.

at being forced to maintain the soldiers upon credit.¹ His answer was an order from Conway to put his men as soon as possible on board ships lying at Plymouth. Holland would sail from Portsmouth, and the whole expedition would meet before St. Martin's.²

Oct. 12.

Charles was growing anxious. "Since I have understood your necessities," he wrote to Buckingham, "for fault of timely supplies, I still stand in fear that these may come too late.³ But I hope God is more merciful to me than to inflict so great a punishment on me." Even yet Wilmot could not start. On the 15th the ships from London had only reached the Downs.⁴
On the same day Holland reported from Portsmouth that nothing was ready, but that, though the captains assured him that it would take ten or fifteen days to remedy the defects of their ships, he hoped to sail in two.⁵

Oct. 13. The King's anxiety.
Oct. 15.

On the 18th the long-expected supplies from the Thames reached Plymouth. Holland, leaving Portsmouth on the 19th, was driven back to Cowes by a storm.⁶ Leaving his windbound ships behind him, he posted to Plymouth to meet Wilmot, who was then ready to sail.⁷ Almost at the moment of his arrival the wind, which had been favourable at Plymouth, chopped round and blew steadily from the south-west.⁸

Oct. 21. Holland unable to leave.

Everything on board the provision ships was in confusion. No bills of lading were on board, no official to take any account of the stores. But it mattered little now. The pitiless wind made the voyage impossible. The Portsmouth squadron, attempting once more to get out, was driven back into the Solent.⁹

---

¹ Wilmot to Conway, Oct. 11, *S. P. Dom.* lxxxi. 13.
² Conway to Wilmot, Oct. 12, *ibid.* lxxxi. 25.
³ The King to Buckingham, Oct. 13, *Hardwicke S. P.* ii. 19.
⁴ Conway to Wilmot, Oct. 15, *S. P. Dom.* lxxxi. 50.
⁵ Holland to Conway, Oct. 15, *ibid.* lxxxi. 5.
⁶ Holland to Conway, Oct. 19, *ibid.* lxxxii. 30, 31
⁷ Wilmot to Conway, Oct. 21, *ibid.* lxxxii. 46.
⁸ Holland to Conway, Oct. 22, *ibid.* lxxxii. 58.
⁹ Wilmot to Conway, Oct. 23; Mervyn to Nicholas, Oct. 23, *ibid.* lxxxii. 66, 68.

The soldiers on board at Plymouth were eating the provisions
designed for the army at Rhé.¹ On the 28th news
from Buckingham reached London. The Duke had
made up his mind to assault the fort. If Holland came in time
with the supplies, he would stay on the island. If not, he
would throw himself into Rochelle, and run all hazards with its
defenders.

Oct. 28.

On the 29th the wind lulled, and Holland's fleet left the
Catwater. In the night the storm raged once more, and the
ships were in great danger from the waves, lashed
into fury in the then open waters of the Sound. The
winds blew loudly for twenty hours. Even if the wind changed,
wrote Wilmot, it would be long before the damaged ships could
be repaired. The soldiers, besides, were ill armed, and there
was no store at Plymouth from which to supply them.²

Oct. 29.

If evidence were still needed of the thorough disorganisation of the Government, it would be found in the circumstance that five or six hundred recruits arrived at
Plymouth without any directions accompanying
them. Nobody had orders to receive them, and Holland was obliged to support them out of his own pocket till he
could persuade the unwilling deputy-lieutenants to force their
maintenance upon the county.³

Nov. 2. Disorganisation of the Government.

No wonder that one more of the Duke's confidants should
be found bewailing to his patron the state of affairs at home.
"In my last," wrote the courtly Goring, "I was bold
to represent unto your Lordship the hazard you
would run if you expected more timely supplies; for
the City, from whence all present money must now be raised,
or nowhere, is so infested by the malignant part of this kingdom, as no man that is moneyed will lend upon any security,
if they think it to go the way of the Court, which now is made
diverse from the State. Such is the present distemper. . . .

Nov. 5. Goring's letter.

¹ Ashburnham to Nicholas, Oct. 25, *S. P. Dom.* lxxii. 87.
² Conway to Holland, Oct. 28; Holland to Conway, Oct. 30; Wilmot to Conway, Oct. 31, *ibid.* lxxxiii. 17, 32, 38.
³ Holland to Conway, Nov. 2, *ibid.* lxxxiv. 12.

In a word, therefore, my dearest Lord, let me tell you what many honest-hearted men, divested of passion or bye-ends, say —that if it be true, as is here conceived, that the fort be again revictualled in such plenty as will force you to a winter siege at the best, before you can hope for any good success, that then your Lordship would rather betake you to a new counsel, and think what way to curb the French insolency some other way than by a wilful struggling against them where the season and place give them such infinite advantage of you. Besides, my dear Lord, here at home—where your judgment is first to reflect—are such desperate obstructions as nothing but your presence can remove, and that will do it, if you will yet be pleased in time to look about you, or let me perish for a false, vile wretch to you."[1]

Whatever others might think of him, Buckingham was still certain of the King's support. The letter written by Charles in the midst of all this uncertainty is very pathetic in its mingled spirit of resignation and confidence. "I pray God," he wrote, "that this letter be useless or never come to your hands, this being only to meet you at your landing in England, in case you should come from Rhé without perfecting your work, happily begun, but, I must confess with grief, ill seconded. This is therefore to give you power—in case ye shall imagine that ye have not enough already—to put in execution any of those designs ye mentioned to Jack Hippesley, or any other that you shall like of. So that I leave it freely to your will, whether, after your landing in England, ye will set forth again to some design before you come hither ; or else that ye shall first come to ask my advice before ye undertake a new work ; assuring you that, with whatsomever success ye shall come to me, ye shall ever be welcome, one of my greatest griefs being that I have not been with you in this time of suffering, for I know we would have much eased each other's griefs. I cannot stay longer on this subject, for fear of losing myself in it. To conclude, you cannot come so soon as ye are welcome ; and unfeignedly in my mind ye have gained as much reputation

Nov. 6. The King's constancy.

---

[1] Goring to Buckingham, Nov. 5, *S. P. Dom.* lxxxiv. 20.

with wise and honest men, in this action, as if ye had performed all your desires."[1]

<small>Oct. 16.
Position of affairs at Rhé.</small>
Charles's forebodings of evil, though he knew it not, were already realised. By the middle of October the condition of the besiegers was pitiable. The weather was cold and wet, and the men were exposed to grievous misery in the trenches. The officers were 'looking themselves blind' by sweeping the horizon with their telescopes for the first signs of Holland's fleet,[2] as in old days the soldiers of Nicias gazed across the Sicilian sea for the triremes of Demosthenes. But for the south-west wind in the Channel, Holland would have been with them in less than a week, and their necessities would have been relieved: but Holland came not, and Buckingham was called on once more to face the question of relinquishing his enterprise.

Everything hung on the chances of Holland's arrival. If he came quickly, all might yet be well. If he delayed, the army might easily be exposed to an irreparable disaster. Was it strange that the officers of Buckingham's council concurred in taking a gloomy view of the situation, while Buckingham himself, upon whom failure would weigh infinitely more heavily than upon all the rest together, hoped against hope, broke out into passionate reproaches against those who seemed to have forgotten him at home, and, whilst prudently making preparations for departure in case of necessity, still clung firmly to the spot on which he was?

<small>Oct. 20.
The French land in the island.</small>
The time was fast passing by when hesitation would be any longer possible. The smaller fort of La Prée had been left unassailed in July, and it now afforded a shelter to the French troops passing over from the mainland. By October 20 nearly 2,000 soldiers had been received within its walls and within the entrenchments which had been thrown up in front of it,[3] and their number might be expected to increase every day.

[1] The King to Buckingham, Nov. 6, *Hardwicke S. P.* ii. 20.
[2] Bold to Nicholas, Oct. 16; Louis to Nicholas, Oct. 16, *S. P. Dom.* lxxxi. 59, 61.
[3] *Isnard,* 177-193. It is not for me, remembering the controversy

It was lamentable for Buckingham to be so near success and yet to miss it. Toiras had only provisions to last him till November 5,[1] and though the exact date was not known in the English camp, the conjectures formed by the besiegers were not far wrong. Between the greatness of the prize and the terrible consequences of exposure to a French attack upon his diminished army, Buckingham was unable to form a resolution. During the week which followed upon the last landing of the French there were continued combats, in which the English held their own. Yet it was certain that when fresh troops arrived at La Prée, Buckingham's position would be untenable, and at last he reluctantly gave way to those who urged him to retreat. Yet in the desperate condition in which he was, he was ready to catch at any straw, and having heard that Toiras had but 500 men left capable of bearing arms,[2] he talked openly of ordering an assault upon the fortress, though an assault had long ago been regarded as a hopeless operation.[3] On the morning of the 27th the attempt was made. Toiras, probably through Buckingham's want of reticence,

*Oct. 27.
Attempted storm.*

about attacking the north side of Sebastopol after the battle of the Alma, to say whether Buckingham was right or wrong in neglecting La Prée. Of course he was blamed after the event for what he did, and Herbert, who represents the talk of the camp, says (p. 50) that 'some of our ancient and well-experienced soldiers thought fit to begin with it,' whilst 'the pretenders to the Duke's favour advised him to begin with St. Martin's.' I do not see, however, that anybody supposed that the Duke was strong enough to attack both at once ; and the only question therefore is, whether he would have been able at the same time to master La Prée and to hinder Toiras from provisioning St. Martin's, so as to make a blockade of that fort practically impossible after La Prée was captured. As matters stood in July, there was no danger of the landing of the French troops at La Prée, because there were none to spare on the mainland. Such a danger did not arise till October. It therefore seems to me to be a perfectly sustainable argument, for those who care to embark on such speculations, that Buckingham took the wisest course. All that I am concerned with, however, is to show that he was not the mere infatuated being that history chooses to represent him.

[1] *Isnard*, 184.
[2] *News-Letter*, Nov. 5, *S. P. Dom.* lxxxiv. 24.
[3] See the account of Courtney's conversation with Eliot, in *Forster*, i. 403.

was amply forewarned, and the troops from La Prée came out to threaten the assailants in the rear. Even if secrecy had been maintained, the operation would probably have failed. The works of the citadel were intact, and the scaling ladders were too short. After a useless butchery, Buckingham was compelled to draw off his men.

Military prudence counselled instant retreat; but Buckingham had not learned to steel his heart against suffering. The Rochellese urged him to protect them a little longer, whilst they gathered in provisions from the island to replace those which they had made over to the English army in the beginning of the month.[1] Neither could he bear to leave his own wounded to the mercies of the enemy. The whole of the next day was spent in shipping the injured men.[2] On the morning of the 29th it was too late. Marshal Schomberg, who had already landed with fresh troops at La Prée, advanced to the attack at the head of little less than 6,000 men.

Oct. 28.

Oct. 29. The retreat from St. Martin's.

Preparations for retreat had been duly made. A wooden bridge had been constructed across the marshes and the narrow arm of the sea which separated the Isle of Rhé from the smaller Isle of Loix,[3] and this bridge was to have been guarded by a fortified work, which would have enabled the troops to embark in safety. Unhappily, by some blunder, the causeway which led to the bridge from the side of the Isle of Rhé was left entirely undefended, whilst only the farther end of the bridge on the lesser island, to which the troops were marching, was guarded by an entrenchment. The French accordingly had but to watch their opportunity. As soon as three regiments were over they charged the handful of horse which had been left to guard the passage.[4] Yielding to the weight of numbers the English

---

[1] *Isnard*, 210.
[2] Crosby to Conway (?), Nov. 14 (?), *S. P. Dom.* lxxxiv. 78.
[3] Now joined to the larger island.
[4] Crosby notes on this leaving sixty horse to meet 200, "An error never to be sufficiently condemned in the Colonel-General and the Sergeant-Major-General, to whom the Duke committed the retreat." If this is true, and not a mere camp rumour, Buckingham was not responsible for the details of the manœuvres of that day.

horse gave way, and dashing in headlong flight towards the bridge, threw the infantry into hopeless confusion. Almost at the same time a body of French, who had pushed round the three English regiments which had not crossed the bridge, fired upon them in the rear. From that moment a sheer massacre ensued. Two colonels were slain upon the spot. Not a horseman succeeded in crossing the bridge. "By this time," wrote the officer who had the command of the work beyond the bridge, "the Rochellese, having found another way on the left hand through the salt-pits, made extraordinary haste to the bridge, and wedged themselves into the flank of Sir Alexander Brett's regiment then passing over, by means whereof, the passage being choked up, the enemy had the killing, taking, and drowning of our men at the bridge at his pleasure, without any hazard, musqueteers being not able to annoy them without endangering our own men." The bridge, too, had no protection at the sides, and large numbers fell over and were drowned. At first the soldiers who guarded the entrenchment beyond the bridge were borne away by the flying rout. But, after a time, a knot of men was rallied by the officers, and the French were driven back. At nightfall the English were still in possession of the entrenchment Early in the morning the bridge was set on fire, and the remains of Buckingham's army were enabled to re-embark at their leisure.[1]

The slaughter on the bridge.

Oct. 30.

Various accounts have been given of the numbers lost in this disastrous retreat. The French claimed to have destroyed 2,000 men. The English authorities would hardly admit that more than 1,000 perished.[2] If, however, the ravages caused by warfare and disease during the preceding weeks be taken into account, the entire English loss must be set down at little less than 4,000 men. On October 20, 6,884 soldiers drew pay at St. Martin's. On November 8 the embarkation was effected without further difficulty, and after a short voyage

Estimate of the loss.

---

[1] Crosby to (Conway ?), Nov. 14 (?), *S. P. Dom.* lxxxiv. 78. Compare *Herbert*, 224. The bird's-eye view given by Isnard brings the whole scene before us.

[2] *Herbert*, 257.

2,989 poor wretches, worn with hunger and enfeebled by disease, were landed at Portsmouth and Plymouth.¹

One of the colonels has left on record his opinion of the proximate causes of the disaster. "It is not to be doubted," he says, "that the Duke had both courage, munificence, and industry enough, together with many other excellent parts, which in time would make him a renowned general. But his prime officers undervaluing his directions because of his inexperience, and taking a boldness in regard of his lenity to delinquents, did not only fail to co-operate with him, but by giving out that he cared not to expose them all for his own vainglory, had infused into a great part of the army a mutinous disposition, insomuch as whatsoever was directed touching our longer abode or any attempt to be made upon the enemy was either cried down, or so slowly and negligently executed as it took none effect. For instance, when it was resolved in council that the little fort should be besieged, they obstinately declined it.² On the other side, whatsoever tended to the retreat was acted with all possible expedition : as for example, the shipping of all the brass cannon, whereunto they had by surprise gotten his consent before the assault, by himself often repented of. In this distraction of affairs, the Duke was forced to resort to new and private counsels, by which he was then so guided that Dulbier, one author thereof, writing to his friend in Holland, used these words :— '*L'ignorance et la dissention qu'est entre les Anglois, m'a faict vendre les coquilles*³ *à bon marché.*'"⁴

Causes of the disaster.

An inexperienced general, discontented commanders, and a half-mutinous soldiery were enough to ruin any undertaking, and it can hardly be denied that Buckingham's hesitation during the last few days went far to convert a necessary retreat

---

¹ Accounts of the number of soldiers, Oct. 20 ; Statement of the numbers, Nov., *S. P. Dom.* lxxxii. 43, lxxxv. 94.

² This cannot refer to the original question of besieging La Prée, but to some later resolution, probably when the French were beginning to land.

³ '*Bien vendre les coquilles*' is '*tirer un profit exagéré d'une opération ou d'un service.*' *Littré*, s.v. *coquille*. Dulbier, on the contrary, sold his shells cheap, *i.e.* got little for his pains.

⁴ Crosby to Conway (?), Nov. 14 (?). *S. P. Dom.* lxxxiv. 78.

into a terrible disaster. Yet neither must it be forgotten that, except when he ordered the assault, his fault lay simply in his miscalculation of chances over which he had no control. But for the persistence of the south-west wind in the Channel, Holland would have been at Rhé about October 24 or 25, and the firmness of Buckingham in resisting the timid counsels of his subordinates would have been one of the commonplaces of history.

As a man Buckingham gains much from an impartial examination of his conduct in this expedition. At least he was no carpet knight, no mere courtier dancing attendance upon the powerful at banquets and festivities. No veteran could have surpassed him in the readiness with which he exposed his person to danger, and in his determination to see all with his own eyes, to encourage the down-hearted, and to care for the suffering of his men. After all, the charge which history has to bring against Buckingham is not so much that he failed in the expedition to Rhé, as that there was an expedition to Rhé at all. The politician, not the man, was at fault. Even if the French war had been justifiable in itself, the idea of undertaking it with no support but that of an alienated nation was hazardous in the extreme. The south-west wind which kept Holland in port was but a secondary cause of the disaster. But for the thorough disorganisation of the English Government, which was the clear result of the quarrel with the House of Commons, Holland would have been able to start at least a fortnight earlier, whilst the wind was still favourable to his voyage. The position at Rhé after the succour had been thrown into the fort was something like that of the allied armies before Sebastopol after the failure of the first bombardment; but the allied armies had powerful Governments behind them, and the British army at least had the support of a nation feverishly anxious for the honour of its arms, and ready to pour forth its treasures without stint to support the enterprise which it had undertaken. Buckingham had nothing behind him but an attached but incapable sovereign, and a handful of officials rendered inert by the dependence in which he had kept them, and by their knowledge of the ill-will with which every act of theirs was scanned by the vast majority of the nation.

CHAPTER LXI.

PREROGATIVE GOVERNMENT IN CHURCH AND STATE.

On November 11 Buckingham landed at Plymouth. Although he was met by information that a plot had been formed to murder him on his way to London, he refused to take any precautions. To his young nephew, Denbigh's son, Lord Fielding, who offered to change clothes with him in order to shield him from danger, he replied that if his enemies believed him to be afraid of danger, he should never be safe.[1]

<small>Nov. 11. Buckingham's return.</small>

The meeting between Buckingham and the King was extremely cordial. Charles threw the whole blame of failure upon the delay in sending supplies. Though Buckingham was well aware of the temper of his officers towards him, he had nothing but commendation to bestow upon them.[2] If he sometimes used hard language, it was directed against the officials at home, and he was even heard to charge the faithful Sir John Coke with stabbing him in the back in his absence.[3] His anger, however, soon cooled down, and the lesson of his failure was quickly forgotten in the excitement of preparation for fresh enterprises. Already he was talking of an attack upon Calais.[4] Whatever the plan finally resolved on might be, he was contemplating nothing but the active resumption of hostilities.

[1] *Rel. Wottonianæ*, i. 229.
[2] Conway to Sir E. Conway, Nov. 20, *S. P. Dom.* lxxxv. 11.
[3] Contarini to the Doge, $\frac{\text{Nov. 22}}{\text{Dec. 2}}$, *Ven. Transcripts.*
[4] The King to Buckingham, Nov. 14; misdated in *Hardwicke S. P.* ii. 21.

Very different was the conclusion drawn outside the charmed circle of the Court. All through the summer news had been eagerly looked for, and rumours, true or false, had spread from mouth to mouth. In spite of the general unpopularity of the Government, sympathy with the Protestants of Rochelle was not dead, and the hopes of success which had been raised from time to time caused the final blow, 'the greatest and shamefullest overthrow,' as one letter-writer described it, 'since the loss of Normandy,' to fall all the more heavily. At first it was rumoured that not a single man or gun had been brought away.[1]

Feeling in England.

Although the exaggeration of the tale was soon discovered, every tongue was loosed in criticism, and the object of every criticism was the Duke. The sins of every officer and soldier fell, as was perhaps inevitable, upon the head of the contriver of the ill-starred expedition. "The disorder and confusion," wrote Denzil Holles to his brother-in-law Wentworth, "was so great, the truth is no man can tell what was done. This only every man knows, that since England was England it received not so dishonourable a blow. Four colonels lost, thirty-two colours in the enemy's possession, but more lost,—God knows how many men slain,—they say not above two thousand on our side, and I think not one of the enemy's."[2]

After this disaster, the resistance to the loan could no longer be treated from a purely legal point of view. The reply given in the summer by George Catesby when his contribution was demanded, "I will be master of my own purse,"[3] would have had a somewhat sordid appearance if Charles had in reality required his money on behalf of an undoubted necessity of State. It was now impossible for the King to place himself before the world as the defender of his country's honour in the face of a factious Opposition. A disaster worse than that of Cecil in 1625, a failure worse than that of Willoughby in 1626, had crowned the efforts of an ill-advised and reckless administration. Whoever favoured

Effect of this feeling in stimulating resistance to the loan.

---

[1] Letters to Meade, Nov. 16, *Court and Times*, i. 285.
[2] Holles to Wentworth, Nov. 19, *Strafford Letters*, i. 41.
[3] Letter to Meade, Feb. 23, *Court and Times*, i. 196.

Buckingham and his designs stood forth, in the eyes of all but a select circle of his admirers, as the worst enemy of his country.

As if to make Charles's difficulties yet greater, he had allowed the political strife between himself and his people to be still further embittered by involving it with the ecclesiastical problem which was already hard enough to solve. As soon as the demand for the loan had been made, each theological party drew instinctively to the side of its natural supporter. The Puritan, sharing as he did in the general sentiment of the House of Commons, and asking for nothing but the exclusive maintenance of a popular form of doctrine, trusted for support to the conservative feelings of the nation. The new school of Churchmen, thirsting for change after the standard of an earlier age, looked to the Royal power as the lever with which they hoped to effect their purposes.

February. Ecclesiastical difficulties.

It is in the nature of things that the political theories and preferences of ecclesiastics should vary with the circumstances in which they find themselves, and it is easy to conceive a state of things in which Puritans would appeal to a Government for support, and their opponents would throw themselves upon popular sympathies. Yet it is difficult to imagine Churchmen of the stamp of Laud and Montague placing any confidence in the general good-will of the people. They were too scholar-like and refined, too much inclined to throw doubt on the sweeping assertions which pass current with the multitude, and at the same time too little conversant with the world, to know how to bring their influence to bear upon those who distrusted or disliked them. As their idea of Church government was the idea of a system controlled by a minority of learned men without any consideration for the feelings and prejudices either of their learned antagonists or of the ignorant multitude, they looked with fondness upon the Royal authority which was alone able to give them the strength which they lacked. "Defend thou me with the sword and I will defend thee with the pen," the sentence with which Montague concluded his *Appello Cæsarem*, expressed the common sentiment of the whole party. The predominance of Charles in the State meant the predomi-

Nature of the Royalism of the Laudian party.

nance of their own way of thinking, and the carrying out of their own principles into action. They did not see how insufficient these principles were for purposes of government. They did not see that, even if their ideas had been all that they fancied them to be, they were pinning their faith to the mere personal prepossessions of the reigning Sovereign. If Charles was their supporter and protector, who could say that his successor might not support and protect their opponents?

The future might take care of itself. For the present, to magnify the King's authority was the one way of safety.

The King the centre of their system. The Laudian party of Charles's reign was the least ecclesiastical of all ecclesiastical parties. The great Popes and Churchmen of the Middle Ages would have branded them as recreants to the cause of spiritual supremacy. It mattered little to them. In the King's authority they saw their only refuge against the tyrannical domination of the multitude, the only fulcrum by the aid of which they could hope to move the world and to settle the English Church in that secure and orderly form which was the object of their aspirations.

Laud, preaching before the King when he opened his first Parliament, chose for his text, "When I shall receive the congregation, I will judge according unto right. The earth is dissolved, and all the inhabitants thereof; I bear up the pillars of it." The king, he declared, "is God's immediate lieutenant upon earth; and therefore one and the same action is God's by ordinance, and the king's by execution. And the power which resides in the king is not any assuming to himself, nor any gift from the people, but God's power, as well in as over him." If the earth was not to dissolve, 'the king must trust and endear his people; the people must honour, obey, and support their king; both king and peers and people must religiously serve and honour God.' The king, however, could not take the whole of the burden of government upon himself. "There must be inferior judges and magistrates deputed by the king for this: men of courage, fearing God and hating covetousness. All judges, even this great congregation, this great council, now ready to sit, receive

1625. June 19. Laud's sermon.

influence and power from the king, and are dispensers of his justice as well as their own, both in the laws they make and in the laws they execute ; in the causes which they hear, and in the sentences which they give : the king God's high steward, and they stewards under him."[1]

Even the Parliament then was but an instrument in the King's hands, for 'counsel not for control,' as Charles afterwards said. Laud's view of the constitution was no new theory evolved out of the recesses of his own mind. It was in the main the doctrine of the Tudor sovereigns, the doctrine under which England had won its national independence from Rome. The authority of the State, according to this view, did not lie in the multitude, necessarily ignorant and driven hither and thither by passion and prejudice. It lay with him whom God had placed at the helm, and who knew better what was good for the people than they could possibly know for themselves. This authority was his not that he might gratify his own will, but that he might do judgment and justice. As long as he did this he would be an instrument in God's hands for bearing up the pillars of the world.

Nature of his theory of government.

Many months had not passed since the delivery of this sermon before everywhere men were beginning to look about for some other theory to live by. Whatever they might think about the King, they had no longer any belief that his ministers wished to do judgment and justice. It was not in the nature of things that these views should be shared by Laud and his friends. To them the House of Commons, which attacked Montague and impeached Buckingham, had ceased to do judgment and justice, and they clung all the more closely to the only power in England which they believed to be willing to do them right.

1626. Influence of current events on him.

In this temper they were found by the forced loan. Looking with admiration upon the King's ecclesiastical policy, they cared little about his foreign policy, and were willing to take it upon trust. The victory of Parliament would be a terrible blow to them, and they threw themselves eagerly upon

1627.

[1] *Laud's Works,* i. 93.

Charles's side. One of them, Dr. Robert Sibthorpe, preaching before the Judges at the Lent Assizes at Northampton, set forth the royal pretensions with irritating plainness of speech. It was the duty of the prince, he said, to 'direct and make laws.' Subjects were bound to pay active obedience to the king, except when his commands were either impossible, or contrary to the laws of God or nature. But even then they were not to resist him.[1]

Feb. 22. Sibthorpe's sermon.

Sibthorpe's sermon was by no means remarkable for ability, but it might be useful as a manifesto in behalf of the loan, and Archbishop Abbot was ordered by the King to license it for the press. The sanction of the highest authority in the Church was thus demanded for the loan, just as the sanction of the highest authority in the law had been demanded a few weeks before.

Abbot refuses to license it.

Abbot, however, proved as impracticable as Crew. He had no objection to make against the ceremonies of the Church, but his austere and ungenial mind was thoroughly wedded to the Calvinistic system of doctrine, and in consequence thoroughly opposed to Laud and his ways. Something, too, of personal bitterness doubtless mingled with nobler motives. Laud had supplanted him with Charles, as Williams had supplanted him with James. Since Buckingham's predominance had been undisputed, he had ceased to attend the Privy Council, where his word was held to be of little worth. He now fancied that the message which he had received was a trick of Buckingham's to bring him into still further discredit with the King, if he refused to do that which his conscience forbade him to do.

Once before in his life Abbot had bearded a king, when he refused to marry Somerset to the divorced Countess of Essex.

July 4. Abbot sent into confinement.

He now again refused to conform to the royal orders. The consequences which he predicted were not long in coming upon him. Independence could not be suffered in the Church any more than on the Bench.

---

[1] Through the kindness of Mr. Wilson, of King William Street, Charing Cross, I was able to obtain a sight of this sermon, *Apostolical Obedience*, which I could not find in the Museum Library.

On July 4 Abbot was ordered to betake himself to Ford, a mansion in Kent belonging to the see of Canterbury, and there to remain in confinement. On October 9 a further indignity was placed upon him. The archbishopric could not be taken away, but he could be deprived of his jurisdiction, on the plea that he was unable to attend to his duties in person. The control of the Church courts was placed in the hands of a commission of which Laud was the leading spirit. Care would now be taken to keep in check those who, contrary to the King's proclamation, ventured to write books against Arminianism.[1]

Oct. 9. Abbot's jurisdiction sequestered.

Laud rose higher in the King's favour as Abbot fell. Hopes had been given to him of succeeding eventually to the Archbishopric of Canterbury, and now, on June 17, just as Buckingham was sent to Rhé, Charles promised him the Bishopric of London as soon as a vacancy occurred.[2] As Buckingham imposed upon Charles by the romantic side of his nature, filling his mind with the promise of those great achievements upon which he loved to dwell, Laud imposed upon him by his love of external authority and his contempt for the popular will. Two such counsellors were enough to ruin any prince.

Laud strong in the King's favour.

By this time a licenser had been found for Sibthorpe's sermon in the least reputable of the prelates then living. Montaigne, Bishop of London, has been severely dealt with by both of the Church parties. "Which," wrote Milton ironically of the condition of a primitive bishop, "what a plural endowment to the many-benefice-gaping mouth of a prelate, what a relish it would give to his canary-sucking and swan-eating palate, let old

May 8. Sibthorpe's sermon licensed by Bishop Montaigne.

---

[1] Commission, Oct. 9, *State Trials*, ii. 1451. Abbot's narrative in *Rushworth*, i. 434. Fuller's blunder (vi. 42), that Abbot was suspended for his 'casual homicide,' has been exposed by Heylyn, *Examen*, 206. But it has probably done more than anything else to keep alive the belief that Abbot's retirement from affairs was owing to that cause. The part which he took in the Parliament of 1628, and which is only known by the revelations of *Elsing's Notes*, shows that he did not shrink from public activity when he expected any good to come of it.

[2] Heylyn, *Life of Laud*, 174; Laud's Diary, *Works*, iii. 196.

Bishop Montaigne judge for me."[1]   Even Laud's admiring biographer, Heylyn, spoke of him as 'a man inactive and addicted to voluptuousness, and one that loved his ease too well to disturb himself in the concernments of the Church.[2] The year before he had made himself notorious by the vigour with which he threw himself into the support of Buckingham's candidature at Cambridge, and he had recently, in sending a present to the Duke, assured him that he could not live if the present were refused. For, he said, when God returns back a man's sacrifice, it is because he is offended with him.[3]

Sibthorpe's sermon had, indeed, done much to exasperate the popular feeling; but there were others who were prepared to go to greater lengths than he. In two sermons preached before the King in July, Dr. Roger Manwaring asserted in the strongest possible terms the duty of obeying the King as the ordinance of God, on pain of eternal damnation. The King represented the rule of justice as opposed to that of mere numbers. He then applied the argument to the refusers of the loan. "First," he said, after a reference to those who appealed to Parliamentary right, "if they would please to consider that though such assemblies as are the highest and greatest assemblies of a kingdom, be most sacred and honourable, and necessary also to those ends to which they were at first instituted; yet know we must, that ordained they were not to this end, to contribute any right to kings, whereby to challenge tributary aids and subsidiary helps; but for the more equal imposing and more easy exacting of that which unto kings doth appertain by natural and original law and justice, as their proper inheritance annexed to their imperial crowns from their birth. And therefore if by a magistrate that is supreme, if upon necessity extreme and urgent, such subsidiary helps be required, a proportion being held respectively to the ability of the persons charged, and the sum and quantity so required surmount not too remarkably the use and charge for which it was levied, very hard would it be for any man in the world

---

[1] *On Reformation in England.*   [2] Heylyn, *Life of Laud,* 174.
[3] Montaigne to Buckingham, March (?), 1627, *S. P. Dom.*

that should not accordingly satisfy such demands, to defend his conscience from that heavy prejudice of resisting the ordinance of God, and receiving to himself damnation; though every of those circumstances be not observed, which by the municipal law is required.

"Secondly, if they would consider the importunities that often may be urgent, and pressing necessities of State that cannot stay without certain and apparent danger for the motion and revolution of so great and vast a body as such assemblies are, nor yet abide their long and pausing deliberation when they are assembled, nor stand upon the answering of those jealous and over-wary cautions and objections made by some who, wedded overmuch to the love of epidemical and popular errors, and bent to cross the most just and lawful designs of their wise and gracious sovereign, and that under plausible shows of singular liberty and freedom, which, if their conscience might speak, would appear nothing more than the satisfying either of private humours, passions, or purposes."[1]

Such was the argument which Charles wished to see printed for the instruction of his subjects. Even Laud remonstrated. There were things in the sermon, he said, 'which would be very distasteful to the people.' Charles was, however, resolute. Montaigne was ordered to license the book, and Montaigne once more did as he was bid.[2]

Posterity has wisely decided against the principles advocated by Manwaring. Whatever the evils were which he attacked, the remedy which he proposed was undoubtedly worse than the disease. Yet it would be unfair to deny that the germ of much that was evil existed in the pretensions of the House of Commons. In defending the rights of the individual against arbitrary taxation, words were sometimes spoken which might be used to countenance that undue reverence for property and vested rights which was the bane of

[1] This extract, brought before the Lords by Pym, is printed in *State Trials*, iii. 346. A copy of the two sermons, printed under the title 'Religion and Allegiance,' is in the Library of Sion College.

[2] *State Trials*, iii. 351. Books might be licensed by the Archbishop of Canterbury or the Bishop of London.

VOL. VI.　　　　　P

a later period, and to discountenance that higher ideal according to which each man is called to justify his claims upon society by arguments founded upon the welfare of the society in which he lives. Nor is it possible to deny that the growing ascendency of the House of Commons, desirable as it was, had yet its ugly side ; that it might come to represent the interests rather than the wisdom of the nation, and that, unless the national mind were aroused to reverence for justice, it might be as arbitrary as Charles had ever been, and as little inclined to deal justly with those who were from any cause regarded with detestation or contempt by any considerable majority of its members.

It may reasonably be allowed that Parliaments no more approach ideal perfection than kings are likely to approach it. It was Manwaring's mistake that he exaggerated that which was worst in the House of Commons, and that he exaggerated still more that which was best in Charles. What he saw in the Royal authority was that which enthusiastic dreamers always imagine that they see in the government of their preference. Royalty was to him what the Republic has been to many a republican. What he sighed for was a ruler who would look beyond the wants of the moment, beyond the petty exigencies of partisan and private objects, to that ideal justice to which the influence of wealth would be no seduction and the clamour of ignorance no hindrance. The authority of kings, he asserts, rising almost into poetic fervour as he utters the words, is derived directly from God. It has no dependence even upon angels. Nothing in the world, nothing in the hierarchy of the Church can restrain them. " No parts within their dominions, no persons under their jurisdictions, be they never so great, can be privileged from their power, nor be exempted from their care be they never so mean. To this power the highest and greatest peer must stoop, and cast down his coronet at the footstool of his sovereign. The poorest creature which lieth by the wall or goes by the highway-side, is not without sundry and sensible tokens of that sweet and royal care and providence which extendeth itself to the lowest of his subjects. The way they pass by is the king's highway. The laws which make provision for their relief take their binding force from the supreme will of their liege lord. The bread that feeds their hungry souls, the poor rags which hide their nakedness, all are the fruit and superfluity of that happy plenty and abundance caused by a wise and peaceable government."

The time would come when a triumphant Parliament would be forced to hear from the lips of Cromwell that a great country cannot be ruled by mere law and custom, whilst those who are entrusted with its guidance are fattening upon the abuses which they have neither the will nor the understanding to remove. In 1627 the immediate danger did not lie here. Whatever Laud or Manwaring might think, Charles's government was in no sense of the word a national government, able to appeal to the higher needs of the people, and to take its stand above disputing factions. How such a government would rise upon the basis of the Parliamentary institutions of the seventeenth century was the secret of the future. The claim of Parliament to predominance had yet to be rendered otherwise than intolerable by the admission of the air of liberty and publicity within its walls to an extent which the foremost men of Charles's reign found it impossible to conceive. Yet even as it was, with all its faults, the hope of England was in the House of Commons and not in Charles. The Commons, it is true, had failed in apprehending the full meaning of religious liberty; they had made mistakes in their mode of dealing with this or that action of the Crown; but the great principle that, when new circumstances call for new modes of action, the course to be pursued must be resolved upon in concurrence with those men whom the nation chooses or allows to represent it, was the principle upon which the greatness of England had rested in past ages, and the vindication of which was the business upon which the Parliaments of Charles's day employed themselves for the benefit of posterity.

Objections to the theory.

It was fitting that the first answer—if not to Manwaring's sermons, at least to the spirit by which those sermons were prompted—should proceed from Eliot, the man to whom the House of Commons was the representative of as high a wisdom as the King was to Manwaring, and to whom the old laws of

England were not records of the dead past, telling a mingled tale of wisdom and folly, but words fraught with stern resolve and prophetic hope, in which a mighty nation had recorded for all future time the conditions on which alone it would deign to live, and from which no subsequent generation, on pain of degradation, might dare to depart.

From his prison in the Gatehouse Eliot's petition was sent to the King,[1] humble in outward form, unbending in its firm reliance on the strength of the position it assumed. "The rule of justice," he declared, "he takes to be the law; the impartial arbiter of government and obedience; the support and strength of majesty; the observation of that justice by which subjection is commanded: whereto religion, adding to these a power not to be resisted, binds up the conscience in an obligation to that rule, which, without open prejudice and violation to those duties, may not be impeached."

Eliot's petition from the Gatehouse.

Then came a string of quotations from statutes of the first and third Edward directed against taxation without the consent of Parliament, followed by the one clause which bore directly upon the question of the loan. In the reign of Edward III., on the petition of the Commons, it had been 'established that the loans which are granted to the King by divers persons be released, and that none from henceforth be compelled to make such loans against their wills, because it is against reason and the franchises of the land; and that restitution be made to such as made such loans.'

Precedents affecting the loan.

Looked at narrowly, it may perhaps be doubted how far these words will bear the interpretation placed upon them. The case in the time of Edward III. appears to have been that the Royal officers first compelled certain merchants to advance beforehand customs which were not due for some months to come, and subsequently refused repayment of the money thus

---

[1] Printed in Forster's *Eliot*, i. 410. The petition seems to have been generally adopted by others in like circumstances (*Forster*, 408, note 4); but the language seems characteristic of Eliot, and I have no doubt that he had at least a main hand in drawing it up, doubtless after consultation with lawyers.

obtained.[1] An advocate of the prerogative might perhaps ask what this had to do with a demand made generally in a case of pressing necessity, when the House of Commons had, as he would say, taken advantage of the King's circumstances to impose its will upon the Crown, in defiance of the constitution of the kingdom. It is, however, needless to pursue further such investigations. The strength of Eliot's case lay precisely in that which even he did not venture to say, that the necessity, so far as it was a necessity at all, had arisen from sheer misgovernment, and that the appeal to a higher law than that of the realm, which Charles was continually making, needed no discussion, because no case had really arisen making such an appeal needful.

Such is the point of view which the modern reader should keep resolutely before his eyes. If the gentry who closed their purses against the loan had believed that a real danger existed, or that Buckingham's policy was really calculated to advance the cause of Protestantism, they would surely not have been extreme to mark any deviation from the strict laws of constitutional propriety. Many of them were the same men who in 1621 and in 1624 had kept silence on the subject of the impositions, deeply as they felt the wrong which had been done to them. Their belief that the whole argument from necessity was based upon a fiction must be taken for granted; but it was none the less present to their minds because they veiled it in silence before that sovereign whom they longed to honour and reverence above all human beings.

Point of view from which the question is to be regarded.

At last five of the prisoners—Sir Thomas Darnel, Sir John Corbet, Sir Walter Erle, Sir John Heveningham, and Sir Edmund Hampden—appealed to the Court of King's Bench for a *habeas corpus*, in order that they might know what their offence had been. On November 15 they were brought to the bar, and the 22nd was appointed for the argument of their counsel.

Five of the prisoners demand their habeas corpus.

Four notable lawyers, Bramston, Noy, Selden, and Cal-

---

[1] 25 Edw. III., *Rolls of Parliament*, ii. 239, compared with ii. 230.

throp appeared for the defence. It was admitted on both sides that the King and the Council had a right to commit to prison; but it was held on the part of the defendants that the cause of committal must be expressed in order that the case might come before the Court of King's Bench, which would proceed to bail the prisoner or to remand him to prison, if it saw fit, till the day of trial came. From this point of view the King and the Privy Council would be reduced to the position occupied in less important cases by ordinary justices of the peace. They would merely prepare the case for the King's Bench, and if they were too long in their preparations, the judges, on being appealed to, would set the prisoner at liberty on bail.

Nov. 22. The defence.

Whether this theory were right or wrong, it is certain that for many years it had not been in accordance with the practice. The Privy Council had again and again kept persons in prison, as dangerous to the State, without attempting to bring them to trial,[1] and those so imprisoned had patiently awaited their deliverance from the King's mercy, without venturing an appeal to a court of justice. On their side the Privy Councillors had taken their own time in preparing accusations, sometimes because fresh evidence was expected, sometimes because they had reasons for keeping the prisoner shut up as long as possible.

Inspired by the indignation which had blazed up everywhere on the imposition of the loan, these four lawyers now stood forward to plead that all this was utterly illegal. They had much to say in defence of their position. The Great Charter, they urged, declared that 'no man should be imprisoned except by the legal judgment of his peers, or by the law of the land,' and these latter words, they said, were interpreted by certain statutes of the time of Edward III. to mean 'due process of law,' which an examination before the Privy Council was not. They then drew attention to the consequences which would result from any other interpretation.

Argument from Magna Carta.

[1] Arabella Stuart, for instance, and more recently the Earl of Arundel, for whom no claim had been put forward, except when Parliament was sitting.

If the Privy Council could imprison without showing a cause upon which the Court of King's Bench could act, a man might never leave his prison till he was released by death. The argument was followed by a long string of precedents in which persons committed by the Privy Council had been brought before the King's Bench to be bailed as a preparation for trial.

and from precedents.

When the argument was concluded, the decorum of the place was startled by unusual sounds. Men shouted out their approval and clapped their hands for joy.[1] Even the judges themselves were shaken. "Mr. Attorney," said Jones, "if it be so that the law of Magna Carta and other statutes be now in force, and the gentlemen be not delivered by this Court, how shall they be delivered? Apply yourselves to show us any other way to deliver them." "Or else," said Doderidge, "they shall have a perpetual imprisonment."

Effect of the argument.

Heath was not likely to startle the Court by placing his argument for the Crown in an extravagant form. The precedents on the other side he met by showing, at least to his own satisfaction, that they were all cases in which the King had voluntarily handed over the prisoners to be dealt with in the King's Bench, and that they therefore proved nothing as to the course which the Court ought to take if the King refused to do so. Further, he urged that due process of law extended to committals by the King, just as it extended to committals by the House of Commons, and that therefore the Court of King's Bench had no right to interfere. In Queen Elizabeth's time the judges, as was proved by a statement alleged—incorrectly as it afterwards appeared—to have been drawn up by Chief Justice Anderson, had decided, after due consultation, that the King was not bound in all cases to show cause. For, as Heath argued, one of two things might happen. There might be persons who had committed no crime which would bring them under the ordinary penalties of the law, but whose liberty would be dangerous to the State. In support of this theory he referred to the children of an Irish chieftain,

Nov. 26. Heath's argument for the Crown.

---

[1] —— to Meade, Nov. 23, *Court and Times,* i. 292.

who had themselves done no wrong, but who had been condemned to a lifelong imprisonment in the Tower, lest their liberation should be the signal for a revolution in Ireland. Upon this branch of his argument, however, the Attorney-General did not lay much stress. The days were long passed when—in England at least—any individual was likely to be dangerous from his social position, and Heath had more to say on the other branch of his argument. It was the duty of the Privy Council to prepare matters for trial. These matters, often involving the discovery of deeply laid plots, frequently demanded a long time to disentangle their intricacies. If the cause of committal were at once signified, and the trial hurried on, accomplices would escape and the ends of justice would be frustrated. All that the judges were asked to do was to trust the King so far as to take it for granted that he had good reasons for withholding the case for the present from their knowledge.

The next day judgment was delivered. If Coke had been upon the Bench he would probably have seized the opportunity of asserting the supremacy of the Court over all causes whatever. But Hyde was not a Coke; and though the other judges—Whitelocke, Doderidge, and Jones—were honourable men, they were not likely to see their way clearly in so difficult a path. The judges took a middle course.[1] Adopting Heath's view of the statutes and

Nov. 28.
The judgment.

---

[1] Whitelocke, when examined in the House of Lords, declared that the prisoners might have had a fresh *habeas corpus* the next day, and that the Judges only took time to advise. "I did never see nor know," he said, "by any record that upon such a return as this a man was bailed, the King not first consulted with in such a case as this. The Commons' House do not know what letters and commands we receive, for these remain in our Court and are not viewed by them." I do not understand these last words as implying that there were private solicitations and threats addressed to the Judges, for these could not be said to remain in court. I fancy the argument is that the Judges had a right to decide whether they would liberate or no, and that they ought to decide in favour of liberty if the prisoner remained in prison too long; but that the special mandate of the King was a *primâ facie* argument that there was a good cause, though it was not expressed. All that was needed was that the Judges should be convinced that there was a good cause, and for this it was not necessary to have the case

precedents, they held that it would be impertinence on their part to hasten the King's proceedings. They therefore refused to admit the prisoners to bail : but, on the other hand, they refused to leave any evidence on the records of the Court that they held that the Crown might persistently refuse to show cause.[1]

The question not settled. It was perhaps best as it was. The question in debate opened up so many issues too wide to be determined by the decision of a purely legal tribunal, that it was well that it should be discussed in an assembly more competent to rise to the height of the great argument. For it is evident that Heath's strongest point as a lawyer would be his weakest when he came to appeal to statesmen. The judges might hesitate to sanction a doctrine which might allow a wily Pretender to the crown to wander about untouched on English soil, or might force on the premature disclosure of the clue by which the Government hoped to come upon the traces of some second Gunpowder Plot. The multitude, which had broken through the stern rules of etiquette by applauding the popular lawyers a week before, knew full well that nothing of the kind was really at issue at the moment. Eliot and Hampden had no influence in England beyond that of the principles which they professed. It was a matter of notoriety that there was no fresh evidence to be collected, no deep conspiracy to be tracked in its secret windings. If all that Charles wanted was to obtain the decision of the Court of King's Bench upon the legality of the loan, he might have sent every one of the prisoners to trial months before as easily as he could now.

Yet the prospect of seeing the legality of the King's proceedings discussed in Parliament seemed more distant than ever. The Duke talked confidently of ruining French commerce, and of carrying on the war for many years.[2] He argued that

argued in open court. This information they would derive from 'letters and commands,' and would exercise the discretion which a police magistrate now exercises when he grants a remand upon application in open court, on the ground that the evidence is not complete. *Rushworth*, i. 560.

[1] *State Trials*, iii. 1.
[2] Contarini to the Doge, Dec. $\frac{4}{14}$, *Ven. Transcripts, R. O.*

what had happened was no fault of his. His honour was safe. He had been deserted by those who ought to have succoured him at home. But, whatever the explanation might be, there was no turn in the tide of his mishaps. In the beginning of December it was settled that Carlisle should go upon the Continent, to take up the web of intrigue which Walter Montague[1] had spun. In a few days news arrived that an officer commissioned by Richelieu had swooped down upon Montague as he was passing through Lorraine, and, in spite of the protection of neutral territory, had carried him and his despatches to Paris. Montague was lodged in the Bastille. His papers, with all they had to tell of intrigues with the Dukes of Savoy and Lorraine and with the French aristocracy, were under the cold, penetrating eyes of the Cardinal.[2]

The Duke's difficulties.

W. Montague seized by the French.

At home matters were in the greatest possible confusion. Before the end of November Buckingham had gone to Portsmouth, and had distributed money in his affable way amongst the soldiers and sailors;[3] but he could do no more than satisfy them for a time. His back was hardly turned when letter after letter came to assure him that everything was in disorder.[4] At Plymouth the sailors were stealing and selling the soldiers' arms; all were without sufficient clothes in the wintry weather; the ships were leaky, and there were scarcely sailors enough on board to carry them round to the Medway to be docked at Chatham.[5] The soldiers were paid till the 10th of December, but there was no means of doing anything more.[6] Captain Mason was sent down to set matters straight, but he reported that Sir James Bagg, whose business it had been to pay the

Want of money at home.

Misery of the sailors.

[1] See page 167.

[2] Contarini to the Doge, Dec. $\frac{4}{14}$; Beaulieu to Puckering, Dec. 12, 19. Meade to Stuteville, Dec. 15, *Court and Times*, i. 303–307. Richelieu, *Mémoires*.

[3] Contarini to the Doge, $\frac{\text{Nov. 22}}{\text{Dec. 2}}$, *Ven. Transcripts, R. O.*

[4] Bagg to Buckingham, Nov. 29; Courtney to Buckingham, Nov. 29, *S. P. Dom.* lxxxv. 61, 64.

[5] Holland to Buckingham, Dec. 5, *ibid.* lxxxvi. 15.

[6] Bagg to Buckingham, Dec. 7, *ibid.* lxxxvi. 27.

men, had received large sums for which he was unable or unwilling to account.¹ At Portsmouth matters were even worse. Many of the ships' companies prepared to desert in a body, and to march up to Whitehall with their complaints. It was only upon a false assurance that money was coming to relieve them at Christmas, that they consented to remain on board. They had not, they said, been paid for ten months. Their clothes were worn out, and they knew not what to do.²

If the sailors were in evil plight no one suffered but themselves. The soldiers billeted about the country spread the mischief in all directions. It was bad enough for a quiet countryman to be forced to entertain, for due payment, a number of rough young men whose character before they were pressed into the service was probably none of the best : but when payment did not come the burden threatened to become utterly unendurable. The Irish quartered in Essex were especially obnoxious to the peasant. They treated him and his family as the dust beneath their feet. They flung about the goodwife's household utensils. They broke the furniture, and threw the meat into the fire if it did not suit their tastes.³ A German peasant would perhaps have wondered at their gentleness, and would have thanked God that they did not proceed to graver outrages still. In England, what was done was enough to rouse public indignation in classes which the loan had hardly reached.

The soldiers' outrages.

At all costs money must be had. The loan had brought in on the whole 236,000*l*., only 52,000*l*. less than the sum originally expected.⁴ There was a talk, if rumour might be believed, of recurring to a fresh loan ;⁵ but the idea, if it was ever seriously entertained, was soon abandoned, excepting so far as 10,000*l*. were extracted on some pretence or other from the Six Clerks of the Court of Chancery.

Means proposed for raising money.

---

¹ Mason to Buckingham, Dec. 13, *S. P. Dom.* lxxxvi. 70, 75.
² Watts to Buckingham, Dec. 16, *ibid.* lxxxvi. 83, 86.
³ The inhabitants of Maldon to the Council, with inclosures, Feb. 10 (?), *S. P. Dom.* xcii. 85.
⁴ State of the loan up to Nov. 30, *ibid.* lxxxv. 77.
⁵ —— to Meade, Nov. 30, *Court and Times,* i. 296.

The only resource left was the mortgage or sale of Crown lands. In this way 143,000*l.* were obtained in the half-year beginning at Michaelmas, and on December 17 the City of London agreed to pay 120,000*l.* by instalments on the security of the King's rents from landed property.[1]

The whole sum thus obtained was 263,000*l.*; but even this amount, large as it was, did not cover the deficit of the past year, the anticipations on the revenue on December 29 amounting to 319,000*l.*,[2] or little less than two-thirds of the whole ordinary revenue of the Crown. Even if this could be paid off, the pressure of the preparations for war was enormous. Together with the recruits which had been levied to reinforce Buckingham at Rhé, there were now 7,557 land soldiers and 4,000 seamen, entitled to pay at the rate of 200,000*l.* a year. If fifty sail were to be sent out in the spring, 110,000*l.* more would be needed for repairs and munitions,[3] and there was besides the immediate necessity of providing and sending out the provisions urgently wanted by Rochelle before its supplies were cut off by the besieging forces.

Pressing necessities.

The one thing needed was to make peace. Peace, however, was the last thing of which either Buckingham or Charles thought. The dislike of the French war, which was universal in the nation, had settled down even upon the Privy Council. Some of its members were less outspoken than others; but those who had the best opportunities of judging were of opinion that Charles and the Lord High Admiral stood alone in their resolution to resist all reasonable overtures of peace.

Not, indeed, that Charles and Buckingham acknowledged the case to be so in their own minds. When the King of France sent back the prisoners taken at Rhé without demanding a ransom,[4] the Venetian ambassador thought it a fair opportunity to urge Charles to meet these advances in a conciliatory spirit. "I will not say," was the King's

Charles determined on carrying on the war.

---

[1] Proceedings of the Common Council, Dec. 17, *S. P. Dom.* lxxxvi. 97.
[2] List of anticipations, Dec. 29, *ibid.* lxxxvii. 63.
[3] Note of charges, Dec. 22, *S. P. Dom.* lxxxvii. 35.
[4] Contarini to the Doge, Dec. $\frac{18}{28}$, *Ven. Transcripts*, R. O.

reply, "that the retreat was fortunate, but neither can I assert that it was ruinous. My intentions were always directed towards the common cause, without the remotest thought of ever gaining a span of territory from France, knowing that circumstances were unsuited to such a design. Had not the King my brother allowed me to give a guarantee for the Huguenots, I should never have stirred. But as his intentions were always false and feigned, as appeared by his actions in the employment of Mansfeld, in the league for the Valtelline, and in the affair of the edicts he promised to the Huguenots, I deemed it a lesser evil to have him for an open enemy than to have him for a false friend, in order that I might prevent his corrupt policy from taking effect. I am aware that this is not the moment for calling him to account for the lesser injuries he has done me. Whenever he makes me think he is of the same mind with myself, I shall readily join him in the relief of Germany.

"But he is determined to destroy Rochelle, and I am determined to support it; for I will never allow my word to be forfeited.

"I believe that the safest plan would be to recommence operations, and to send an army of 20,000 men to Rochelle, from which point succour could be given to the whole Huguenot body. I am convinced that in this way I and the King of France will be the sooner friends."

In much the same way Buckingham spoke "The French," he said, "have vowed to destroy Rochelle, and we to preserve it. As long as this punctilio exists there is no use in treating or speaking of peace. Let all men beware of dealing with Frenchmen, for they are thoroughly false." [1]

Buckingham's views.

With such sentiments as these peace was hopeless. Yet how were the growing expenses of the war to be met? Buckingham, audacious as ever, advocated the calling of a Parliament. The last of all men to believe that his actions would not stand the light, he threw himself on his knees before the

---

[1] Contarini to the Doge, $\frac{\text{Dec. 23}}{\text{Jan. 2}}$, *Ven. Transcripts, R. O.* As I have merely a translation of a translation to give, I have altered some of the less important words, so as to bring out the sense more clearly.

King. If he were found worthy of death, he said, let them not spare him.[1] After Christmas he made the same proposal in open council, but the King would not hear of such a measure. The Councillors knew not what to think when they heard the great Duke pleading for once in vain. They fancied there was some collusion, and that the scene had been pre-arranged for the purpose of winning popularity for the favourite. Then was seen the effect of such predominance as Buckingham's upon the men whom he had trained to flatter, not to counsel. Not a man ventured to open his mouth to give advice. The sovereign and the favourite were isolated at the council board as they were in the nation.[2]

It is far more likely that Buckingham expressed his real opinions. The Council, however, had to obey the King, and they were called upon to discuss the best means of filling up the deficiency irregularly.[3] They were first asked to declare whether they would themselves render obedience to any resolution which might be taken. Upon their answering in the affirmative, they came to the conclusion that some excise upon commodities —beer or wine to begin with—would be necessary. And yet how was it to be done? Persuasion, it was generally recognised, would be of no avail. Any attempt to impose the new taxes by force would be met by an appeal to the courts of law, and the courts of law were certain to decide against the Crown. The only resort from this difficulty would be a proclamation, the contravention of which would be punishable in the Star Chamber.

Debate in the Council on taxation.

Proposed excise.

---

[1] Meade to Stuteville, Dec. 15, *Court and Times*, i. 304.

[2] Contarini to the Doge, Jan. $\frac{1}{11}$, *Ven. Transcripts, R. O.*

[3] This debate in the Council is from a paper which was used by Hallam (*Hargrave MSS.* 321, p. 300). It is a modern copy taken by some one who could not properly read the original, and is in some parts unintelligible. Its date is not given; but from a statement in Contarini's despatch last quoted, that the Council had been occupied with schemes for laying impositions on commodities, I have no doubt that the discussion took place in the last week of the year. At all events, as the King's last words show, it must have been before Jan. 30.

It would be interesting to know from whom the last recommendation proceeded ; but the brief notes which alone have reached us are silent on this head. Whoever the bold man may have been, the King felt himself called upon once more to justify so unheard-of a proceeding. "If there were any other way," he said, "I would tarry for your advices. I can find no other real way. For the particulars, I have thought of some. If you can find any easier, I will hearken to it. To call a Parliament, the occasion will not let me tarry so long."

Was it really only the want of time which hindered the calling of a Parliament? At all events the courtiers were bound to believe that it was so. When the King proceeded to support the plan for an excise upon beer and wine, they all assented to the wisdom of the proposal. Suffolk, Laud, and Weston agreed that something of the kind must be done. Buckingham spoke at greater length. In obedience to Charles he had by this time abandoned the idea of a Parliament, and he fell back upon the idea of strengthening the throne by military force, which he had entertained in 1624.[1] "Had you not spent all your own means," he is reported to have said, addressing the King, "and yet your friends lost, I would not have advised this way. But being raised to defend religion, your kingdoms, and your friends, I see no other way but this. Neighbour kings are now beyond you in revenue ... therefore, not I, but necessity of affairs." The army, he went on to say, would require 200,000*l.*, and 300,000*l.* would be needed for the navy. The army would be kept at home as a standing force of 11,000 men,

A standing force proposed. in readiness to be employed in the relief of Rochelle or of the King of Denmark, as the case might require. On December 29 it was formally resolved that a fleet of 100 sail should be got ready in the ensuing summer.[2] To the demand for an army, apart from any expeditionary force to be actually employed for a definite purpose, all who spoke, with the single exception of Sir John Savile, gave their approbation. As a military measure it would be an admirable precaution to have a standing depôt at home; but what would

---

[1] See Vol. V. p. 195.   [2] *Council Register*, Dec. 29.

be its effect upon the civil constitution? Were the armed men, in the intervals of fighting at Rochelle or in Denmark, to force the new taxes upon England in defiance of courts of law and universal indignation?[1] Nor was this the only danger. Dulbier, now Buckingham's chief military adviser, was to be sent over to Germany with Sir William Balfour to levy a thousand German horse, who were to form the cavalry of this force. It would probably be hard to convince those who heard the news that nothing more than a mere measure of military precaution was intended. That Dulbier's horsemen were intended as a threat to the English opponents of the Government is a belief which has been frequently adopted by modern writers. But, after all, there is one circumstance which militates against this interpretation. Already, on December 29, the King had declared his intention of reviewing the cavalry of the militia of the ten counties nearest London;[2] and it seems incredible that, if Charles had really intended to suppress resistance by the sword, he should think of calling out a body of armed men who, as drawn from a class whose possessions were larger than those of the foot militia, were hardly likely to stand by in silence whilst their countrymen were being trodden down by a handful of German horse. Probably, after all, nothing more was meant by Balfour and Dulbier's commission than met the eye. It would only be one more example of Charles's extreme ignorance of the people amongst whom he lived if he fancied that he could summon

margin: 1628. January. German horse sent for.

---

[1] Conway to the Clerk of the Signet, Jan. 14, *S. P. Dom.* xc. 80. The last suspicion was strongly entertained by Contarini in his despatch of $\frac{\text{Jan. 28}}{\text{Feb. 7}}$. Mr. Forster (*Sir J. Eliot*, i. 417) has suggested that they were intended to overawe the Parliament. But the arrangements were made before a Parliament was determined on. Still there may have been some eventual intention of this kind. Mr. Forster was aware that the order for the money for Balfour and Dulbier was signed on the 30th of January. But he does not seem to have noticed Conway's letter for its preparation as early as the 14th. That Dulbier's horsemen were to be Roman Catholics is a later invention. They were levied in North Germany, and were subsequently transferred to the army of Gustavus. Dulbier was taken prisoner by Tilly at New Brandenburg. Charles wrote in vain to request his liberation.

[2] *Council Register*, Dec. 20.

them to his defence at the same time that he was pressing them down with illegal taxation, and flaunting in their eyes the banners of his foreign mercenaries.

The deliberations of the Council about raising money dragged on more slowly than their deliberations about raising men. The more the subject was discussed the less easy it must have seemed to venture upon so flagrant a breach of the law as the scheme which had been mooted. Avowedly or tacitly the proposed excise was abandoned for a time. The next scheme which rose and died away was one to compel every parish to keep three armed men in readiness at its own cost, thus producing a force of rather more than 30,000 men. Towards the end of January the Council assembled daily. One plan after another was discussed, and some even took heart to maintain, in the face of the King and the Duke, that it would be better to withdraw altogether from the Continent, and to be content with maintaining a strong defence at home. No names are given, but the counsel is attributed to the Spanish faction, the old opponents of the war, of whom Weston was the sole remaining Privy Councillor, though he may possibly have been supported by other voices at such a time.[1]

The proposed excise abandoned.

Nor was this the only unpalatable advice to which Charles was compelled to listen. Those who were disinclined to withdraw altogether from interference on the Continent told him plainly that the only alternative was a Parliament.[2] One obstacle, indeed, no longer stood in the way. On January 2 orders[3] had been given that the prison doors should be opened to those who had been confined for their refusal to pay the loan. Seventy-six persons in all, some imprisoned, some in banishment in different counties, were permitted to return home, but we may be certain that not one of the whole number felt the slightest gratitude for

Release of the prisoners in confinement about the loan.

---

[1] Contarini to the Doge, Jan. $\frac{10, 20, \text{Jan. } 28}{20, 30, \text{Feb. } 7}$, *Ven. Transcripts, R. O.*

[2] *Council Register*, Jan. 2.

[3] The King to the Council; the King to Worcester, Jan. 25, *S. P. Dom.* xci. 52. *Docquet Book*.

the word which had unbarred the doors closed upon them by the decree of arbitrary power.

On January 25 the King, who had not yet consented to summon Parliament, ordered a fresh issue of Privy seals, the old resource of the forced loan under another form. The next few days were spent in urging upon the unwilling Charles the necessity of calling a Parliament. The leading personages at Court [1]—their names have not reached us—gave their personal guarantee that no attempt should be made to renew the Duke's impeachment. At a late hour on the night of the 30th Charles gave way, and orders were given that writs should be issued for a new Parliament.[2]

Jan. 25 Privy seals proposed.

Jan. 30. Parliament to meet.

Nothing, however, was further from Charles's intention than to place himself without conditions in the hands of the House of Commons. As sheriffs were chosen in November, it was too late to have recourse in January to the manœuvre which had been practised two years before; but various schemes were canvassed for making the Lower House pliable. It is even said that it was proposed to issue a proclamation excluding all lawyers from sitting, and it was decided that any attempt to touch the Duke should be followed by an immediate dissolution. In that case the King would consider himself no longer bound by the laws and customs of the realm.[3]

Parliament was not even to be allowed the option of giving or refusing. It was to meet on March 17, and the fleet was to put to sea on the 1st. A scheme for levying subsidies before they were granted approved itself highly to Charles's mind. His fleets since 1625 had been largely composed of vessels demanded from the port towns and the maritime counties. The idea of a universal ship-money to be levied in every county in England seemed to him to be merely a further extension of

---

[1] Pembroke, one would guess a likely man.

[2] The date, with the rest of the facts, I get from Contarini's despatch of $\frac{\text{Jan. 31}}{\text{Feb. 10}}$. He is more likely to know than Meade, who gives Jan. 28.

Contarini to the Doge, $\frac{\text{Jan. 21}}{\text{Feb. 10}}$, *Ven. Transcripts, R.O.*

the old principle. On February 11 letters were issued to all the shires. The distress of the King of Denmark, the ruin of English commerce in Germany and the Baltic, the danger to Rochelle and the Protestant religion, and the possibility of invasion from France and Spain were made the most of. It was asserted that the fleet must go to sea before Parliament could be brought together, and it was stated that if the money were paid at once the King would allow Parliament to meet; if not, he would think of some other way. The sum assessed upon each county must be levied and paid into the Exchequer by March 1. The whole sum demanded in England was 173,000*l.*[1] On the 15th the clergy were ordered to pay 20,000*l.* as a free gift.[2]

<small>Feb. 11. Ship-money to be collected.</small>

A few days brought wiser counsels. Lord Northampton, when he made the unheard-of demand in Warwickshire, of which county he was Lord Lieutenant, was told to his face that he had promised that the last loan should be repaid, and was asked how he could expect to draw more money from the subjects' purses. In Berkshire the Earl of Banbury, the honest Wallingford of James's reign, refused to raise his voice in favour of ship-money, on the ground that he had engaged, if the loan were paid, never to ask anything unparliamentary again. Such words were doubtless but samples of others uttered all over England. Charles swiftly drew back, revoked his letters, and hung up ship-money in the Royal armoury of projects to be used as occasion might require.[3]

<small>The orders revoked.</small>

Charles, however, could not understand that the insuperable objection which his subjects appeared to entertain towards the payment of ship-money extended to all unparliamentary taxation whatever. On February 29 he issued a commission to the leading members of the Privy Council, directing them to consider all the best and speediest ways and means of raising money 'by impositions or

<small>Feb. 29. Commission for excise.</small>

---

[1] The King to the Sheriffs of Anglesea, Feb. 11; List of the sums levied on the counties (Feb. 11), *S. P. Dom.* xcii. 88, 93.

[2] The King to Archbishop Abbot, Feb. 15, *S. P. Dom.* xciii. 39.

[3] Beaulieu to Puckering, Feb. 20; Meade to Stuteville, Feb. 22, *Court and Times,* i 322 324.

otherwise' as they might think best, 'in a case of this inevitable necessity, wherein form and circumstance must be dispensed with rather than the substance be lost or hazarded.'[1]

That Charles should have imagined it to be possible that he could raise money in such a manner is indeed strange. All that can be said is that he was in desperate straits. While he was racking his brains Rochelle was perishing. Ever since November the city had been blockaded. A line of entrenchments cut it off from all communication with the country around, and the Cardinal, in the midst of the winter storms, restlessly superintended the erection of two vast piers projecting from either side of the long harbour to bar the passage of succours from without. The Rochellese, bold seamen as they were, had not force enough to resist the Royal fleet. Their deputies reminded Charles that they had deprived themselves of provisions to supply Buckingham's wants, and Charles felt it a point of honour to restore the means of subsistence of which he had stripped them.

The blockade of Rochelle.

Denbigh was to take command of the convoy which was to protect the store-ships laden with supplies for Rochelle; but the same causes which had hindered Holland stood in the way of his departure. The convoy was not ready, and the bread, beer, and cheese were spoiling in harbour.[2] On March 15 everything was in disorder. The ships needed repairs. Men ran away as soon as they were pressed. The 26th was talked of as the day on which all would be ready. But unless six hundred men could be pressed and kept from deserting, the fleet could not sail.[3]

Denbigh at Plymouth.

March 15.

On land matters were as bad. At Banbury, encouraged perhaps by the near neighbourhood of Lord Saye, men refused to contribute to the billeting of the soldiers. In Dorsetshire, when the promised payments from the Exchequer were not forthcoming, the men were turned out of doors to steal or

[1] Commission, Feb. 29. *Parl. Hist.* ii. 417.
[2] Burlamachi to Conway, Feb. (?), *S. P. Dom.* xciv. 103.
[3] Denbigh to Buckingham, March 15; Manwaring to Buckingham, March 16, *S. P. Dom.* xcvi. 3, 11.

starve.[1] It might be feared that, unless money could be found speedily, all England would be in an uproar.

All this while the elections were going on, and with a few rare exceptions they went against the Crown. Those who had refused the loan were sure of seats. The House when it met would be as stern in its opposition to illegal measures as the Parliament of 1626.

[1] Banbury to Manchester, Feb. 28; Deputy Lieutenants of Dorsetshire to Suffolk, March 1, *S. P. Dom.* xciv. 73, xcv. 8.

CHAPTER LXII.

THE PARLIAMENTARY LEADERSHIP OF SIR THOMAS WENTWORTH.

ON March 17 the Houses met. The sermon was preached by Laud, on the text, "Endeavour to keep the unity of the Spirit in the bond of peace." The tone of the sermon was somewhat plaintive. Three years before he had set forth, in the presence of the first Parliament of the reign, his theory of the constitution.[1] The King was to do judgment and justice ; the Parliament, by its knowledge of all that was passing in the realm, was to give him information which would enable him to govern with full understanding. The hope that this would be a picture of Charles's reign had turned out to be a dream, and the preacher had no other explanation to give than the evils of distraction and discord against which he warned his hearers.[2]

March 17. Laud's sermon.

It never entered into Laud's head that he was doing his best to foment the distraction and discord which he deplored, by teaching Charles the lesson which he was already too prone to learn, that he had nothing but information to look for from his subjects. The events of the past year had brought the King's authority in question in a way in which it had not been brought in question before. A few days before the opening of the session a meeting of the leading members of the House of Commons had been held at the house of Sir Robert Cotton. There was a general feeling

The meeting of the leaders of the Commons.

---

[1] See p. 204. [2] *Laud's Works,* i. 149.

that the attack upon Buckingham should not be repeated, and
Eliot, who was of the contrary opinion, withdrew his opposition
in the face of the general sentiment, reserving his right to revert
to his original position at some future time. To the others it
was becoming clear, notwithstanding their reluctance to face
the truth, that the main struggle was with the King and not
with Buckingham. The gravity of the situation impressed itself
on their minds. A whole range of questions opened up before
them, every one of them possibly leading to a complete disloca-
tion of the relations existing between the King and his people.
Coke and Phelips, Wentworth and Selden, concurred in the
opinion that the violated rights of the subject must first be
vindicated. The very being of the commonwealth, they declared, was at stake.[1]

If there had been any doubt before of the difficulty of the
work to which the new Parliament had to address itself, there
could be none after the King's speech was delivered.

March 17. The King's speech. Charles seemed determined to console himself for the unpleasant necessity of calling Parliament at all by treating the Houses with studied rudeness. He at least did not 'endeavour to keep the unity of the Spirit in the bond of peace.' He had called his subjects together, he said, in order that means might be provided to meet the common danger. If they failed to do their duty in this, he must, in discharge of his conscience, use those other means which God had put in his hands. They were not to take this as a threat, 'for he scorned to threaten any but his equals;' but he wished them to understand that, though he was ready to forget their distractions in
the last Parliament, he expected them to alter their conduct.[2]

This time there had been no attempt to exclude anyone
from the House of Commons. Yet in spite of all that had
been said and done in the last Parliament, when the

Certain Peers absent. Lords took their seats, Abbot and Williams, Arundel, Bristol, and Lincoln were absent from their places. The Peers quickly called the roll of the House, and instituted inquiry into the reasons of their absence. In a few days the missing

---

[1] Forster, *Sir J. Eliot*, ii. 1.   [2] *Lords' Journals*, iii. 687.

members took their places without further hindrance. Since the last Parliament every one of the five had suffered much from the Government. Abbot had been suspended from the exercise of his functions; Williams had been kept in banishment in his diocese; Arundel had been placed under restraint, nominally for his part in his son's marriage—in reality, it would seem, as an opponent of the warlike policy of the Court; Lincoln had resisted the loan, and had been sent to the Tower; Bristol had been summoned before the Star Chamber to answer to the charges which Charles had been driven to bring against him in the last session. He had, however, fallen seriously ill, and his illness had been taken as an excuse for postponing the prosecution indefinitely. It is hardly likely that it was more than an excuse. He had professed his readiness to produce the private correspondence relating to the journey to Madrid, and it would scarcely be pleasant to Charles to see that mystery laid open, even before a Court as devoted as the Star Chamber.[1]

<small>Bristol's Star Chamber prosecution.</small>

The ability and tact of Bristol alone might make a great difference to the Government if its fortune ever came to depend on the opinion of the Upper House. For the present the main interest was in the Commons. The root of the evils complained of lay in the King's claim to withdraw from the cognisance of the judges all cases of imprisonment by his own command. If Charles could be deprived of the assumed right of punishing offenders against his will, it would matter little what commands he might choose to give. He might ask for loans and taxes as he pleased. No one would be the worse, if the judges invariably liberated persons committed to prison for refusing to comply with his illegal requirements. Such at least seems to have been Coke's opinion. On the 21st he brought in a Bill providing that, except by the sentence of a Court, no person should be detained untried in prison for more than two months if he could find bail, or for more than three months if he could not.[2]

<small>March 21. Coke's Bill on imprisonment.</small>

Whether Coke intended by this Bill to meet all the difficul-

---

[1] Interrogatories to Porter, *Sherborne MSS.*
[2] *Harl. MSS.* 4771, fol. 15. *Nicholas's Notes.*

ties of the case we cannot tell, but it was certain that the burning indignation which was in men's hearts would soon find expression in a more sweeping form. The next day something was said about supply. "If his Majesty," said Seymour, "shall be persuaded to take what he will, what need we to give?" Sermons had been preached to persuade the people that all they had was the King's. The question of supply was one to be discussed seriously in committee.[1]

<small>March 22. Seymour on supply.</small>

In vain Edmondes and May, on the part of the Government, pleaded that the House should forget and forgive. In a speech of wondrous power and comprehensiveness, Eliot drew a lively picture of the past misgovernment. It was no question, he told his hearers, whether they would forget and forgive. The question at issue was the very existence of the ancient laws and liberties of England. If these laws were set aside, all right of property was at an end. "It falls," he said, "into the old chaos and confusion, the will and pleasure of the mightier powers." It was no mere question of money, no mere temporary breach of the law under pressure of necessity, which might be considered as being of no more consequence than any other accident. "Yes," he cried, "it is of more; more than is pretended; more than can be uttered. Upon this dispute not alone our lands and goods are engaged, but all that we call ours. These rights, these privileges, which made our fathers freemen, are in question. If they be not now the more carefully preserved, they will I fear render us to posterity less free, less worthy than our fathers. For this particular admits a power to antiquate the laws. It gives leave to the State"—the Government, as we should now say—"besides the Parliament, to annihilate or decline any Act of Parliament; and that which is done in one thing, or at one time, may be done in more or oftener."

<small>Eliot declares against arbitrary taxation,</small>

---

[1] This debate is not given by Nicholas. I have adopted the order of speeches in the *Harl. MS.*, which is confirmed by Phelips, who at the end of the debate referred to the principal speeches in the same order as that given above. The ordinary arrangement, which was adopted by Mr. Forster, is, I believe, quite wrong.

All the evil, the great orator went on to say, sprang from the danger of innovation in religion. Favour had been shown within the Church to those who were most in unison with Rome, and even to Rome itself. No man in England had any interest in attacking the ancient liberties of the kingdom 'but that false party in religion which to their Romish idol sacrifice all other interests and respects.' There was a danger therefore in 'the habit of disregarding and violating laws.' "Apply to religion," said Eliot, "what has been propounded as to moneys exacted for the loan. We possess laws providing first in general against all forms of innovation, and also careful in particular to prevent the practice of our enemies by exclusion of their instruments, by restraining of their proselytes, by restricting their ceremonies, by abolishing their sorceries. Sir, while these laws continue, while they retain their power and operation, it is impossible but that we should in this point be safe. Without that change also in our policy by which law is set at nought, there could not be an innovation in religion."

and speaks of the state of religion.

The attack upon the liberties of the subject, and the attack upon the religion of the nation, were in reality, he argued, an attack upon the King. To discuss these matters was the truest service to the King, and the whole complicated subject should be referred, in its several divisions, to the committees of the House.[1]

Rudyerd followed, in his feeble way, trying to reconcile things that could not be reconciled. The danger of the kingdom was great; the danger of offending the King was also great. It was the crisis of Parliaments, by which men would know whether parliaments would live or die. "Men and brethren," he said in his distraction, "what shall we do? Is there no balm in Gilead?" On the whole, he thought the best thing would be to vote a large sum of money, and then to ask the King to set everything straight that had gone wrong.

Rudyerd preaches union.

[1] Forster, *Sir J. Eliot*, ii. 8. Mr. Forster has given an abstract of the part of his speech which referred to Laud and the clergy. It is a pity that he did not give Eliot's own words.

Rudyerd was succeeded by a speaker of a different order. The business of Parliament, said Wentworth, was to produce union between the King and his people. Both had been injured by past evils. Both were interested in finding a remedy for those evils. "The illegal ways," he exclaimed, "are punishments and marks of indignation. The raising of loans strengthened by commissions with unheard-of instructions and oaths, the billeting of soldiers by the lieutenants and deputy-lieutenants, have been as though they could have persuaded Christian princes, nay worlds, that the right of empire had been to take away by strong hand, and they have endeavoured, as far as was possible for them, to do it. This hath not been done by the King, under the pleasing shade of whose crown I hope we shall rather gather the fruits of justice, but by projectors. They have extended the prerogative of the King beyond its just symmetry, which makes the sweet harmony of the whole. They have rent from us the light of our eyes, inforced a company of guests worse than the ordinances of France, vitiated our wives and daughters before our faces, brought the Crown to greater want than ever it was by anticipating the revenue. And can the shepherd be thus smitten and the flock not be scattered? They have introduced a privy council,[1] ravishing at once the spheres of all ancient government,[2] imprisoning us without banks or bounds.[3] They have taken from us—What shall I say? Indeed, what have they left us? They have taken from us all means of supplying the King and ingratiating ourselves with him by tearing up the roots of all property; which, if they be not seasonably set into the ground by his Majesty's hand, we shall have, instead of

---

[1] A reference to the secret councils of Buckingham and his friends.

[2] Mr. Nutt, of Rugby, has pointed out to me that this phrase is founded on one in Bacon's *Essay on Superstition*. "Superstition hath been the confusion of many states, and bringeth in a new *primum mobile*, that ravisheth all the spheres of government." Compare also in the *Essay on Counsel*: "For which inconveniences, the doctrine of Italy, and the practice of France in some kings' times, hath introduced cabinet councils; a remedy worse than the disease."

[3] This is the reading of some MS. authorities. The ordinary 'bail and bond' is probably the corruption of a prosaic copyist.

beauty, baldness. To the making of all these whole I shall apply myself, and propound a remedy to all these diseases. By one and the same thing hath the King and people been hurt, and by the same must they be cured.[1] To vindicate what? New things? No. Our ancient, sober and vital liberties, by reinforcing of the ancient laws of our ancestors: by setting such a stamp upon them as no licentious spirit shall dare hereafter to enter upon them. And shall we think this a way to break a Parliament. No,—our desires are modest and just. I speak truly, both for the interest of the King and people. If we enjoy not these, it will be impossible to relieve him."

Wentworth and Eliot were heartily at one in denouncing the evils of the times; but the difference between the modes in which the two men regarded the grievances of the nation was ominous of coming division between them. Wentworth had nothing to say about religion, nothing to say about the large constitutional groundwork on which Eliot founded his conclusions. Both were loyal to King and Parliament alike; but, whilst Eliot was thinking chiefly of Parliament as the mirror of the national will and the guardian of ancient law, Wentworth was thinking chiefly how the King's government was to be carried on. With him the practical mischief was of more importance than all theoretical considerations, as throwing obstructions in the way of the true work of government, as well as inflicting the most exasperating injuries upon the people. Different as were the points of view from which the events of the past year were regarded by the two men, the remedies which they proposed were no less different. Eliot would have had the whole state of the nation discussed in committee; Wentworth, having very little confidence in committees, and very great confidence in himself, stepped forward to offer his own guidance to the House. There must, he said in conclusion, be no more illegal imprisonment, no more compulsory employments abroad, no forced loans, no billeting of soldiers without the assent of the householder.

Comparison between Wentworth and Eliot.

Wentworth's remedies.

[1] There seems to be something omitted here, but I have been unable to recover it.

In a few short words Wentworth had laid the foundation of the great statute which afterwards assumed the form of the Petition of Right. A condemnation of martial law was afterwards added. If Coke was finally to give to the Petition its form, Wentworth was the originator of its substance.

The debate still rolled on for some little time. Phelips did his best to reinforce Eliot's argument by protesting against the sermons of Sibthorpe and Manwaring.[1] Coke, on the other hand, seems to have been unwilling to go as far as Wentworth. He was not able, he said, in allusion to the words of Phelips, 'to fly at all grievances, but only at loans.' He recommended that subsidies should at once be granted, but that a statement of the illegality of the late loan should be inserted in the preamble of the Bill. In reply Secretary Coke made an admission most damaging to the King. He could not deny, he said in pressing for an immediate supply, that the law had been broken, but he could say that it had been broken under necessity. It would not be very long before Sir John's acknowledgment that the law had been broken would be thrown in his teeth as a complete abandonment of the case set up by the King.

Speeches of Phelips and Coke.

In the end Sir Henry Mildmay suggested that nothing should be done hastily. The King should have time given him to consider what had been said.

Charles's wisest course would evidently have been to close promptly with Wentworth. He did not understand that Wentworth's demand was the measure of the House's determination. As in 1625 he had agreed to persecute the Catholics in order to persuade the Commons to give him money to send out the fleet to Cadiz, so he would do now. Eliot and Phelips should learn that against the Catholics at least they had the King upon their side.

March 24. The King's reception of the demands.

---

[1] Phelips's speech is curious as enouncing, in opposition to Manwaring, a doctrine which afterwards became famous. "It is well known," he said, "the people of this state are under no other subjection than what they did voluntarily assent unto by their original contract between king and people."

A few days before the meeting of Parliament a discovery had been made, that a house at Clerkenwell, belonging to the Earl of Shrewsbury, was being used by a small party of Jesuits as a place of meeting. The Jesuits were at once arrested and their goods and papers seized. As there was nothing treasonable in the papers, some clever scoundrel thought fit to forge a letter from one of the community, in which it was told how the Jesuits had a plot on hand for keeping alive the quarrel between Buckingham and the House of Commons, and the forged letter was widely circulated.[1] Buckingham, when he saw it, was highly offended, as the unskilful forger had allowed expressions about Dulbier's horse to slip in which might be more damaging to him than to the Jesuits.

The Jesuits at Clerkenwell.

Neither Buckingham nor Charles, however, cared to protect the Catholics,[2] and they may very likely have instructed the

---

[1] The whole story was told by Mr. J. G. Nichols in the *Camden Miscellany*, vols. ii. and iv. Sir J. Maynard seems to have had something to do with the forgery, if he was not himself the forger. Mr. Nichols printed at the same time a curious letter from the Council to Falkland, which he held to be a forgery also. But the grounds he alleged were manifestly insufficient. He argued, in the first place, that the letter had an impossible date. This would be worth attending to if we had the original. But the hasty copy which is all we have may easily have substituted the 2nd for the 22nd of March. Mr. Nichols's second argument is that the letter is signed by Suffolk, Salisbury, Morton, and Durham. The latter, he said, if meant for the Bishop of Durham, would scarcely have come last. But surely earls would come before bishops. "Morton," too, he argued, "is a name not familiar to the history of the period." He was, however, a Privy Councillor, being the Scotch earl who commanded the reinforcement which was to have joined Buckingham at Rhé. The letter is very characteristic of Buckingham's off-hand way of treating serious matters. I incline to think it genuine. I may add that the last letter I ever wrote to Mr. Nichols was to call his attention to these points, being unaware at the time of his illness. Those who had the good fortune to know him will be sure that, if he had been convinced by its arguments, he would have accepted the correction with pleasure. Truth was the one thing which he cared for in his investigations.

[2] The Northern Commission, of which the Earl of Sunderland was the nominal chief and Sir J. Savile, the acting head, was, I fancy, intended

Secretary to make the most of the affair of the Jesuits at Clerkenwell; but Sir John had not the light hand which was needed to deal with the discovery so as to make a good impression. On the 24th, after promising that if the House would take the question of supply into immediate consideration, his Majesty would then be ready to redress all grievances, he proceeded to unfold his tale. "You little think," he said, "there was another pretended parliament of Jesuits, and other well-willers to that party, within a mile of this place." The House was not to be frightened with this bugbear. Not one of the speakers who followed even referred to the terrible portent. There was much sharp speaking about the Arminian divines, and the House gave it to be understood that it meant to discuss its grievances before doing anything about supply.[1]

<small>Sir J. Coke tries to frighten the House.</small>

<small>Grievances to precede supply.</small>

This was a bitter pill for Charles. Denbigh's mournful letters were pouring in day by day, to plead for the necessities of his charge. The council of war, too, had just sent in an estimate of little less than 600,000*l.* for the military and naval service of the coming year, besides an immediate demand for nearly 700,000*l.* for repairs and munitions of war.[2] Charles was thus in much the same difficulty as he had been in 1625. If he asked for all that he wanted, he would get a refusal. If he asked for less, the service would be starved. The course adopted was to lay before the House the heads of expenditure, without any mention of the sums required for each.

<small>March 25. Necessities of the Government.</small>

On points of form the Commons were not willing to contend with the King. At the urgent entreaty of Secretary Coke, they

<small>simply to get money. By taking less than the legal fines directly from the recusants, a whole set of informers would be discountenanced, and more money come actually to the Crown. See the Commission, June 23, 1627; *Patent Rolls*, 3 Charles I., Part 35, No. 7. The affair, however, seems to have been mismanaged.

[1] *Harl. MSS.* 4771, fol. 24.
[2] Estimate, March 22, *S. P. Dom.* xcviii. 1. It is one of the few important errors in Mr. Bruce's *Calendar*, that he overlooked the first of these demands, and so under-estimated the whole sum required.</small>

resolved that the Grand Committee which was to discuss grievances should also discuss supply. It soon appeared that Charles had gained but little. As soon as the House had gone into committee, speaker after speaker announced his full belief that their property in their goods and the liberty of their persons must be placed beyond dispute before it would be fit to mention supply. Phelips, with his usual proneness to seize upon questions which were not yet ripe for solution, even asked what was the use of ascertaining the law if the judges could expound it as they pleased.

On Charles's request the committee ordered to consider both grievances and supply.

Debate in committee on the liberty of the subject.

It was but the natural result of Charles's system of government that he was as ill-served in the House of Commons as he was everywhere else. To Eliot and Wentworth and Phelips he had nobody to oppose but Secretary Coke. May and Edmondes contented themselves with general exhortations to concord; and Weston, who, as Chancellor of the Exchequer, had no love for the war expenditure for which he was expected to provide, sat silent by their side. To the great lawyers of the Opposition, with Coke and Selden at their head, there was no one to reply except the Solicitor-General, and Shilton was an example how easily incompetency could float to the surface when buoyed up by Royal favour. When he rose it was only to say that he had not been present when the case of the habeas corpus was argued in the King's Bench, but that if they would give him time to consult Heath, he would see what Heath had to say about the matter.

The King almost without support in the Commons.

Shilton's verbal admission of his own incompetence brought up Sir Edward Coke. The old lawyer contemptuously replied that he too would be glad to know what the Attorney-General had to say. In the meanwhile, he had something worth his consideration to tell him. Whenever the old law-books spoke of the King's imprisoning a man, they meant that the King's command was signified through his judges. "The King," said Coke, "can arrest no man, because there is no remedy against him." He then produced a precedent from the reign of Edward III., according to which a

Coke's statement of the law.

committal without cause named had been deemed insufficient by the judges. Scripture too was on his side. Had not Festus said to Agrippa, "It seemeth to me unreasonable to send a prisoner, and not withal to signify the crimes laid to his charge?" Coke ended by saying that he had given the Attorney-General a preparative, but he had more physic in store for him.

Coke's argument was another warning to Charles to close with Wentworth quickly. If Eliot would have placed the direction of affairs in the hands of the House of Commons, Coke would have placed the final decision in the hands of the judges. The question asked by Phelips earlier in the day had to be answered in favour of the judges before they could be considered competent to the task assigned them.

As Charles made no sign, the Commons stepped boldly forward. They refused even to consider the Secretary's heads of expenditure for the present, and they passed a resolution condemnatory of taxation without a Parliamentary grant.

March 26. Resolution on taxation.

The question of imprisonment was not so easily settled. There was something to be said on the side of the King. In ordinary times it might be all very well that the King should not imprison without showing cause, and that the judges should be called upon at once to decide whether the accused person should be admitted to bail or kept in prison. Would not this, however, be dangerous in extraordinary times? In the last two reigns there had been grave conspiracies affecting the well-being of the whole nation. There had been plots to assassinate Elizabeth, and more recently a plot to blow up King, Lords, and Commons with gunpowder.

March 28.

Nethersole's argument.

"I will put my case," said Nethersole, in evident allusion to the position of Northumberland in connexion with the Gunpowder Plot: "there is amongst us a great party of Jesuits and priests, and the scholars of Jesuits are about to question the King's title to the crown; and suppose some friends of some one great man and allied to the Crown, do conspire against the King and Crown. Now, to keep that great man out of danger, they never acquaint him with the plot. Will not all men confess that a warrant in this case is both lawful and necessary to secure this great man? And what reason of his imprisonment can be added?"

In the course of the debates which followed, this argument was put again and again in every possible form. It is childish to ignore its weight. The conclusion to which it points has been embodied in that unwritten constitution under which Englishmen are content to live. In ordinary times the rule which Coke advocated suffices; but when any extraordinary commotion makes itself felt in the depths of society, when some great conspiracy is on foot, the ministry of the day comes to Parliament for a suspension of the *Habeas Corpus* Act, and arbitrary committals find no impediment.

Estimate of its force.

There are occasions on which the historian has to acknowledge that no complete solution of existing difficulties was possible at the time. Practically the great evil of the day was that Charles was not fit to be entrusted with powers which had been wielded by former sovereigns. He had acted as if there had been an emergency, when, if there was an emergency at all, it was one of his own creation. Even if the leaders of the Commons had looked fairly into Nethersole's argument, all that they could have said was that, by some possible re-arrangement of the constitution, by some form of government hitherto untried, that which he asked for might beneficially be granted. Sufficient for the day was the evil thereof. The Commons had come to consider that it was more important for them to bind the King's hands than to arm them against conspiracies which, in their time at least, had no existence except in the fertile imagination of Secretary Coke.

No complete solution then possible.

The legal aspect of the question was by this time coming to the front. It was in vain for Eliot to appeal to the high position of Parliament as the interpreter of the national conscience, in vain for Wentworth to lay the foundations of a new settlement in an intelligent perception of the requirements of the State, if Charles refused to take account of their just demands. It remained for the great legal authorities of the Commons to lay down the law as it stood, to trace out

The legal question.

the long tradition of legality which in the course of ages had raised a barrier against arbitrary power.

That the barrier thus raised had not always been firmly maintained it is impossible to deny. Precedents were not always consistent, and the weak side of the legal argument was that it attempted to reduce the fluctuations of social forces to a uniform system, and to account for the constitution of England in the Middle Ages without mentioning those revolutionary disturbances which had supplemented the decisions of the judges.

In the Commons Coke had no adversary worthy of his steel. Yet even Shilton contrived to embarrass him for the moment by producing a resolution of the King's Bench in 1615, in which Coke himself expressed approval of the doctrine that when the Council sent a man to prison the cause of the imprisonment need not be disclosed. At the same time Shilton quoted the opinion of Chief Justice Anderson, to which Heath had referred triumphantly in Westminster Hall.

<small>March 29. Coke and Shilton.</small>

Even Coke was for once disconcerted by the attack. The report, he said, was not yet twenty-one years old. Then floundering still more deeply in the mire, and forgetting dates and everything else in his confusion, he began talking wildly of the necessity of dealing strictly at that time with the traitors concerned in the Gunpowder Plot, as if, in 1615, every one of them who had fallen into the hands of the Government had not been executed nine years before.

It was a fine opportunity for Shilton. "What!" he might have said, "do you really hold that in times such as that of the Gunpowder Plot, the strict law for which you are pleading cannot be executed?" Shilton, however, was no debater, and sat silent. Wentworth came to Coke's rescue with a few sarcastic words. "Mr. Solicitor," he said, "hath done that which belongs to his place, but not so ingeniously as he might." [1]

---

[1] *Harl. MSS.* 4771, 45 b. The word is "ingeniously," which in those days bore the signification of "ingenuously" as well as that of "ingeniously." Probably Wentworth meant to reflect on Shilton's want of skill. The *Harl. MS.* gives the only satisfactory account of the affair.

Two days later Coke was himself again. He had the right, he said, of changing his opinion when his knowledge was increased. Since he signed the resolution referred to, he had seen members of Parliament imprisoned. He had himself only just escaped imprisonment. He had gone to his law-books, and there he had found that the boasted resolution of Anderson and the judges of his day was apocryphal. Anderson's words were very different from those which had been cited in Court.

March 31. Coke's justification.

Coke had risen above the weakness which led him to claim infallibility in matters of law. "I cannot think of flattery," said Eliot, "but we may here thank him now whom posterity will hereafter commend."[1] Eliot, in fact, had a great part in the old lawyer's triumph. A report of Anderson's resolution in his own handwriting had been treasured up as a precious possession by his heirs. They now sought out Eliot and placed the manuscript in his hands. On the morning of April 1 Eliot laid it before a Committee of the House. If it was not by any means so explicit as the popular lawyers would have drawn it, it was more in their favour than the note which had been cited by Heath.[2] Coke

April 1. Anderson's judgment produced.

---

[1] *Harl. MSS.* 4771, fol. 46 b. Coke's speech has a wrong date in *State Trials,* iii. 82.

[2] "And where it pleased your Lordships to will divers of us to set down in what cases a person sent to custody by her Majesty, her Council [or] some one or two of them, are to be detained in prison and not delivered by her Majesty's Courts or Judges, we think that if any person be committed by her Majesty's commandment from her person, or by order from the Council Board, or if any one or two of her Council commit one for high treason, such persons, so in the case before committed, may not be delivered by any of her Courts without due trial by the law and judgment of acquittal had. Nevertheless the Judges may award the Queen's writ to bring the bodies of such prisoners before them; and if upon return thereof the causes of their commitment be certified to the Judges, as it ought to be, then the Judges in the cases before ought not to deliver him, but to remand him to the place from whence he came, which cannot be conveniently done unless notice of the cause in generality or else specially be given to the keeper or gaoler that shall have the custody of such prisoner." *Anderson's Reports,* i. 298. Upon this, Hallam (i. 387), observes: "For though this is not grammatically worded, it seems impossible to doubt that it acknow-

interpreted the words entirely as he wished them to be interpreted. The old man was more than triumphant. "Of my own knowledge," he said, "this book was written with my Lord Anderson's own hand. It is no flying report of a young student. I was Solicitor then, and Treasurer Burghley was as much against commitment as any of this kingdom. ... Let us draw towards a conclusion. The question is, Whether a freeman can be imprisoned by the King without setting down the cause? I leave it as bare as Æsop's crow, they that argue against it."[1]

Coke's appeal to Anderson's opinion swept everything before it. In three resolutions the Committee unanimously resolved that no freeman might be committed without cause shown; that every one, however committed, had a right to a writ of *habeas corpus*; and that, if no legal cause of imprisonment appeared, he was to be delivered or bailed.

Resolutions on imprisonment.

These three resolutions on imprisonment, together with the resolution on taxation, constituted the main part of the case of the Commons with regard to the liberty of the subject. The ledges the special command of the King, or the authority of the Privy Council as a body, to be such sufficient warrant for a commitment as to require no further cause to be expressed, and to prevent the Judges from discharging the party from custody either absolutely or upon bail." The consequence, he goes on to say, would be to render every statute by which the liberties of Englishmen were protected, a dead letter. The effect of Anderson's report depends on whether he meant 'the cause in generality' to apply merely to the order of the Queen or Privy Council, or to some general statement of the offence committed. In any case, however, Anderson seems to have had in view a trial before the King's Bench as the proper result, and to have been thinking rather of saying that bail ought to be refused to persons so committed, till the time for trial came on, than of the further question whether they could be kept back entirely or for any long time from the jurisdiction of the Court. Anderson's assertion that the cause of commitment ought to be certified, would be the part of the report on which the Commons would probably lay stress.

[1] There is some difficulty about this speech (*State Trials*, iii. 76). Part of it, *Humores moti*, &c., occurs in a speech of the 29th, and the rest is not mentioned by Nicholas or in the copy in the Harleian MSS. But it can hardly have been spoken except on the production of Anderson's original MS.

day before, the King had accorded a gracious reception to the joint petition of the two Houses for the strict execution of the Recusancy laws.¹ On April 2 the Commons took into consideration the heads of expenditure presented on behalf of the King. The general opinion was that provision should be made for the defence of the kingdom, but that no encouragement should be given to Charles to launch out into another of those great expeditions which had hitherto ended in such disastrous failure. Sir John Coke indeed argued that attack was often the best defence. It might be so, retorted Eliot, but attacks conducted after the fashion of the late attempts upon Cadiz and Rhé could defend nobody. "Consider," he said, "in what case we are, if on the like occasion, or with the like instruments, we shall again adventure another expedition. It was ever the wisdom of our ancestors here to leave foreign wars wholly to the State, and not to meddle with them. There may be some necessity for a war offensive, but, looking on our late disasters, I tremble to think of sending more abroad." ² Wentworth took a course of his own. He would have nothing to say to Eliot's investigations into the past. "I will not fall," he said, "into the deep of foreign actions, but address myself to particulars. I cannot forget the duty I owe to my country, and unless we be secured in our liberties we cannot give." Wentworth recommended that there should be no attempt to enter upon the heads of expenditure. He also recommended that a bountiful supply should be given ; but he reminded the committee that the list of grievances was not yet exhausted, and that there was no security that, if money were voted, their grievances would be redressed. He therefore moved and carried the adjournment of the debate to the 4th. He held, in fact, that the House should not make itself responsible for the mode in which the money voted would be spent. He did not care enough for the war to think it worth while to inquire whether Rochelle was likely to be lost or saved ; but he did care for the settlement of those domestic difficulties which

---

¹ *Parl. Hist.* ii. 248.   ² Forster, *Sir J. Eliot,* ii. 22.

made all healthy government impossible, and though he was not likely to abet any movement which would have placed the House of Commons in direct opposition to the Crown, he was quite ready to use the refusal of subsidies as a lever to obtain that which he regarded as advantageous to the Crown and the Commons alike.

As the result of the adjournment the committee betook itself to supplement its previous resolutions. The practice of confining a person obnoxious to the Court to his own house, or to the house of any other private person, which had been recently practised in the cases of Bristol and the refusers of the loan, was voted to be illegal.

<small>Resolution on confinement.</small>

<small>Billeting soldiers.</small> The warmest discussion, however, arose on the billeting of soldiers and the malpractices connected with it. Eliot related, with striking effect, a circumstance of which he was cognisant. The house of a gentleman near Plymouth, he said, had been attacked by a band of soldiers, and its owner forced to fly from their fury. A few days afterwards he was recognised in Plymouth by the same soldiers, and assaulted by them. He complained to the Mayor, and was by him referred to the Commissioners appointed for the government of the troops. Not only did the Commissioners give him no redress, but they sent him and his servant to prison. "Little difference I see," said Eliot, "between these and the old Roman soldiers. Can this people give supply that are not masters of themselves?"

Complaint waxed louder and louder. "If we go on in particular," said Digges, "we shall never come to an end. It is too common for the commanders to deny all justice." Phelips said that the deputy lieutenants had no right to make rates for the maintenance of the soldiers. Yet there was something in the defence of Sir Edward Rodney, himself a deputy lieutenant. The soldiers, he said, came with empty stomachs and with arms in their hands. If the King's orders had not been obeyed, the men would have seized by force all that they wanted. It had always been the custom to levy money for the support of soldiers on the understanding that it would be repaid from the Exchequer. If the men had been billeted in private houses it was because no money had come down from the King to support them in inns.¹

No money had come down. That was the gist of the whole grievance. And why had no money come down? Because, the King would say, the Commons, in neglect of their duty, had refused to vote it. The Commons held that it was because the King had engaged in an expenditure of which they were in the right in disapproving. Do what they would, the deep question of sovereignty—of the right of saying the last word when differences arose—was for ever cropping up.

Question of authority opened up.

The next morning a message was delivered from the King by Secretary Coke. His Majesty, he said, had heard that there were rumours that he was angry with what the House had been doing, and that Buckingham had spoken malicious words against the Parliament. He assured them that this was not the case. Sir John added that the King wished them to vote him a supply the next day, without any condition. He would then assure them that he had no intention of intrenching upon their liberties. Charles, in short, could not see that their liberties were at all in danger. "For God's sake," he had said, "why should any hinder them of their liberties? If they did, I should think they dealt not faithfully with me."

Satisfaction expressed by the King.

There is no reason to accuse Charles of hypocrisy in these words. He did not yet fully understand where the struggle really lay. He had regarded the loan as an irregular expedient, forced upon him by the course taken by the Commons in the first two Parliaments of his reign, much as the King of Prussia regarded the unparliamentary budget arranged by himself before the campaign of 1866. Now that the Commons appeared likely to resume their proper functions, there would be no need for him to revert to such unusual proceedings. They would vote him the supplies which he needed, and he would assure them that he would not again put in force the extraordinary powers of which they

What did Charles mean?

---

¹ *Harl. MSS.* 4771, fol. 51–57 b. *Nicholas's Notes.*

complained; but which he firmly believed to be part of the inheritance of the Crown, of which he was resolved not to divest himself.

In the course of the day the four resolutions on imprisonment and taxation were formally reported to the House. The debate on forced employment on foreign service took an unexpected turn when Selden called in question the existing system of pressing men for military and naval service which had grown up since the commencement of the Tudor reigns. Even Phelips was startled by the prospect which had been opened by Selden. Without compulsory service, he asked, how was an army to be maintained? Wentworth gave expression to the same doubt. If Selden was right, and the King had no power to press, the sooner the power was given to him the better. The only point to be considered was how such a power could be moderately exercised. On Wentworth's motion a committee was appointed to consider the question.[1]

Question of pressing men for the army.

The position thus taken up by Wentworth is significant. Above the question of Royal or Parliamentary authority, above the question of law and precedent, he kept ever steadily before him the necessity of an intelligent perception of the wants of the country. Parliaments might be merely the reflection of the interests and passions of an ignorant nation. Lawyers might appeal to the dry records of a dead past which could give no rule to the living present; but intelligence could not fail. The strength and the weakness of Wentworth lay in this doctrine, so true when intelligence takes account of the elements of passion and prejudice, zeal or sluggishness in the nation, so false when it deals with a people as mere brute matter, to be handled and directed as the man of wisdom thinks best.[2]

Wentworth's position.

Wentworth's motion had at all events, by taking up the time of the House, made the completion of the list of grievances

---

[1] *Harl. MSS.* 4771, fol. 57 b; 2313, fol. 28.

[2] The modern idea of statesmanship, in fact, looks upon government as a μαιευτικὴ τέχνη. But the Socrates of politics was yet in the future in Wentworth's days.

impossible for the present. The next morning had been fixed for the debate on supply. It was accordingly resolved to suspend the consideration of the military grievances for the present, and to lay the four resolutions on taxation and imprisonment before the Lords.

April 4. Separation of civil from military grievances.

Before the House went into Committee of Supply, a fresh message from the King came to give assurance that they should enjoy their liberties under him as fully as under the best of their former kings. Though the House was in a liberal mood, there were many to whom the heads of expenditure seemed excessive, many too in whose minds they awakened memories of disaster and defeat. Wentworth recommended that the heads of expenditure should be quietly shelved. The House should grant a large supply, and ask no questions how it was to be employed. The recommendation had a marked success. Eliot said that he had intended to say something about the heads of expenditure, but that he had no wish to interpose any further delay. Wentworth's motion was carried, and the House was thus relieved from all responsibility for the prosecution of the war. What was given would be a free gift, binding no one for the future.

Debate on supply.

Then followed a discussion on the number of subsidies to be granted. Some said five, others less. Eliot, frightened at the excessive liberality of the House, moved the adjournment of the debate. Wentworth supported the largest grant suggested, and he had the House with him. Eliot protested in vain that so much could not be raised without the aid of military force; but he did not venture to appeal to a division, and five subsidies were unanimously voted.

Five subsidies voted.

The leadership of the Commons was clearly in Wentworth's hands. He represented the desire of the majority of the members to carry conciliation to the utmost possible limits; but he also represented their desire to have a full and effective remedy for their grievances. As soon as the motion for the subsidies was carried, he proposed that no report of the vote should be made to the House. What had been done, he said, was done

Wentworth's leadership.

The grant not to be reported.

conditionally on the King's agreement to settle the fundamental liberties of the subject. The proposal thus made was practically if not formally adopted.[1] No report was made, and there was thus no official record that the subsidies had ever been voted at all. It would be impossible for Charles, if matters went ill, to levy the subsidies as he had attempted to do in 1626, on the ground that they had been offered by the House.

Charles's hopeful picture of an immediate grant of supply, followed by a vague declaration of his own intention to maintain the liberties of his subjects, was therefore not to be realised. Though Wentworth had no wish to reduce the Royal authority to a shadow, it was by his hand that the cup had been dashed from the King's lips. He had been one of the committee which had unanimously recommended that the four resolutions should be laid before the House of Lords.[2] He may have thought that such a course was unavoidable under the circumstances, or he may have been unwilling to lose his influence by openly differing from the great lawyers of the House. At all events he had something more definite to propose. "He would," he said, "have the Grand Committee appoint a sub-committee to draw into a law what may assure us of our liberty of our persons and property of our goods before we report the resolution of our gift."

Wentworth proposes a Bill on the liberties of the subject.

Here then, at last, was Wentworth's scheme. Not a humble petition to the King, not a legal argument to accompany the four resolutions when they were laid before the Peers, but a law to provide for the future, was his solution of the difficulty. Whatever might come of the argument before the Upper House, it would be certain to offend the King. He would have to be

---

[1] There is a discrepancy in the authorities. The *Harleian MS.* 4771 (60 b–63 b) ends with an order for a report. Nicholas gives the further speech noticed above, and then says, "the Speaker goeth unto the chair and the House riseth." Another *Harleian MS.* (4313, fol. 34 b) gives the order for the report with Wentworth's speech following. As no report appears to have been made, there can be no doubt that the order was dropped on Wentworth's intervention, though it may not have been formally rescinded.

[2] *Commons' Journals*, i. 879.

told that he had been utterly in the wrong, and that he had broken a whole series of laws, from Magna Carta downwards. It might indeed prove that Charles was not to be conciliated, and then it might be necessary to go through all this. Wentworth may well have thought that there was a better way. If once it became statute law that the King might not levy loans without the consent of Parliament, and that he might not imprison men without allowing them to seek their trial in open court, all the learning in the world about the constitution of England in the Middle Ages would be no more than an antiquarian investigation, more interesting to Englishmen but not more practically important than an inquiry into the laws of Solon or the procedure of the Roman prætors.

A Bill, moreover, would have the advantage in Wentworth's eyes of being capable of limitation. Nethersole's argument was not likely to pass unheeded by Wentworth, and he was sure to regard with special favour a mode of procedure by which it would be possible to consider not merely what the law was, but what the law ought to be.

For the present, however, the lawyers had it all their own way. A day was fixed for their argument before the Lords.

<small>April 7.
The King pleased with the subsidies.</small> Even Charles was in high good humour. Either he did not yet see how far the claims of the Lower House would reach, or he confided in the firmness of the Peers to reject anything which in his eyes was clearly unreasonable. The five subsidies had surpassed his expectations. "By how many voices was it carried?" he asked Secretary Coke, who brought the welcome news. Sir John could afford to jest, and replied, "By one." Then, having frightened the King for a moment, he explained that the Commons had voted with one voice and one assent.

All this and more Coke garrulously reported to the House; but he had not the tact to be content with singing the praises <small>Coke reports Buckingham's speech.</small> of the King. He added that Buckingham had joined in a hope that the desires of the House would be granted. If the spirit which had animated the last Parliament was asleep it was not dead. Eliot sprang to his feet and protested against the mediation of a subject between

King and Parliament. His words found an echo in the cries of "Well spoken, Sir John Eliot!" which arose on every side.[1]

That day brought knowledge to the King that more was meant by the Commons than he had hitherto supposed. Coke, Selden, and Littleton laid the resolutions of the House before the Peers. Much new light had been thrown on the subject since the proceedings in the King's Bench, and the lawyers of the Commons made a strong case in behalf of the absolute illegality of committals without cause shown. The next day Heath commenced his argument on the other side, contending that the King had never relinquished the right of interfering with the ordinary jurisdiction of the Courts when the necessity of the State so required.

The resolutions before the Lords.

Charles was beginning to open his eyes to the magnitude of the issues at stake. It was something more than a mere question of the legality of this or that action. It was sovereignty itself, the right of deciding in the last resort, which he was required to abandon. He was ready to promise that no more loans or taxes should be levied without the consent of Parliament ; and that in all ordinary imprisonments he would leave the decisions to the judges ; but he was not ready to promise that, in questions in which the fortunes of the whole realm were interested, he would stand aside and descend from the high position which his predecessors had occupied with general consent.

Charles sees the extent of the concessions required.

Nor was it on the question of imprisonment alone that the Commons were pressing upon him. Whilst the argument was proceeding before the Lords, the Lower House had again taken up the grievance of billeting. "In my county," said Sir Walter Erle, speaking of Dorsetshire, "under colour of placing a soldier, there came twenty in a troop to take sheep. They disturb markets and fairs, rob men on the highway, ravish women, breaking houses in the night and enforcing men to ransom themselves, killing men that have assisted constables to keep the peace." Other members had tales equally bad to tell. Sir Edward Coke proposed to petition

April 8. Billeting soldiers.

[1] *Parl. Hist.* ii. 274. Meade to Stuteville, April 12, *Court and Times* i 336.

the King against the abuse. Wentworth, true to his principles, suggested that a Bill should be drawn up to regulate the mode of quartering soldiers for the future. Soldiers must live, and Wentworth seems to have thought it useless to attack the evil unless provision were made for the necessity which had caused it. He proposed a petition to the King, to be followed by a Bill in due course of time. Orders were at once given to draw up the petition. This time, at least, Wentworth had succeeded in keeping the whole subject from the cognisance of the Lords till the Bill was in existence.[1]

Charles's hopefulness was beginning to fail. As the requirements of the House became plainer to him, the prospect of supply grew more distant. Yet money was sadly needed. Denbigh had not left Plymouth. The pressed men were still deserting daily. The ships laden with corn for Rochelle were reported to be unfit for sea.[2] April 10 was Thursday in Passion week, and the House had already made provision for the Easter recess ; but a message was brought from the King conveying his pleasure that there should be no recess. Not even on Good Friday were the Commons to have rest. The members were ill pleased to be deprived of their holiday. Eliot suggested that worse was behind. He believed that the King's message had been in the hands of the Privy Councillors for two days. Why had it not been delivered before, unless it were with the expectation that when many members had left town it would be easy to hurry a vote of supply through a thin House? He moved that no vote of supply should be taken till the House was again full. Though his motion was not formally adopted, the House had been put upon its guard.[3]

April 10. The Easter recess forbidden.

Martial law, not supply, was the subject of that Good Friday's debate. Eliot placed the whole subject on the right footing.

---

[1] *Harl. MSS.* 4771, fol. 67–69 b.

[2] Denbigh to Buckingham, April 8, *S. P. Dom.* c. 56.

[3] Meade says that the motion was adopted. Meade to Stuteville, April 19, *Court and Times,* i. 342. Nethersole (*S. P. Dom.* ci. 4), who was himself a member, says that it was rejected, and this is confirmed by the absence of any mention of its adoption in the *Harleian MS.* 4771, fol. 74.

A paper of instructions had been read, appointing special
punishments for military crimes. Mutiny, disregard
of orders, and such offences, were to be punished in
soldiers as they are now punished in every army in the
world. To all this Eliot raised no objection, but he held that
when a soldier committed an offence against a civilian, the
civilian should have his remedy in the ordinary course of law,
and not be dependent for justice on the good pleasure of the
officers. Thus stated, the case against the Government involved
the whole of the relations between the civil and the military
power. Were soldiers to be subject to the laws, or were they
to be a law to themselves? If the latter view was to prevail,
how long would the laws of England subsist in their presence?

April 11. Debate on martial law.

The debate was interrupted in the strangest manner. In
spite of Eliot's warning of the previous day Sir Edward Coke,[1]
of all men in the world, started up to propose that
the dates for the payment of the subsidies should be
fixed. In vain Eliot explained that the business
before the committee was not supply. Secretary Coke rap-
turously echoed the proposal and it seemed difficult to get rid
of it decently. At last Wentworth rose. "I must confess," he
said, with a bitter allusion to the day on which they were sitting, "I expected within myself this day to hear a sermon."
As, however, the thing had been said, let the dates be fixed.
But let them not be reported any more than the grant itself.
Though even this was too much for some, Coke's untoward
proposal was eventually disposed of as Wentworth suggested.

Coke's proposal about supply.

Charles grew impatient, and sent a fresh message reproving
the Commons for spinning out their time, and ordering them
to vote the subsidies at once. 'Notice,' the
Secretary explained, was taken 'as if this House
pressed not upon the abuses of power, but upon
power itself.' Sir John was asked to explain what
he meant by power. The word, he replied, came from his
Majesty, and to his Majesty alone belonged the explanation.
Wentworth knew that he was himself the author of the

April 12. Impatient message from Charles.

[1] *Harl. MSS.* 4771, fol. 75 b, 78. That it was Sir Edward, and not Sir John, seems to be settled by Nethersole's letter just quoted.

motion against reporting the subsidies which had given such offence to the King. He moved for a committee to explain that there had been no intentional delay, and a statement to the effect that grievances took precedence of supply, was prepared for the Speaker to present together with the petition on billeting.[1]

The House was growing accustomed to Wentworth's leadership. A letter-writer of the day speaks of him as the man 'who hath the greatest sway in this Parliament.'[2] Would he be able to force his policy on the King as well as on the Commons? It seemed as if Charles would soon receive a powerful ally in the House of Lords. The Peers listened to Heath's argument, and arranged that the opinion of the judges of the King's Bench should be heard. Buckingham and his friends pleaded for a decision without admitting the Lower House to a further reply. Eliot took alarm, and carried a motion for a message begging the Peers to decide nothing without hearing the Commons once more.[3]

The Lords incline towards the King.

The temper of the courtiers in the Upper House was growing warm. "Will you not hang Selden?" said Suffolk, the son of James's Treasurer; "he hath razed a record, and deserves to be hanged." Selden, in his place in the Commons, indignantly denied the imputation. Suffolk was too cowardly to stand by his words, and denied that he had spoken them. The Commons took up the defence of their member, but in the midst of more pressing business they were unable to bring the accusation home.[4]

Suffolk attacks Selden.

On the 14th the judges appeared before the Lords. They did not bring much help to either party. They said that they had not given a final judgment, and that the prisoners might have applied for a *habeas corpus* the next day if they had pleased. The Court only meant to take further time to consider.

April 14. The judges heard by the Lords.

That afternoon Charles received the explanation of the Commons, that they were right in considering grievances before

---

[1] *Harl. MSS.* 4771, fol. 78–81.
[2] Nethersole to Elizabeth, April 14, *S. P. Dom.* ci. 4.
[3] *Elsing's Notes. Harl. MSS.* 4771, fol. 81.
[4] *State Trials*, iii. 156.

supply. He replied sharply, that he did not question their right. "But, for God's sake," he said, "do not spend so much time in that as to hazard the ruin of your liberties and my prerogative by a foreign army." He was as careful of their liberties as they were themselves.

The King expostulates with the Commons.

Charles spoke under the influence of the disheartening news which came to him from Plymouth. He had just sent an order to Denbigh to sail at all risks, and he had been told that the fleet might put to sea, but that there was no chance of its being able to fight its way into Rochelle.[1] All this made no impression on the Commons. They did not know what the King understood by the liberties which he said he was ready to maintain, even if they had been inclined to trust his unsupported promise. They accordingly took no notice of his words, but went quietly on with the debate on martial law, as though he had never pressed them for money at all.[2]

The Commons again refuse to proceed with supply.

On April 16 and 17, in consequence of the message from the Commons, there was a fresh argument by the lawyers before the House of Lords. On the one side it was maintained that the King could in no circumstances commit without showing cause. On the other side it was alleged that, though the King might not abuse his power by imprisoning men for ever without allowing them to appeal to the Courts, he might exercise a discretion in keeping back any particular case from the cognisance of the judges.[3]

April 16. Fresh legal argument before the Lords.

On the existence of this discretionary power the battle was to be fought. The bare assertion of a right in the King to override the laws would not meet with the support of the Upper House. A statement made by Serjeant Ashley in the course of his argument for the Crown, to the effect that the question was too high to be determined by a legal decision, was at once checked by Manchester and disavowed by Heath.

---

[1] *Council Register*, April 12. Clarke to Buckingham, April 12, *S. P. Dom.* c. 64.
[2] *Harl. MSS.* 4771, fol. 91.   [3] *Lords' Journals*, iii. 746.

Ashley was committed to prison by the Lords till he had apologised for his offence.¹

On the 21st the great subject was merely approached by the Peers. They resolved that the King and Council had power to commit upon just cause. On the 22nd they considered whether it was necessary for the cause to be expressed or not ; in other words, whether the judges or the King were to decide upon the legality of the commitment.

April 21. Debate in the Lords.

April 22.

It was generally believed that the majority would be on the King's side. Heath's arguments had told, and the influence of the Court was strong. Within the last few days four new Peers, Coventry and Weston amongst them, had taken their seats. The Commons, in alarm, sent to beg for another conference before the vote was taken.

The opposition, minority as it was, stood firm. Saye was foremost in the combat ; and he was warmly supported by those who had suffered from Buckingham's domination. Williams pronounced strongly for the popular interpretation of the law. Abbot was equally decided. The first hand held out to the King outside the ranks of the Court was that of a man whom he had deeply wronged. Bristol argued that they were simply discussing the limits of the King's legal power. Behind that was a regal power upon which he could fall back in extraordinary cases. "As Christ," he said, "upon the Sabbath healed, so the prerogative is to be preserved for the preservation of the whole." Bristol, in short, proposed that the law should be declared according to the demand of the Commons, but that an acknowledgment should be made that if a really exceptional state of things arose, the King might boldly set aside the law for the sake of the nation. The Lord Keeper would have none of such help as this. For the Privy Council to commit without showing cause, he said, was only in accordance with the ordinary law. Upon this, Buckingham, confident in the support of the majority, moved

Resistance of the minority.

Middle course proposed by Bristol.

Rejected by Coventry.

---

¹ *Lord's Journals,* ii. 759. *Elsing's Notes.*

that the debate be closed. The next step would have been to
reject the Commons' resolutions, but Saye interposed with a
motion for delay till the judges had been consulted. If this
were not done, those who were in favour of the resolutions
would enter their protests. It was thought that, if it had come
to a division, there would have been fifty-six votes recorded
in opposition to the Court, against sixty-six in its
favour. Buckingham did not venture to divide in
the face of so formidable an opposition, and the debate was
adjourned.[1]

<small>The debate adjourned.</small>

When the discussion was re-opened the next day, Arundel
declared his concurrence in the general doctrine of the
Commons ; but he thought that some modifications
might be introduced into the resolutions. At Pembroke's suggestion a Committee was appointed to
examine the whole bearings of the question. Before this examination Buckingham's majority melted away. It is said that
when he went down to the House he assured the King that
the resolutions would be rejected before he came away. For
ten hours the debate swayed to and fro. The decisive impulse
came at last from Abbot, who pointed out the ruinous consequences of a breach with the Lower House in the face of
so many enemies abroad.[2] It was resolved that,
instead of rejecting the resolutions of the Commons,
counter-propositions should be drawn up in lieu of
them. As Harsnet, the Bishop of Norwich, was employed
to put them into shape, it may be supposed that there was a
defection on the Episcopal Bench, which, as a rule, was the
chief support of the Court. The defection, however, was not
universal. To Laud, at least, Harsnet's desertion seemed a
base concession to expediency, sinning against the principle

<small>April 24. Arundel's proposal.</small>

<small>April 25. The Lord's propositions.</small>

---

[1] *Elsing's Notes. Harl. MSS.* 4771, 102 b. Meade to Stuteville.
May 3, *Court and Times,* i. 348.

[2] This debate is not reported by Elsing. The account in the text is
taken from Contarini's despatch of May $\frac{5}{15}$. He gives no date, but his
description will not suit any other day than this.

that the King is above all laws, even above Magna Carta itself.[1]

The first four propositions were intended to secure the subject against all interference with the ordinary course of justice. The Great Charter, and six other statutes by which it had been interpreted in early times, were asserted to be in force. Every freeman was declared to have 'a fundamental property in his goods, and a fundamental liberty of his person.' His Majesty was to be requested to confirm the 'ancient just privileges and rights of his subjects in as ample and beneficial manner' as 'their ancestors did enjoy the same under the best of his Majesty's most noble progenitors;' and to promise that 'in all cases within the cognizance of the common law concerning the liberty of the subject, his Majesty would proceed according to the laws established in this kingdom, and in no other manner or wise.'

The fifth proposition ran thus: " And as touching his Majesty's royal prerogative intrinsical [2] to his sovereignty, and entrusted him from God *ad communem totius populi salutem, et non ad destructionem*, that his Majesty would resolve not to use or divert the same to the prejudice of any of his loyal people in the property of their goods or liberty of their persons; and in case, for the security of his Majesty's Royal person, the common safety of his people, or the peaceable government of his kingdom, his Majesty shall find just cause, for reason of State, to imprison or restrain any man's person, his Majesty would graciously declare that, within a convenient time, he shall and will express the cause of the commitment or restraint, either general or special; and, upon a cause so expressed, will leave him immediately to be tried according to the common justice of the kingdom."

The fifth proposition.

---

[1] A copy of the propositions (*S. P. Dom.* cii. 14) is endorsed by Laud, as 'penned by Dr. Harsnet, Bishop of Norwich.' Amongst other notes in Laud's hand, is one referring to the confirmation of Magna Carta:—
" Yes, but *salvo jure coronæ nostræ* is intended in all oaths and promises exacted from a sovereign."

[2] So in *Harl. MSS.* 4771, fol. 110, and so quoted by Coke. The *Parl. Hist.* has 'incident.'

In sending these propositions to the Commons, the Lords assured them that they had prejudged nothing. They were ready to hear anything that might be said on the other side.[1]

It is only fair to the authors of these propositions to acknowledge that they seem to have been actuated by a serious wish to mediate between the opposing parties. Whilst they wished, in opposition to Coventry and Buckingham, to exclude the Crown from all interference with the ordinary administration of the law, they also wished that the King should enjoy a right, analogous to the right of suspending the *Habeas Corpus* Act in our own times, of overriding the law in any special State emergency. Whether such a middle course was possible may well be doubted. The Lords who proposed to entrust Charles with extraordinary powers forgot that he had already ceased to inspire confidence. Even if this had not been the case, the language of the propositions was not felicitous. The prerogative referred to was spoken of as intrinsical to sovereignty and was traced to a Divine origin. It was therefore entirely different from that prerogative which was considered as part of the law, and as liable to discussion in the Courts.

Spirit of the propositions.

When the propositions came before the Commons, they were savagely criticised by Coke. Was the confirmation of the Great Charter to be accorded as a grace? What were just liberties? Who were the best of his Majesty's predecessors? "We see," he said, "what an advantage they have that are learned in the law in penning articles above them that are not, how wise soever." Coming nearer to the heart of the matter, he asked what was intrinsical prerogative. "It is a word," he said, "we find not much in the law. It is meant that intrinsical prerogative is not bounded by any law, or by any law qualified. We must admit this intrinsical prerogative, and all our laws are out. And this intrinsical prerogative is intrusted him by God, and then it is *jure divino*, and then no law can take it away." His Majesty could commit when he pleased. It was the very thing for which King John had striven in vain. If the Lords refused

April 26. They are criticised in the Commons.

[1] *Parl. Hist.* ii. 329.

their concurrence in the resolutions of the Commons, it would be better to go directly to the King for redress. Selden spoke in the same tone. "At this little gap," he said, referring to the words 'convenient time,' "every man's liberty may in time go out."

In the main, most of the speakers took the same view of the case. But there were some who were still seeking for a middle course more satisfactory than that which had been proposed by the Lords. Let the old laws, argued Noy, be recited and declared to be in force. Then let a provision be made for the more ready issue of writs of *habeas corpus*, and let it be enacted that 'if there be no cause of detaining upon that writ,' the prisoner 'is to be delivered.'

Noy's proposal of a Habeas Corpus Act.

Wentworth was less explicit than Noy. He said that he had no wish to dive into points of sovereignty or divine right. He hoped that the question 'whether the King be above the law or the law above the King' would never be stirred. Though he rejected the fifth proposition as entirely as Coke or Selden, and would have nothing to do with it 'but only to disclaim it,' he doubted the wisdom of Coke's proposal to petition the King. Perhaps he thought that such a petition was sure of rejection; but he merely argued that the petition, even if granted, would only be laid up in a Parliament Roll, and so remain practically unknown. Once more he declared that what was wanted was a Bill. There must be a clearer explanation of the words 'law of the land' in the Great Charter, and they might confer with the Lords about that. It should be ordained in the Bill 'that none shall be committed without showing cause.' A penalty must be set on those who violated it. Then speaking in his grand, impetuous way of the possible breach of the law in extraordinary cases—'When it shall,' he said, 'on any emergent cause, he thinks no man shall find fault with it.'[1]

Wentworth's speech.

Wentworth's idea was much the same as Bristol's. The law must be clear against arbitrary committals. If the time came

[1] *Harl. MSS.* 4771, fol. 112 b, 116. *Nicholas's Notes.*

when the good of the State imperatively demanded its violation, let the King violate it openly and boldly, and trust to the good sense of the nation for his justification.[1]

To Charles there was but little to choose between Coke and Wentworth. On the 28th he summoned the Commons before him in the Upper House. It was a point, said the Lord Keeper in the King's name, of extraordinary grace and justice in his Majesty to suffer his prerogative 'to rest so long in dispute without interruption.' But the delay could be borne no further, and he was therefore commanded to declare that his Majesty held the Great Charter and the six statutes to be in force, and would 'maintain all his subjects in the just freedom of their persons and safety of their estates, according to the laws and statutes of the realm.' They would 'find as much sincerity in his Royal word and promise as in the strength of any law they could make.'[2]

April 28. Coventry's declaration that the King's word must be taken.

It was characteristic of Charles to suppose that his word

---

[1] It is worth noticing how this idea of a law binding for all ordinary purposes, which might yet be broken 'on any emergent cause,' was Wentworth's to the last. On September 13, 1639, he wrote about ship-money to Judge Hutton: "I must confess in a business of so mighty importance, I shall the less regard the forms of pleading, and do conceive that the power of levies of forces at sea and land for the very not feigned relief and safety of the public, is such a property of sovereignty as, were the Crown willing, yet can it not divest itself thereof. *Salus populi suprema lex*; nay, in case of extremity even above Acts of Parliament." *Strafford Letters*, ii. 388. Ship-money, to Wentworth, was money levied for a real necessity. The forced loan was levied for a feigned necessity. One was for defence, the other for aggression. The difference between Wentworth in office and Wentworth out of office must also be taken into account. Laud's opinions were much the same. In his 'History of the Troubles' (*Works*, iii. 399) he says: "By God's law and the . . . law of the land, I humbly conceive the subjects met in Parliament ought to supply their prince when there is just and necessary cause. And if an absolute necessity do happen by invasion or otherwise, which gives no time for counsel or law, such a necessity—but no pretended one—is above all law. And I have heard the greatest lawyers in this kingdom confess that in times of such a necessity, the King's legal prerogative is as great as this."

[2] *Parl. Hist.* ii. 331.

could stand in the place of a formal enactment. Yet the actual intervention of the King was not without its effect. Rudyerd urged a fresh conference with the Lords, in the vague hope that some plan would be discovered which might please everyone. There was something, he thought, in the King's offer. He would be glad 'to see that good old decrepit law of Magna Carta, which hath been so long kept in and bedrid, as it were,' walking abroad again with new vigour and lustre, attended by the other six statutes. But even Rudyerd thought there must be a Bill forbidding imprisonment for refusing to pay loans or Privy seals.

Debate in the Commons.

To confer with the Lords, after the experience lately gained, was poor advice. "I cannot conceive," said Eliot of the propositions, "how they can be of use to us." He adhered to Wentworth's suggestion of proceeding by Bill.

Wentworth's views were thus at last adopted by the House. Resolutions and propositions were to drop together. Theories of law, theories of government, were to be left untouched. The Commons were to prepare a practical solution of the difficulty, and to send it up to the Lords for their acceptance or rejection. A sub-committee, in which Eliot, Wentworth, Pym, and Phelips, and a few others of the leading members sat with all the lawyers in the House, was to draw up a Bill expressing the substance of the old statutes and of the recent resolutions of the Commons.[1]

A Bill to be prepared.

On the morning of the 29th the Bill which was to assure the liberties of the subject was brought into the Grand Committee by Coke, in the name of the sub-committee. "In this law," said the old lawyer, as he stood with it still in his hand, "we looked not back, for *qui repetit separat.* We have made no preamble other than the laws, and we desired our pen might be in oil, not in vinegar."[2]

April 29. The Bill on the liberties of the subject.

[1] *Commons' Journals,* i. 890; *Harl. MSS.* 4771, fol. 120; *ibid.* 2313, fol. 65. *Nicholas's Notes.*

[2] As the Bill never got out of Committee, it is not mentioned in the Journals. It has hitherto been confused with the subsequent Petition of Right, and only fragments of the debates which followed have been known.

Unlike the subsequent Petition of Right, the Bill contained no recital of grievances. Charles was not to be told that he had broken the law; but he was plainly to acknowledge that he had no right to billet soldiers without the householder's authority; to levy loans or taxes without consent of Parliament; or to commit a man to prison. If he did commit a man to prison the judges were to bail him, or deliver him, without paying regard to the King's orders.

The question of imprisonment gave rise to some difference of opinion in committee. The declaration that the King could not commit seemed to many to be harsh and uncalled for; and there were some who argued that it would be enough if provision were made for the due granting of the *habeas corpus*, whether the prisoner had been committed by the King or by a subject.

Debate on the Bill.

There was an evident division in the House. Eliot and Coke were for taking the Bill as it stood. Noy and Digges and Seymour were in favour of a modification. The party which afterwards passed over to the Crown was already forming.

The following is the only form in which I have met with it. *Harl. MSS.* 4771, fol. 123:—

 "An Act for the better securing of every freeman touching the propriety of his goods and liberty of his person.

 "Whereas it is enacted and declared by Magna Carta that no freeman is to be convicted, destroyed, &c., and whereas by a statute made in E. 1, called *de tallagio non concedendo*: and whereas by the Parliament, 5 E. 3, and 29 E. 3, &c., and whereas by the said great Charter was confirmed, and that the other laws, &c.

 "Be it enacted that Magna Carta and these Acts be put in due execution, and that all allegements, awards, and rules given or to be given to the contrary shall be void; and whereas by the common law and statute, it appeareth that no freeman ought to be committed" (convicted in *MS.*) "by command of the King, &c.; and if any freeman be so committed and the same returned upon a *habeas corpus*, he ought to be delivered or bailed; and whereas by the common law and statutes every freeman hath a propriety of his goods and estate, as no tax, tallage, &c., nor any soldier can be billeted in his house, &c.; Be it enacted that no tax, tallage, or loan shall be levied &c. by the King or any minister without Act of Parliament, and that none be compelled to receive any soldiers into his house against his will."

On the third day of the debate Wentworth rose. "We are here," he said, "to close up the hurt and danger of his Majesty's people. All our desires are but to this Bill; and this left unsecured makes us lose all our labour. We shall tread the olive and lose all the oil. I agree the resolutions are according to law, and that we cannot recede a tittle. We can lay no other foundation than what is already laid. But here let us see how this misery comes on us; first by the too speedy commitments at Whitehall, and by too slow bailments at Westminster Hall. If we secure the subject at Westminster by a good law, it will satisfy and regulate the sudden commitments at Whitehall. We have by this Act a security by Magna Carta and the other laws. Let us make what law we can, there must—nay there will—be a trust left in the Crown. Let us confirm Magna Carta and those other laws, together with the King's declaration, by this Act. Let us provide by this law to secure us that we may have no wrong from Westminster. Let it be enacted that we shall be bailed if *habeas corpus* be brought and no sufficient cause. Such a law will exceed all the laws that ever we had for the good of the subject; and if it be so, I desire to know whether our country will not blame us if we refuse it. I am to be changed by better reason if I see it."[1]

May 1. Wentworth proposes to modify the Bill.

Wentworth, it would seem, would have made the form of the Bill even more conciliatory than it was. He would have confined himself to a bare recital of the statutes confirmed, and would have added the words in which the King had declared his intention to observe them. But he would have omitted the denial of the King's right to commit. With a good *Habeas Corpus* Bill such a right would be perfectly harmless. If the prisoner committed without sufficient cause shown were liberated at once by the judges, the committals complained of would soon come to an end of themselves.

Value of the proposal.

It would have been curious to have seen Wentworth's pro-

[1] The reports in the *Harleian MS.* and *Nicholas's Notes* differ verbally from one another. I have pieced the two together, taking the one or the other as it seemed more full, and changing connecting words to fit the sentences together.

posal in its complete shape. The judges would have had the ultimate decision of the legality of the committal in their hands. We know that Wentworth spoke of the trust to be reposed in the King, and that he had spoken before of circumstances in which a breach of the law would be a commendable action. In his present speech there was no provision for such a case. Yet the omission is perhaps one which strikes us more than it was likely to strike Wentworth. In those days the communication between the judges and the Government was much closer than it is now, and Wentworth may have thought that if special precautions were needed, the King would lay the grounds upon which he proposed to suspend the law privately before the judges, and thus obtain their consent to the interruption of the ordinary course of justice.

However this may have been, Wentworth's plan undoubtedly contemplated the transfer of authority from the King to the judges. It was enough for him that he could leave to the Crown all authority worth having. It must not be forgotten that no proposal had as yet been made for abolishing the power of fine and imprisonment possessed by the Star Chamber. Wentworth, at least, would have had no difficulty in ruling vigorously under such conditions. But he had forgotten that the shadow of authority was as dear to Charles as its substance. It was not from Coke or Eliot that the blow came which levelled to the dust the edifice which he was constructing with such toil. For all we know, his sway over the House may have been as absolute as ever; but as soon as he sat down the Secretary rose, declaring to the committee that he was entrusted with a message from his Majesty. When the Speaker had taken the chair, Sir John stated that the King wished the question to be put 'whether they would rest on his Royal word and promise.'

<small>The King's message.</small>

The text was bad enough. The Secretary's comment was far more irritating. The House, he said, could not expect to place the King in a worse position than he had been in before. He had a sword in his hand for the good of his subjects. Make what law they pleased, they could not alter that. He was himself a Privy Councillor, and

<small>Sir John Coke's comment.</small>

it would be his duty under any circumstances to commit without showing the cause to anyone but the King.[1]

After such a message the Commons had but one course to pursue. They adjourned to consider their position. One gleam of hope remained. It was known that the Secretary had been in the House for some time, and it did not appear that any fresh communication had reached him after Wentworth began to speak. It was therefore just possible that, if Wentworth's overtures were allowed to reach Charles, they might still be accepted.

The House adjourned.

When the House met the next day the case against Charles was put in the plainest terms by Sir Walter Erle. "It is conceived," he said, "that the subject had suffered more in the violation of the ancient liberties within these few years than in the three hundred years before." Charles, in short, could not be trusted with powers which had been conceded to Henry and Elizabeth. The debate which followed showed how completely he had succeeded in throwing a chill over the sentiment which was rising in his favour. Those who thought that some moderate latitude should be allowed to the action of the Government were repelled by Charles's claim to be above all constitutional restrictions. Noy and Digges remained silent. Seymour spoke in defence of the Bill. The awkward advocacy of the Solicitor-General only served to irritate his hearers. The King, he said, was certain to keep his word as long as he lived. A bad king in future times would not be bound by any law which they might make.

May 2. Debate on the message.

The doctrine that the King was permanently above law was as offensive to those who, like Wentworth, recognised the fact that all possible cases could not be provided for by legislation, as to those who, like Coke, would reduce all government to the observation of the law. Wentworth, persisting in his opinion, almost smothered the King in compliments. Let them thank his Majesty, he said, for his gracious message. Never House of Parliament trusted

Wentworth's appeal to the King.

[1] *Parl. Hist.* ii. 342.

more in his goodness than they did as far as their own private interests were concerned. "But," he added firmly, "we are ambitious that his Majesty's goodness may remain to posterity, and we are accountable for a public trust; and therefore, seeing there hath been a public violation of the laws by his ministers, nothing can satisfy them but a public amends; and our desires to vindicate the subjects' right by Bill are no more than are laid down in former laws, with some modest provision for illustration, performance, and execution." As if to suggest that the Bill, as it stood, was not altogether such as he approved of, he added that the King should be informed that the House had not yet agreed upon its terms. When it had been discussed and perhaps amended in the two Houses, the King would have it before him in its final shape.

Nothing could be firmer in substance or more conciliatory in form. Even Coke, touched by the solemnity of the occasion, was conciliatory too. Let the Bill, he said, be couched in the form of a promise. "We will grant, for us and our successors, that we and our successors will do thus and thus." "It is to the King's honour," said Coke, "that he cannot speak but by record."

<small>Coke's proposal.</small>

All respect, in short, should be shown to the King. The House was ready to trust his word; but his word must be given and his authority exercised as part of the constitutional system of the country, and not as something outside of it.

Against the determination of the House it was useless to strive. Sir John Coke contented himself with denying the correctness of Wentworth's assertion that the laws had been violated. Wentworth proudly answered that he had not said that the laws had been violated by his Majesty. They had been violated by his ministers. Seymour reminded the unlucky Secretary that he had himself acknowledged the violation, and had been content to excuse it on the plea of necessity.[1]

<small>Had the laws been violated?</small>

A sub-committee was appointed to draw up a Remonstrance on the basis of Wentworth's speech. The House answered

---

[1] In his speech of March 22, *Parl. Hist.* ii. 233. See p. 237.

readily to the hand of its leader. Charles, however, would have none of such mediation. He knew well that whatever his ministers had done, had been done with his approbation. He therefore anticipated the Remonstrance by a message that he was ready to repeat the promise he had made, but that he would not hear of any encroachment upon that sovereignty or prerogative which God had put into his hands for the good of his people. On May 13 the session must be brought to a close.[1]

<small>Wentworth's speech to be turned into a Remonstrance.
The King objects.</small>

The Commons could not but stand firm. They ordered the Remonstrance to be presented in spite of the message, adding a few words of assurance to the King that they had no wish to encroach on his sovereignty or prerogative. Charles held his ground. He would confirm Magna Carta and the six statutes, but it must be 'without additions, paraphrases, or explanations.' For the rest he had given his Royal word, and that was enough.[2]

<small>May 5.
The Remonstrance presented.
The King's reply.</small>

In the Remonstrance of May 5 Wentworth spoke for the last time in the name of the House of Commons. On that day his leadership came to its inevitable end. He had hoped to reconcile the King and his subjects. His idea of kingship was a high one—too high, indeed, for the circumstances of the time ; but he regarded it, as Bacon had regarded it, as part of the constitution of England, as restricted to action in consonance with the laws, and only rising above them because no written laws could possibly provide for all the emergencies which might occur. For Charles the kingship was something different from this—something divine in its origin and unlimited in its powers. Therefore, even if he was willing to agree that he would not repeat the actions which had given just offence in the preceding year, he was not willing to bind himself to more. He would surrender the abuse. The authority from which the abuse sprang he would not surrender.

<small>End of Wentworth's leadership.</small>

Wentworth's hopes were thus baffled. There was to be no

---

[1] *Harl. MSS.* 4771, fol. 129–136 ; *Nicholas's Notes* ; *Parl. Hist.* ii. 345.
[2] *Parl. Hist.* ii. 347.

provision for the future with Charles's consent, no great constructive measure which would lay afresh the foundation of a higher union between King and people in accordance with the wants of the age and the experience of the past. Wentworth must step aside and make room for another policy and other men. The Commons, if they were to carry their point at all, must set their teeth hard and declare war to the end against their sovereign. It would have been well for Wentworth if he had recognised once for all that no stable constitutional edifice could be raised with Charles for its foundation, if the bitter cry "Put not your trust in princes" which was to be wrung from him when at last he stooped his proud head before an angry and triumphant nation, had risen to his lips as he sat moodily watching the troubled assembly which it was now no longer his to guide.

CHAPTER LXIII.

THE PETITION OF RIGHT.

WHEN the King's answer to the Remonstrance was read, Sir John Coke proposed that it should be debated in the House and not in committee, as being more for the King's honour. Against this proposal Eliot protested. There was greater freedom of speech in committee. If a member changed his views, he could say so, though he had already spoken. "For my part," said Eliot, "I am often converted."

<small>May 6.
The King's answer to be considered.</small>

It was no hypocritical affectation of humility which brought these words to Eliot's lips. The records of this session are the highest witnesses to the moral worth of the patriotic orator. No man was ever placed in more trying circumstances than Eliot during the first weeks of this session. He had been the life and soul of the last Parliament. It had thought with his thoughts and spoken with his words. Now other men were listened to more than himself. Policy which he thought unwise was frequently adopted. Yet all this he had borne without the slightest sign of self-will or petulance. He had spoken his opinion freely, and had frankly acknowledged that his opinion was changed whenever he saw that the argument was going against him.

<small>Eliot's moral worth.</small>

After Wentworth's failure it was not likely that the House would again ask for anything short of the extreme measure of its claims. The discussion in committee was opened by an appeal from Alford to the lawyers present to inform him what benefit would accrue to the subject by the

<small>Debate in committee.</small>

confirmation of the statutes without explanation. Lyttelton promptly answered that the subject would be in a worse condition than before, as the abandonment of the resolutions would imply a doubt whether they were a correct interpretation of the statutes confirmed. Other members dwelt upon the vagueness of the King's offers. The King, said Sir Nathaniel Rich, was like a debtor who said, 'I owe you nothing, but pray trust me.' They must know what the King offered before they could say whether they would trust him or not. Another member pointed to the difference of opinion on the meaning of the words 'the law of the land' in Magna Carta. "We all," he said, "agree what it is. But have the Lords and the judges so agreed?" Pym pushed the argument still further home. "Our assurance," he said, "in the King's word were sufficient, if we knew what the King's sense and meaning is. We have not his word only, but his oath also at his coronation." If the law had been broken, it was clear that the King did not know what the law was. "We complain," he added, "of unjust imprisonment upon loans. I hear not any say we shall be no more, or that matter of State shall be no more pretended when there is none. . . . We all rest on the King's royal word. But let us agree in a rule to give us satisfaction."

Sir John Coke remonstrated. Did Pym mean that the King's word added no force to a law? Sir Harbottle Grimston threw back upon the Secretary the words which he had recently spoken. "The King's ministers," he replied, "tell us here they must commit." Till the law on the point of committal was clearly understood, it was hopeless to expect an agreement. Even Sir John saw that something must be conceded. The loan, he said, was the original grievance. Let them petition his Majesty not to repeat it.

The Secretary little thought what echo his words would have. Sir Edward Coke rose at once.[1] Yes, he said, let us

[1] Mr. Forster (*Sir J. Eliot*, ii. 47) is evidently mistaken in speaking of Coke as rising with the draft in his hand. The Bill had been before the Committee for some days, and the petition was not yet in existence. It must be remembered that without the use of *Harl. MS.* 4771, or *Nicholas's Notes*, Mr. Forster had a very limited amount of straw to make his bricks

rely on the King. "Under God, he is God's lieutenant. Trust him we must." Yet what was an answer in general words to particular grievances? A verbal declaration was not the word of a king. "Did ever Parliament rely on messages? They ever put up petitions of their grievances, and the king ever answered them? The King's answer is very gracious. But what is the law of the realm? that is the question. I put no diffidence in his Majesty. The King must speak by a record and in particulars, and not in general. Let us have a conference with the Lords, and join in a Petition of Right to the King for our particular grievances. Not that I distrust the King, but because we cannot take his trust but in a Parliamentary way."

<small>Coke proposes a Petition of Right.</small>

The word had at last been spoken which the House could accept as its only safe guidance. The King would not allow them to consider what was right and what was wrong; at least they could ask that the meaning of the existing laws should be placed beyond doubt, and that they should know whether the interpretation of Heath or the interpretation of Coke and Selden was to prevail. The acceptance of the proposal was general and immediate. Eliot, Seymour, Glanville, Littleton, Phelips, Pym, Hoby, Coryton, and Digges adhered to it at once. Even Wentworth accepted it as now inevitable, though he reserved for himself the right of reconsidering his position after the King's answer had been received.

<small>General acceptance of the proposal.</small>

The leaders of the House had all declared that they were ready to trust the King, and they doubtless persuaded themselves that it was really so. Sir Nathaniel Rich rose at the end of the debate to tear away the veil. A petition, he said, was better than a Bill, for by it they would have an answer before they sent up the subsidies. A petition, in fact, would receive an immediate answer. A Bill would be sent up at the end of the session, and what was

<small>Was the King really trusted?</small>

---

with. A great part of the speech he attributes to Coke does not seem to stand on any evidence, and I fancy he must inadvertently have carried his marks of quotation too far.

there to hinder the King from accepting the subsidies and rejecting the Bill?[1]

A Petition of Right to be prepared.

The sub-committee which had drawn up the previous Bill was entrusted with the preparation of the petition. A protest against forced loans, arbitrary imprisonment, and compulsory billeting was to form its substance. To these heads was to be added another against the late commissions for the execution of martial law. After recent experience it was hopeless to guard the broad assertion of their illegality by any provision for the maintenance of proper discipline in the army, and all that could be done was to declare that the exercise of martial law was absolutely illegal.

May 7. Martial law to be protested against.

There was no delay in the labours of the sub-committee. On the 8th the Petition of Right was brought in by Selden, and the House of Lords was asked to appoint a day for a conference upon it. In order to make the medicine more palatable to Charles, the resolution for the five subsidies was at last reported to the House.[2]

May 8. The petition brought in.

There was, indeed, need to render the medicine palatable if Charles was to accept it willingly. Everything to which he had objected in the Bill re-appeared in the petition in a harder and more obnoxious form. He was no longer asked merely to regulate the course of his future action. He had to allow that actions done by his orders had been in direct opposition to the law of England. His acceptance of the Bill would have been a friendly agreement to order his relations with the nation on new terms. His acceptance of the petition would be a humble acknowledgment of error.

The petition contrasted with the Bill.

During these days, when his proposals had been flatly rejected by the House, Charles lost all patience. A draft exists of a declaration which was to explain the causes of the dissolution which had been resolved on; but better counsels prevailed, and the breach was averted for a time.[3]

A dissolution resolved on.

---

[1] *Harl. MSS.* 4771, fol. 137–140 b. *Nicholas's Notes.*

[2] *Commons' Journals,* i. 894. *Harl. MSS.* 4771, fol. 144.

[3] The draft is in Heath's hand (*S. P. Dom.* cxxxviii. 45, i.), and was calendared by Mr. Bruce, and quoted by Mr. Forster as applying to the

The petition was at once sent up to the Upper House. On the 10th a Committee of the Lords reported that they left the question of imprisonment to the House. The rest of the petition they accepted with a few amendments, most of which were intended to render the condemnation of the past conduct of the Government less abrupt, whilst there were two which had been drawn up with the object of retaining for the King the power of exercising martial law over soldiers, though not over civilians.[1]

May 10. The petition before the Lords. Report of the Lords' Committee.

Coming from such a source the report was clearly more condemnatory of the Government than the petition itself. As we read over the list of the committee—Coventry, Manchester, Arundel, Bedford, Bristol, Saye, Paget, Weston, with Bishops Harsnet and Williams[2]—we feel that Charles must indeed have stood alone in England before such names would be appended to words which even in their modified form contained the severest censure to which any King of England had submitted since the days of Richard II.

Composition of the Committee.

Before such a demonstration of opinion it was impossible for Charles to maintain his ground. In a letter to the Lords he condescended to argue the point of his right to imprison. "We find it insisted upon," he wrote, that "in no case whatsoever, should it ever so nearly concern matters of State or Government, neither we, nor our Privy Council, have power to commit any man without the cause be showed, whereas it often happens that, should the cause be showed, the service itself would thereby be destroyed and defeated. And the cause alleged must be such as may be determined by our Judges of our Courts of Westminster in a legal and ordinary way of justice;

May 12. The King argues on his right of imprisonment.

dissolution in 1629. I find it hard to believe that either Mr. Bruce or Mr. Forster ever seriously examined the paper. There is not a word referring to the second session, whilst everything would be in place in May 1628. The paper is undated, but if it belongs to this session must have been drawn up in the week following May 2; I suspect after the petition was known to the King.

[1] *Parl. Hist.* ii. 351.   [2] *Lords' Journals*, iii. 788.

whereas the causes may be such as those Judges have not the capacity of judicature, nor rules of law to direct and guide their judgment in cases of so transcendent a nature; which happening so often, the very intermitting of that constant rule of government practised for so many ages within this kingdom, would soon dissolve the foundation and frame of our monarchy." Yet Charles was ready to engage that he would never again imprison anyone for refusing to lend him money, and that when he did imprison he would always disclose the cause as soon as it could be done conveniently for the safety of the State.

The King's letter was forwarded to the Commons by the Lords. The Commons would not hear of such a basis of settlement. When the petition was complete they would ask for the King's assent. A letter was of no value. The Lords replied that they did not place more weight than the Commons upon the letter. All that they wished was to bring the petition into conformity with the letter, so as to give it a chance of securing the King's assent.[1]

<small>May 14. His overture rejected by the Commons.</small>

The Lords were about to try what they could do to give effect to their wishes; but though they had been apparently unanimous in supporting the proposed course, the unanimity was greater in appearance than in reality. Saye and his friends agreed to allow the attempt to be made, on the express understanding that if it failed they might fall back on the petition as it stood.

<small>The Lords will try an accommodation.</small>

That there was a strong element in the Upper House which desired to take a middle course was manifest. Though men like Williams and Bristol and Arundel had suffered too much from the unrestrained exercise of the King's authority not to join heartily in the main demands of the petition, they were too old statesmen not to be aware that a discretionary power must be lodged somewhere, and they laboured hard to discover some formula which should restrict it to real cases of necessity. At first it seemed that the

<small>May 15. Debate in the Lords.</small>

---

[1] *Harl. MSS.* 4771, fol. 155. *Lords' Journals,* iii. 796.

Lord Keeper would meet them half-way. "No man," said Coventry, "ought to be imprisoned but a clear and direct cause ought to be showed, unless the very declaration of the cause will destroy the business, and in such a case, for a time, a general cause may serve." A committee was appointed to draw up a form of words in which Coventry's view might be embodied.

It was no such easy matter. The Committee for a long time was unable to agree upon anything. At last they reported a clause proposed by Williams.[1] Thus it ran :—"That no freeman be—for not lending money or for any other cause contrary to Magna Carta and the other statutes insisted upon, and the true intention of the

<small>May 16. Williams's clause.</small>

---

[1] There are two clauses in the *Lords' Journals* (iii. 799, 80) with no names to them. Compare *Elsing's Notes*. The second, the one finally adopted, is twice claimed by Weston. From the same notes we learn that there had been two forms before, the one proceeding from Williams and the other from Arundel, the latter of which was probably in some way or other amended by Weston. Williams's speeches, as there reported, leave no doubt that his was the one in which the King's sovereignty is not mentioned. The usual attribution to Williams of the clause about sovereignty falls to the ground, and that theory, in fact, is directly contradicted by Williams's notes on the King's letter as given by *Hacket*, ii. 77. Of the supposed intrigues of Williams, and his alleged efforts at this time to bring Wentworth over to the Court, I know nothing. Hacket's account of a later reconciliation with Buckingham will be given in its proper place. Williams, no doubt, acted with Bristol and Arundel, but to act with Bristol and Arundel was to be opposed to Buckingham and the Court, though not so decidedly as Saye. The true story of William's proposed clause is told in a paper in *Harl. MSS.* 6800, fol. 274, under the heading "The offer of accommodation made by the Bishop of Lincoln." He would have left the preface to the petition as it stood, adding a complaint that divers of his Majesty's subjects had been imprisoned without cause shown, and would then have inserted the clause in the text for 'that no freeman in any such manner as is before mentioned be imprisoned or detained.'

He also proposed a form for the King's reply, as follows: "Neither we nor our Privy Council shall or will at any time hereafter commit or command to prison, or otherwise restrain the persons of any for not lending of money unto us, nor for any other cause contrary to the true intention of Magna Carta and those other six statutes insisted upon to be expounded by our judges in that behalf."

same, to be declared by your Majesty's judges in any such matter[1] as is before mentioned—imprisoned or detained."

Its intention.
The clause was certainly not clear, and needed all Williams's explanations; but its intention was manifestly that which he said it was. While he believed, as Wentworth believed, that in very special cases the King had by his prerogative the right of suspending the action of the ordinary law, he shrank from affirming this in so many words. The result was ambiguity itself. The author of the clause was the first to discover that his meaning had been misunderstood.

May 17. Explanation of Williams.
He had to explain that in referring the decision of the legality of a commitment to the judges he had no thought of countenancing the idea that they might refuse bail on the old ground of want of cause expressed. He meant, he protested, nothing of the sort. If his proposition meant that, it was 'the idlest that ever was offered.'

A medium of agreement which needs explanation from its author is self-condemned; but it was probably not its obscurity which rendered it unpalatable to the majority of the Upper House. "Power," said Weston, "which is not known and confessed, cannot be obeyed." The following clause, probably originally drawn up by Arundel and finally brought in by Weston,[2] left no doubt of the reservation of authority. It ran thus:—"We humbly present this petition to your Majesty, not only with a care of preserving our own liberties, but with due regard to leave entire that sovereign power wherewith your Majesty is trusted for the protection, safety, and happiness of your people."

Arundel's clause adopted.

Was even this free from ambiguity? On the 19th, the Commons having asked leave to argue against the proposed amendments in the body of the petition, Williams moved that those amendments should be withdrawn and the new additional clause alone discussed. Buckingham rose to give his approval to the proposal, on the understanding that the reservation of sovereignty applied to the whole petition. Such a demand undeniably went far

May 19. Its meaning doubted.

---

[1] "Matter" in the *Harl.* copy; "manner" in the *Lords' Journals*.
[2] As I have said, he twice claims the authorship in *Elsing's Notes*.

beyond the intention of all members of the House who were more than mere courtiers. If it was granted, the King would be at liberty not merely to imprison without showing cause whenever he thought that the safety of the State so required, but to collect forced loans, to issue commissions of unlimited martial law, and to billet soldiers by force, whenever, in his judgment, such a contingency might arise.

Buckingham's interpretation.

"If you extend this addition to every particular in the petition," said Saye, "the petition is quite overthrown. Your expressions were to reserve the sovereign power only in emergent cases, and not in the particulars mentioned in the petition, for then a man may be, for any particular mentioned in the petition, committed hereafter."[1]

Saye dissents.

Saye's objection was certain to find an echo in the Lower House. With a comparatively unimportant exception, all the amendments to the body of the petition were rejected by the Commons, and their rejection was acquiesced in by the Lords. The additional clause now formed the only point in dispute between the Houses.[2] It was soon evident that the Commons would have nothing to say to it. They professed themselves unable to discover what sovereign power might mean. According to Bodin, said Alford, it means that which 'is free from any condition.' "Let us give that to the King that the law gives him, and no more." "I am not able," said Pym, "to speak to this question. I know not what it is. All our petition is for the laws of England, and this power seems to be another distinct power from the law. I know how to add sovereign to his person, but not to his power. Also we cannot leave to him sovereign power, for we never were possessed of it."[3] Then, showing how well he was in-

May 20. Debate in the Commons.

---

[1] *Elsing's Notes.*

[2] Rushworth, whom Mr. Forster had no choice but to follow, gives a debate as taking place on the 17th, which is really the debate of the 20th, together with a jumble of two speeches of Wentworth's foisted in from the 22nd and 23rd, and a speech of Selden's from the 22nd.

[3] Mr. Forster corrects 'he never was' for 'we never were' (*Sir J. Eliot*, ii. 55, Note 8); but "we never were" has the authority of MSS. otherwise varying from one another; and Pym may have meant, 'We can only leave what we have control over. This is beyond our control.'

formed of what had passed in the Upper House, Pym went on to allude to Buckingham's explanation. "We cannot," he said, "admit of these words with safety. They are applicable to all the parts of our petition." The clause, in fact, was of the nature of a saving, and would annul the whole. Coke followed in much the same way. The prerogative, he said, was part of the law, but sovereign power was not.

Without a dissentient voice, therefore, the clause was rejected by the House of Commons. Coke had clearly taken the right ground when he said that the prerogative was part of the law. As Wentworth had said before, if an actual emergency occurred, no man would dispute what the King did. Yet to insert a special saving of such a right as being above the law was to make all law uncertain.[1]

The clause rejected.

When the answer of the Commons was carried up to the Lords, many a tongue was loosed to speak against Weston's clause. "The prerogative of the Crown," said Williams, "is a title in law, and those learned in the law do know the extent of it as well as of any other articles." "The saving," declared Bristol, "is no way essential to the business." Might not, he suggested, the petition be sent up as it was, accompanied by a verbal statement that the Houses had no intention of infringing upon the prerogative. To such a solution as this, however, Buckingham would not listen. "Let it be resolved here among us," he said, "that there be a saving." He was not allowed to have his way. The House adjourned, at the joint motion of Saye and Arundel.

Objection to the clause in the Lords.

Buckingham stands by it.

The next day Buckingham expressed his willingness to make a great concession. He was ready to change the words 'sovereign power' into 'prerogative.' The House seems to have been fairly puzzled. Paget suggested that the judges should be asked their opinion. Abbot said he had heard a learned peer say that they could not destroy the prerogative, even by an Act of Parliament. Bridgewater naïvely expressed his opinion that after so long a debate

The Lords try to explain it away.

---

[1] *Harl. MSS.* 4771, fol. 166.

they ought to 'resolve of some addition or other,' and 'to think of fitting reasons.' Williams said he would not vote till it was made plain to him that the addition 'did not reflect nor any way operate upon the petition;' and Weston, the author of the clause, together with Dorset, usually one of the most determined partisans of the Government, expressed their full concurrence in this view of the case. No wonder that the original Opposition pushed their advantage home. Saye and North urged that before going in search of reasons for the addition, they had better decide whether the addition was necessary at all. Buckingham begged the House to vote at once whether there was to be a saving of the King's power or not. Rather, urged Essex, let us vote first whether we will agree to the petition or not. In this chaos of opinion a proposal of Coventry's was finally adopted, that the addition should be again commended to the Lower House, but that he should be authorised to explain that it really meant as little as possible.[1]

Buckingham had clearly lost his hold upon the Lords. As far as it is possible to judge from the debates, the prevailing opinion was that the law was as it was stated in the petition, although a loophole ought to be left for sudden and unforeseen emergencies. Yet the moment they came to put this upon paper the difficulty of not yielding more than they intended to yield was altogether insuperable.

The Lords no longer under Buckingham's control.

Insuperable, at least, the difficulty seemed to the Commons. In the debate which followed the Lord Keeper's communication, not a single voice was raised in favour of the clause. Lawyers and country gentlemen argued alike that the additional clause would destroy the whole petition. The King, it would be understood to say, cannot billet soldiers or force loans upon us by the law; but he can by his sovereign power. Sir Henry Marten stripped the whole question of its techicalities. According to Æsop, he said, the lion, the ass, and the fox went out hunting together. The booty was taken, and the ass having divided it into three equal

May 22. The addition rejected by the Commons.

---

[1] *Elsing's Notes.*

portions, told the lion that it was his prerogative to choose between them. The lion took it ill that only a portion was offered him, and saying, "It is my prerogative to choose," tore the ass in pieces. The fox, taught by the ass's calamity, contented himself with a little piece of skin. Such, implied Marten, would be the fate of the English people if they once acknowledged a power superior to the laws. To this view of the case Wentworth gave his hearty approval. "I think," he said, "we all agree we may not admit of this addition. If we do, we shall leave the subject worse than we found him, and we shall have little thanks for our labours when we come home. I conceive this addition, as it is now penned, amounts to a saving, whereas before the law was without a saving. I am resolved not to yield to it; but let us not vote it; let a sub-committee collect the reasons already given."[1]

Wentworth was unwilling to come into unnecessary collision with the Lords, and as the House was of the same opinion, he had no difficulty in carrying his point so far as its immediate action was concerned. The clause was not rejected, but a sub-committee was to prepare an argumentative answer to be laid before the Lords.

<small>Arguments to be presented to the Lords.</small>

The next morning the sub-committee reported the heads of the answer which they proposed that Glanville and Marten should deliver. Before they had been adopted by the Grand Committee, Wentworth rose. "We are now fallen," he said, "from a new statute and a new law to a Petition of Right, and unless the Lords co-operate with us, the stamp is out of that which gives a value to the action. If they join with us it is a record to posterity. If we sever from them it is like the grass upon the house-top, that is of no long continuance. And therefore let us labour to get the Lords to join with us. To this there are two things considerable; first not to recede in this petition either in part or in whole from our resolutions; secondly, that the Lords join with us, else all is lost. We have protested we desire no new thing;

<small>May 23. Wentworth proposes a further accommodation.</small>

[1] This is from *Harl. MSS.* 4771, fol. 176 b, except the words 'as it is now penned,' which come from *Nicholas's Notes.* The debate is headed in *Nicholas,* May 23.

we leave all power to his Majesty to punish malefactors. Let us clear ourselves to his Majesty that we thus intend. It is far from me to presume to propound anything. I dare not trust my own judgment, only to prevent a present voting [1] with the Lords. Let us again address ourselves to the Lords that we are constant in our grounds that we desire no new thing, nor to invade upon his Majesty's prerogative : but let us add, though we may not admit of this addition, yet if their Lordships can find out any way to keep untouched this petition, we will consider of it and join with them." [2]

Wentworth was consistent with himself in attempting to provide for all emergencies. To Eliot the suggestion was a mere machination of evil, for he saw, what Wentworth did not see, that these emergencies must be left to future generations to provide for ; and he saw too, in a dim way, that the House of Commons was the heir of the Tudor monarchy, and would be the depositary of those extraordinary powers which Charles had forfeited the right to exercise. Thus, without knowing it clearly, he became the advocate of change in the frame of the State, which should indeed maintain old principles and should operate within the lines of the old constitution ; whilst Wentworth, whose mind was full of schemes for alteration and reform, was an advocate of the constitutional forms which had existed in the days of his youth. Early in the session he had announced that the Commons could do nothing without the King. He now announced that they could do nothing without the Lords.

To Eliot such a suggestion was intolerable. "As though," he said, "the virtue and perfection of this House depended upon and were included in their Lordships ! Sir, I cannot make so slight an estimation of the Commons as to make them mere cyphers to nobility ! I am not so taken with the affectation of their Lordships' honour, so much to flatter and exalt it. No ! I am confident that, should the Lords desert us, we should yet continue flourishing and green." At the proposal itself, he went on to say, he could not but be

Eliot's rejoinder.

---

[1] Voting a rejection of the clause in opposition to them.
[2] *Harl. MSS.* 4771, fol. 176 b.

amazed. It was to throw them back after so long a debate into new rocks and difficulties.¹ Eliot then insisted on the danger of making the slightest change in the petition, and charged Wentworth with deserting the cause which he had once espoused. Then addressing himself to the substance of the proposal, he exposed in masterly language its entire futility. "No saving in this kind," he said, "with what subtlety soever worded, can be other than destructive to our work."

These last words contain the true vindication of the persistency with which the Commons held to their determination. Not that Wentworth, looking at the question from a different point of view, was without excuse. Whether the Commons were right or wrong, their petition contained within it the germs of a revolution. As a matter of fact no man then living could remember the time when the discretionary power which Charles claimed had not been exercised by the Crown. Wentworth at once rose to vindicate his motives. Declaring that he had merely meant by his metaphors that without the assent of the Peers the petition would have no statutory force, he explained his own position. "My proposition," he said, "is for no moderation, but preserve the petition in the whole or the parts of it. I will never recede from it. Put it not in extremity to have it voted against us. It was wondered I spake after so long a debate. I have discharged my conscience and delivered it. Do as you please. God, that knows my heart, knows that I have studied to preserve this Parliament, as I confess the resolutions of this House, in the opinion

[margin: Wentworth's reply.]

¹ There is evidence here that Eliot's speeches in the *Port Eliot MSS.*, though in the main correct, were subject to some manipulation. He is there made to refer to that which had been done ' by the Grand Committee this morning in direction of those arguments to the Lords which they framed.' When Eliot wrote this down, he must have fancied that the speech had been delivered in the House itself, and Mr. Forster thereupon (ii. 68) supposed that Wentworth's speech to which Eliot replied was delivered in support of a fresh proposal of the Lords which was really not discussed till the 24th. But unless the whole debate is a dream of the Harleian reporter, the debate was in committee, and the direction of the committee was not given till after Eliot's speech was finished. The end of Eliot's speech, too, seems to have been altered in the same way.

of wise men, stretch very far on the King's power, and if they be kept punctually, will give a blow to government. The King said that if government were touched, he was able to protect us; and by[1] this saving indeed is added nothing to him."[2]

It was quite true; the bare law of the petition could never be the rule for all future time. Martial law would have to be executed upon soldiers if discipline was to be maintained. Provision must somehow be made for lodging the men when they were brought together, and, if extraordinary evils demanded extraordinary remedies, men must be imprisoned without much regard for their legal rights. What Eliot saw and Wentworth did not see, was that these powers could no longer safely be entrusted to Charles. When the law was once made without exception, exceptional cases could be settled as they arose with consent of Parliament. To us the change seems simple enough. But the change was great in those days. By making the consent of Parliament necessary to the King, it deprived him of that right of speaking in all emergencies as the special representative of the nation, which he held from custom if not from constitutional law.

How far was there weight in it?

Wentworth's argument made no impression on those who heard it. Seymour alone supported it; but he met with no response, and Glanville and Marten were despatched to lay their long train of reasoning before the Lords.

The Commons decide against Wentworth.

It was impossible for the Lords to maintain the addition any longer. As far as we can judge, the great majority of the House, with Bristol and Williams at its head, was of the same opinion as Wentworth. Argument and the current of events had made Buckingham powerless. Whilst, however, this majority was strong enough to refuse to follow Buckingham, its weakness, like Wentworth's weakness, lay in the impossibility of placing ideas upon paper without surrendering to the King more than it was willing to surrender. Weston's clause had merely been

---

[1] "to" in MS.
[2] *Harl. MSS.* 4771, fol. 176 b. *Parl. Hist.* ii. 364.

thrown out as a feeler, and the moment it was seriously assailed it was dropped without difficulty. Yet the Lords felt that something must be done. Clare proposed that a Committee of both Houses should draw up another form upon which they could all agree. Abbot suggested that a conference should be held to see 'if there be any that can find a more commodious way of accommodation.' There was plainly nothing definite fixed, nothing which it was possible to ask the House to stand on. Laud's old friend, Bishop Buckeridge, of Rochester, made a very different proposal. Let the petition, he said, be delivered to the judges, that they may give their opinion whether anything in it 'do intrench upon the King's prerogative.' Their opinion could then be entered on the roll, 'and then this petition can no way prejudice the King's right.' The idea here was much the same as Wentworth's: the idea of an inalienable prerogative, not above the law but part of the law, and which it was therefore not necessary to express in words. Clare's suggestion was the one adopted. The Commons were asked to join the Lords in a committee, 'to see if, by manifestation and protestation or declaration or any other way, there could be any way found out to satisfy his Majesty.'[1]

The Lords make a fresh proposal,

The proposal was elastic enough. The reasons for rejecting it were admirably put by Phelips. "What," he said, "should be the subject of this accommodation? It must be somewhat like the last addition. If it be so put into other words and acted otherwise, yet virtually and actually it will be interpreted to amount to the very same thing. Also we have already expressed as much care over his Majesty's prerogative as can be made. We have obliged ourselves by our oaths, and how apt have we been to defend it upon all occasions!" Wentworth and Seymour were in favour of appointing the joint committee; but they found no support, and the proposal of the Lords was rejected.

which is rejected by the Commons.

The action thus taken by the Commons was in little danger of meeting with a repulse in the House of Lords, as Wentworth

---

[1] *Elsing's Notes; Harl. MSS.* 4771, fol. 193 b.

had feared. The leaders of that middle party, which was now able to command a majority, declared that they would push their desire for an accommodation with the King no further. Arundel explained that he had now no wish to press the Lower House 'with an addition to this petition.' "We do hold it fit," he added, "to declare to the King that we intend not to prejudice his prerogative in this petition, in regard we are exempted from the oath of supremacy." The Lords, in fact, would practically join in that oath to which Phelips had appealed, and the right of the prerogative would be left as vague as before. Bristol accepted the way of escape offered. The Commons, he said, had declared that they had no intention of prejudicing the prerogative. Let the Lords make the same declaration at once.

<small>May 25. The middle party in the Lords agree with the Commons.</small>

Would this view of the case be acceptable at Court. Dorset, impulsive as when he had gone forth to the bloody duel which has fixed a stain on his name for ever, or when he declared in the Parliament of 1621 that the passing bell was tolling for religion, stood foremost in the breach. "My Lords," he said, "if I did not believe this petition would give the King a greater wound here in his government than I hope ever an enemy shall, I would hold my peace."[1] Buckingham himself declared firmly against the course proposed. "The business," he said, "is now in your hands alone, which gives me comfort. It now remains whether you will depart from your addition. If we now depart from our addition, we do in a manner depart from ourselves. The addition must[2] be either in the preamble, or in the body, or the conclusion. If it be nowhere I cannot give my vote to it. The reason is[3] that it carries words in it not expressed in Magna Carta and the other six statutes. Let them go their way and we make a petition, and then we may make a protestation as we please."

<small>Resistance of Buckingham and his friends.</small>

If anything were needed to justify the resolution of the

---

[1] The report ends at "shall." The five following words are added from conjecture.

[2] "to be," MS.   [3] "Reason that," MS.

Commons, it was these words of Buckingham. He, at least,
wanted something more than the prerogative which
Bristol and Arundel were ready to allow. But the
days were gone by when Buckingham could hope
to carry the House with him. Abbot advised the Peers to
'join with the Commons in the petition, though we would
have had also some demonstration of their saving of the King's
just prerogative.'[1] "When their liberties," said Northampton,
"have been trenched upon, their goods have been taken away
not by a legal course, I will desire that it may be amended.
When the subjects' liberty is in question, I will creep upon my
knees with a petition to his Majesty with all humility. When
the King's prerogative is in question, I will get upon my horse
and draw my sword, and defend it with my life and estate."
After this a motion was made by another peer that a declaration
might be prepared for clearing the King's prerogative.[2]

The Lords adopt the view of the Commons.

The advice thus given was taken. The next day a form
was unanimously adopted by which the Lords declared, altogether apart from the petition, that their intention
was not to lessen or impeach anything which by
the oath of supremacy they had 'sworn to assert
and defend.'

May 26. Declaration of the Lords.

It was not much. The oath of supremacy simply bound
those who took it to defend the authority of which the Crown
was already possessed, without specifying what that authority
was. The declaration, however, left it open to those who held
that the Crown had a right to override the law in cases of
emergency, to assert that they had not sacrificed their consciences to political conveniency. The Commons on their
part had no desire to push matters farther. On the
28th the petition was brought up to the Lords, and
was by them adopted without more discussion.

May 28. The petition passes both Houses.

Three or four weeks earlier, Charles would probably have
refused even to consider the petition in the form in which it
now reached him; but the last week had brought
news of disaster which would hardly allow him to
turn his back so easily upon the proffered subsidies. In

The King's difficulties.

---

[1] Minute Book, *House of Lords MSS.*   [2] *Elsing's Notes.*

Germany Stade was lost. In France Rochelle was still unsuccoured.

The disasters of the autumn of 1627 had converted the war in North Germany into a succession of sieges. Whilst Schleswig and Jutland were overrun by the Imperialists, Christian clung with the grasp of despair to the fortresses by which the mouth of the Elbe was guarded. Krempe and Glückstadt on the eastern side were supplied with money and provisions by the Dutch. Stade, near the western bank, had the misfortune to be confided to Morgan's English garrison. Every disposable penny in the Exchequer had been applied to the French war, and since August the little force—4,000 men in all—was left to shift for itself.[1] Anstruther and Morgan raised a little money on their own credit, not enough to do more than to procure a fresh supply of shoes and stockings. Even though no actual siege was opened, the enemy lay closely around the town, and provisions were not to be obtained from the surrounding country. Yet the brave old Morgan showed no signs of flinching. "If it must be my extreme hard fortune," wrote the General, "to be thus abandoned, I will not yet abandon myself, nor this place, as long as with cat and dog—our present diet—we shall be able to feed an arm to that strength that it may lift a sword."[2]

January. Morgan at Stade.

Week after week slipped away, and help came not. Want and disease were doing their fell work, and Morgan had little hope of holding out. Before the end of March Anstruther received a little money from England. It was now too late. The town was closely blockaded and no supplies could be sent in. On April 27 Stade was formally surrendered to Tilly.[3] The garrison was allowed to march out with all the honours of war, and a month later, whilst the Lords and Commons were fighting their last battle over the Petition of Right, the whole sad story was known in England.[4]

April 27. Surrender of Stade.

[1] At the beginning of the year the garrison numbered 3,900, viz. 2,700 English, 700 Scots, 500 Germans. Anstruther to Conway, Jan. 5, *S. P. Denmark.*
[2] Morgan to Conway, Jan. 25, *S. P. Denmark.*
[3] Anstruther to Conway; Morgan to Conway, May 3, *ibid.*
[4] Woodward to Windebank, May 21, *S. P. Dom.* civ. 47.

Thus dropped the curtain, amidst gloom and disaster, upon the scene of English history on which Charles and Bucking-
End of English intervention in Germany. ham had entered so hopefully four years before. The war for the deliverance of the Palatinate, to be waged whether the nation supported it or not, had come to this. The sixteen hundred brave men, worn with toil and hunger, who stepped forth from Stade with colours flying and with arms in their hands, the noble old General who had held his own so long, abandoned as he was by King and country, had no need to feel the shame of failure. The shame was for those who had directed the course of war so aimlessly, and who had so erroneously judged the conditions of the contest.

Even now Charles thought but little of the disaster in Germany compared with the other disaster in France. The deliverance of the Palatinate had come to be for him a matter of secondary importance, in which he had long since ceased to expect success. The deliverance of Rochelle was a matter of personal honour.

Before the end of April Denbigh's fleet, sixty-six vessels in all, had at last left Plymouth Sound. The crews were pressed men, carried off against their wills from their daily occupations to a service of danger in which the reward was but scanty pay, or most probably no pay at all. Many of them were soldiers converted forcibly into sailors from very necessity. Such a fleet was hardly likely to overcome even moderate opposition.

May 1. Denbigh's fleet at Rochelle. When, in the afternoon of May 1, Denbigh's force ranged up in front of the port of Rochelle, the danger was plainly seen to be of the most formidable description. The passage up the harbour, narrow enough of itself, was still further narrowed by moles jutting out from either side, *Defences of the French.* and the opening between them was guarded by palisades, in front of which were vessels, some of them sunken, some floating at the level of the water. Even to reach such a formidable obstruction it would be necessary to beat down the fire of twenty armed vessels, supported by crowds of musqueteers, who were in readiness either to fire upon the enemy from the shore or to float off in barges to the succour of their friends. It may be questioned whether Drake or Nelson, followed by crews as high-spirited and energetic as themselves, could have made the attack successfully. It is certain that Denbigh's force, composed as it was of men without heart in the matter, could not but fail.

Of the details of the failure it is hardly possible to decide in the midst of the conflicting evidence. The English officers, when they came home, threw all the blame upon the Rochellese who accompanied them, whilst the Rochellese bitterly retorted the accusation. It is, however, plain that the English officers had no confidence in their chance of success, and Denbigh was not the man to inspire those beneath him with a more daring spirit. A resolution was taken to wait till the next spring-tides made the attack easier for his fire-ships. On the morning of the 8th a fresh apprehension seized upon the commander. The wind was blowing from Rochelle, and if he could not set fire to the ships of the enemy, the French might possibly set fire to his. He therefore gave the order to weigh anchor, that the fleet might retire to a little distance. When the minds of men are in a state of despondency the slightest retrograde movement is fatal. The Rochellese weighed anchor as they were told, but they understood that the expedition had been abandoned, and made all sail for England. Thus deserted, the whole fleet followed the example.[1]

May 8. Failure of the undertaking.

The first news of difficulty had only served to sharpen Charles's resolution. On the 17th he issued orders to Denbigh to hold on at Rochelle as long as possible, and to ask for reinforcements if he found them needful.[2] On the 19th he knew that the fleet was on its way home.[3] Never before had he been so angry. "If the ships had been lost," he cried, impatiently, "I had timber enough to build more." He at once despatched Denbigh's son, Lord Fielding, to Portsmouth with orders to press into the

May 17. Determination of Charles not to give way. May 19.

---

[1] Examinations of Ramboilleau and Le Brun, May 16. Denbigh, Palmer, and Weddell to Buckingham, June 2, *S. P. Dom.* civ. 2 i., 3 i., cvi. 11.

[2] The King to Denbigh, May 17, *S. P. Dom.* civ. 8.

[3] The date we learn from Contarini. The news, as we know from the examinations cited above, reached Plymouth and Dartmouth on the 16th.

King's service every vessel he could meet with, and to direct his father to go back at all hazards to Rochelle, and there to await the further supplies which would be sent.¹ Secretary Coke himself was sent down to Portsmouth to hurry on the reinforcements. On the 27th Denbigh was off the Isle of Wight, professing his readiness to return as soon as his shattered fleet could be collected.² It was easier for him to talk of returning than actually to return. Three of his vessels laden with corn for Rochelle were snapped up by the Dunkirk privateers within sight of the English coast.³ The ships which remained were full of sick men, and in urgent need of repair. The fire-ships were not ready. There were not enough provisions on board to enable the fleet to stay long at Rochelle, even if it returned at once. Although the ships were in want of water, Denbigh dared not send his men on shore, lest they should run away from so unpopular a service. Before this combination of difficulties even Charles was compelled to give way, and orders were despatched to Denbigh to refit his squadron, but to remain in England till the whole available maritime force of the country could be got ready to accompany him.⁴

<small>May 27.</small>

<small>May 28.</small>

<small>May 30.</small>

Such were the tidings pouring in upon Charles during the days when he was considering the answer which he would give to the Petition of Right. Unless he gave his consent to that, he would never touch a penny of the subsidies, and without the subsidies the relief of Rochelle was absolutely hopeless. Everything combined to make him anxious to assent to the petition, if he could do it without sacrificing the authority which he believed to be justly his. The one point which still appeared necessary to him to

<small>May 26. The King's difficulties about the petition.</small>

---

¹ Fielding to Buckingham, May 20; Woodward to Windebank, May 21, *S. P. Dom.* civ. 34, 47. Contarini to the Doge, May $\frac{20}{30}$. *Ven. Transcripts, R. O.*

² Denbigh to Buckingham, May 27, *S. P. Dom.* cv. 29.

³ The Council to Buckingham, May 30, *Rushworth,* i. 587.

⁴ The letters of Denbigh and Coke containing these details will be found in *S. P. Dom.* cv. and cvi.

granted there is no fear of conclusion as is intimated in the question."[1]

The day after the last reply was given in was Whit Sunday, a day spent as busily by the King as Good Friday had been spent by the House of Commons. At the council table the whole question of the petition was discussed, and the forms of answer drawn up by Heath to suit every possible contingency were doubtless laid before the board. Of these forms[2] there was probably only one which, to any extent, suited the exigencies of Charles's position. "Since both the Lords and Commons," it was proposed that the King should say, "have severally, with dutiful respect to us, declared their intentions not to lessen our just power or prerogative as their sovereign, we do as freely declare our clear intention no way to impeach the just liberty of our subjects ; and therefore, this right undoubtedly being so happily settled between us and our people, which we trust shall ever continue, we do freely grant that this petition shall in all points be duly observed."

<small>June 1. The Council consulted.</small>

<small>Heath's suggested answer.</small>

By these words the petition would become the law of the land, especially if the old words of Norman French, "*Soit droit fait comme est desiré,*" had been added. The claim to special powers would still have been maintained, but by the use of the word 'prerogative' Heath not only borrowed the expression of the House of Commons itself, but placed the King's claim under the special guardianship of the judges, who were constantly accustomed to decide on the extent of the prerogative.

It may be that Charles shrank from subjecting his authority to the decision of the judges. It may be that he had little taste for a clear and definite restriction upon his powers. The day before, too, had been spent in Buckingham's company,[3]

---

[1] *Ellis*, ser. 2, iii. 250. The original copy of the questions and answers is in *Hargrave MSS.* 27, fol. 97.

[2] The first one in *S. P. Dom.* cv. 95. Others will be found in this and the following papers.

[3] Contarini's Despatch, June $\frac{7}{17}$.

and Buckingham had no wish to see the King give way. The form finally adopted, with the full consent of the Privy Council,[1] united all the objections it is possible to conceive. "The King willeth," so it was determined that the Lord Keeper should speak, " that right be done according to the laws and customs of the realm ; and that the statutes be put in due execution, that his subjects may have no cause to complain of any wrongs or oppressions contrary to their just rights and liberties, to the preservation whereof he holds himself in conscience as well obliged as of his prerogative." [2]

<small>Answer agreed on.</small>

Such an answer meant nothing at all. The petition was not even mentioned. It was Charles's old offer of confirming the statutes whilst refusing the interpretation placed upon them by the Commons. Its words breathed an entirely different spirit from the questions to the judges. The King no longer asks for a limited power to meet special emergencies, which Bristol and Wentworth, if not Eliot and Coke, would have been willing to grant him, but he throws back not merely the question of imprisonment, but every question which the petition professed to answer, into the uncertain mazes of his own arbitrary will. If nothing better than this was to be had, the Commons had toiled in vain.

<small>Its worthlessness.</small>

The next morning the Peers and Commons were in the King's presence in the House of Lords. "Gentlemen," he said, "I am come here to perform my duty. I think no man can think it long, since I have not taken so many days in answering the petition as ye spent weeks in framing it ; and I am come hither to show you that, as well in formal things as essential, I desire to give you as much content as in me lies." Then, after a few words from the Lord Keeper, the answer agreed upon the day before was read.

<small>June 2. The answer given.</small>

When this answer was read the next morning in the Commons, Eliot, representing the general dissatisfaction, moved

---

[1] The part taken by the Council is gathered from the subsequent debates in the House of Lords.
[2] *Lords' Journals,* iii. 835.

that its consideration should be postponed till Friday, June 6.[1]

June 3. Its consideration postponed. He had, however, something more to say than that. The breach with the King against which he had struggled so long seemed now inevitable. But was it really the King who was to blame? Eliot must have known at least as well as we can know how Buckingham had been the soul of the opposition to the petition in the House of Lords, and how he had struggled to the last to make it meaningless; and he must have suspected, if he did not know, that the last unsatisfactory answer had been dictated by the favourite.[2] If this were so, Eliot may well have thought that the time was come when the legal claims on which the Commons had been hitherto standing must be reinforced with other arguments, reaching far more widely than any which that Parliament had yet heard. He would again stand forward as the Eliot of 1626. Subsidies must be refused—if they were to be refused at all—not merely because the King's part of the bargain, tacitly made, had not been fulfilled, but because, as the last Parliament had declared, they would be utterly wasted if they were to pass through Buckingham's hands. What danger he might draw on his own head, Eliot recked nothing. Like the great Scottish reformer, he was one who 'never feared the face of any man.' As he spoke he felt within him the voice of an offended nation struggling for utterance.[3]

Buckingham's part in the matter.

[1] *Nicholas's Notes.* This, with the King's answer, and a short note of Eliot's second speech, is all that Nicholas gives us between May 26 and June 6. The invaluable Harleian report, too, deserts us at May 27; so that we are by no means so well informed about these later proceedings as about the earlier ones.

[2] Whether it was so or not, I cannot say; but the contrast between the spirit of the questions to the judges, and that of the answer adopted by the Council where Buckingham was supreme, is very suspicious.

[3] See Mr. Forster's remarks on this speech (*Sir J. Eliot*, ii. 78). On one point I am almost inclined to go beyond him. He thinks that Eliot's 'fearless spirit could discern the safety that lay beyond the danger,' as if he had expected to frighten the King into giving way. I fancy that, judging by past experience, he could have little hope of this, and if he spoke from a sheer sense of duty, without expectation of success, his conduct is all the more admirable.

He began by reminding his hearers that they met there as the great Council of the King, and that it was their duty to inform him of all that it was well for him to know. That duty it was now for them to fulfil. At home and abroad everything was in confusion. At home true religion was discountenanced. Abroad their friends had been overpowered, their enemies had prospered. Rash and ill-considered enterprises had ended in disaster. In Elizabeth's days it had not been so. She had built her prosperity upon a close alliance with France and the Netherlands. Now France was divided within herself, and driven into war with England. To this French war the Palatinate had been sacrificed. Such a policy might well be regarded rather 'a conception of Spain than begotten here with us.'

Eliot on the state of the nation.

On foreign policy.

At these words Sir Humphrey May rose to interrupt the speaker. Knowing as he did how closely this French war was entwined round the King's heart, he was perhaps anxious to check words which would only widen the breach which he so much deprecated. But the House was in no mood to listen to a Privy Councillor. Eliot was encouraged with cries of "Go on!" from every side. "If he goes on," said May, "I hope that I may myself go out." "Begone! begone!" was the reply from every bench; but the spell of the great orator was upon him, and he could not tear himself away.

May's interruption.

When Eliot resumed he was prepared to try a higher flight than even he had hitherto ventured on. He had no longer to speak merely of disaster and mismanagement, which might be plausibly at least accounted for by the niggardliness of the Commons. Striking at the very heart of the foreign policy of the Government, he asked why the moment when Denmark had been overpowered at Lutter had been chosen for the commencement of a fresh quarrel with France. Was it credible that this had been advised by the Privy Council? With full knowledge doubtless how completely the French war had been the act of Buckingham, with less knowledge, it may be, how completely it had also been the act of the

Eliot on the French war.

King, he turned upon the councillors present, perhaps specially upon May. "Can those now," he said, "that express their troubles at the hearing of these things, and have so often told us in this place of their knowledge in the conjunctures and disjunctures of affairs, say they advised in this? Was this an act of Council, Mr. Speaker? I have more charity than to think it; and unless they make a confession of themselves, I cannot believe it."

Asks who had advised it.

The main error in policy, if it was but an error, having been thus exposed, Eliot turned to the mismanagement of the war. The expedition to Cadiz, the expedition to Rhé, the latest failure at Rochelle, he painted in the gloomiest colours. Buckingham's name was not mentioned, but it must have been branded in letters of flame upon the mind of every man who sat listening there. At home, too, the Court, the Church, the Bar, the Bench, the Navy, were handed over to men ignorant and corrupt; the Exchequer was empty, the crown lands sold, the King's jewels and plate pawned. "What poverty," he cried, "can be greater? What necessity so great? What perfect English heart is not almost dissolved into sorrow for the truth? For the oppression of the subject, which, as I remember, is the next particular I proposed, it needs no demonstration. The whole kingdom is a proof. And for the exhausting of our treasures, that oppression speaks it. What waste of our provisions, what consumption of our ships, what destruction of our men have been! Witness the journey to Algiers! Witness that with Mansfeld! Witness that to Cadiz! Witness the next![1] Witness that to Rhé! Witness the last!— And I pray God we shall never have more such witnesses.— Witness likewise the Palatinate! Witness Denmark! Witness the Turks! Witness the Dunkirkers! Witness all! What losses we have sustained! How we are impaired in munition, in ships, in men! It has no contradiction. We were never so much weakened, nor had less hope now to be restored."

Misconduct in military operations.

Such was the terrible catalogue of grievances flung forth,

---

[1] This contemptuous reference is to Willoughby's fleet, which only reached the Bay of Biscay.

one after another, in words which pierced deeply into the hearts of those who heard. To the end Buckingham's name had not been mentioned. Whatever Eliot's secret thoughts might have been he said nothing of reviving the impeachment of the unpopular minister. He asked that a Remonstrance—a statement of grievances, as we should now say—might be drawn up, in order that the King might be informed what the Commons thought of his policy.

A Remonstrance to be prepared.

There were many among Eliot's hearers who shrank from so bold a step. Some thought it would be better to ask for a fuller answer to the petition. Sir Henry Marten suggested that Eliot's speech proceeded from disaffection to his Majesty, whilst others looked upon it as an angry retort upon the King's answer. Eliot rose to explain. So far from his words having been called forth by the King's answer, he and others had long ago formed a resolution to call attention to these grievances when a fit opportunity occurred ; and the truth of this statement, which doubtless referred to the line taken by Eliot at the private meeting before the opening of the session,[1] was attested by Wentworth and Phelips. In spite of all that had been said, Eliot's proposal was adopted, and the next day was fixed for the discussion of the Remonstrance.[2]

Feeling of the House.

Even as an answer to the King's reply, it might fairly be argued that Eliot's proposal was well-timed. The King had claimed to be possessed of special powers above the law, for the honour and safety of the realm. Such powers he had wielded for more than three years, and the Remonstrance would tell him what had come of it.

Bearing of the proposal.

Charles fancied himself strong enough to drive back the rising tide. Believing, as he did, that all the disasters which had happened had arisen from the reluctance of the Commons to vote him money, he now sent to tell them that the session would come to an end in a week, that he had given an answer to their petition 'full of justice and grace,' and would give no other. They were therefore seriously to proceed to business, without enter-

June 4. The King tries to stop the Remonstrance.

---

[1] See page 230.   [2] Forster, *Sir J. Eliot*, ii. 79.

taining new matters; in other words, to pass the Subsidy Bill, and let the Remonstrance alone.[1]

The House was now in Eliot's hands. The silence to which Wentworth was self-condemned since the failure of his conciliatory efforts, was the measure of the downward progress which Charles had been making since the days of the leadership of the member for Yorkshire. After listening to a report from the Committee of Trade,[2] strongly condemnatory of the cruel treatment to which shipowners and mariners had been subjected when pressed into the King's service, the House, taking not the slightest notice of the Royal message, went into committee on the Remonstrance.[3]

The House refuses to stop.

The next morning a sharper message was delivered from the King, positively forbidding the House to proceed with any new business which might spend greater time than remained before the end of the session, or which might 'lay any scandal or aspersion upon the State, Government, or ministers thereof.'

June 5. Sharper message from the King.

It was a terrible awakening for the leaders of the Commons; the more painful because, in their simple loyalty, they would not open their eyes to its real meaning. If they could have fully realised the fact that their King was against them; that even without Buckingham's intervention, Charles would have closed his ears to their prayers; that Charles, if he was not the originator, was the most obstinate defender of all that had been done, they might have nerved themselves with pain and sorrow to the conflict before them. It was because they could not see this that a feeling of helplessness came over them. The King, they earnestly attempted to believe, was good and wise; but he was beyond their reach. Between him and them stood the black cloud of Buckingham's presence, impenetrable to their wishes, and

Distress of the House.

---

[1] *Parl. Hist.* ii. 388.

[2] *Commons' Journals*, i. 909; and more fully in *Harl. MSS.* 6800, fol. 353.

[3] Except from a few words in Nethersole's letter (*S. P. Dom.* cvi. 55) I know nothing of this debate.

distorting every ray of light which was suffered to reach the place in which Charles remained in seclusion. Before this grim shadow, almost preternatural in its all-pervading strength, bearded men became as children. Sobs and tears burst forth from every side of the House.

Phelips declares the misfortune of the House. With quivering voice and broken words Phelips strove to give utterance to the thoughts within him. There was little hope, he said; for he could not but remember with what moderation the House had proceeded. "Former times," he said, mournfully, "have given wounds enough to the people's liberty. We came hither full of wounds, and we have cured what we could. Yet what is the return of all but misery and desolation? What did we aim at but to have served his Majesty, and to have done that which would have made him great and glorious? If this be a fault, then we are all criminous." It was their duty, he proceeded, to give advice to the King. If they were to be stopped in doing this, let them cease to be a council. *Proposes to ask leave to go home.* "Let us presently," he concluded by saying, "inform his Majesty that our firm intents were to show him in what danger the commonwealth and state of Christendom stands; and therefore, since our counsels are no better acceptable, let us beg his Majesty's leave every man to depart home, and pray to God to divert those judgments and dangers which too fearfully and imminently hang over our heads."

Perhaps it would have been better, if anything could have been better with such a king as Charles, that Phelips's proposal should have been adopted on the spot. But whatever reticence the leaders may have deliberately imposed upon themselves, there was too much angry feeling against Buckingham to be long suppressed. Eliot pointed out that there had been misrepresentation to the King, as was especially shown in the clause of the message forbidding them to lay aspersions on the Government. They had no such intention. "It is said also," he added, "as if we cast some aspersions on his Majesty's ministers. I am confident no minister, how dear soever, can——"

The sentence was never ended. Finch, the Speaker,

started from his chair. He, too, felt the weight of the issues with which the moment was fraught. "There is command laid upon me," he said, with tears in his eyes, "to interrupt any that should go about to lay an aspersion on the ministers of State."

<small>Eliot stopped by the Speaker.</small>

What Eliot meant to say can never be known. He had too much self-command to make it likely that he was going beyond the position he had assumed in the former debate. Probably he was but about to express an opinion that no minister could stand higher with his Majesty than the needs of his subjects. But the ill-timed intervention of Finch had done more than Eliot's tongue could have done. It was one more proof how impossible it was for the Commons to reach the King.

Eliot sat down at once. If he was not to speak freely, he would not speak at all. What Eliot expressed by his silence, Digges expressed in words: "Unless we may speak of these things in Parliament, let us arise and be gone, or sit still and do nothing." Then there was a long pause. At last Rich rose to protest against the policy of silence. It was most safe for themselves, he said, but not for their constituents. Let them go to the Lords and ask them to join in the Remonstrance.

<small>Digges declares their remaining useless.</small>

<small>Rich wishes to consult the Lords.</small>

In the despondent mood in which the members were, there were not wanting a few who thought Eliot had been to blame. It was that terrible speech of his on the 3rd,[1] they said, which had done the mischief. The House would not hear of such an explanation. From the first day of the session, it was resolutely declared, no member had been guilty of undutiful speech. Others again essayed to speak. Old Coke, with the tears running down his furrowed face, stood up, faltered, and sat down again. At last it was resolved to go into committee to consider what was to be done.

Finch, thus released from his duties, asked permission to leave the House. The permission was not refused. With streaming eyes he hurried to the King to tell what he had heard and seen. To him too, and to all real

<small>The Speaker leaves the House.</small>

[1] See page 299.

friends of the prerogative, the breach between the Crown and so thoroughly loyal a House must have been inexpressibly sad.

The impression left by the Speaker's departure was that a dissolution was imminent. Men waxed bolder with the sense of coming danger. "The King," said Kirton, "is as good a prince as ever reigned. It is the enemies to the commonwealth that have so prevailed with him, therefore let us aim now to discover them ; and I doubt not but God will send us hearts, hands, and swords to cut the throats of the enemies of the King and State." Wentworth, rejecting Rich's proposal, moved to go straight to the King with the Remonstrance. Were they not the King's counsellors?

Debate in the committee.

Coke was the next to rise, his voice no longer choked by his emotions. He was about to say that which Eliot had refrained from saying. He quoted precedent after precedent in which the Commons had done the very thing that the King had warned them against doing. Great men, Privy Councillors, the King's prerogative itself, had once not been held to be beyond the scope of Parliamentary inquiry. "What shall we do?" he cried; "let us palliate no longer. If we do, God will not prosper us. I think the Duke of Bucks is the cause of all our miseries, and till the King be informed thereof, we shall never go out with honour, or sit with honour here. That man is the grievance of grievances. Let us set down the causes of all our disasters, and they will all reflect upon him." Let them not go to the Lords. Let them go straight to the King. It was not the King, but the Duke, who had penned the words, 'We require you not to meddle with State government, or the ministers thereof.' Did not the King once sanction the principle which this message condemned? Did he not, as Prince of Wales, take part as a Peer of Parliament in the proceedings against Lord Chancellor Bacon and Lord Treasurer Middlesex?

Coke names the Duke.

Amidst expressions of approbation from every side, Coke sat down. At last the word which was on all lips had been spoken. Then, as a contemporary letter-writer expressed it, 'as when one good hound recovers the scent, the rest come in with a full cry, so they pursued it, and every one came on home, and laid the blame where they thought the fault was.' Selden but put into shape what Coke had suggested. "All this time," he said, "we have cast a mantle on what was done last Parliament; but now, being driven again to look on that man, let us proceed with that which was then well begun, and let the charge be renewed that was last Parliament against him, to which he made an answer, but the particulars were sufficient that we might demand judgment on that answer only."[1]

Resolution to name Buckingham.

As Charles had made Wentworth's leadership impossible, so, it seemed, he would now make Eliot's leadership impossible. The mere representation of the evils of the State seemed tame after what had taken place that day. The remaining heads of the Remonstrance were hurried over, and just as a final clause, condemnatory of Buckingham, was being put to the vote, the Speaker reappeared with a message from the King, ordering them to adjourn till the following morning. In doubt and wonder the members departed to their homes.

The King stops the debate.

It was but eleven o'clock when the debate that morning was forcibly interrupted. It may be that if the words spoken in the Commons had reached the King alone, the Houses would have met the next day only to be dissolved. But the Commons were not alone. In the other House a message from the King demanding an adjournment had been interpreted as ominous of a dissolution. Bristol at once interposed the weight of his authority. It was indiscretion, he said, to speak of such a thing as a dissolution from conjecture. If it was true that the Privy Council had advised it, the Lords were greater than the Privy Council. They were the great council of the kingdom, and it was for them to lay before the King the true state of the kingdom. There was danger from Spain, danger from France, danger from the Dunkirk privateers. "The whole Christian world," he said,

Debate in the Lords.

Bristol proposes a representation to the King.

---

[1] *Parl. Hist.* ii. 401. *Rushworth*, i. 605–610. Meade to Stuteville, June 15, *Court and Times*, i. 359. Meade is plainly mistaken in assigning Coke's speech to the 4th.

"is enemy to us. We have not in all the Christian world but one port to put a boat into, Rochelle. We have been like the broken staff of Egypt to all that have relied upon us. The distress of our friends lies before us, the power and malice of our enemies. Now, if we return home, when God had put it into the King's heart to call a Parliament, what disadvantage will it be unto us when our adversaries shall observe that the King and his people have three times met, and departed with no good? Whosoever shall say that a monarch can be fed by projects and imaginations, knows not of what he is speaking." [1] Bristol concluded by moving for a Select Committee to 'represent unto the King the true state of the kingdom, to be humble suitors unto him to let things pass as they have done in the times of his ancestors. To be likewise suitors unto the King, that [2] if there have been any carriage of any private persons displeasing to him, he will not make a sudden end of this Parliament.' [3]

The Lord Keeper ordered to acquaint the King with the feeling of the House.
Charles withdraws from his ground.

Although, from motives of respect to Charles, Bristol's motion was not formally adopted, the Lord Keeper was directed to acquaint the King with the feeling of the House. [4]

Even Charles, self-willed as he was, could not venture to stand up against both Houses. Thanking the Lords for the respect which they had shown him by refusing to appoint the committee which Bristol had proposed, he assured them that he was as fully aware as they were of the dangers of the kingdom—a message which drew from Essex the demand that Bristol's motion for a committee should be put again, and from Bristol himself the expression of a hope that they would at least petition the King not to put a sudden end to the Parliament. [5]

By the Lower House, too, a message had been received

---

[1] The words after "imaginations" are added by conjecture.
[2] The word 'that' is not in the *MS*.
[3] The report ends at "carriage." The rest of the sentence is filled in from Bristol's speech of the next day.
[4] *Elsing's Notes*.   [5] *Ibid.*

qualifying the one which had given such offence the day before. The King, according to this explanation, had no wish to debar the Commons from their right of inquiry, but wished merely to prohibit them from raking up old offences by looking into counsel which had been tendered to him in past times. The explanation was gravely accepted. "I am now as full of joy," said Eliot, "as yesterday of another passion." But the Commons went steadily on with their Remonstrance. On the morning of the 7th they had gone so far as to inquire into the levy of Dulbier's German horse, intended, as one member said, 'to cut our throats or else to keep us at their obedience.'[1]

The Commons go on with the Remonstrance.
June 7.

The House of Lords again intervened. Bishop Harsnet, the author of the Lords' propositions, from which the controversy had by this time drifted so far, now stood up in defence of the Petition of Right. Hateful to the Calvinists on account of his bold attacks made in early life upon the extreme consequences of their cherished doctrine of predestination, he was no less distrusted by Laud for his refusal to entertain the extreme consequences of the opinions which they held in common. The answer to the petition, he said, was full of grace, but it did not come home or give the satisfaction which was expected. Let the Commons be asked to join in a petition to the King for another answer. Williams supported the proposal. It was rumoured, he said, that the answer was not the King's, but had been voted by the Council.[2] "I do not see," he added, "in all the learning I have, that this is at all applicatory to the petition or any part of it." "I conceive," said Bristol, "the answer to be rather a waiving of the petition than any way satisfactory to it. I believe that those distractions and fears which since have sprung amongst us took their original from that answer." The House was unanimous in its desire for a clearer reply. Even Buckingham was unable to oppose himself to the current. The Commons, as soon as they were

Intervention of the Lords.

The King asked for a clear answer to the petition.

---

[1] *Parl. Hist.* ii. 406. *Nicholas's Notes.*
[2] "An assembly which I reverence," is the periphrasis.

invited, gladly gave their consent, and a deputation, with Buckingham at its head, was sent to ask Charles for a clear and satisfactory answer to the petition.[1] They returned with the news that the King would bring his own reply to their request at four o'clock.

At four o'clock, therefore, on that eventful day, Charles took his seat upon the throne. The Commons came troop-ing to the bar, ignorant whether they were to hear the sentence of dissolution or not. They had not long to wait. "The answer I have already given you," said Charles, "was made with so good deliberation, and approved by the judgment of so many wise men, that I could not have imagined but that it should have given you full satis-faction; but, to avoid all ambiguous interpretations, and to show you that there is no doubleness in my meaning, I am willing to please you in words as well as in substance. Read your petition; and you shall have such an answer as I am sure will please you." Then after it had been read, as the shouts of applause rang out loud and clear from the Commons, the clerk pronounced the usual words of approval, '*Soit droit fait comme est desiré.*'

<small>Charles assents to the Petition of Right.</small>

Charles had yet a few more words in reserve. "This," he said, "I am sure is full; yet no more than I granted you on my first answer; for the meaning of that was to confirm all your liberties; knowing, according to your own protestations, that you neither mean nor can hurt my prerogative. And I assure you that my maxim is, that the people's liberties strengthen the King's prerogative, and that the King's prerogative is to defend the people's liberties. You see how ready I have shown myself to satisfy your demands, so that I have done my part; wherefore if the Parliament have not a happy conclusion, the sin is yours; I am free from it."[2]

Once more the acclamations of the Commons rose. The shout was taken up without as the news spread from street to street. The steeples of the City churches rang out

<small>General joy.</small>

---

[1] *Elsing's Notes. Lords' Journals*, iii. 842.
[2] *Lords' Journals*, iii. 843.

their merriest peals. As the dusk deepened into darkness bonfires were lighted up amidst rejoicing crowds. Since the day when Charles had returned from Spain no such signs of public happiness had been seen.[1]

[1] Nethersole to the titular Queen of Bohemia, June 7; Conway to Coke, June 9, *S. P. Dom.* cvi. 55, 71.

CHAPTER LXIV.

REMONSTRANCE AND PROROGATION.

WHATEVER interpretation might still be placed by the King on the concession which he had made, it was undeniable that the House of Commons had gained a great advantage. It might still be doubtful whether, in case of necessity, the King might not break the law, but it could never again be doubtful what the law was.

June 7. Importance of the petition.

The Petition of Right has justly been deemed by constitutional historians as second in importance only to the Great Charter itself. It circumscribed the monarchy of Henry VIII. and Elizabeth as the Great Charter circumscribed the monarchy of Henry II. Alike in the twelfth and in the sixteenth century the kingly power had been established on the ruins of an aristocracy bent upon the nullification of government in England. Alike in the thirteenth and in the seventeenth century, the kingly power was called to account as soon as it was used for other than national ends. Like the Great Charter, too, the Petition of Right was the beginning, not the end, of a revolution.

Comparison with the Great Charter.

So far as in them lay the Commons had stripped Charles of that supreme authority which he believed himself to hold. Their action had, however, been purely negative. Somewhere or another such authority must exist above all positive law, capable of setting it aside when it comes in conflict with the higher needs of the nation. Charles was right enough in thinking that the Commons were

Supreme authority in abeyance.

consciously or unconsciously tending to seize upon this authority themselves; but as yet they had not done so. They had cried, as it were, The King is dead! They had not cried, Long live the King! The old order had received a deadly blow, but it had not given place to the new. Many a stormy discussion, many a sturdy blow, would be needed before the Commons seated themselves in the place of the King.

In every nation supreme authority tends to rest in the hands of those who best respond to the national demand for guidance. Would the House of Commons be able to offer such guidance? Could it represent the wishes, the wisdom, the strength, it may be the prejudices, of the nation, as Elizabeth had represented them? At least it could throw into disrepute those theories upon which the King's claim to stand above the laws was founded, and set forth its policy and its wishes so as to be understood of all men. On June 9, Pym carried up to the Lords the charges which had been gradually collected against Manwaring, and on the same day the Commons went steadily on with their Remonstrance, as if nothing had happened to divert them from their purpose.

<small>June 9. Impeachment of Manwaring.</small>

It was certain that Manwaring would find no favour in the House of Lords. More clearly than many others whose theological opinions coincided with his own he had allowed political speculation to follow in the train of doctrinal thought. The notion that the clergy had an independent existence apart from the rest of the community easily led to the conclusion that that community had no rights which it could plead against the King, by whom the clergy were protected. The theory that the King had a divine right to obedience apart from the laws of the realm was one which had failed to find support amongst the lay Peers in the discussions on the Petition of Right. Manwaring was therefore condemned to imprisonment during the pleasure of the House, to pay a fine of 1,000*l*., to acknowledge his offence, to submit to suspension from preaching at Court for the remainder of his life, and from preaching elsewhere for three years. He was further forbidden to hold any ecclesiastical or civil office, and the King was to be

<small>June 14. Sentence against him.</small>

asked to issue a proclamation calling in all copies of his book in order that they might be burnt.¹

That Manwaring should be impeached and condemned was a matter of course. His offence and his punishment are of little interest to us now; but it is of great interest to know what answer his challenge provoked, what political principle was advocated by the House of Commons in reply to the political principle which it condemned.

The accusation had been entrusted to Pym, and by Pym's mouth the Commons spoke. "The best form of government," he said, "is that which doth actuate and dispose every part and member of a State to the common good; and as those parts give strength and ornament to the whole, so they receive from it again strength and protection in their several stations and degrees. If this mutual relation and intercourse be broken, the whole frame will quickly be dissolved and fall in pieces; and instead of this concord and interchange of support, whilst one part seeks to uphold the old form of government, and the other part to introduce a new, they will miserably consume and devour one another. Histories are full of the calamities of whole states and nations in such cases. It is true that time must needs bring about some alterations, and every alteration is a step and degree towards a dissolution. Those things only are eternal which are constant and uniform. Therefore it is observed by the best writers on this subject, that those commonwealths have been most durable and perpetual which have often reformed and recomposed themselves according to their first institution and ordinance, for by this means they repair the breaches and counterwork the ordinary and natural effects of time."²

Pym's reply to Manwaring's declaration of principle.

What then was the first institution and ordinance of the

---

¹ *Parl. Hist.* ii. 388, 410.

² Bacon has the same conservatism as Pym, but more appreciation of the need of reform. "It is good also not to try experiments in States, except the necessity be urgent, or the utility evident; and well to beware that it be the reformation that draweth on the change, and not the desire of change that pretendeth the reformation."—*Essay on Innovations.*

laws of England? Pym's answer was ready. "There are plain footsteps," he said, "of those laws in the government of the Saxons. They were of that vigour and force as to overlive the Conquest; nay, to give bounds and limits to the Conqueror. . . . It is true they have been often broken, but they have been often confirmed by charters of Kings and by Acts of Parliaments. But the petitions of the subjects upon which those charters and Acts were founded, were ever Petitions of Right, demanding their ancient and due liberties, not suing for any new."

A far nobler view this than Manwaring's. In the historical past of the English people lay the justification of its action in the present. Beyond the precedents of the lawyer and the conclusions of the divine, the eye of the statesman rested on the continuity of responsibility in the nation for the mode in which it was governed. It may be that many things seem otherwise to us than they seemed to Pym, and that we should condemn actions which to him appeared worthy of all praise; but our sympathies are nevertheless with Pym and not with Manwaring. If there were faults in the House of Commons, if there was a danger of the establishment of a self-seeking aristocracy in the place of a national government, it was not from Charles that the remedy was likely to come. Whatever justification might be put forth, Charles's assumption of power had been clearly revolutionary. To conduct war and to extort money in defiance of the nation was an act which had nothing in common with those acts which had been done by former sovereigns with the tacit assent of the nation. The root of the old constitution was the responsibility of the Crown to the nation, a responsibility which, it is true, was often enforced by violence and rebellion. Yet a view of the constitution which takes no account of those acts of violence is like a view of geology which takes no account of earthquakes and volcanoes. There was indeed a certain amount of unconscious insincerity in the legal arguments adduced on either side, which, though dealing with the compacts which sanctioned the results of force, yet shrank from the acknowledgment that the force itself, the steady determination that a king who

Superiority of his view.

spoke for himself and acted for himself should not be permitted to reign, was part of that mass of custom and opinion which, varying in detail from age to age, but animated in every age by the same spirit, is, for brevity's sake, called the English constitution. To the spirit of this constitution the Tudor princes had, even in their most arbitrary moods, sedulously conformed. No rulers have ever been so careful to watch the temper of the nation as were Henry VIII. and Elizabeth. That the King was established by God Himself to think and act in opposition to the thoughts and acts which the nation deliberately chose to think best, was a new thing in England, and even when the King was right and the nation was wrong, it was a change for the worse.

The Commons did their best to persuade themselves from time to time that every step taken in the wrong direction had been owing to the King's ministers rather than to himself ; but it was growing hard for them to close their eyes much longer to the truth. A discovery was now made that Manwaring's sermons had been licensed for printing by the King's special orders, and that too against Laud's remonstrances, for even Laud had warned him that many things in the book would be 'very distasteful to the people.' [1]

The King's part in the issue of Manwaring's book.

In one respect Charles had gained his object by his acceptance of the petition. As soon as it was ascertained that it was to be enrolled like any other statute, the Subsidy Bill was pushed on, and on the 16th was sent up to the Lords.

Subsidies voted.

Of the Remonstrance, however, Charles had not heard the last. It is true that Selden's proposal for renewing the impeachment of Buckingham was quietly dropped, but it was certain that the name of Buckingham would appear in the Remonstrance. All that Charles

June 9. The Remonstrance proceeded with.

---

[1] *Lords' Journals,* iii. 856. Manwaring's absolute appeal to first principles would probably not be agreeable to Laud, who preferred leaving such matters to the schools, and basing his demands upon the authority of established institutions.

had gained was that the name would appear in a statement made to himself, not in an accusation addressed to the Lords.

The King, in fact, had never understood the reasons which had induced the House, under Eliot's guidance, to prepare this Remonstrance. He had fancied that it was a mere weapon of offence intended to wrest from him a better answer to the petition, and certain to be let drop as soon as its purpose had been accomplished. He could not perceive how deeply the disasters of the years in which he had ruled England had impressed themselves upon the mind of the nation, and so far as he took account of those disasters at all he argued that they had resulted from the niggardliness of the Commons, not from the incapacity of his own ministers.

On June 11[1] the Remonstrance was finally brought into shape. First came the paragraphs relating to religion, including the inevitable demand for the full execution of the penal laws against the Catholics and a special complaint against the commission which had been issued for compounding with recusants in the northern counties, of which Sir John Savile had been the leading member, and which had been warmly attacked by Wentworth. Still more bitter was the cry against Arminianism. The Calvinistic preachers had not, it is true, been actually persecuted. They had, however, been discountenanced. Books written by their opponents easily found a licenser. Books written by themselves were scanned more strictly. Laud and Neile were in high favour with the King, and those who adopted their opinions were on the sure road to promotion. Before long the high places of the Church would be occupied exclusively by men whose opinions were those of a minority of the clergy and of a still smaller minority of the laity.

June 11. The Remonstrance voted.

Attack on the Arminians.

It is easy to see that these complaints were not without

---

[1] The debate in committee is given by Nicholas, and the adoption of the Remonstrance is in the Journals of the same day. Rushworth is clearly wrong in saying the charge against Buckingham was voted on the 13th. We here take leave of Nicholas, who gives nothing later than the 11th.

foundation. It is easy to see, too, that the course of silencing the Arminians, suggested rather than advised by the Commons, would have been of little avail. But for the present the main stress of the petition was directed to another quarter. The whole history of the past three years was unrolled before the King, and, after a warm debate, the blame of all the mischief was laid upon the Duke. "The principal cause," so the House declared, "of which evils and dangers we conceive to be the excessive power of the Duke of Buckingham, and the abuse of that power;[1] and we humbly submit unto your Majesty's excellent wisdom, whether it be safe for yourself or your kingdoms that so great a power as rests in him by sea and land should be in the hands of any one subject whatsoever. And as it is not safe, so sure we are it cannot be for your service ; it being impossible for one man to manage so many and weighty affairs of the kingdom as he hath undertaken besides the ordinary duties of those offices which he holds ; some of which, well performed, would require the time and industry of the ablest men, both in counsel and action, that your whole kingdom will afford, especially in these times of common danger. And our humble desire is further, that your excellent Majesty will be pleased to take into your princely consideration, whether, in respect the said Duke hath so abused his power, it be safe for your Majesty and your kingdom to continue him either in his great offices, or in his place of nearness and counsel about your sacred person."[2]

Position taken by the Commons. The Commons had thus returned to the position which they had taken up at the close of the last session, as soon as it had become evident that the impeachment would not be allowed to take its course. They passed what in modern times would be called a vote of want of confidence in Buckingham. They brought no criminal charges. They asked for no punishment. But they demanded that the man under whose authority the things of which they complained

---

[1] These words were inserted after a proposal from Phelips that on'y the Duke's power, and not the abuse of his power, should be complained of. [2] *Rushworth*, i. 619.

had been done, should no longer be in a position to guide all England by his word.

On minor points Charles was willing to gratify the Commons. He allowed his ministers to give out that he was ready to discountenance the Arminians, which he might easily do, as Laud and his friends entirely disclaimed the title. He cancelled the patent by which certain Privy Councillors had been empowered, before the meeting of Parliament, to consider the best way of raising money by irregular means,[1] and he announced that Dulbier should not bring his German horse into England.[2] But he would not give up the Duke. To abandon Buckingham was to abandon himself.

Charles will not give up Buckingham.

Before the Remonstrance was presented to the King an event occurred which must have served to harden Charles in the belief that the movement against Buckingham was nothing more than a decent veil for an outbreak of popular anarchy which if it were not checked might sweep away his throne and all else that he held sacred. Dr. Lambe, an astrologer and quack doctor, a man too, if rumour is to be believed, of infamous life, had been consulted by Buckingham, and was popularly regarded as the instigator of his nefarious designs. Things had now come to such a pass that nothing was too bad to be believed of the Duke. Men declared without hesitation that Buckingham had caused the failure of Denbigh's expedition to Rochelle, out of fear lest, if the town were relieved, a peace might follow.[3] His luxury, his immoralities, his bragging incompetence, once the theme of Eliot's rhetoric, were now sung in ballads passed from hand to hand. In these verses it was told how he had poisoned Hamilton, Southampton, Oxford, Lennox, and even King James himself; how he had sat in a boat out of the way of danger, whilst his men were being slaughtered in the Isle of Rhé; how he was indifferent to the

---

[1] *Parl. Hist.* ii. 417; *Lords' Journals,* iii. 862. See p. 224.
[2] *Rushworth,* i. 623.
[3] Contarini to the Doge, June $\frac{5}{15}$, *Ven. Transcripts, R. O.*

ravages of the Dunkirkers and to the ruin of the country,[1] whilst he employed Dr. Lambe to corrupt by his love-charms the chastest women in England. Even at Cambridge the judicious Meade found himself treated with contempt for venturing to suggest that the Duke's faults arose from incapacity rather than from any settled purpose to betray the kingdom.[2]

June 13. Murder of Dr. Lambe. Whilst such thoughts were abroad, Dr. Lambe stepped forth one evening from the Fortune Theatre. A crowd of London apprentices, ever ready for amusement or violence, gathered round him. hooting at him as the Duke's devil. Fearing the worst, he paid some sailors to guard him to a tavern in Moorgate Street, where he supped. When he came out he found some of the lads still standing round the door, and imprudently threatened them, telling them 'he would make them dance naked.' As he walked they followed his steps, the crowd growing denser every minute. In the Old Jewry he turned upon them with his sailors, and drove them off. The provocation thus given was too much for the cruel instinct of the mob. A rush was made at him, and he was driven for refuge into the Windmill Tavern. Stones began to fly, and the howling crowd demanded its victim. In vain the landlord disguised him before he sent him out. There was another scamper through the streets, another attempt to find refuge. The master of the second house satisfied his conscience by dismissing him with four constables to guard him. Such aid was of little avail. The helpless protectors were dashed aside. The object of popular hatred was thrown bleeding on the ground. Blows from sticks and stones and pieces of board snatched up for the occasion fell like rain upon his quivering flesh. After he could no longer speak to plead for mercy, one of his eyes was beaten out of its socket. No man would open his doors to receive the all but lifeless body of the detested necromancer. He was at last carried to the Compter prison, where he died on the following morning.

[1] Fairholt's Poems and Songs relating to the Duke of Buckingham, *Percy Society.*
[2] Meade to Stuteville, July 12, *Court and Times,* i. 373.

Charles, when he heard the news, was greatly affected. The murderers had been heard to say that if the Duke had been there they would have handled him worse. They would have minced his flesh, and have had everyone a bit of him. He summoned before him the Lord Mayor and Aldermen, bidding them to discover the offenders,[1] and he subsequently imposed a heavy fine upon the City for their failure to detect the guilty persons.

June 16. The King's displeasure.

The King's heart was hardened against the assailants of the Duke. To sift the statements of the Remonstrance, or to promise an inquiry into the cause of the late disasters, would be beneath his dignity. He determined to meet the charges of the Commons as a mere personal attack upon innocence.

The 17th was the day fixed by Charles for the reception of the Remonstrance. The day before, he sent to the Star Chamber an order that all documents connected with the sham prosecution of Buckingham which had followed the last dissolution, should be removed from the file; 'that no memory thereof remain of the record against him which may tend to his disgrace.'[2]

Orders the proceedings in the Star Chamber against the Duke to be taken from the file.

When the reading of the Remonstrance was ended, Charles answered curtly. He did not expect, he said, such a remonstrance from them after he had so graciously granted them their Petition of Right. They complained of grievances in Church and State, 'wherein he perceived they understood not what belonged to either so well as he had thought they had done. As for their grievances, he would consider of them as they should deserve.' When he had finished, Buckingham threw himself on his knees, asking permission to answer for himself. Charles would not allow him to do so, giving him his hand to kiss in the presence of his accusers.[3]

June 17. Answers the Remonstrance.

If it had not been too late for anything to have availed

---

[1] Meade to Stuteville, June 21, June 29, *Court and Times*, i. 364, 367. Diary, *S. P. Dom.* cii. 57. *Rushworth*, i. 618.

[2] *Rushworth*, i. 626.

[3] Meade to Stuteville, June 21, *Court and Times*, i. 364.

Buckingham, it might be thought that he had judged better for himself than his master had done. His way was to meet charges boldly and defiantly. Charles's way was to relapse into silence, to fall back upon his insulted dignity, and to demand the submission to his mere word which argument could alone have secured for him. His own notions were to him so absolutely true that they needed no explanation.

Contrast between Buckingham and Charles.

So far as Buckingham was able, he sought to meet the charges against him. It had been rumoured in the House of Commons that the Duke had said, "Tush! it makes no matter what the Commons or Parliament doth; for without my leave and authority they shall not be able to touch the hair of a dog." In vain Buckingham protested that the slander was absolutely untrue.[1] The accusation was repeated in verses drawn up to suit the popular taste, in which the Duke was made to declare his entire independence of the popular feeling. "Meddle," he is made to say to his opponents—

Buckingham denies a slanderous story.

> "Meddle with common matters, common wrongs,
> To the House of Commons common things belongs.
> They are *extra sphæram* that you treat of now,
> And ruin to yourselves will bring, I vow,
> Except you do desist, and learn to bear
> What wisdom ought to teach you, or your fear.
> Leave him the oar that best knows how to row,
> And State to him that best the State doth know.
>
> . . . .
>
> Though Lambe be dead, I'll stand, and you shall see,
> I'll smile at them that can but bark at me."[2]

Though in reality these words applied far more correctly to the King than to Buckingham, so long as Buckingham was in favour no man would believe how great a part Charles had in his own calamities. "Who rules the kingdom?" were the words of a pasquinade found nailed to a post in Coleman

---

[1] *Lords' Journals*, iii. 897.
[2] Poems on Buckingham, *Percy Society*, 30.

Street. "The King. Who rules the King? The Duke. Who rules the Duke? The devil. Let the Duke look to it."[1]

Under the influence of the feeling provoked by the rejection of the Remonstrance the Commons went into committee on the Bill for the grant of tonnage and poundage which had been brought in at the beginning of the session, but had been postponed on account of the pressure of other business. With the exception of the merest fragment, no record of the debates in this committee has reached us; but we learn from a contemporary letter[2] that the Commons, whilst making a liberal grant, equal to the whole of the customs and imposts put together, wished to alter the incidence of some of the rates, partly because they considered them too heavy on certain articles, partly for the preservation of their own right to make the grant.

June 14. Tonnage and poundage.

As soon as it appeared that the work to which the Commons had set themselves would take two or three months, they proposed to pass a temporary Bill to save the rights which they claimed, leaving all further discussion till the next session. When the King refused to assent to this proposal, they expressed a wish that they might have an adjournment instead of a prorogation. In this way the Act, when finally passed at their next meeting, would take effect from the beginning of the session in the past winter, and the illegality, as they held it, of the actual levy would be covered by it.

Dissatisfaction of the King.

It may be that the Commons did not at the time mean more than they said, and had no fixed intention of using their claim to be the sole originators of the right to levy customs' duties in order to compel the King to attend to their political grievances. It may very well have seemed to Charles that the case was otherwise; and the more persistent they were in asserting their right, the more determined he was not to give way on a point where concession would make it impossible for him to govern the kingdom except in accordance with their views. If the Commons saw fit at their next meeting to vote him less than the old tonnage and poundage and the new im-

---

[1] Meade to Stuteville, June 29, *Court and Times,* i. 367.
[2] Nethersole to Elizabeth, June 30, *S. P. Dom.* cviii. 52.

positions put together, he would be landed in a perpetual deficit, even if a treaty of peace could be signed at once with France and Spain. For Charles a perpetual deficit meant the expulsion of Buckingham from his counsels and the domination of Puritanism in the Church; in other words, it meant his own surrender of that Royal authority which had been handed down to him from his predecessors—a surrender far more complete than he had contemplated in giving his assent to the Petition of Right.

Accordingly, on the 23rd Charles sent a message once more declaring that he had fixed a date for the prorogation. The Houses might sit till the 26th, but they should sit no longer.

June 23. The prorogation determined on.

The Commons at once proceeded to draw up another Remonstrance. They would not have complained, they asserted, if an adjournment and not a prorogation had been offered. In that case the matter would have been taken up when they met again, and the Act when passed would have given a retrospective sanction to all duties levied under it since the commencement of the session. The Commons then proceeded to declare that no imposition ought to be laid upon the goods of merchants, exported or imported, without common consent by Act of Parliament; which, they said to the King, 'is the right and inheritance of your subjects, founded not only upon the most ancient and original constitutions of this kingdom, but often confirmed and declared in divers statute laws.' They had hoped that a Bill might have been passed to satisfy the King in the present session. "But not being now able," they concluded by saying, "to accomplish this their desire, there is no course left unto them, without manifest breach of their duty both to your Majesty and their country, save only to make this humble declaration: That the receiving of tonnage and poundage and other impositions not granted by Parliament, is a breach of the fundamental liberties of this kingdom, and contrary to your Majesty's Royal answer to their late Petition of Right; and therefore they do most humbly beseech your Majesty to forbear any further receiving the same; and not to take it in ill part from those of

June 25. Remonstrance on tonnage and poundage.

your Majesty's loving subjects who shall refuse to make payment of any such charges without warrant of law demanded. And as, by this forbearance, your most excellent Majesty shall manifest unto the world your Royal justice in the observation of your laws, so they doubt not but hereafter, at the time appointed for their coming together again, they shall have occasion to express their great desire to advance your Majesty's honour and profit." [1]

Rather than listen to such words as these, Charles determined to hasten the end of the session by a few hours. Hurriedly, and without taking time to put on the usual robes, he entered the House of Lords early the next morning, almost as soon as the Peers had met.

"My Lords and Gentlemen," he said, when the Commons had been summoned, "it may seem strange that I come so suddenly to end this session; wherefore, before I give my assent to the Bills, I will tell you the cause; though I must avow that I owe an account of my actions but to God alone. It is known to everyone that a while ago the House of Commons gave me a Remonstrance, how acceptable every man may judge; and for the merit of it I will not call that in question, for I am sure no wise man can justify it.

June 26. The King's speech.

"Now, since I am certainly informed that a second Remonstrance is preparing for me, to take away my chief profit of tonnage and poundage—one of the chief maintenances of the Crown—by alleging that I have given away my right thereof by my answer to your petition: this is so prejudicial unto me that I am forced to end this session some few hours before I meant it, being willing not to receive any more Remonstrances to which I must give a harsh answer.

"And since I see that even the House of Commons begins already to make false constructions of what I granted in your petition, lest it might be worse interpreted in the country I will now make a declaration concerning the true meaning thereof:—

"The profession of both Houses, in time of hammering

---

[1] *Parl. Hist.* ii. 431.

this petition, was no ways to entrench upon my prerogative, saying they had neither intention nor power to hurt it: therefore it must needs be conceived I granted no new, but only confirmed the ancient liberties of my subjects; yet, to show the clearness of my intentions, that I neither repent nor mean to recede from anything I have promised you, I do here declare that those things which have been done whereby men had some cause to suspect the liberty of the subjects to be trenched upon —which indeed was the first and true ground of the petition— shall not hereafter be drawn into example for your prejudice: and in time to come, on the word of a King, you shall not have the like cause to complain.

"But as for tonnage and poundage, it is a thing I cannot want, and was never intended by you to ask—never meant, I am sure, by me to grant.

"To conclude, I command you all that are here to take notice of what I have spoken at this time to be the true intent and meaning of what I granted you in your petition, but especially you, my Lords the Judges—for to you only, under me, belongs the interpretation of laws; for none of the House of Commons, joint or separate—what new doctrine soever may be raised—have any power either to make or declare a law without my consent."[1]

After the Royal assent had been given to a few Bills the session was formally brought to an end by prorogation to October 20. It was the first time in his reign that Charles had ended a session otherwise than by a dissolution. Yet the crisis was more serious, the breach more complete and hopeless, than ever before. In 1625 the King had been asked by the Commons to take counsel with persons upon whom dependence could be placed. In 1626 he had been asked to dismiss one unpopular minister from his service. In 1628 his whole policy was to be changed at home and abroad, his whole personal feeling was to be sacrificed by the condemnation of Laud and Neile as well as of the great Duke himself. Statesmen and divines who were

Parliament prorogued.
Breach between the King and the Commons.

[1] *Lords' Journals*, iii. 879. The last clause is corrected from *Parl. Hist.* ii. 434.

pleasing to the Commons were to be promoted: statesmen and divines who were displeasing to them were to be discouraged and silenced. The will of the Lower House was to be the rule by which all that was taught and all that was done in England was from henceforward to be gauged; and this claim to sovereignty—for it was nothing less—was backed by the ominous claim to relieve individual persons from the duty of paying to the Crown dues which, though they had been declared illegal by a resolution of the House of Commons, had been declared to be legal by the judges. It would have taxed the Commons to the utmost, if the opportunity had been afforded them, to answer the King within the lines of existing constitutional practice. That the judges, and not the King, were to decide questions affecting the liberty of the subject had been the point pressed most firmly by the Commons in the debates on the Petition of Right. Yet now they proceeded to ignore entirely the fact that the unreversed decision of the judges in the case of impositions was clearly on the King's side. If the Commons were to suspend the payment of these duties by their own resolution in the face of a judicial decision, why might they not suspend the operation of any law whatever against which they entertained objections? And, unless new checks were provided, what would government by the resolutions of a single House lead to but the tyranny which enabled Cromwell to turn the key on the expelled Long Parliament, and which in the following century roused the thinking part of the nation to take up the defence of a man so unworthy as Wilkes?

Charles formally in the right.

Nor was it only in his resolution to leave the interpretation of the laws to the judges that Charles took ground which was at least formally defensible. That the words of the Petition of Right, praying that 'no man hereafter be compelled to make or yield any gift, loan, benevolence, tax, or such like charge, without common consent by Act of Parliament,' ought to have covered the case of customs' duties is a proposition from which few would now be inclined to dissent. Yet amongst the words used, only 'tax' was sufficiently general to be supposed for a moment to

Was tonnage and poundage included in the Petition of Right?

cover the case of duties upon imports and exports, and even that word, though often used loosely to apply to payments of every kind, had the specific meaning of direct payments, and in this sense would not be at all applicable to the dues which were levied at the ports.[1] When, therefore, Charles said that in granting the petition he had never intended to yield on this point, he undoubtedly said nothing less than the truth. He might have said even more than he did. It is as certain as anything can well be that, either because they did not wish to enhance the difficulty of obtaining a satisfactory answer from the King, or because they expected to gain their object in another way, the Commons never had any intention to include the question of tonnage and poundage in the Petition of Right. The Tonnage and Poundage Bill had been brought in early in the session. From time to time it had been mentioned, but, except a few words from Phelips, nothing had been said to give to it any sort of prominence. What would have been easier than, by the addition of one or two expressions to the petition, to include the levy of these duties amongst the grievances of the House? Yet nothing of the kind was done, though the words of the petition, as was known to every lawyer, if not to every member of the House, were such as would not be acknowledged by the King to cover the case of tonnage and poundage. What was still more important was that the Petition of Right, like every other statute, was subject to the interpretation of the judges, and that it was well known that the judges were in the habit of deciding every doubtful point in favour of the Crown. It was therefore with full knowledge that the ambiguous word 'tax' would not carry with it the consequences which they now wished to derive from it, that the framers of the petition, themselves being lawyers of the highest eminence, had abstained from strengthening their work with other words which would have put an end to all doubt. For these reasons, the insertion of the appeal to the Petition of Right in the final Remonstrance can only be regarded as a daring attempt to take up new ground

[1] The notes of Montague's speech in the *Parl. Debates in* 1610 give: "Tax or tallage only by Parliament. Custom or imposition proceed from a regal power, and matter of inheritance in the King."

which would place the right of the House above that decision given in the last reign by the Court of Exchequer, which they had hitherto contested in vain.[1]

<small>The case for the Commons.</small>

It by no means follows, however, that the Commons, if formally in the wrong, may not have been materially in the right. Legal decisions cannot bind a nation for ever, and the power of saying the last word, with all the terrible responsibilities which weigh upon those who pronounce it, must be with those by whom the nation is most fully represented. The Commons had at least shown that they had confidence in the English people. In every petition which had come before them relating to the exercise of the franchise, they had always decided in favour of the most extended right of voting which it was in their power to acknowledge. Great as was the influence of wealthy landowners in returning members to the House, those members had no wish to be anything else than the representatives of the nation.[2] With the nation their conservatism placed them at a great advantage as the defenders of what to that generation was the old religion and the old law. In his resistance to Calvinistic dogmatism, in his desire to make the forces of the nation more easily available for what he conceived to be national objects, Charles was the advocate of change and innovation. His weakness lay in his utter ignorance of men, in his incapacity to subordinate that which was only desirable to that which was possible, and above all, in his habitual disregard of that primary axiom of government, that men may be led though they cannot be driven. He looked upon the whole world through a distorting lens. If

---

[1] The wording of this clause in the petition is 'that no man hereafter be compelled to make or yield any gift, loan, benevolence, tax, or such like charge without common consent by Act of Parliament.' In the Tonnage and Poundage Act of the Long Parliament we hear 'that no subsidy, custom, impost, or any charge whatsoever ought to be laid or imposed upon any merchandise exported or imported.' In the debates in 1610 the question was almost entirely debated, especially on the side of the Crown, as if customs' duties were to be treated apart from other taxation.

[2] For the results of this work in committee I must refer to Mr. Forster, *Sir J. Eliot*, ii. 119.

Buckingham was far from being the scoundrel which popular opinion imagined him to be, his failures could not be ascribed, as Charles thought fit to ascribe them, to mere accident. If Calvinistic orthodoxy must, sooner or later, be struck down in England, it was not from Laudian uniformity that the blow could come. In Charles blindness, narrow-mindedness, and obstinacy, combined with an exaggerated sense of the errors of his opponents, were laying the sure foundations of future ruin. Then would come the turn of the Commons, the day when they too would learn that sovereignty is only permanently entrusted to those who can represent the nation with wisdom as well as with sympathy. The secret of the future was with those who could guide England into the sure haven of religious liberty. It was not enough to say that the Commons represented England in 1628 as well as Elizabeth represented England in 1588. Elizabeth at least took care that all manner of complaints should reach her ears, and that no man should be excluded from her Privy Council on account of his opinions. If the preponderance in the constitution was to pass from the King to the House of Commons, many a compensating change would be needed before the great alteration could be safely effected. Above all, opinion must be set free to an extent of which Pym and Coke never dreamed, if it were only that the nation might itself receive that enlightenment which had in old times been thought necessary for the sovereign.

Such considerations, however, were still in the future. Though men were beginning to feel, and sometimes to act, as if some constitutional change was necessary, they had not yet learned to give verbal expression to their thoughts. If Charles was still sovereign of England in the eyes of others, more especially was he sovereign in his own eyes. Unhappily he did not see in past events a reason for acting so as to regain the hearts of his people. Having the opportunity of flinging defiance in the face of the Commons, he chose to place in high positions in the Church the men whom he knew to be most unpopular. Not long ago Neile had been transferred from Durham to Winchester; and now Montaigne, the old, infirm, luxurious Bishop of London, who was

<small>Ecclesiastical appointments.</small>

at the moment best known as the licenser of Manwaring's sermons, was promoted first to Durham, and then to the Archbishopric of York :[1] whilst the See of London, with all its authority over a more than ordinarily Calvinistic clergy and people, was handed over to Laud.[2] Howson, one of Laud's chief supporters amongst the bishops, was raised to the important See of Durham;[3] Buckeridge, another of his supporters, having been recently translated to Ely.[4] Yet the promotion which gave the greatest offence was undoubtedly that of Richard Montague to the bishopric of Chichester.[5] Whatever Montague's merits may have been, a wise king would not have chosen such a moment to promote a man so unpopular. The very circumstance which should have told most against him was doubtless that which most recommended him to Charles's favour. The Puritans must be made to understand that they had no standing ground in the English Church; and how could that be brought more clearly before their eyes than by the promotion of a man who openly declared them to be a usurping faction?

Scarcely less unwise was Charles's course with Manwaring. It can hardly be wondered that he desired to relieve the unlucky divine from the penalties which had befallen him for advocating a doctrine which in the King's eyes had only been pushed too far. Charles was indeed careful to mark his dissent from the extreme form which that doctrine had taken. In the pardon which he caused to be drawn up for Manwaring, he stated that the ground on which it was based was his recantation of the most objectionable part of his opinions.[6] But Charles did not stop here. He conferred upon Manwaring the rectory of Stanford Rivers, just vacated by Montague,[7] again confirming the assertion of the Commons, that promotion in the Church was becoming the exclusive property of that section whose opinions were regarded with abhorrence by the majority of the clergy and of the religious laity.

[1] Date of *congé d'élire*, June 5.   [2] July 4.
[3] July 4.   [4] April 8.   [5] *Congé d'élire*, July 8.
[6] The King to Heath, July 6, *S. P. Dom.* cix. 42.
[7] Docquet, July 18.

These promotions in the Church had been made in the first swing of indignation against the Puritans, to whom Charles and Buckingham [1] traced all their calamities. Of the two men, Buckingham, though his impetuousness and self-confidence were perpetually leading him astray, was more accessible than Charles to statesmanlike considerations. When Charles was inclined to treat the unpopularity of his government as a matter of no moment, and to regard the objections raised against his proceedings with the cool contempt of silence, Buckingham was always ready to give a reason for his actions, with the firm assurance that he needed only a fair hearing to set him right with those who disapproved of his conduct. To him, too, the war in which he had engaged was now a matter rather of necessity than of enthusiasm, and he had for some time been seeking to limit its operations. The correspondence Gerbier continued to carry on with Rubens gave some reason to believe that Spain would still be induced, through jealousy of France, to make peace with England; and, whatever Buckingham may have thought of the matter, the sanguine mind of Charles was not without some hopes of obtaining in this way the restitution of the Palatinate and an acknowledgment of the independence of the Dutch republic.[2] Circumstances, too, had occurred in Italy which made it not impossible that Spain might be brought to make unusual concessions. In December the Duke of Mantua had died, leaving as the undoubted heir to his possessions a distant kinsman, the Duke of Nevers, whose family had long been settled in France. Against this extension of French influence in Italy the Emperor interfered, claiming the right, as King of Italy, to dispose of vacant fiefs, a right which he was inclined to exercise, as far as Mantua was concerned, in favour of another candidate who would have been entirely

---

[1] Laud, in his *History of the Troubles* (*Works*, iv. 273), says that Montague's appointment was procured by Buckingham.

[2] The papers translated in Mr. Sainsbury's *Rubens* should be compared with Contarini's despatches, after making allowance for the anti-Spanish feeling of the Venetian, and his consequent tendency to suspect all sorts of treachery in Charles and Buckingham.

under the influence of Spain. At the same time the Duke of Savoy, who had lately been swinging round in his political alliances, proposed to divide with Spain the territory of Montferrat, which had formed part of the dominions of the deceased Duke.

Charles was still anxious to push on the war in all directions. Though it was a point of honour with him to succour Rochelle at all risks, he would gladly have saved the King of Denmark and the German Protestants as well, if he had only known how to do it. Carlisle was therefore sent in April on a special mission to Savoy. He was to visit the Duke of Lorraine on his way, in order to stir him up against France; and when he reached Turin he was to take advantage of the disturbances in Italy to embitter the rising quarrel between France and Spain, and thus to leave room for the freer action of England at Rochelle and in the North of Germany.[1]

April. Carlisle's embassy.

Whatever might come of these various negotiations, the idea of a forced retirement from Continental affairs was not entertained either in the Court or the Council of Charles. As soon as the acceptance of the Petition of Right had given assurance that the subsidies would be really voted, the Privy Council began to discuss the best mode of sending a force to assist the King of Denmark to maintain himself in Glückstadt and Krempe, which were still holding out. Morgan's men who had surrendered at Stade were to be employed for the purpose; and Dulbier's horse, which could not now be landed in England, were to be kept in Germany or the Netherlands, in order that they might be used in defence of the North German Protestants as soon as Rochelle had been either captured or relieved.[2] The belief, in fact, was rapidly gaining ground that the war with France

June. Warlike projects.

---

[1] Carlisle's instructions, March 10, *Harl. MSS.* 1584, fol. 173.

[2] Conway to Carleton, June 7, 10, *S. P. Holland.* Morgan's men were to be reduced to one regiment of 1,500 men, and were offered temporarily to the Dutch, to be paid by England and lodged and fed by the States-General. D. Carleton to the States-General, July $\frac{6}{16}$, *Add. MSS* 17,677, M. fol. 256.

would not be of long continuance. It was hardly thought possible that the great expedition now preparing could fail to relieve Rochelle ; and if Rochelle were once relieved, whether peace were formally concluded with France or not, there would be no further need for any great exertions in that quarter. If, on the other hand, the attempt ended in failure, Rochelle must of necessity submit, and the same result would ensue. In either case, Charles would be at liberty to turn his attention to Germany.

July. Prospects of peace with France

The only question therefore was whether the opening of negotiations with Spain should be encouraged. Buckingham had now veered round to his earlier policy of 1622, and was hoping everything from the friendliness of Spain. " Let us make peace with Spain, and settle the affairs of the Palatinate," he said to the Savoyard ambassador, the Abbot of Scaglia, "and then the Dutch will do as we please." At all events, he assured the Abbot, there should be no peace with France till an answer had been received to the offer about to be addressed to Spain.[1] It was finally arranged that Endymion Porter, once the messenger who had made arrangements for Charles's journey to Madrid, should make his way to Spain in order to come to an understanding with Olivares, and to assure him that, if it were thought necessary, Buckingham would come in person to carry on the negotiation for peace.[2] The hope entertained in England seems to have been that the Spaniards would throw their whole strength into Italy, thus leaving Germany free.

and with Spain.

Buckingham was far more anxious than Charles for the success of these negotiations. Yet not long after the prorogation, Charles sent a message to the Prince of Orange, informing him that, 'being unable to bear the burden of war against two such great kings,' he had resolved to listen to the Spanish overtures for a treaty in which the restoration of the Palatinate and the pacification of the Nether-

Charles informs the Prince of Orange.

---

[1] Statement enclosed in a letter from the Infanta Isabella to Philip IV., June, $\frac{\text{Aug. 27}}{\text{Sept. 6}}$, *Brussels MSS.*

[2] The Infanta Isabella to Philip IV., Oct. $\frac{14}{24}$, *Brussels MSS.*

lands would be expressly included.¹ The proposal was received with astonishment and indignation at the Hague, where the circumstance that Carlisle, in passing through Brussels, had an audience of the Infanta was considered as enough to indicate the intention of Charles to conclude a separate peace. The Dutch ambassadors in England were accordingly instructed to remonstrate all the more warmly against any such purpose, because it was believed by the States-General that even a peace in which they were themselves included would be most deleterious to their interests, as leaving the Spaniards free to act in aid of the Emperor in Germany. Naturally enough, too, the Dutch found a warm advocate in the Venetian ambassador, to whom Charles's project of putting an end to the troubles of the North by fanning the flames of war in Italy appeared to be an act of the blackest ingratitude. Neither he nor the Dutch ambassadors were inclined to believe Charles's assurances that nothing should be done without the knowledge of his allies. Yet there is no reason to doubt Charles's sincerity. As he had scarcely as yet opened his eyes to the absolute necessity of putting an end to the war on account of the poverty of his exchequer, he was likely enough to flatter himself that it was in his power to continue fighting on his own terms, and to reject any offers from Spain which might be disagreeable to his sense of right.²

It is impossible to disconnect these diplomatic efforts from the personal changes which at the same time took place in the Government. The anxiety for the future which led Buckingham to attempt to impose a limit upon his military operations abroad, was also shown in his desire to meet Parliament, when it re-assembled, in something like a conciliatory spirit. Although in the King's present temper it would be impossible to expect that Charles would consent to give much satisfaction to the Puritans, it might be

Changes in the Government.

¹ Extract from a despatch of the Prince of Orange in Contarini's despatch of July $\frac{18}{28}$.

² The Dutch Ambassadors to the States-General, $\frac{\text{July } 22}{\text{Aug. } 1}$, *Add. MSS.* 17,677, M. fol. 266; Contarini to the Doge, July $\frac{18, \text{July } 28}{28, \text{Aug. } 7}$, *Ven. Transcripts, R.O.*

possible, if once success at Rochelle should have limited the extent of the war, to restore order to the finances, and also to gain the good-will of men whose names would seem to be a guarantee for the strict execution of the Petition of Right, and who would yet be the last to acquiesce in the claim of the House of Commons to direct the external policy of the kingdom.

Such men were to be found in the leaders of the majority of the House of Lords. Bristol and Arundel were therefore restored to favour, and Weston, who was practically one in policy with them, became Lord Treasurer.

<small>Weston, Lord Treasurer.</small>

Marlborough, old and thoroughly inefficient, found a place as President of the Council, and Manchester became Privy Seal, Worcester having died some months before. It was certain that the influence of these men would be exerted in favour of economy and peace, and that they would give their countenance to an understanding with the House of Commons, if they could attain that object without diminishing that which they regarded as the legitimate authority of the King. A paragraph in a letter written by Weston to the Duke, doubtless expressed the feelings of the others as well. "I long to see you at home again with honour, in a quiet and settled Court, studying his Majesty's affairs, which require two contrary things to cure them—rest and vigilancy."[1]

The letter-writers of the day are full of news of these changes at Court, and of others which have less interest in our eyes. On one promotion, which has never ceased to engage the attention of Englishmen, they are entirely silent. Not one of them notices the fact that on July 22 Sir Thomas Wentworth became Lord Wentworth, and was, on Weston's introduction, received into favour by Charles.

<small>July 22. Wentworth created a Peer.</small>

From that time to this no word has been found too hard for the great apostate, the unworthy deserter of the principles of his youth. Those who have studied the true records of the session which had just come to an end are aware that he was neither an apostate nor a deserter. The

<small>Was he an apostate?</small>

[1] Weston to Buckingham, Aug. 18, *S. P. Dom.* cxiii. 14.

abuses struck at by the Petition of Right he regarded as prejudicial to government as well as injurious to the subject. When they had been swept away he was free to take his own course; and that course must have been greatly determined by the proceedings of the Commons in the last days of the session. With Puritanism he had no sympathy whatever. He had no confidence in the House of Commons as an instrument of government, and must have regarded its claim to strip the Crown of tonnage and poundage, and its declaration that subjects were released from the obligation of paying those dues, as a proclamation inviting to anarchy. If, however, he thought the Lower House unfit to govern England, he was equally of opinion that Buckingham was unfit to govern England. We may well believe, therefore, that he had no anxiety to accept a share in the responsibilities of a Privy Councillor's place at a time when the duties of a Privy Councillor were reduced to the uncongenial task of echoing the words of the all-powerful minister. Many months were yet to pass before Wentworth would be asked to take his seat at the Council board.[1] The position which he was now called upon to occupy exactly suited his present mood. His peerage removed him from the House of Commons, where he had been isolated ever since the failure of his effort to mediate between the Crown and the nation. In the House of Lords he would find, in the lately formed majority, a body of men with whom he could cordially co-operate. Bristol and Arundel were as opposed as he was to the extravagances by which the policy of the Crown had lately been disfigured, whilst they were of one mind with himself in resenting any attempt of the House of Commons to make itself master of the State.

Although it is likely enough that Wentworth had no immediate wish to gain that admittance to the Council which was

[1] That he became a Privy Councillor at this time is a mistake. Sir G. Radcliffe (*Strafford Letters*, ii. App. 430) having put together the two years 1628 and 1629, seems to say that he became a Privy Councillor in Michaelmas term, 1628. The true date, as we learn from the *Council Register*, is Nov. 10, 1629, a fact of considerable importance in an estimate of Wentworth's character.

denied him by Charles, it is also likely that he aspired, at a not distant future, to a higher post than any which was for the present open to him. No man knew better than he that the war must soon come to an end for want of supplies, and that the policy of abstention from interference with the Continent which he had advocated from the beginning would be forced upon Charles. When peace was restored the hour of Wentworth would come. For the present he was content with the promise that he should before long succeed the Earl of Sunderland as President of the Council of the North. At York he would be far removed from all responsibility for the general government. At York, too, he would be able to carry out those principles which he had professed in the House of Commons. One of the grave complaints made by the Lower House at the close of the session had been against the leniency shown by Sunderland to the recusants, and Wentworth's voice had been raised as loudly as Pym's against this leniency. In times of difficulty Charles was always ready to throw the recusants over, and there was now an understanding between him and Wentworth that, in this matter at least, the will of the House of Commons should prevail.

He expected Presidentship of the North.

To Wentworth himself this temporary abstraction from all public consideration of national affairs was doubtless extremely grateful. We are tempted to ask whether it was equally beneficial to the nation. In the last session he alone amongst the leaders of the House had shown anything like powers of constructive statesmanship. Coke and Eliot, Pym and Phelips, had been content with the negation of misgovernment. Their wish was simply that the law and religion of England should remain as it was. Wentworth had not shown himself content with this. An active, wise, and reforming Government was the ideal after which he strove from first to last.

Wentworth as a Parliamentary leader.

In that session, too, Wentworth had developed powers for which those whose knowledge of him is acquired only from the acts of his later life must have some difficulty in giving him credit. The impetuous haughtiness of his disposition had been curbed before that great assembly which he was learning to lead. There he could be silent and patient, could watch his opportunity till the time arrived when he could express his special thought in harmony with the thoughts of those around him. Whatever mistakes may have been committed in judging Wentworth's career, those are not wrong who hold that his leadership of the Commons in the early part of the session of 1628 was the brightest, noblest period of his life.

From all this Wentworth was now cut off, not by his peerage or by the allurements of power, but by the impossibility of finding a common ground upon which the King and the House of Commons could work together. If Charles had abandoned him, as he was to abandon him again, he was still drawn to Charles by every tendency of his nature. He could persuade himself, as the Commons had persuaded themselves in 1625, that Charles had erred from want of counsel, and he could hope to breathe into his soul a higher, loftier spirit. Even whilst he had played the foremost part amongst the Commons, he had never been one with them in heart. He could make use of their power over the grant of subsidies to put an end to the folly and violence of which he complained; but he could not lift up the standard of Puritanism as Pym or Eliot could lift it up. He could not believe in the capacity for government of a House composed for the most part, as it was of necessity, of men of ordinary abilities. He could not see that in the face of a Government which was hurrying a nation against its will into a path from which it recoiled, the mere conservatism of the Lower House, the simple determination to stand in the old paths and to cling to the old familiar religious and political traditions, might be, for the moment, the highest political virtue.

Causes which estranged him from the House of Commons.

Wentworth's acceptance of a peerage marked to a great extent the choice which he had made; but more than thirteen months—momentous months for England—were to elapse before he took his place in the Privy Council and finally threw in his lot with Charles. As yet Buckingham stood in the way. A Council controlled by a minister so incapable and so headstrong was no place for Wentworth.

His time not yet come.

CHAPTER LXV.

THE ASSASSINATION OF THE DUKE OF BUCKINGHAM.

WOULD the policy foreshadowed in the names of Bristol and Weston be sufficient to save the King from the difficulties which would stare him in the face when Parliament met again? Even if an attempt were made to effect some compromise about tonnage and poundage, the religious difficulty remained unsolved. There was one man at least in the party which had played so stirring a part in the House of Lords who had no confidence in the system of giving promotion to a small minority amongst the clergy. Williams had sense enough to
<small>Views of Williams.</small> see that the favour shown to Manwaring and Montague was no road to a settled government. For the high dogmatic ways of Calvinism he had little taste; but he could not ignore the fact that Calvinism was a great power in England, and he had too much of the instinct of a statesman to treat with contempt the religion of the large majority of the English people.

Already, before the session was at an end, overtures had been made to Williams by Buckingham's mother. The Countess
<small>May. Overtures of the Countess of Buckingham.</small> had in old days been on familiar terms with him, and she may well have looked at that sagacious counsellor as the most likely man to save her son from the ruin which she saw approaching. Before the end of May, at a time when the Petition of Right, if not accepted by the King, had been definitively accepted by the House of Lords, she had a long interview with him, whether at her son's instigation

or not we cannot say.¹ The result was that Williams, being allowed to kiss the Duke's hand, made use of the opportunity to urge the wisdom of a policy of indulgence towards the Puritans.

Reconciliation between Buckingham and Williams.

Unless there is some error in the report which has reached us, Williams had already recommended that Eliot rather than Wentworth should be selected to receive tokens of the Royal favour. Though it may be doubted whether Eliot, as matters stood, would have responded to the call, the suggestion, if it was really made, showed a clear insight into the political situation. The fact that English Calvinism existed was one which no wise Government could pass by, and though Williams would not have been likely to advise Charles to silence Laud and Montague to please the House of Commons, he would have advised that Laud and Montague should not be permitted to impose their opinions on the rest of the clergy. Williams would, however, have changed his nature if some intrigue had not been mingled with the wise counsel which he gave. He suggested that his reconciliation with Buckingham should be veiled in profound secrecy, in order that when he supported a compromise on the dispute about tonnage and poundage in the next session, he might speak with greater authority as an independent member of the Upper House.²

Whatever may be the truth about the proposal made relating to Eliot, there can be no doubt that Williams's counsel was worthy of acceptance. As far as it is possible to argue from cause to consequence, if Williams had been trusted by Charles instead of Laud, there would have been no civil war and no dethronement in the future.

¹ The fact of the interview between them is all that is known. Woodward to Windebank, May 28, *S. P. Dom.* cv. 55.

² *Hacket*, ii. 80, 83. Mr. Hallam, who has been followed by Mr. Disraeli and Mr. Forster, fancied that this promise of support referred to Williams's behaviour in the debates on the Petition of Right; whereas anyone who will read Hacket's words with the least attention will see that it refers to the 'next session.' Williams's conduct is, perhaps, open to censure, but it does not deserve all the blame which has been bestowed upon it. He was perfectly straightforward about the petition.

It is needless to pursue the speculation further. How could
Eliot trust the overtures of a King who had just given
a bishopric to Montague and a rich living to Manwaring? Nor could Williams be sure even of Buckingham. If Williams could speak of wise toleration, he could
not speak otherwise than as an advocate of peace, and peace
would be the ruin of the Duke. During the whole of the last
five years Buckingham had been planning some effective blow
against Spain or France, some brilliant achievement which was to
fix upon himself the admiring gaze of a whole continent. How
could he settle down to the ordinary drudgery of attending to
the administration of the law, of balancing arguments for or
against religious liberty, of improving the finances, and banishing
corruption from the machinery of government? On all these
questions Williams and Laud, Wentworth and Weston, would
have something to say. The brilliant Duke, who had for more
than three years been in the King's stead in the eyes of the nation, would have to sit as a learner at the feet of those towards
whom he had hitherto played the part of a providence upon earth.

Buckingham's difficulties.

There was one man, with little real knowledge of England,
who was eager to lead Buckingham in a more congenial path.
In the middle of June Carleton had returned from
the Hague. He soon gained Buckingham's entire confidence, and received from him a promise that before long he
should be Secretary in place of Conway, whose health had lately
become impaired. He was soon raised, as Viscount
Dorchester, to a higher step in the peerage. The
new Viscount was too completely dependent on Court
favour to advocate a policy which would be unpalatable to his
patron; but there could be no doubt that if he found a favourable moment he would advocate, not a general peace such as
Wentworth and Williams desired, but a peace with France
which would enable Buckingham to turn his attention to Germany and to reconquer popularity by achieving the recovery of
the Palatinate.[1]

Carleton's influence.

July 25. He is raised to a Viscountcy.

---

[1] After Buckingham's death Dorchester wrote as follows: "My private
respects are many testimonies of his love, and none greater than a purpose
he declared unto me upon my last return from your Majesty and hath

One step was taken by Buckingham to conciliate popular opinion. His retention of many offices had long been matter of complaint, and he now divested himself of the Wardenship of the Cinque Ports. That which might have gained him credit in 1625 could gain him no credit now, even if he had not chosen as his successor Suffolk, the cowardly Peer who had brought a false charge against Selden, and had shrunk from supporting the accusation.[1]

Buckingham's surrender of the Cinque Ports.

Almost at the same time an attempt was made to win back the friendship of the Dutch Government. The East Indiamen seized in the autumn were restored, on an engagement that effectual steps should be taken to investigate the truth of the massacre of Amboyna.[2]

Restoration of the East Indiamen to the Dutch.

Was it indeed possible for Buckingham to shake off his past and to replace himself in the position from which he had started in 1624? One terrible object must have been ever before his eyes to remind him that things were not as they had been then. Rochelle was suffering the horrors of starvation, and he could not act as though he had no part in the matter.

Progress of the siege of Rochelle.

The city was by this time in great distress. Before the end of June famine was making fearful ravages. Grass and roots, with a little shell-fish and boiled leather, formed the only food of the women and children, the weak and infirm, though men

since often reiterated unto me, of making me by his favour with the King, our gracious master, an instrument of better days than we have seen of late, he having had a firm resolution, which he manifested to some other persons in whom he reposed trust and confidence, as well as to myself, to walk new ways, but upon old grounds and maxims both of religion and policy, finding his own judgment to have been misled by errors of youth and persuasions of some persons he began better to know, so as I must confess to your Majesty, knowing otherwise the nobleness of his nature and great parts, and vigour both of mind and body, as I had full satisfaction in him myself, so I made no doubt but the world would soon have, notwithstanding the public hatred to which he was exposed."—Dorchester to Elizabeth, Aug. 27, *S. P. Dom.* cxiv. 17.

[1] Suffolk's appointment, July 14, *Patent Rolls*. 4 *Charles I*. Part 28.

[2] Contarini to the Doge, Aug. $\frac{4}{14}$, *Ven. Transcripts, R. O.*

with arms in their hands were able to take advantage of their strength to extort for a time the means of subsisting on a somewhat better fare. Guiton, the champion of resistance, had held out bravely as yet; but now, for a moment, even Guiton's iron resolution gave way. He sent to ask Richelieu for terms.[1] Before the answer reached him he had changed his mind, and had resolved to resist to the uttermost. A month later the starving crowd was crying out for surrender, and the cry of misery awoke the pity of men in high office. Guiton called upon his armed followers for support, and drove the officials from the town. Yet from what quarter could assistance be hoped for? In the South of France Rohan was still in arms, but he was utterly unable to make head against the forces opposed to him. In other quarters Richelieu's success was telling. The incapable Soissons, who the year before had been meditating an attack upon France with the aid of England and Savoy, made his peace with the Cardinal, and the Duke of La Tremoille, a leader amongst the Huguenot aristocracy, came into the camp before Rochelle to profess himself a convert to the religion which was accompanied by the sure tokens of victory. Yet it was not on victory alone that Richelieu rested, so much as on the conviction which he was able to impart that he was not engaged in a war of religion. After Rochelle was taken, the French Protestants should be free, as before, to worship after their own fashion; but the King's authority must be supreme.

Amongst the French Protestants outside the city the resistance of Rochelle came to be regarded as a great misfortune, increasing their prospect of hard treatment from their Catholic neighbours.[2] Even in Rochelle itself the same opinion was gaining ground. At last, even Guiton could not prevent the opening of negotiations with Richelieu, though he contrived to delay them till he knew that the English fleet was really coming to his aid.

---

[1] That the offer came from Guiton, and not from Richelieu, is **proved** by M. Avenel. *Lettres de Richelieu*, iii. 125.

[2] Substance of letters from Niort, July $\frac{4}{14}$, *S. P. France.*

The enterprise in which Buckingham was now engaged was one in which success or failure would be equally ruinous. To allow the great Protestant city, which was suffering untold misery in reliance upon his plighted word, to be taken before his eyes, was to confirm the settled belief of the world in his incompetence if not in his treachery. Yet what would be the result of his success? If the arms of the national King were beaten back from the walls of Rochelle, the innocent Protestant populations scattered over France would be regarded as the traitorous allies of the foreign enemy. It would be well if the horrors of the Revocation of the Edict of Nantes, combined with the horrors of the rule of the Jacobin Committee of Public Safety, were not anticipated Royal indignation would combine with popular bigotry to mark the Huguenots out for destruction. All this would happen because Buckingham and his master had failed to read the signs of the times, and had thought that it was as easy for them to interfere to prevent the national consolidation of France as it was for them to interfere to prevent the merely military consolidation of Germany.

Buckingham's prospects.

Some perception of the dangers upon which he was running was beginning to dawn upon Buckingham. The Dutch and Venetian ambassadors had warned him from time to time that he was throwing away his chances of again interfering in Germany. If once Catholic and Protestant were exasperated to the utmost against one another in France, there would be little hope of obtaining French co-operation against the House of Austria in the Empire, even if France did not throw all her weight on the side of Spain and the Emperor. Buckingham listened to what they said without impatience, though he had no definite plan to propose. Evidently he would have been glad to be relieved from the duty of succouring Rochelle, if only he could be relieved without dishonour.

Dangers in his way.

Difficulties of another sort now came upon Buckingham. 'During the summer months the trusty Sir John Coke had been at Portsmouth, toiling in vain to re-organise the fleet. " Give me leave to say freely," he had written to his patron on June 25, "that not only my abode here will now be of no use, but that every day whilst the fleet stayeth in this harbour it will be less ready and worse provided to set to sea. The victuals and provisions daily waste, and supplies cannot be made so fast; and if it linger till towards autumn, when the winds will blow high, they will require more supplies of anchors, cables, and all things else than I fear all the stores of the navy can supply; and, what is most important, the men, part by sickness, part by running away, do every day grow fewer." [1]

<small>August. Slowness with which the fleet is fitted out.</small>

At last, at the beginning of August, an effort was to be made to bring order out of chaos. The King went down to Southwick, a house of Sir Daniel Norton, in the neighbourhood of Portsmouth, to superintend the fitting out of the fleet, whilst Buckingham remained in London to hasten the supplies which were needed for the expedition. The great Duke had to learn the weakness of the omnipotence which he was accused of possessing. No man in England believed any longer in him or his undertakings. His own officers opposed the force of inertia to his reiterated commands. "I find nothing," he was reduced to write, "of more difficulty and uncertainty than the preparations here for this service of Rochelle. Every man says he has all things ready, and yet all remains as it were at a stand. It will be Saturday night before all the victuals will be aboard, and I dare not come hence till I see that despatched, being of such importance." [2]

<small>Aug. 6. Buckingham's despondency.</small>

On the day on which Buckingham wrote these despairing lines, Dorchester received a visit from Contarini, the Venetian ambassador, which threw a ray of light into the darkness. Contarini had been horror-struck at the idea of Buckingham's cold-blooded scheme for making Italy the battle-ground between France and Spain, and he now brought with him nothing less than a project of pacification with France which had been forwarded to him by Zorzi, the representative of the Republic in France. Dorchester

<small>Contarini proposes peace with France.</small>

---

[1] Coke to Buckingham, June 25, *Melbourne MSS.*
[2] Buckingham to Conway, Aug. 6, *S. P. Dom.* cxii. 32.

received Contarini with open arms, and assured him that the Duke would always prefer a peace with France to a peace with Spain, if it could be had on honourable terms. The moment the fleet was no longer needed at Rochelle it would steer to the aid of the King of Denmark.

Contarini then had an interview with Buckingham himself. The only difficulty in the way seemed to be that the King of France would make it a point of honour not to treat with a foreign sovereign on the conditions to be granted to his own subjects. It was at last agreed to propose that the Rochellese should treat directly with Louis. Nothing, said Buckingham, would satisfy him better than to find when he arrived at Rochelle that the citizens had received satisfaction from their own king. Zorzi should be entrusted with the negotiation, and if there was not time to settle everything before the Duke sailed, the good news might meet him when he arrived on the coast of France. Care, however, must be taken not to effect peace between Louis and the Huguenots without making peace between France and England at the same time. When everything was arranged there might be an interview between Buckingham and Richelieu to conclude peace under the walls of Rochelle.[1]

His interview with Buckingham.

Buckingham welcomes the idea of peace.

Once more the sanguine Buckingham was looking forward to carry out his old scheme of a Protestant war. Morgan was ordered to gather together the remains of the garrison of Stade, and to carry them back to the aid of the King of Denmark. Dalbier had letters of credit

Preparations for war in Germany.

---

[1] Contarini to the Doge, with enclosures, Aug. $\frac{10}{20}$, *Ven. Transcripts, R. O.* Carleton to Wake, Sept. 2, *Court and Times*, i. 391. *Carleton Letters*, xxi. Mr. Forster saw treachery in all this; I see none. There was no intention to withdraw from fighting unless the negotiation was satisfactory, as is shown in a letter from Peblitz and Knyphausen to the King, in which the details of Buckingham's plans are given, Aug. 25, *Melbourne MSS.* The facts must be taken in connection with Clarendon's statement that the Duke, shortly before his death, thought of turning against Weston. If Cottington, as is most likely, was Clarendon's informant, the story doubtless originated with Weston, and may be taken as Weston's interpretation of the probable result of Buckingham's change of policy.

given him, with orders to keep his men on foot till the end of October.[1]

> Aug. 15. Buckingham says the King wishes delay.

Buckingham's authority was great in England, but it was not everything. It was necessary for him to go down to Portsmouth to consult the King. On the 15th he was back in London, and told Contarini that Charles was in no hurry. He was afraid that if the negotiations began before the fleet arrived, the Rochellese would be disheartened and the French inspirited to make exorbitant demands.

On the 17th Buckingham was again at Portsmouth. Soubise, backed by two of the deputies from Rochelle, spoke vehemently against peace. Buckingham himself was to some extent shaken. He told Contarini, who had followed him, that it was impossible to trust Richelieu, who might communicate the whole negotiation to Spain if time were allowed him. Contarini was perfectly satisfied that Buckingham wished for peace, and was not making difficulties in order to create delay. He left him on the understanding that they were to meet the next morning in the King's presence at Southwick, to come to a final decision on the matter.[2]

> Aug. 17. Buckingham at Portsmouth.

> Aug. 22. Contarini's last interview with the Duke.

That interview was never to take place. Before the hour for the meeting arrived the great Duke had been struck down by the knife of a fanatic.

The members of Buckingham's family had long been prepared for coming evil. Strange fancies, the offspring of despondency, lay, doubtless, at the root of the wild stories which have floated into the history of the time. Clarendon himself

---

[1] Contarini to the Doge, Aug. $\frac{12}{22}$, *Ven. Transcripts*, R. O.

[2] Contarini to the Doge, $\frac{\text{Aug. 23}}{\text{Sept. 2}}$, *ibid.* It does not appear from these letters what terms Contarini proposed; but we know from another source that he meant to suggest that the King of France should raise the siege of Rochelle and grant religious liberty to the Protestants, on condition that the King of England should renounce all pretensions to interfere between Louis and his subjects. Contarini to Dorchester, $\frac{\text{Aug. 27}}{\text{Sept. 6}}$, *S. P. France.*

gravely told how the ghost of Sir George Villiers appeared to an ancient servitor, commanding him to warn his son to propitiate the nation which he had offended; and Buckingham's sister, the Countess of Denbigh, writing to him on the fatal 23rd of August, 'bedewed the paper with her tears,' and fainted away as she thought of the dangers of his voyage. Even Buckingham himself, fearless as he was, was haunted by a feeling of insecurity. In taking leave of Laud he begged him to put his Majesty in mind of his poor wife and children. "Some adventure," he explained, " may kill me as well as another man."[1]

Yet he was not prepared for assassination. Some weeks before, Sir Clement Throgmorton had begged him to wear a shirt of mail beneath his clothes. "A shirt of mail," answered the Duke, "would be but a silly defence against any popular fury. As for a single man's assault, I take myself to be in no danger. There are no Roman spirits left."[2] On the 22nd he had nearly fallen a victim to that popular fury which alone he dreaded. A sailor who had affronted him a fortnight before was condemned to death by a court-martial. As he was led to execution, an attempt was made to rescue him by force, and the guard was attacked by an angry mob of his comrades. Buckingham, followed by a train of mounted attendants, rode hastily to the defence. The assailants were driven on board ship. Two of them were killed in the struggle, and many more were wounded by the armed horsemen. Buckingham then accompanied the procession to the gibbet. But for the mutiny the poor man's life would have been spared, as the Duchess had interceded for him. The pardon could no longer be granted, if discipline was to be maintained.[3] Yet, even after this vindication of his authority, Buckingham was still in danger. The officers formed a circle round him, and brought him in safety to the house in the High Street, in the occupation of Captain Mason, the treasurer of the army, in which he was lodging.

That night Buckingham was restless in his sleep, as well he

Aug. 22. Mutiny at Portsmouth.

[1] *Rel. Wottonianæ,* i. 335.
[2] *Ibid.* i. 233. D'Ewes, *Autobiography,* 381.
[3] A letter from one of the Highams. *Rous's Diary.*

might be. The Duchess, anxious as ever, adjured him in the morning to take more precautions. At first he spoke harshly to her. Then, softened by her manifest affection, he told her that he would take her importunity as a sign of her love.[1] About nine o'clock he came down to breakfast, in a room com-municating by a dark passage with the central hall.

Aug. 23. Rumour of the relief of Rochelle.

As he breakfasted news was brought that Rochelle had been relieved. Such news, if it had been true, would have set him free at once from the burthen which he had found too heavy to bear. A peace with France—a triumphant peace—would have speedily followed, and the fleet would have steered for the mouth of the Elbe, where Glückstadt still held bravely out for the King of Denmark and the Protestant cause. But, alluring as the prospect was, it was all the more necessary for Buckingham to be on his guard against false rumours. Soubise and the deputies of Rochelle protested warmly that the tale could not be true, and their vehement gesticulations gave rise, with those who were alike ignorant of the French language and the French temperament, to the supposition that their eagerness to bear down contradiction was passing into angry menace.

The breakfast party was soon at an end. Dorchester had come in from Southwick to fetch the Duke to the conference with Contarini, which was to settle the terms on which Charles would be ready to agree to peace when the fleet arrived at Rochelle. Buckingham rose to follow him. As he stepped into the crowded hall he stopped for an instant to speak to one of his colonels, Sir Thomas Fryer. Fryer was a short man, and the Duke stooped to listen to him. As his attention was thus engaged, a man who had been standing at the entrance of the passage into the breakfast room stepped forward, and struck him heavily with a knife in the left breast, saying, "God have mercy upon thy soul!"[2] as he dealt the blow. Buckingham had strength enough to draw the knife out of the wound, and crying 'Villain!' attempted to follow the assassin. But the blow had been struck by no feeble arm.

Murder of the Duke.

[1] Johnston's *Hist. Rerum Britannicarum*, 722.
[2] *Clarendon*, i. 55.

Tottering on for a step or two, the Duke fell heavily against a table and sank dead upon the ground.[1]

All was confusion for a moment; the immediate bystanders thought that Buckingham had been seized with a stroke of apoplexy; but the blood gushing from his mouth and from the wound soon undeceived them. The murderer had slipped away into the kitchen, and men who had witnessed the quick words and flashing eyes of Soubise in the breakfast room, fancied that they had found there the explanation of the mystery. Shouts of "A Frenchman! a Frenchman!" were mingled with "Where is the villain? Where is the butcher?" In the excitement of the moment, the assassin fancied that his own name, Felton, was pronounced. He was no coward, and, stepping calmly into the hall with his sword in his hand, he confronted the crowd with the simple words, "I am the man. Here I am." But for the intervention of Dorchester and a few others, he would have been cut down on the spot. It was only with difficulty that he was rescued and carried off for examination.

The murderer seized.

Then followed a scene the like of which had never been witnessed by any present. Lady Anglesea, the Duke's sister-in-law, was watching the crowd in the hall from a gallery into which the sleeping apartments opened. Flinging open the door of the chamber in which the Duchess was, she told her that the sad day which her loving heart had so long foreboded had come at last. Rushing out in her night-dress with a bitter cry, the poor lady, now a widow, looked down upon the bleeding, lifeless corpse of him who had been her only joy. "Ah, poor ladies!" wrote one who was present; "such was their screechings, tears, and distractions that I never in my life heard the like before, and hope never to hear the like again."[2]

The Duchess of Buckingham in the gallery.

In a few minutes the body was taken up and removed to the room in which the Duke had breakfasted. There was no one there who thought it his duty to watch by the corpse

---

[1] Meade to Stuteville, Sept. 20, *Ellis*, ser. 1, iii. 261.

[2] Dorchester to Elizabeth, *Ellis*, ser. 1, iii. 256, Aug. 27, *S. P. Dom.* cxiv. 20.

of him who had been the greatest man in England. The throng, amongst which were so many who had received everything at his hand, poured forth to spread the news or to provide for the dangers of the hour. The mortal remains of him who had stood apart in life from his fellow-men were left for the moment untended by any friendly hand.[1]

In the meanwhile the news was on the way to Southwick. The messenger who bore the tidings found the King at morning prayers, and whispered the tale of horror in his ear.

The King informed.

If the workings of his countenance betrayed the emotion within, he did not rise or leave the room till the service was at an end. Then going into his own apartment he threw himself upon his bed, and with bitter tears and lamentations gave free vent to his sorrow.[2]

Charles might well grieve for the loss of the only real personal friend he ever had; but with personal sorrow was doubtless mingled another feeling. "His Majesty," says a contemporary letter-writer, "since his death, hath been used to call him his martyr, and to say the world was much mistaken in him. For whereas it was commonly thought he ruled his Majesty, it was clear otherwise, having been his Majesty's most faithful and obedient subject in all things; as his Majesty would make hereafter sensibly appear to the world."[3] There was doubtless much exaggeration in the view that Buckingham did no more than carry out the King's orders. Charles was the last person to discover how much he had been influenced. There was, however, more truth in it than history has been willing to acknowledge. The secrets of the intercourse between the two men will, in all probability, never be revealed; but there is every reason to believe that Charles's tenacity and self-sufficiency had to the full as large a share in the mischief as the presumptuous optimism of his favourite.

---

[1] *Rel. Wottonianæ,* i. 234.

[2] *Clarendon,* i. 62. Contarini distinctly speaks of the King as showing trouble in his countenance; and it is likely enough that the contrary story, which has been usually accepted, was an exaggeration based upon the fact that the King did not leave his place.

[3] Meade to Stuteville, Sept 20, *Court and Times,* i. 395.

It was for Charles a melancholy duty to discover the motives of the assassin. John Felton, a gentleman springing from an old Suffolk family, had served as a lieutenant in the expedition to Rhé. The captain of his regiment had been killed and he had expected promotion. But promotion, on account of some rule of the service, was refused him. When he applied a second time, the Duke, to whom he appealed asking how he was to live, had, according to one account, told him that he might hang himself if he could not live.[1] Returning to England, he remained in London, a moody, discontented man, whiling away his time by much reading. At last he could bear his misery no longer. Besides his own special grievance, he was weighed down by the common misfortune of all who entered the King's service. His pay amounted to some seventy or eighty pounds, and not a penny of it was forthcoming. At the beginning of August he was deeply in debt, and he saw no means of sustaining life much longer. His reading brought to him the persuasion that the man who had cut short his career was a public enemy. The Remonstrance of the Commons taught him that the Duke was the cause of all the grievances of the kingdom. A book written by Dr. Eglesham, a physician of James I., in which Buckingham was accused of poisoning the late King, and the Marquis of Hamilton as well, painted his oppressor in still darker colours.[2] Certain propositions culled out of a book called the *Golden Epistles*, which taught him that all things done for the good, profit, and benefit of the commonwealth should be accounted lawful, confirmed him in the resolution to rid the country of its tyrant.[3]

Story of Felton.

On the 19th his resolution was finally taken. He himself always ascribed his determination to the reading of the Remonstrance. One who saw him in his disconsolate condition not

---

[1] This is but a way of reconciling Wotton's statement that Felton was satisfied with the Duke's answer with the other story that he received from the Duke the reply which is given above, and which he could not have regarded as satisfactory. He said he was twice rejected, so both accounts may be true.

[2] *Rel. Wottonianæ*, i. 232.

[3] Inclosure (Sept. 19) in Meade's letter to Stuteville, *Court and Times* i. 399. *Duppa's Report*, Sept. 11, *S. P. Dom.* cxvi. 101.

long before, had told him that it was not fit for a soldier to want courage. "If I be angered or moved," replied Felton, "they shall find I have courage enough." It was quite true. At a cutler's shop on Tower Hill he bought a tenpenny knife, and, as his left hand was maimed, he sewed a sheath for it into his pocket, that he might draw it easily with one hand. As he passed through Fleet Street he went into a church and left his name to be prayed for as 'a man much discontented in mind.' So he passed on to Portsmouth, making his way mostly on foot, but riding whenever he fell in with a friendly waggoner. On the morning of the 23rd he was at Mason's house, ready for his victim.

The writing in the crown of his hat. Felton's only care was to assure the world that he was an executioner, not an assassin. In the crown of his hat he had sewn a paper on which he had written, to persuade others as he had persuaded himself, that

Nought he did in hate, but all in honour :—

"If I be slain, let no man condemn me, but rather condemn himself. It is for our sins that our hearts are hardened and become senseless, or else he had not gone so long unpunished.

"JOHN FELTON."

Then again, as if he had just risen from the perusal of those propositions in the *Golden Epistles*, of which he kept a copy in his trunk :—

"He is unworthy of the name of a gentleman or soldier, in my opinion, that is afraid to sacrifice his life for the honour of God, his King, and country.

"JOHN FELTON."[1]

His popularity. If Felton stood alone in conceiving his murderous purpose, he did not stand alone in regarding it with complacency after it was accomplished. The popular feeling about Buckingham was something like that with which the despot of an old Greek city was regarded. He had placed himself above his king, his country, and the laws of his country, and

[1] Dorchester to Elizabeth, *Ellis*, ser. 1, iii. 256.

he had no right to the sympathy of honest men. When the news was known in London, men went about with smiling faces, and healths were drunk to Felton on every side.[1] "God bless thee, little David!" cried an old woman to the slayer of the Goliath of her time, as he passed through Kingston on his way to the Tower. Outside the Tower itself a dense throng was gathered to see him, and friendly greetings of "The Lord comfort thee! The Lord be merciful unto thee!" were the last sounds which rang in his ears as the gates closed upon him.[2] Nor was the feeling of exultation confined to the illiterate and uneducated. Even Nethersole, courtier as he was, spoke of the murder as the removal of the stone of offence by the hand of God, and as a means by which the King might be brought to join in perfect unity with his people.[3] Verses expressive of satisfaction were passed in manuscript from hand to hand. One of these copies was believed, even in such a well-informed company as that which met at Sir Robert Cotton's at Westminster, to have been the work of Ben Jonson himself, who, as poet laureate, was officially bound to abstain from sympathy with the national rejoicing. The charge was thought sufficiently serious to demand inquiry by the Attorney-General, and the verses were finally traced to a minister, Zouch Townley, a devoted admirer of the poet, who had caught the ring of Jonson's versification. Townley avoided punishment by a prudent flight to Holland; but his words remain as a startling memorial of what a student of Christchurch and a minister of the gospel could write under the impressions caused by Buckingham's rule. The poem is a long exhortation to Felton to enjoy his bondage and to bear with courage the tortures preparing for him. Townley ended with words of encouragement which doubtless met with a hearty reception from their readers :—

> "Farewell! for thy brave sake we shall not send
> Henceforth commanders enemies to defend;

---

[1] Nethersole to Carlisle, Aug. 24, *S. P. Dom.* cxiv. 7.
[2] Meade to Stuteville, Sept. 13, 20, *Court and Times.* i. 394, 395.
[3] Nethersole to Carlisle, Aug. 24, *S. P. Dom.* cxiv. 7.

>   Nor would it our just monarchs please
>   To keep an admiral to lose the seas.
>   Farewell! Undaunted stand, and joy to be
>   Of public sorrow the epitome.
>   Let the Duke's name solace and crown thy thrall,
>   All we for him did suffer—thou for all;
>   And I dare boldly write, as thou darest die,
>   Stout Felton, England's ransom he doth lie." [1]

When assassination was thus lauded, it is no wonder that those few to whom Buckingham was not a monster regarded with horror the deed which threatened to refer political disputes to the arbitration of the dagger. To Charles and Laud this outburst of hatred conveyed no warning of the risk of conducting a government in defiance of opinion ; it was simply the opening of the floodgates of iniquity, which they were in duty bound to keep closed at all hazard to themselves. Such a feeling as this could alone account for a strange passage in the life of William Chillingworth, the divine whom all men now combine to honour. He was at this time a Fellow of Trinity at Oxford, and to his argumentative mind, with its eagerness to try every conclusion by its own logical tests and its dislike of foregone conclusions, the Puritan dogmatism was extremely hateful, especially when it was found in conjunction with a noisy, irreverent temper.

Gill at Oxford. Amongst the members of the College was a certain Alexander Gill, a man of some abilities, who was assistant to his father, the head master of St. Paul's School, and who, in that capacity, had contrived to impress at least one of his pupils, John Milton, with the idea of the splendour of his talents. The younger Gill, however, was much given to bluster and wild talk of every kind, and one day towards the end of August he came down to Oxford full of delight at the Duke's murder. "The King," he said, "is fitter to stand in a Cheapside shop, with an apron before him, and say 'What lack ye?' than to govern a kingdom." Then he proposed Felton's health, and talked rashly about the Duke and the late King being in hell together. All this Chillingworth, in disgust at the ribaldry, related to Laud. Gill was brought before the Star

---

[1] Preface to Bruce's *Calendar,* 1628-9, viii. *Court and Times,* i. 427.

Chamber, and only escaped the full infliction of a terrible sentence by Laud's intercession on the ground of his father's position and services.[1]

The day before Felton was brought to the Tower, the Duke's funeral was hurried over 'in as poor and confused manner as hath been seen.' At ten o'clock at night a coffin was brought to Westminster Abbey, attended by only about a hundred mourners. Yet even this, if the story told can be believed, was mere show. The body had the day before been privately interred in the Abbey, lest the people in their madness should rise to offer insult to the remains of the man whom they hated. Even the sham funeral was attended with marks of extraordinary precaution. "To prevent all disorders," we are told, "the trainbands kept a guard on both sides of the way all along from Wallingford House to Westminster Church, beating up their drums loud, and carrying their pikes and muskets upon their shoulders as in a march, not trailing them at their heels, as is usual in mourning."

Sept. 11. Ceremony of Buckingham's funeral.
Sept. 10. His body buried the day before.

The dishonour shown to the remains of the Duke ceased at the Abbey doors. His place had already been marked out by the excessive favour of his sovereign. In the Chapel of Henry VII., set apart in older days for members of the Royal house, Buckingham had received permission to take possession of a vault for his own family. It had already been twice opened. There lay his eldest son, a child who had died in infancy. There lay his sister's son, young Philip Fielding. Now the vault was open for the third time, to receive the mortal remains of him who whilst living had stood amongst kings, and who was not to be divided from them in his death.

Charles at first spoke of erecting a stately monument to the memory of him whom he had loved so well; but he had no money to spare, and Weston warned him against the costly project. "I would be loth," said the Lord Treasurer, "to tell your Majesty what the world would say, not only here, but all Christendom over, if you

Buckingham's monument.

---

[1] The facts are collected from Meade's letters and the State Papers in Masson's *Life of Milton*, i. 177.

should erect a monument for the Duke before you set up one for King James, your father." Charles took the warning to heart, and left his friend without the token of respect with which he had intended to honour him.[1] At last, the widow to whom he had ever been the most loved of husbands, in spite of his many infidelities, stepped in and built that pretentious tomb in which the bad taste of an age in which grace and beauty were forgotten was signally manifested. Yet with an unconscious irony the piled marble points the moral of the story of him who sleeps below. Unlike the figure of the Duke of Lennox on the opposite side of the chapel, the form of Buckingham lies open to the eye of day without the superincumbent shadow of a canopy to shroud him from the crowd whose observation in life he loved to court. The report of his actions is committed not to some 'star-ypointing pyramid' firmly and immovably based upon the firm earth, but to a sprightly Fame, who, with bursting cheeks, proclaims with a trumpet the great deeds of the Duke. On either side of her are two slender obelisks, which would evidently succumb to the first gust of wind that blew, and which rest upon a foundation of skulls. "Dust thou art, and to dust thou shalt return," is the sentence written upon the works of him who has built his house upon the sand. The one touch of human interest in the tomb is the attendance of the children, who had been taught by their loving mother to reverence their father's name. The Duchess, in truth, had no doubt of her lost husband's perfections. In the inscription which she caused to be affixed to the monument, she spoke with sweet remembrance of his gifts of mind and body, of his liberality, and above all of his singular humanity and incomparable gentleness of disposition. To her he was still the enigma of the world, who had been styled at one time the parent, at another time the enemy, of his country. She, at least, herself cherishing in her heart a warm attachment for the ancient forms of religion, could speak with wonderment, if not perhaps with half-concealed sarcasm, of the strange fate which caused him to be charged with attachment to the Papacy whilst

---

[1] Meade to Stuteville, Nov. 1, *Court and Times*, i. 419.

he was making war against Papists, and to be slain by a Protestant whilst he was doing what he could to give assistance to Protestants.[1]

Career of Buckingham.

The solution of the enigma is not to be found in the popular imagination of the day, and still less in the popular history which has been founded upon it. Buckingham owed his rise to his good looks, to his merry laugh and winning manners; but to compare him with Gaveston is as unfair as it would be to compare Charles with Edward II. As soon as his power was established, he aimed at being the director of the destinies of the State. Champion in turn of a war in the Palatinate, of a Spanish alliance, and of a breach first with Spain and then with France, he nourished a fixed desire to lead his country in the path in which for the time being he thought that she ought to walk. His abilities were above the average, and they were supported by that kind of patriotism which clings to a successful man when his objects are, in his own eyes, inseparable from the objects of his country. If, however, it is only just to class him amongst ministers rather than amongst favourites, he must rank amongst the most incapable ministers of this or of any other country. He had risen too fast in early life to make him conscious of difficulty in anything which he wished to do. He knew nothing of the need of living laborious days which is incumbent on those who hope to achieve permanent success. He thought that eminence in peace and war could be carried by storm. As one failure after another dashed to the ground his hopes, he could not see that he and his mode of action were the main causes of the mischief. Ever ready to engage in some stupendous undertaking, of which he had never measured the difficulties, he could not understand that to the world at large such conduct must seem entirely incomprehensible, and that when men saw his own fortunes prospering in the midst of national ruin and disgrace, they would come to the mistaken but natural conclusion that he cared everything for his own fortunes and nothing for the national honour.

[1] Keepe, *Monumenta Westmonasteriensia*, 283. Compare Stanley's *Memorials of Westminster Abbey*, 236.

Buckingham's ignorance of the real basis of the popular indignation was fully shared by the King. The explanations of Felton, natural as they were, were received with deep incredulity by Charles. He could not but believe that Felton was the instrument of a widespread conspiracy. Dorset, who was one of the councillors employed to examine the prisoner, threatened him with the rack. Felton replied that if he were put on the rack he would accuse Dorset himself of being his accomplice.[1] Still the wish to wring the supposed truth out of the murderer was strong with Charles.

Nov. 13. The judges consulted. On November 13 he ordered that the judges should be consulted whether Felton could be tortured by law, as he was not inclined to use his prerogative as it had been so often used in former reigns. To this question the judges unanimously returned an answer in the negative.[2] On the 27th, therefore, Felton was at last brought up for trial. He pleaded guilty. Some compunction he showed for his deed, though the repentance was probably not very deep. He asked that the hand which had been the instrument of the crime might be cut off before he suffered. His request was, of course, refused, as contrary to the law.[3] On the 29th he was hanged at Tyburn. The body was then carried down to Portsmouth, to be suspended in chains in the sight of those amongst whom his crime had been committed.

Nov. 14. Nov. 27. Felton condemned and executed.

The murdered Buckingham had no successor in Charles's

---

[1] —— to Stuteville, Sept. 19, *Court and Times*, i. 399.

[2] Mr. Jardine, in his *Reading on the use of Torture*, has reduced this matter to its true dimensions. Torture had been allowed by custom as inflicted by the prerogative, but not by law. The judges only said what Charles ought to have known already. Torture was inflicted as late as 1640 by prerogative. I do not agree with Mr. Jardine in throwing discredit on Rushworth's narrative, or in connecting the inquiry which was made on Nov. 13 with the affair about the hand which took place on the 27th. The position Charles was in after the grant of the Petition of Right would make him shy of using his prerogative unless he felt himself to be unquestionably justified in doing so.

[3] Whitelocke's story that Charles wished the hand to be cut off is no doubt a mere substitution of Charles for Felton.

affections. No other man could bring with him the long habitude of personal friendship, or the promptness of decision made palatable by winning gracefulness of manner, which had enabled the late Lord Admiral, under the show of deference, to guide his sovereign at his pleasure.

<small>September. Buckingham not replaced in Charles's favour.</small>

It was easy to dispose of Buckingham's offices, to give the Mastership of the Horse to Holland, and to place the Admiralty in commission, in order that the profits of the place might be applied to the payment of debts which Buckingham had contracted, for the most part in his master's service. Charles, however, marked his sense of personal loss by refusing to give away the vacant Garter which his friend had worn.[1]

<small>His offices given away.</small>

Buckingham had been more than a Master of the Horse or a Lord Admiral. He had been even more than a Prime Minister is in a modern Cabinet. His word had given the impulse to the whole machine of government. Every act had been submitted to his approval. Every office had been filled by personal followers, who had learned that their fortunes could be made or marred by his nod. Into this supreme direction of affairs Charles stepped at once. He announced his intention of presiding continually at the Council, and ordered each minister to report directly to himself on the business entrusted to his charge.

<small>The government undertaken by the King.</small>

Of industrious attention to business Charles was eminently capable. Countless corrections upon the drafts of despatches and state papers show how diligent he was in moulding the minutest turns of expression to his taste, and how little latitude he allowed to those who served under him. For government in the higher sense he had no capacity. He was as obstinate in refusing to abandon any plan which he had once formed, as he was irresolute in the face of any obstacles which might arise in the way of its execution. Hence the contrast between his treatment of difficulties at home and abroad. Within the kingdom, where his authority

<small>Charles as a director of government.</small>

---

[1] Contarini to the Doge, $\frac{\text{Sept. 28}}{\text{Oct. 8}}$, *Ven. Transcripts, R. O.*

was undisputed, he required prompt obedience without troubling himself about the growing ill-will which was storing itself up to become the source of future trouble. With the Kings and States of the Continent, who had no thought of taking his word for law, he never succeeded in gaining his ends. Constant repetition of the same demand without any intention to offer advantages in return, or any power to extort by prompt action the object which he sought, made Charles's diplomacy a byword on the Continent, as his father's had been before.

From the beginning of the reign it had been the fault of Charles's foreign policy that it rested rather on the supposed necessity of giving satisfaction to the personal honour of the King than on the well-understood interests, either of England or of the nations of the Continent. Because he had himself failed to secure a wife at Madrid, and because the Elector Palatine was his brother-in-law, he had engaged in war with Spain. Because his guarantee to the treaty between Louis XIII. and his Huguenot subjects had been disregarded, he had engaged in a war with France. As long as Buckingham lived Charles had struck blow after blow in the vain hope of recovering the Palatinate and saving Rochelle. With Buckingham no longer at his side, it was likely that words would take the place of deeds, and that he would write despatches and instruct ambassadors, instead of arming fleets and appointing generals; but it was not likely that he would frankly acknowledge that events were stronger than himself, or that he would give up the hope of obtaining objects which he still believed to be desirable, because they were beyond his reach.

Charles's foreign policy.

Everything thus combined to increase the influence of the minister whose voice was persistently raised in favour of peace. Weston, the Lord Treasurer, was neither a high-minded nor a far-sighted politician. His wife and some of his children were acknowledged recusants; and though he himself conformed to the English Church, it was generally believed that but for the allurements of temporal interest he would have followed in their steps. He was outrageously rude to those whom he could afford to despise, and obsequiously

Character of Weston.

subservient to those upon whom he was obliged to depend. He alone of all who had advocated the maintenance of peace n 1624 had contrived to keep his place in Buckingham's favour by promptly accommodating his actions to the wishes of the favourite; and men were already beginning to laugh at the timidity with which he shifted his ground whenever a persistence in the course which he had adopted would be likely to be accompanied by consequences unpleasant to himself.

Like Middlesex, Weston was a careful and economical administrator of the treasury, though he took good care to fill his own pockets, by means even more unscrupulous than those to which Middlesex had resorted. Like Middlesex, too, he was now endeavouring to impress upon the Government the policy of complete abstention from foreign complications, except when intervention was absolutely required by the material interests of England. The men of the sixteenth century had handed down traditions of heroism displayed on behalf of the Continental Protestants. Weston wished to hear of nothing of the kind. He cared for England alone; but he cared for England with no exalted patriotism. It was not to him the land of ordered liberty and ancient pre-eminence in arts and arms. It was a land the people of which it was his business to make rich, in order that they might be more easily made obedient.

<small>His political influence.</small>

The influence of Weston would thus bring itself to bear on that side of Charles's character which had been neglected by Buckingham. Buckingham had encouraged Charles's unyielding persistency, and had relieved his helplessness by his own promptness in action. Weston taught him that inactivity was in itself a virtue, and that the best policy was to do nothing. But he did not weary him by contradiction. He offered himself as the instrument of his will, whatever it might be, certain that something would occur in the end to throw insuperable difficulties in his way. No minister, in fact, could hope to keep his place for an hour who should venture to inform Charles that the recovery of the Palatinate was beyond his power to effect.

<small>His influence upon Charles.</small>

For the present, however, it was evidently not in Charles's

power to do anything for the Palatinate. When great men die, or are driven from office, their works survive them. The testament of Richelieu was written in the triumphant story of victory which decorated the annals of his weaker successor. The legacy of Buckingham to his country was failure and disgrace. All through August the misery of Rochelle was growing blacker. The inhabitants were dying by hundreds. Rats and other unclean animals were no longer to be met with. Leather and parchment boiled up with a little sugar were regarded as delicacies. Entire families perished together. Even the soldiers, for whom the scanty supplies in the town had been husbanded to the utmost, were dying of sheer starvation. Voices were everywhere raised for a surrender, and it was with difficulty that Guiton was able to induce his fellow-citizens to hold out till the English fleet appeared.[1]

August. Misery at Rochelle.

Charles had thrown himself eagerly into the preparations for succouring the beleaguered town, and on September 7 the fleet weighed anchor. Buckingham's place as Admiral was filled by the Earl of Lindsey, who, as Lord Willoughby, had commanded the futile expedition which had been driven back by a gale in the Bay of Biscay in the summer of 1626.[2]

Sept. 7. Sailing of the fleet.

On the 18th Lindsey anchored off St. Martin's, the scene of Buckingham's failure of the year before. Baffling calms and contrary winds prevented an immediate attack, and it was not till the 23rd that any attempt was made to succour the starving city. The difficulties were almost if not entirely insuperable. Up the narrow channel which led to the port lay the two moles advancing from either side, the space left between them to admit of the scour of the tide being covered by a palisade. In front of the moles were thirty or forty vessels, which in themselves would have been unable to oppose a persistent

Sept. 18. Anchors off St. Martin's.

Sept. 23. Prospects of the attack.

---

[1] Pory to Meade, Nov. 28, *ibid.* i. 437. Arçere, *Hist. de la Rochelle*, ii. 306.

[2] Dorchester to Carlisle, Aug. 30; Meade to Stuteville, Sept. 23, *Court and Times*, i. 388, 398.

resistance to the far more numerous English force; but the harbour swarmed with boats and small craft laden with armed soldiers, and artillery was posted on each point of vantage at the entrance of the harbour, so that an advancing squadron could only reach the enemy under a cross fire of cannon and musketry from either side, as well as under the fire of the guns upon the moles.

Lindsey, unhappily for his chances, had other risks to encounter besides those which awaited him from the enemy. His crews were no more ready to follow him into danger than Denbigh's had been to follow their commander in the spring. The system which had ruined the Cadiz expedition was still at full work. Now, as then, men had been brought together by compulsion, and those in authority had fancied that human valour and enthusiasm could be had to order, like so much wood and iron. When the word was given to attack, the masters of the merchantmen which had been pressed into the service complained that they were being exposed to danger by being ordered to the front, where they might possibly be deserted by the King's ships, which had been directed to follow in support. The King's ships drew too much water to come to close quarters, and the Admiral could only order them to go as near the danger as possible without running aground. It was to no purpose. The merchantmen remained at such a distance that after firing for two hours the whole fleet lost but six men. No attempt was made to board the enemy, though Lindsey believed the operation to be perfectly feasible.

Want of enthusiasm in the fleet.

Ineffectual attack.

The next day's attack was equally ineffectual. In vain orders were issued to the commanders to carry their vessels nearer to the danger and to send in fire-ships to grapple with the enemy. Five or six fire-ships were sent drifting in, without any attempt to direct their course, and the Frenchmen in the boats easily towed them aside and ran them ashore where they could do no harm. Not one ship of the French fleet was set on fire. Not one Englishman was slain in the attempt.

Sept. 24. Second attack fails.

In spite of these pitiable results Lindsey could not make

up his mind to relinquish hope. In a few days the spring tide would enable him to bring his largest ships nearer to the mole. Time, however, pressed. A messenger from the town succeeded in reaching the English fleet with a tale of desperate misery, whilst the deputies who had accompanied the fleet from England talked of placing the town in the hands of the King of England, as if he had any chance of taking possession of it in any other than a figurative way.[1]

Sept. 26. News from the town.

Walter Montague had accompanied the fleet in order to carry out the negotiations which had occupied Buckingham on the eve of his assassination. Hitherto no use had been made of his services; but, as the prospect of relieving Rochelle was becoming dubious, Lindsey resolved to send him to the Cardinal on pretence of effecting a change of prisoners, to see what the French might have to say. Montague had no reason to complain of his reception. Richelieu received him with all courtesy, showed him over the moles, and convinced him that the works were impregnable by any force which Lindsey could bring against them.[2] Naturally Richelieu refused to quit his hold upon Rochelle. The city, he said, must surrender to its own sovereign. It was not to Charles's interest to support rebellion. He would, however, assure him that there should be no persecution. As soon as the King returned to Paris after the town had yielded, he would issue a declaration confirming to the Huguenots freedom of worship in the places in which they had formerly enjoyed it. The prizes taken at sea, with the exception of the ship unfairly seized in the neutral waters of the Texel,[3] might be kept by the captors. The Queen's household might be regulated on the scheme negotiated by Bassompierre. The moment that these terms were accepted Louis would turn his arms against Spain in Italy, and would come to an understanding with

Oct. 5. Montague's negotiation.

Oct. 7. Richelieu's terms.

---

[1] Lindsey to the King, Oct. 3, *S. P. Dom.* cxiii. 7. Soubise to the King, Oct. 2, *S. P. France.*

[2] —— to the Count of Morette, Oct. $\frac{8}{18}$, *S. P. France.*

[3] See page 187.

England and her allies on the best mode of assisting the King of Denmark.[1]

With these terms Montague was despatched to England, with instructions to inform the King that the fleet was in need of victuals and munitions. On October 14 he appeared before Charles. His message could hardly fail to carry conviction that the relief of Rochelle was hopeless, and that it was absurd to expect better terms than those which were now offered. Charles, too, had need of his forces in another direction. In the beginning of September a Danish ambassador, Rosencrantz, had arrived to represent Christian's urgent need of men and money. Charles accordingly desired Morgan to carry to Glückstadt the 1,200 men who formed the shattered remains of the garrison of Stade, and to do his utmost to relieve Krempe. Before the end of the month, commissioners were appointed to treat with Rosencrantz on the best means of rendering more considerable assistance.[2] They would find their task all the lighter if the ships and men under Lindsey could be spared for service in the North. Contarini too continued to offer the mediation which had been interrupted by Buckingham's assassination. He had the unusual satisfaction of finding his advances accepted by men of every shade of opinion. Weston was delighted to help on peace in any shape; whilst Pembroke and Dorchester looked upon a treaty with France as a necessary preliminary to an active co-operation with the German Protestants.

Oct. 14. Montague in England.

September. Mission of Rosencrantz.

In the view taken by Pembroke and Dorchester Charles apparently concurred. In conversation with Contarini he even went so far as to express a preference for the plan which he had rejected when proposed by Gustavus in 1624, that France should carry on war against Spain in Italy, whilst

---

[1] Propositions sent by Montague, Oct. 7 (?); Lindsey to the King, Oct. 7, *S. P. Dom.* cxviii. 27.

[2] Proposition by Rosencrantz, Sept. 4; Commission to Weston and others, Sept. 28, *S. P. Denmark.* Carleton to the Privy Council, Oct. 20, *S. P. Holland.*

England and the Protestant Powers combated the Emperor in Northern Germany.[1]

Contarini had further found a warm ally in the Queen. Henrietta Maria had been gradually accustoming herself to the loss of her French attendants. Buckingham's death had been the removal of a wall of separation between herself and her husband. When the confidential friend was gone, Charles turned for consolation to his wife. At last he tasted the pleasures of a honeymoon. She was now in her nineteenth year, ignorant and undisciplined, but bright and graceful, with flashing eyes and all the impulsive vehemence of her race. Her pouting sulkiness had been the response to her husband's cold assertion of superiority, and when he threw aside his reserve, and sought but to bask in the sunshine of her smiles, she repaid him with all the tenderness of a loving woman. Courtiers had many stories to tell of the affection of this pair so long estranged, and it was soon announced that a direct heir to the English throne was to be expected.

The Queen supports the French alliance.

October.

Of politics the Queen was completely ignorant, and it was always difficult to interest her in them, unless some personal question was involved; but she could not be indifferent to the continuance of strife between her brother and her husband.

In spite, however, of all the influence brought to bear upon him, Charles received the overtures brought by Montague coldly. Montague carried back to France the following reply: "His Majesty cannot admit to hearken to any accommodation wherein his Majesty shall leave those of the Religion in worse condition than he found them when he was invited by the King of France to treat for them, and his ambassadors were received to stand as pledges for the performance of the conditions. If, therefore, his brother the King of France will show his affection to the common good of Christendom by taking away the cause of the difference, and put those of the Religion into their promised liberties, and dis-siege Rochelle, his Majesty will not only re-

Oct. 14. Charles rejects the French terms.

---

[1] Contarini's despatches give full particulars of his conversations with the King and others.

enter into a strong league and friendship with his dear brother, but will endeavour to draw not only the Duke of Savoy, but all his other friends and allies into a resolution for the re-establishing of the affairs of Italy and Germany, and to enter into it with united counsel and forces as to the defence of the common cause : and therein, in respect of the near correspondence that is between them, his Majesty doubts not to prevail with them."[1]

Evidently his Majesty was fitted to control the affairs of some other than this world of ours, where men have to submit to superior force, if they will not yield to superior reason. More ridiculous demand was never made than this, that after all that had passed Louis should raise the siege of a city which would in a few days be in his hands.

Charles's letter to Lindsey did not echo the despondent tone of the Admiral's despatches. "We will give you no other charge or advice," he wrote, "than that you take care of our honour, the honour of our nation, and your own honour, according to the rules of wisdom and reason and the ancient practice of former generals. We see that the passage must be opened before the town can be relieved. And we conceive the French ships must be beaten before the passage can be opened, which we think can best be done while they are on float, but cannot be done without hazard of some of our ships, and loss of our subjects whom we much more tender. But our honour and our pious intention to relieve those distressed churches give way to such actions as may clear our affections and intentions in that point. And therefore we do call for it at your hands, that, according to your wisdom and noble disposition, upon which we rely, you make a vigorous trial for beating of their ships, and that being done, and when you shall have applied your engines of war and your courage and industry to force the passage for the relief of the town—to which we pray God give success—if it prove unfeasible, we shall hold ourself to be excused to the world, and that you have worthily acquitted yourself to us. We will only add

Orders Lindsey to persevere.

[1] The King's answer, Oct. 14 (?), *S. P. Dom.* cxviii. 68.

this word, that whereas the French [1] have often made the work feasible to us, and offered to lead on our men, and instruct their courages by example, we would have you let them know that we expect at their hands that they do now by some notable action make good their former boastings, howsoever we do rely upon the courage of our own subjects, which we hope will never deceive us, and particularly in this occasion of the relief of Rochelle." [2]

It was not a very useful letter to address to a commander whose chief difficulty was that he could not persuade three quarters of his force to go into action. Its effect was never to be tried. The Rochellese had discovered for themselves the futility of Charles's efforts to save them. On October 18 the capitulation was signed which put an end to their long and heroic resistance.

Oct. 18. Surrender of Rochelle.

Externally Rochelle was treated like a conquered city. The massive walls which had bid defiance to so many armies were destroyed. The privileges of the town were cancelled, and the King's officers governed the Protestant municipal republic as they governed Paris or Rouen. Richelieu had, however, set his heart on showing to the world an example of toleration, and his influence with Louis was great enough to enable him to have his way. He, at least, was no dreamer, and he knew that if France was to be strong against her enemies without, she must be at peace at home. Those who expected that the victory of a Cardinal would be the signal for outrages upon the Huguenots found that they were much mistaken. Wherever the French Protestants had enjoyed liberty of worship before, they were to enjoy it still. Protestant and Catholic would be equally welcome to aid their common country with their services; but there was to be no more political independence, no more defiance of the sovereign who represented, in the eyes of all, the unity of France.

Treatment of the city.

The fall of Rochelle was a bitter draught for Charles. Whilst he had grown weaker, Louis, who had rejected his mediation and

---

[1] *i.e.* the refugees from Rochelle.
[2] The King to Lindsey, Oct. 14, *S. P. Dom.* xviii. 66.

frustrated his efforts, was growing stronger. Nor was Charles's military and naval failure the measure of his disaster. The French king's declaration of tolerance was an announcement to the world that the war which Charles and Buckingham had persistently waged had been a blunder from the beginning. All for which Charles could reasonably ask was now given to the Huguenots without his intervention. There need have been no forced loan, no arbitrary imprisonments, no expedition to Rhé, no attempt to goad unwilling mariners to break through the guarded barrier at Rochelle. Charles's fancy that Richelieu was a mere emissary of the Roman See, was shown beyond question to have been an entire delusion. He had proved himself as incompetent to recognise the conditions under which war ought to be waged as Buckingham had proved himself incompetent to carry it to a satisfactory conclusion.

<small>Charles's failure.</small>

Yet even the news of the fall of Rochelle did not at once convince Charles that it was necessary to come to terms with France. He took it ill that Richelieu did not immediately despatch messengers to England to sue for peace,[1] and began to cast about for other means than French aid by which to recover the Palatinate. In Buckingham's lifetime Endymion Porter had been sent to Madrid, and Carlisle, after passing through Brussels and Lorraine, had arrived at Turin, to knit together, if possible, a general league of the enemies of France. Ever since the failure of the French alliance, which he had negotiated in 1624, Carlisle had thrown himself warmly into opposition to Richelieu, by whose arts, as he held, the honest intentions of the English Government had been thwarted. There was, indeed, much to complain of on both sides. If Charles had broken his word in the matter of the marriage treaty, Louis had broken his word in the matter of Mansfeld's expedition; and whilst the expulsion of the Queen's attendants and the renewed persecution of the English Catholics were bitterly remembered at the Louvre, the utter failure of

<small>November. Effect of the news of the capture of Rochelle.</small>

---

[1] Contarini to Zorzi, Nov. $\frac{11}{21}$; Contarini to the Doge, $\frac{\text{Nov. 22}}{\text{Dec. 2}}$, *Ven. Transcripts, R. O.*

the first military expedition of the war was by no means forgotten at Whitehall. Carlisle now urged the continuance of the war with France. "If the present
Government of France," he wrote, "were such as
good and honest patriots do wish and desire, many questions
would fall to the ground." The King of France, however, he
continued, had neither the power nor the will to recover the
Palatinate, and he certainly designed the ruin of Protestantism
in his own country. If Charles listened to the overtures of
Spain, without accepting them too impatiently, he might have
full satisfaction in all that he desired. Charles caught at the
suggestion. He hoped that no one would suspect him of 'so
great a villainy' as a peace with France which failed to secure
terms for the Huguenots. He at once invited the Savoyard
diplomatist, the Abbot of Scaglia, to England, to act as an
intermediate agent between Spain and himself, and he assured
the Duke of Rohan that he would continue to support him in
spite of 'the late mis-accident of Rochelle.'[1]

He suggests a Spanish alliance.

It was the fundamental weakness of Charles's foreign policy
that he had no moral sympathy with any single party on the
Continent. The States which he courted were nothing more
in his eyes than instruments which might help him to gain his
own objects. If one King would not help him, another might.
He forgot that it was unlikely that anyone would care to help
him at all, unless he had something to offer in return.

In the meanwhile, Weston's influence was daily growing.
He effected a complete reconciliation between the King and
Arundel. That stately nobleman once more took his
place at the Council board, ready when the moment
came to give his vote in favour of peace. He was
soon joined there by Cottington, a man of the world
without enthusiasm, believing that the Roman Catholic belief was the safest to die in, and that Weston's policy ran
less risk than any other in the immediate present. Weston was

October. Arundel in the Council.

Nov. 12. Cottington a Councillor.

---

[1] Carlisle and Wake to Conway, Nov. 1; Conway to Carlisle and Wake, Nov. 23; The King to Carlisle, Nov. 24, *S. P. Savoy*. Conway to Rohan, Nov. 23, *S. P. France*.

thankful for his support, and marked him out for the Chancellorship of the Exchequer as soon as a vacancy could be made.

Weston's voice was always raised in favour of economy. With as great persistency as he had shown in opposing the erection of a monument to Buckingham, he now opposed every enterprise which was likely to require fresh warlike expenditure. Rosencrantz was urgent that some of the ships and troops returning from Rochelle might be sent to the King of Denmark's assistance. Weston hastened to pay off the landsmen, and gave an unfavourable answer about the ships.[1]

Weston's economy.

He holds back from interference in Germany.

When news arrived that Krempe had surrendered to the Imperialists, Charles resolved to send no present aid to Denmark, and Morgan was ordered to keep quiet at Glückstadt till the winter was over. Yet though Charles allowed himself to be persuaded into inaction for the present, he could not be induced to forego the luxury of promising large aid in the future. His ambassador, Anstruther, was directed to inform the King of Denmark that though the aid which he sorely needed was postponed, it was not refused. Parliament would, doubtless, grant the necessary supplies, and help would be sent in the spring. Morgan's regiment should be reinforced, and a fleet of forty ships should be despatched to the Elbe.[2]

Nov. 24.

In the course of December a nomination was made which showed that Charles did not place himself unreservedly in Weston's hands. Conway was old and sickly, and was removed from the Secretaryship to the less troublesome office of President of the Council, which the still older Marlborough was induced to vacate. He was succeeded by Dorchester, a warm advocate of the French alliance. It was not long before Dorchester had the satisfaction of seeing the difficulties in the way of peace with France

Dec. 14. Dorchester Secretary.

---

[1] *Council Register*, Oct. 26, Nov. 12. Contarini to the Doge, $\frac{\text{Oct. 24}}{\text{Nov. 3}}$, $\frac{\text{Nov. 22}}{\text{Dec. 2}}$, *Ven. Transcripts, R. O.*

[2] Coke to Morgan, Nov. 24; Anstruther to Conway, Dec. 29. Answer of the Commissioners, Jan., *S. P. Denmark.*

gradually removed; and in January a treaty sent over by Richelieu was, with the exception of one not very important particular, agreed to by the English Council.[1]

1629. January.

Almost at the same time Carlisle and Porter returned from their respective missions. The most dazzling offers were dangled before Charles's eyes as the price of an alliance with Spain. With the help of Olivares, Frederick and Elizabeth would soon be reinstalled at Heidelberg, whilst Denmark and the Dutch Republic should be relieved from the attack of the Catholic Powers. Already the two great rivals, Richelieu and Olivares, were measuring one another's strength with hostile glances, and were anxious to secure the neutrality, if not the alliance, of England in the inevitable conflict.

Return of Carlisle and Porter.

A negotiation almost completed and publicly avowed for a treaty with France, which might possibly lead to an alliance against Spain and the Emperor—an inchoate and unavowed negotiation for a treaty with Spain, which might possibly lead to an alliance against France—and a promise to send active aid to Denmark in its war against the Emperor; such were the bewildering results of three months of Charles's diplomacy since he had lost Buckingham's assistance. What likelihood was there that he would succeed in making his policy intelligible to the House of Commons, or that he would gain the support of the nation for his plans?

Progress of the negotiation with France.

Results of Charles's diplomacy.

As far as it is possible to gauge the feeling of the nation, it may be asserted that, though any favour shown to Spain would be unpopular, there was no longer that burning zeal for war which had animated the political classes when the news of the loss of the Palatinate first reached England. Not only had the thoughts of the nation been diverted to domestic affairs, but Spain herself was far less formidable in 1629 than she had been in 1621. The reduction of Breda in 1625 had been followed by a

Feeling of the nation.

Growing weakness of Spain.

---

[1] Contarini to the Doge, $\frac{\text{Dec 30}}{\text{Jan. 9}}$, Jan. $\frac{10}{20}$. *Ven. Transcripts, R. O.*

long period of quiescence, during which the Spanish generals had not even attempted to push home the advantage which they had gained. In Germany, though Spanish troops continued to occupy Frankenthal and the Western Palatinate, they stood aloof from all active participation in the war, and left Tilly and Wallenstein to stamp out, if they could, the last embers of resistance on the coasts of the Baltic Nor, if Spain failed to make any show of strength in Germany or the Netherlands, was she able to explain her inertness by any increased activity in opposing England. Even at the height of Buckingham's mismanagement, when Cecil returned discomfited from Cadiz, when Buckingham brought back the beaten remnants of his army from Rochelle, she had not ventured on a single aggressive movement. Now at last it was seen that she could no longer hold her own. In the summer of 1628, the stadtholder, Frederick Henry, for the first time, quitting the defensive tactics which necessity had for so many years imposed on the guardians of the Dutch Republic, had attacked and taken Grol under the eyes of Spinola. Before the year was out, still more glorious tidings were wafted across the Atlantic. The prize which Drake and Raleigh had failed to secure, and for which Cecil had waited in vain, had been secured by the skill and courage of a Dutch mariner. Peter Hein had captured the Plate fleet, and the treasure which had been destined for the payment of Spanish soldiers was on its way to support the arms of the Republic in a more daring campaign than any Dutchman had ventured to contemplate since the day when Ostend had surrendered to the skill and resources of Spinola.

1628. The fall of Grol.

Hein's capture of the Plate fleet.

It had thus become plain in England that the danger of the erection of a universal monarchy having its seat at Madrid had passed away. Nor were the imaginations of Englishmen much moved by the risk of the establishment of a strong military and Catholic empire having its seat at Vienna. No doubt there was sympathy with the German Protestants, and much angry talk about the devastations of Wallenstein and Tilly. But, after all, the coast of the

1629. English sympathy with the German Protestants limited.

Baltic was far away, and the fall of Krempe did not touch Englishmen as the fall of Ostend had touched them in earlier days. It did not bring home to them any sense of immediate danger to themselves, nor were the conquerors men of that race whose very existence had been a standing menace to England ever since the early days of Elizabeth's reign. Tilly's veterans were not the military representatives of the troops who had contended with Sidney under the walls of Zutphen, or had waited on the Flemish sandhills under Parma till the Armada should appear to convey them to the invasion of the island realm.

Above all, neither the King of Spain nor the Emperor threatened now to undermine the institutions of England by secret sap. There was no longer any fear of the arrival of an Infanta to be the bride of a King of England: and it is difficult to say how much of the warlike ardour of 1621 was to be attributed rather to the fear of the intrigues of Spain in the English Court, than to the fear of its warlike predominance in Germany and the Netherlands. Those who in 1621 were eager to avert a domestic danger by engaging in a foreign war, were ready in 1628 to allow the Continental nations to shift for themselves.

The fear of Spanish interference at home removed.

Whatever might be the ultimate result of Charles's diplomacy, there could be no doubt that the period of history which began with the meeting of the Parliament of 1624 was at an end. The war fever had died down upon its embers. A few months might pass before peace would be actually signed with France and Spain, but sooner or later peace was inevitable. Charles had no longer the means of carrying on war. Would he be able to lead the nation in time of peace? The man was dead who had concentrated upon his own person the general hatred, and it might seem as if Charles would start fairly upon a new course. Such an expectation, if it really existed, was founded on a delusion. In all the mischief of the past years Charles had had his share, and the qualities which had combined with Buckingham's presumption to bring about the ruin, were not likely to assist him when he undertook to calm the excitement and discontent of an

End of the war period.

alienated people. James had been regarded with disfavour because, with all his knowledge and shrewdness, he had no resolute energy to give effect to his determinations. Charles had forfeited his popularity because he refused to look facts in the face, or to acknowledge that opinions other than his own had either a right to exist or strength to compel their recognition. When the war was at an end questions about internal government and legislation, questions especially about Church doctrine and discipline, would be certain to come into the fore ground; and there was unfortunately no chance that the man who had dealt so unwisely with foreign opposition to the wishes which he had conceived, would deal more wisely with the opposition of his own subjects to the principles which he believed to be true. The years of unwise negotiation in James's reign led up to the war and desolation which followed. The years of unwise war in the reign of Charles were leading up to divisions and distractions at home, to civil strife, and to the dethronement and execution of the sovereign who had already given such striking proofs of his incapacity to understand the feelings of those whom he was appointed to govern.

END OF THE SIXTH VOLUME.

PRINTED BY
SPOTTISWOODE AND CO., NEW-STREET SQUARE
LONDON

www.ingramcontent.com/pod-product-compliance
Lightning Source LLC
Chambersburg PA
CBHW030342230426
43664CB00007BA/503